Prophecy and Discernment

If people claim to speak for God, what enables us to know when to credit or discredit the claim? This book analyses the criteria for discernment of prophetic authenticity in the Old Testament, and for discernment of apostolic authenticity in the New Testament; and also considers their validity and viability in a contemporary context.

After explaining the biblical concept of prophetic and apostolic speech on God's behalf, Moberly offers close readings of the biblical text so as to bring to life the distinctive voices, especially those of Jeremiah and St Paul, which speak of critical discernment. He addresses contemporary difficulties with the whole idea that humans might speak for God and analyses the nature of authentic spirituality. Throughout the discussion the premise is that the biblical treatment of discernment illuminates the fundamental human issue of the need to know who may be trusted and why.

R. W. L. MOBERLY is Professor of Theology and Biblical Interpretation at the University of Durham. He is author of *The Bible, Theology, and Faith: A Study of Abraham and Jesus* (2000), also in the Cambridge Studies in Christian Doctrine series.

Cambridge Studies in Christian Doctrine

Edited by
Professor Daniel W. Hardy, *University of Cambridge*

Cambridge Studies in Christian Doctrine is an important series which aims to engage critically with the traditional doctrines of Christianity, and at the same time to locate and make sense of them within a secular context. Without losing sight of the authority of scripture and the traditions of the church, the books in this series subject pertinent dogmas and credal statements to careful scrutiny, analysing them in light of the insights of both church and society, and thereby practise theology in the fullest sense of the word.

Titles published in the series

1. Self and Salvation: Being Transformed
   DAVID F. FORD
2. Realist Christian Theology in a Postmoderm Age
   SUE PATTERSON
3. Trinity and Truth
   BRUCE D. MARSHALL
4. Theology, Music and Time
   JEREMY S. BEGBIE
5. The Bible, Theology, and Faith: A Study of Abraham and Jesus
   R. W. L. MOBERLY
6. Bound to Sin: Abuse, Holocaust and the Christian Doctrine of Sin
   ALISTAIR MCFADYEN

7. Church, World and the Christian Life: Practical-Prophetic Ecclesiology
NICHOLAS M. HEALY

8. Theology and the Dialogue of Religions
MICHAEL BARNES, SJ

9. A Political Theology of Nature
PETER SCOTT

10. Worship as Meaning: A Liturgical Theology for Late Modernity
GRAHAM HUGHES

11. God, the Mind's Desire: Reference, Reason and Christian Thinking
PAUL D. JANZ

12. The Creativity of God: World, Eucharist, Reason
OLIVER DAVIES

13. Theology and the Drama of History
BEN QUASH

14. Prophecy and Discernment
R. W. L. MOBERLY

Forthcoming titles in the series

Remythologizing Theology: Divine Action and Authorship
KEVIN J. VANHOOZER

A Theology of Public Life
CHARLES T. MATHEWES

Theology, Society and the Church
D. W. HARDY

Prophecy and Discernment

R. W. L. MOBERLY

CAMBRIDGE UNIVERSITY PRESS
Cambridge, New York, Melbourne, Madrid, Cape Town, Singapore, São Paulo

Cambridge University Press
The Edinburgh Building, Cambridge CB2 8RU, UK

Published in the United States of America by Cambridge University Press, New York

www.cambridge.org
Information on this title: www.cambridge.org/9780521859929

First published 2006
This digitally printed version (with corrections) 2008

A catalogue record for this publication is available from the British Library

ISBN 978-0-521-85992-9 hardback
ISBN 978-0-521-05104-0 paperback

To *R. B. M.*

magna cum pietate

Contents

Preface

This book is a sequel to my *The Bible, Theology, and Faith,* in which I argued the in-principle case for, and sought to demonstrate in practice, a robust contextualization of academic biblical study within the theology and spirituality of the Christian Church; hence the presence of works of biblical interpretation within a series on Christian doctrine. Unfortunately, this sequel is unlikely to be placed on the library shelf next to its predecessor, even though in my mind they belong together. Here I seek to extend the thesis of the first book by showing how a key issue within Christian theology and spirituality – the critical discernment of claims to speak on God's behalf – might be articulated and developed within the context of Christian Scripture as a whole, with a view to its contemporary appropriation. I have tried throughout to keep in appropriate tension both the concern to read the biblical texts as ancient texts and the concern to read them for their bearing upon the present within the context of the continuing Christian tradition; the fusion of ancient and modern is fraught with difficulties, and yet is a nettle which the Christian theologian must firmly grasp. Although most of the book is a cumulative sequence of exegetical studies of prophetic and apostolic texts, its stance and thesis are alike theological, hermeneutical, and spiritual in outlook.

The content of this book has been germinating steadily over the last decade or so, primarily in the context of my Biblical Theology lectures in Durham; I am grateful to my students whose questions always force me to become clearer in my own thinking. However, the material was for the first time brought together in something like its present shape in the context of my delivering the Speaker's Lectures in Oxford in late October and early November 2002. I am grateful for the honour of being invited to give these lectures; and I am grateful to Ernest Nicholson, the then Provost of Oriel College, and to John Barton, the Oriel and Laing Professor of the Interpretation of Holy Scripture, for their generous hosting of me in Oriel College and for chairing my lectures. Although the book considerably expands, and sometimes modifies, the content of those lectures, I hope it will be recognizable to any who were present as the book of those lectures.

Quality time for reading and writing is ever harder to come by in the contemporary university – or so, at least, it feels to me (and the failure of half a dozen grant applications in relation to this project has not exactly helped). So I am the more grateful to my friends and colleagues who have generously given of their scarce time to read and comment on draft chapters of this work as it progressed: John Barclay, Stephen Barton, David Day, William Ford, Richard Hays, Robert Hayward, Paul Joyce, Joel Kaminsky, Paul Murray, Michael Sadgrove; and my eagle-eyed wife Jenny. I have, I think, incorporated suggested improvements from all of them; and if at times I declined their suggestions, there is only myself to blame for the result. I am also grateful to my CUP editors, Kate Brett and Jackie Warren, and copy-editor, Pauline Marsh, whose friendly efficiency has made it a pleasure to work with them. My thanks too to William Ford for compiling the indices.

I have tried to write with two audiences in mind. One is my fellow professional scholars, the other is interested non-specialists – clergy, teachers, students, general readers. Whether I have succeeded must, of course, be decided by my readers. My basic strategy has been to try to keep the main text accessible to the non-specialist, while including in footnotes and excursus extra material for the specialist; though some of the footnotes and some of the excursus are there not because they are technical but because their content is interesting yet did not conveniently fit within the main flow of the argument. Because I recognize that many read a book such as this without a biblical text open beside them, I have included an English translation (NRSV) of every passage that I discuss in the main text; though I have indicated with a broken underlining where I think the NRSV translation is open to question and have suggested an improvement in a footnote, or occasionally, if sufficiently significant, in the main text.

Despite the numerous footnotes and the reasonably substantial bibliography, I am aware that all this gives a quite inadequate guide to my real intellectual debts. For example, a seminal moment for me was my sitting in on Rowan Williams' lectures on Christian spirituality at Westcott House in early 1979 (subsequently published as Williams 1979) where, among other things, I was first introduced to critical discernment within the Carmelite tradition. Subsequent reading of literature in this tradition, both the classics of the sixteenth century and their twentieth-century interpreters, has been of enormous heuristic significance in helping me recognize what was going on in certain biblical texts with which I was familiar but whose pattern of thought had hitherto eluded me. Since none of this receives reference or footnoting in the following argument, it seems to me important to acknowledge it here at the outset. My hope is that the book may contribute as much to spirituality as to theology or to biblical study, or rather that it will help hold together that which too often is inappropriately put asunder.

Finally, two technical notes. First, in the biblical exegeses it has sometimes been important to note the usage of particular words, and so there is some Hebrew and Greek in transliteration. Although transliteration of Greek is relatively straightforward, I to-ed and fro-ed about the best way to render the Hebrew. Although almost all Hebraists prefer proper diacritical marks, these tend to be off-putting for the non-specialist; while Hebraists can always recognize what a transliteration without diacritical marks is meant to be. So I have eschewed regular diacritical marks but put in indications of vowel length to assist pronunciation; thus, for the Hebrew verb 'to turn/repent', instead of *šûb* I have used *shūv*, with the macron on the *u* to indicate that the pronunciation is 'shoov' rather than 'shove'.

Secondly, although not unaware of feminist difficulties, I refer to God with a masculine pronoun. However, I periodically, though not consistently, capitalize it – partly as a small gesture towards the recognition that gendered language is applied analogically to God who is beyond gender, but also to stand in the tradition of reverential reference to God.

Abbreviations

AB	Anchor Bible
AV	Authorized Version
BADG	*A Greek–English Lexicon of the New Testament and other Early Christian Literature*, 3rd edn, revd and ed. by F. W. Danker, based on the 6th edn of Walter Bauer's *Griechisch–Deutsches Wörterbuch*, Chicago & London, Chicago University Press, 2000
BB	Biblische Beiträge
BDB	*A Hebrew and English Lexicon of the Old Testament*, by Francis Brown, S. R. Driver, and Charles A. Briggs, Oxford, Clarendon, 1953 (1907)
BFCT	Beiträge zur Förderung christlicher Theologie
BHS	*Biblia Hebraica Stuttgartensia*, ed. K. Elliger, W. Rudolph et al., Stuttgart, Deutsche Bibelgesellschaft, 1984 (1967/1977, 1983)
BI	*Biblical Interpretation*
BNTC	Black's New Testament Commentaries
BWANT	Beiträge zur Wissenschaft vom Alten und Neuen Testament
BZAW	Beihefte zur Zeitschrift für die alttestamentliche Wissenschaft
CCT	Challenges in Contemporary Theology, ed. Gareth Jones and Lewis Ayres
EQ	*Evangelical Quarterly*
ESV	English Standard Version
ET	English Translation
ExpT	*Expository Times*

FAT	Forschungen zum Alten Testament (ed. B. Janowski and H. Spieckermann)
FOTL	The Forms of the Old Testament Literature
FRLANT	Forschungen zur Religion und Literatur des Alten und Neuen Testaments
GKC	*Gesenius' Hebrew Grammar, as Edited and Enlarged by E. Kautzsch, and Revised by A. E. Cowley*, Oxford, Clarendon, 1976 (1910)
HAT	Handbuch zum Alten Testament
HTR	*Harvard Theological Review*
HTS	Harvard Theological Studies
IBCTP	Interpretation: A Bible Commentary for Teaching and Preaching
ICC	International Critical Commentary
JB	Jerusalem Bible
JBL	*Journal of Biblical Literature*
JM	*A Grammar of Biblical Hebrew*, by Paul Joüon and T. Muraoka, SB 14, Rome, Pontifical Biblical Institute, 1991
JR	*Journal of Religion*
JSNTSS	Journal for the Study of the New Testament Supplement Series
JSOTSS	Journal for the Study of the Old Testament Supplement Series
JTS	*Journal of Theological Studies*
KAT	Kommentar zum Alten Testament
KHAT	Kurzer Hand-Commentar zum Alten Testament
LF	Library of Fathers of the Holy Catholic Church
LXX	Septuagint
MT	Masoretic Text
NCB	New Century Bible
NIBC	New International Biblical Commentary
NICNT	New International Commentary on the New Testament
NICOT	New International Commentary on the Old Testament
NIGTC	New International Greek Testament Commentary
NIV	New International Version
NovT	*Novum Testamentum*
NRSV	*Holy Bible: New Revised Standard Version*, Oxford, Oxford University Press, 1995
NTS	*New Testament Studies*

NTT	New Testament Theology
OBO	Orbis Biblicus et Orientalis
OBT	Overtures to Biblical Theology
OTL	Old Testament Library
REB	Revised English Bible
RSV	Revised Standard Version
RV	Revised Version
SB	Subsidia Biblica
SBT	Studies in Biblical Theology
SCHNT	Studia ad Corpus Hellenisticum Novi Testamenti
SJT	*Scottish Journal of Theology*
SNT	Supplements to *Novum Testamentum*
SNTSMS	Society for New Testament Studies Monograph Series
SO	*Symbolae Osloenses*
SVT	Supplements to *Vetus Testamentum*
TBS	Tools for Biblical Study
TDOT	*Theological Dictionary of the Old Testament*, ed. G. Johannes Botterweck, Helmer Ringgren, and Heinz-Josef Fabry (Grand Rapids: Eerdmans, 1974– ; ET from German of 1970–)
TNTC	Tyndale New Testament Commentaries
TynB	*Tyndale Bulletin*
Vg	Vulgate
VT	*Vetus Testamentum*
WBC	Word Biblical Commentary
WUNT	Wissenschaftliche Untersuchungen zum Neuen Testament
ZAW	*Zeitschrift für die alttestamentliche Wissenschaft*
ZNW	*Zeitschrift für die neutestamentliche Wissenschaft*

1

What is prophecy, and can it be validated?

> If truth be told, the contemporary academy does not find the appeal to divine revelation at all attractive. Outside theology, and often within theology itself, the appeal to revelation is simply not permissible.
>
> — WILLIAM J. ABRAHAM (2002:254)

In this study I wish to examine how the Bible presents the phenomenon of human speech on behalf of God – for which the prime biblical designation is 'prophecy' – and its disciplined critical appraisal – 'discernment'. My purpose is to understand the Bible in its own right with a view to being able to appropriate it and bring it to bear upon issues of contemporary understanding and practice: how, in a contemporary context where, as in antiquity, numerous different conceptions of life and reality jostle in the market place, may it be possible to speak meaningfully of Christian faith in God and divine revelation as a matter of public, albeit contested, truth?[1]

In this first chapter, there are three main aims. First, I wish to set out a preliminary biblical portrayal of the phenomenon of prophecy, in such a way as to clarify its basic conceptuality. Secondly, I will consider some of the obvious prima facie difficulties that are raised by attempts to regard the biblical conceptuality as genuinely meaningful and potentially valid, and look at the handling of these issues in some modern scholarship.

1. The issues with which I engage are, in certain forms, live issues for Jews and Muslims as well as for Christians. Yet the ways in which they are configured within the wider contexts of Jewish and Muslim thought and practice may make profound differences, and these lie beyond my remit and competence. My focus is on the disciplines of Christian thought and life (hence my usage of 'Bible' is in the Christian sense of Old and New Testaments together), where there are quite sufficient divergences on the issues of prophecy for a Christian theologian to be going on with. I will, however, sometimes touch on issues within Judaism and Islam where it seems appropriate.

Thirdly, I will briefly suggest a possible way ahead. Taken together these will set the stage for the more extended engagement with selected portions of both Old and New Testaments in the chapters that follow.

1 Preliminary outline of the conceptuality of prophecy

Human speech on God's behalf: two succinct biblical depictions

A convenient starting point is afforded by some words of St Paul in 1 Thess. 2:13:

> We also constantly give thanks to God for this, that when you received the word of God that you heard from us,[2] you accepted it not as a human word but as what it really is, God's word, which is also[3] at work in you believers.

The context of these words (to which we will return later) is Paul's moving exposition of his apostolic lifestyle among the Thessalonians, a lifestyle characterized by integrity and practical concern for his converts (2:1–12). For the present, what matters is the pure statement of one of our prime concerns: the word of God in human words. Paul's claim is as fundamental and far-reaching as could be – that when the Thessalonians heard his human words, they rightly heard these words as the address of God to them.

Paul expresses himself with a favourite rhetorical idiom of emphasis, '*not* a human word *but* . . . God's word', an idiom whereby Paul does not deny the human reality of his words, but transforms their significance. In other words, his idiomatic meaning is that the words are *not only* human

2. Perhaps preferable is 'the word which you heard from us, which is from God'. This attempts to draw out the significance of the awkward word order, in that 'of God' (*tou theou*) is directly adjacent not to 'word' but to 'from us' (*par' hēmōn*) (my Greek may be at fault, but I am unpersuaded by Richard 1995:112, who says that 'the entire, compact construction, *logon akoēs par'hēmōn tou theou*, conforms to classical usage'). This awkwardness, which was not modified in the manuscript tradition, is smoothed by NRSV. Yet it deserves attention since *tou theou* might easily have been omitted altogether, as *logos akoēs* could stand on its own (as in Heb. 4:2), and the juxtaposition of 'us' with 'God' is probably intentional. This means that 'the awkwardness of the construction . . . draws attention to Paul's concern to bar any distinction between his and God's word' (Malherbe 2000:166). In grammatical terms, as J. B. Lightfoot (1895:31) puts it, '*tou theou* is emphatic by its position, and is intended to deprecate any false deduction from *par' hēmōn* . . . *Tou theou* is therefore a subjective genitive "proceeding from God, having God for its author", as its emphatic position requires.'

3. The precise sense of this *kai* is debatable, but I am inclined to take it to be ascensive, i.e. 'indeed'.

but also divine;[4] or, the nature of his human words is so constituted by God that their full reality is not adequately rendered by an account which does not simultaneously depict the divine as well as the human. Moreover, the divine nature of his words is implicitly attested by their continuing impact amongst the believing Thessalonians; there is thus an implicit nexus between divine origin ('God's word'), transformative impact ('at work'), and the responsiveness of faith ('in you believers'). Paul is of course well aware that the hearing of his words as the word of God may not happen – as it did not happen on numerous occasions during his ministry, as both Acts and his letters make clear. This is why he in no way takes such hearing for granted but sees it as the cause of thanksgiving, a thanksgiving which for him is not a one-off but a continuing reality.

Beyond the immediate context of 1 Thessalonians, the 'deep' context for Paul's words is a Jewish conceptuality that is rooted in Israel's scriptures. For here we find articulated that conceptuality which Paul presupposes – that is the concept of prophecy.[5] The prime Hebrew term for 'prophet' is *nāvi'*, and the basic characteristic of the *nāvi'* is nicely captured in Exod. 7:1, a passage frequently cited in this regard.[6] The context is the renewed commissioning of a reluctant, professedly tongue-tied, Moses to act as God's agent in delivering Israel from Egypt and the power of Pharaoh.

4. For Paul's idiom 'not . . . but' meaning 'not only . . . but also' with reference to the presence of God/Christ in his life see, e.g., Gal. 2:20, 'I live – no longer I, but Christ lives in me', or 1 Cor. 15:10, 'I toiled more than them all – though not I but the grace of God which is with me.' For a comparable idiom within the Old Testament, see, e.g., Deut. 8:17–18.

5. 'In many respects the NT apostle was the functional equivalent of the OT prophet' (Aune 1983:202, cf. 248).

6. For example, in the seventeenth century, Hobbes in *Leviathan*, ch. 36 (1996:290) says, 'The name of PROPHET, signifieth in Scripture sometimes *Prolocutor*; that is, he that speaketh from God to Man, or from man to God: And sometimes *Praedictor*, or a foreteller of things to come: And sometimes one that speaketh incoherently, as men that are distracted. It is most frequently used in the sense of speaking from God to the People.' Hobbes then proceeds to cite Exod. 4:16, 7:1 in illustration of the primary sense. Similarly Spinoza says at the very outset of ch. 1 of his *Tractatus Theologico-Politicus* (1951:13): 'Prophecy, or revelation, is sure knowledge revealed by God to man . . . The Hebrew word for prophet is "*nabi'*", i.e. speaker or interpreter, but in Scripture its meaning is restricted to interpreter of God, as we may learn from Exodus vii. 1.' It is not possible here to look at the fascinating treatment of prophecy by Hobbes and Spinoza, but in their different ways they shared a concern (if one may be permitted a sweeping simplification) to disengage questions of religious truth from the public life of the state. Whatever good reasons they may have had for so doing in their respective historical contexts – not least, of course, the 'wars of religion' fuelled by ambitious nation-states – the legacy of their arguments has been to contribute to the ultimate marginalizing of the biblical conception of prophecy in the public life of modern Western culture.

> The LORD said to Moses, 'See, I have made you like God[7] to Pharaoh, and your brother Aaron shall be your prophet [*nāvi'*].'

Moses will be the godlike figure of authority and power, but it will be Aaron who will do the talking, who will speak on Moses' behalf.[8] Thus the *nāvi'* is in essence *one who speaks for God*, a spokesman (or spokeswoman, since the Old Testament recognizes several female prophets, *nevi'āh*). When Paul speaks of his ministry as an apostle, he is not in principle, *mutatis mutandis*, speaking of anything different from the Old Testament conception of a prophet.

Closely linked to the notion of speaking for God is the natural correlative notion that the initiative for such speech lies with God. This is characteristically expressed in terms of the prophet being 'sent' by God, as a messenger by his/her master. The verb 'send' (*shālah*) appears at the heart of God's commissioning of Moses, Isaiah, Jeremiah, and Ezekiel.[9] In the New Testament the very term 'apostle' means 'one who is sent' (*apostolos* is etymologically related to the verbal root *apostellō*), and so the New incorporates within its depiction of those who foundationally speak for God in Christ the conceptuality of the Old.[10]

Human speech on God's behalf: Moses as paradigmatic prophet in Deuteronomy 5

The basic conceptuality of prophecy as articulated in Exod. 7:1 receives what is perhaps its fullest depiction in Deuteronomy, a book which presents Moses as *the* prophet *par excellence*.[11] The passage in question is Deut. 5:22–33, which develops and transforms a shorter account of the same issue in Exod. 20:18–21. Its nature as a paradigmatic portrayal of prophecy is not at all well known – I can find no discussion of it in any of

7. Or perhaps 'a god'. The generic use of *'elōhim* does not require capitalization.
8. Compare Exod. 4:15–16, 'You [Moses] shall speak to him [Aaron] and put the words in his mouth; and I [YHWH] will be with your mouth and his mouth, and will teach you what you shall do. He indeed shall speak for you to the people; he shall serve as a mouth for you, and you shall serve as God [*or* a god] for him.' Interestingly, as the narrative of the encounters with Pharaoh unfolds, Moses in fact regularly speaks on his own behalf – perhaps because, in context, YHWH's words in 7:1 are a reassurance to overcome Moses' sense of inadequacy as a speaker (6:30, cf. 6:12), and so it may be that we are to imagine Moses gaining confidence as events proceed and no longer needing the help of Aaron in this way.
9. Exod. 3:13, 15, Isa. 6:8, Jer. 1:7, Ezek. 2:3.
10. Representative accounts of the divine initiative are Gal. 1:1, John 20:21.
11. So, perhaps most famously, Deut. 34:10, 'Never since has there arisen a prophet in Israel like Moses, whom the LORD knew face to face.'

the standard studies of prophecy on my (reasonably well-stocked) shelf.[12] Yet its significance is considerable.[13]

The context is as important as it could be – Israel gathered at Horeb to hear the Ten Words of YHWH that constitute the covenant.[14] Moses is speaking, and he retells the scene to make clear its enduring significance and its consequences:

> 22 These words the LORD spoke with a loud voice to your whole
> assembly at the mountain, out of the fire, the cloud, and the thick
> darkness, and he added no more. He wrote them on two stone tablets,
> and gave them to me. 23 When you heard the voice out of the darkness,
> while the mountain was burning with fire, you approached me, all the
> heads of your tribes and your elders; 24 and you said, 'Look, the LORD
> our God has shown us his glory and greatness, and we have heard his
> voice out of the fire. Today we have seen that God may speak to
> someone and the person may still live.[15] 25 So now why should we die?
> For this great fire will consume us; if we hear the voice of the LORD our
> God any longer, we shall die. 26 For who is there of all flesh that has
> heard the voice of the living God speaking out of fire, as we have, and
> remained alive? 27 Go near, you yourself, and hear all that the LORD our
> God will say. Then tell us everything that the LORD our God tells you,

12. It would be tedious to list books in this context, though they include Buber 1949, Heaton 1958, Heschel 1962, Lindblom 1962, von Rad 1965, Koch 1983, Blenkinsopp 1996, Petersen 2002; also Neumann 1979, which is an overview of modern German research on prophecy. The reason for the neglect of Deut. 5:22–33 is not hard to discern, at least in general terms. The common modern approach has been to offer a historical, developmental, and thematic account of prophecy in Israel and its world. The recognition that the biblical portrayal of Moses as a *nāvi'* may well belong less to the origins than to the flowering of Israelite prophetic thought (though the case for this is not straightforward, at least within Exodus) has tended to mean that the portrayal, especially in Deuteronomy, is treated dismissively as a (mere) rationalization or retrojection (or whatever other term indicates a lack of fit with the modern historian's priorities in unscrambling Israel's religious history). If, however, one seeks to work with the biblical text as the mature distillation of what is of enduring value in Israel's religious history, in a portrayal which may in varying degrees invert and transpose the course of that history but which has value in its own terms, then the depiction of Moses as *nāvi'* can properly become a key to discerning the nature and meaning of biblical prophecy for those who wish to appropriate its legacy.

13. Von Rad's only discussion of the passage is in his commentary on Deuteronomy. Here he notes that 'the report of these events is far from being an historical report in our sense; instead it is a complete theological statement' (1966:60). But this recognition of the text's genre and function – 'a complete theological statement' – does not lead him to make the kind of use of it which one might have expected.

14. For some reason the Hebrew of Exodus and Deuteronomy consistently depicts YHWH's direct address to Israel as 'words' (*devārim*) rather than 'commandments' (*mitswōt*) – which does not, of course, mean that the familiar labelling 'Ten Commandments' fails to capture the nature of the text.

15. Perhaps preferable is 'a deity may speak to humanity and humanity may still live'. The concern of the text is the communication between two generically different realities, deity (*'elōhim*) and humanity (*hā'ādām*).

> and we will listen and do it'. [28] The LORD heard your words when you spoke to me, and the LORD said to me: 'I have heard the words of this people, which they have spoken to you; they are right in all that they have spoken. [29] If only they had such a mind as this, to fear me and to keep all my commandments always,[16] so that it might go well with them and with their children for ever! [30] Go, say to them, "Return to your tents." [31] But you, stand here by me, and I will tell you all the commandments, the statutes and the ordinances, that you shall teach them, so that they may do them in the land that I am giving them to possess.' [32] You must therefore be careful to do as the LORD your God has commanded you; you shall not turn to the right or to the left. [33] You must follow exactly the path that the LORD your God has commanded you, so that you may live, and that it may go well with you, and that you may live long in the land that you are to possess.

YHWH spoke directly, 'face to face', with Israel, out of the fire upon the mountain (Deut. 5:4, 22). The fire is the awesome symbol of the divine presence, as in YHWH's initial appearance to Moses at the burning bush (Exod. 3:1–6);[17] here its combination with cloud and darkness is in some ways suggestive of the visual accompaniments of a volcanic eruption, the point being that these most awesome of phenomena convey something of the awesomeness of the divine presence and speech. Although YHWH 'only' (so to speak) spoke the Ten Commandments – the continuation 'and he added no more' (5:22aβ) draws a clear line under the divine address, as does the writing of the divine words on stone tablets (5:22b) – the experience of hearing YHWH speak was utterly overwhelming for Israel. They felt that in hearing the deity speak[18] they had gone to the

16. 'Always' should surely qualify Israel's state of mind, i.e. 'If only they had such a mind as this always.' YHWH's wish is that Israel's present correct attitude should be enduring.

17. Presumably one reason for the appropriateness of fire as a prime symbol of YHWH's presence is that it is something that both attracts (by its colour, movement, and warmth) and repels (by the intensity of its heat and the danger of burning if one comes too close). It thus embodies that polarity which was famously depicted by Rudolph Otto (1924) in relation to holiness as *mysterium tremendum et fascinans*.

18. Interestingly the formulation of Israel's leaders uses the generic terms 'deity' and 'humanity', not the specific terms 'YHWH' and 'Israel', and uses the imperfect/*yiqtol* form of the verb for open-ended, repeated action, not (as one might expect) the perfect/*qatal* form for completed action. The point would seem to be to locate Israel's encounter with YHWH within basic conceptual and existential categories, so that the unparalleled nature of their specific encounter with YHWH may best be appreciated. There is a similar use of generic categories in Deut. 4:32–40, esp. 32–4a (and compare 4:7–8), where the point seems to be to express YHWH's dealings with Israel in categories which allow for comparison with other accounts of deity and humanity, but only so as to emphasize the unrivalled nature of what YHWH has done with Israel, so that Israel is to recognize YHWH not just as a deity (*'elōhim*, i.e. 'god') but rather *the* deity (*hā'elōhim*, i.e. 'God'), the one and only, the incomparable (4:35, 39; see MacDonald 2003:79–81).

very edge of endurable human experience, so that any further divine speech would risk destroying them entirely – to hear the words was to be exposed to the heart of the fire that is the divine presence and so they wanted henceforth to withdraw to a safer distance (5:24–6). This led to their crucial request to Moses (verse 27):

> Go near, you yourself, and hear all that the LORD our God will say. Then tell us everything that the LORD our God tells you, and we will listen and do it.

Moses is to be so close to God that he is able to hear what God is saying – the assumption is that, with the possible exception of the direct address of YHWH to Israel in the Ten Commandments, God does not (as it were) shout, so that proximity to God matters for hearing God. The purpose of this is that Moses can then transmit what he has heard to Israel, with a view to Israel thus knowing what God wants of them so that they can live accordingly. Here we have, spelled out with clarity and precision, the prime sense of what it is to be a particular kind of mediator – not a priest (though a priest may speak for God, Mal. 2:4–7), but one whose prime responsibility is to speak for God, a prophet (*nāvi'*).

Israel's request is then approved by God (5:28–9), with an approval that is the more striking because so consistently elsewhere in the surrounding context Israel is depicted as hard-hearted, stiff-necked, and persistently rebellious (esp. 9:7–10:11); presumably this approval is at least in part because the requested mediator is to enable Israel's obedience to YHWH's will, an obedience which Israel undertakes to live out.[19] The approval leads directly into instructions to Moses to carry out what has been approved. Israel is to disperse, while Moses fulfils his commissioned role (verse 31):

> But you, stand here by me, and I will tell you all the commandments, the statutes and the ordinances, that you shall teach them, so that they may do them in the land that I am giving them to possess.

19. It is, of course, possible to read this (as indeed everything within the Bible) in an oblique way, with an eye to the human interests (of varying, often problematic, kinds) that 'must' underlie the text; so, e.g., even Alter 2004:909 (perhaps drawing on Levinson 1997:145), 'One may detect in all this the interest of a royal scribal elite promoting itself as the necessary authoritative mediators of God's words for the people.' Insofar as such comments are not merely reductive and dismissive, they serve as a reminder that, among other things, there are heavy moral and spiritual responsibilities laid upon those who put forward such a text to be taken seriously.

This restates verse 27 in terms of YHWH's directive rather than the people's request, but the content remains the same in depicting Moses' role as mediator: Moses' proximity to YHWH is to enable him to receive that divine teaching which will guide Israel in living faithfully in accordance with the divine will.

The section then concludes with a general exhortation by Moses to Israel to obey what he will mediate to them from God (5:32–3) – the content of which Moses immediately goes on to convey to them in the form of a brief preamble (6:1–3) followed by the Shema (6:4–9), which thus becomes the keynote of Moses' commissioned prophetic teaching of the will of God for Israel.

Three reflections on this passage.[20] First, although the specific term *nāvi'* is not used here, the conceptuality is unambiguous. Moreover, later in Deuteronomy, there is an important section to do with YHWH's future guidance of Israel (18:9–22), where Israel is forbidden to follow the practices of other nations in trying to get some leverage upon divine guidance (verses 9–14), but is promised that YHWH will raise up other Israelites to be to Israel as Moses has been:

> [15] The LORD your God will raise up for you a prophet (*nāvi'*) like me from among your own people; you shall heed such a prophet. [16] This is what you requested of the LORD your God at Horeb on the day of the assembly when you said: 'If I hear the voice of the LORD my God any more, or ever again see this great fire, I will die.' [17] Then the LORD replied to me: 'They are right in what they have said. [18] I will raise up for them a prophet (*nāvi'*) like you from among their own people; I will put my words in the mouth of the prophet, who shall speak to them everything that I command.'

Moses is described as a *nāvi'* himself and as the model for Israel's other prophets,[21] all with explicit reference to the scene at Horeb where Israel's request (5:24–6), YHWH's approval (5:28–9), and the depiction of the *nāvi'*

20. See also Excursus 1 for a remarkable misreading.

21. The numerically singular and anarthrous form in Deut. 18:15, 18, 'a prophet' (*nāvi'*), has not infrequently encouraged interpreters to see reference to one particular prophetic figure who would definitively reveal God's will; and the text is certainly open to such a reading. Within the deuteronomic context, however, the prime sense must be that the singular is collective, as is the 'I' voice with which Israel speaks in 18:16. Thus the reference is to a succession of prophets over time, raised up by YHWH as and when Israel needs appropriate guidance. This portion of Deuteronomy speaks of various kinds of leadership within Israel, judges (16:18–17:13), kings (17:14–20), priests (18:1–8), prophets (18:9–22); the depiction of the king in 17:14–20 is consistently singular, yet the possibility of more than one king seems clearly to be envisaged.

as the one who speaks YHWH's words to Israel (5:27, 31) constitute the basis for God's continuing provision of prophets.

Secondly, Moses' prophetic role is explicitly based upon his proximity to God, his standing in the divine presence. Although this could be construed geographically, in terms of being on, or close to, the holy place, Mount Horeb, there is remarkably little emphasis upon this in the narrative,[22] especially when this account is compared to the narrative of Exodus 19 with its numerous references to approaches to, and ascent and descent of, the mountain. This suggests that, even if a geographical element is not entirely lacking, the concept of proximity to God is primarily a 'moral' and 'spiritual' concept,[23] to do with a certain mode of being, i.e. attentiveness, faithfulness, and obedience to God. To put the matter differently, and to anticipate subsequent discussion, the portrayal here of Moses' proximity to God that enables knowledge and communication of God's will is a portrayal that is not in essence different from the perhaps better-known depiction in prophetic literature of the 'divine council'. For the point of the divine council, that prophets may have appropriate proximity to God such that they come to know God's will, is identical to the point of Moses' proximity to YHWH at Horeb. Prophets, as we will see, need proximity to Horeb not geographically but morally and spiritually, in terms of obedience to the divine instruction associated with Horeb.[24]

22. It is perhaps most explicit in the instructions to Israel to depart for their tents (verse 30).

23. I put the adjectives 'moral' and 'spiritual' in inverted commas in order to indicate that they are in important ways problematic. For they very readily conjure up certain modern categories and classifications which may all too quickly skew the sense of the biblical text by construing it in inappropriate ways, predominantly through greatly narrowing the sense and scope of the terms. Nonetheless it is difficult to deny the contemporary interpreter any use of modern abstract or general categories, potentially misleading though they may be (what about 'history' or 'theology'?). As long as the terms are used tentatively and heuristically, with the sense that is to be ascribed to them being allowed to arise inductively out of immersion in the biblical text, I hope the terms will be helpful rather than misleading.

24. The obvious exception that proves the rule is Elijah in 1 Kgs. 19. However, one possible way of understanding the richly suggestive story of Elijah's journey to Horeb, and the theophany there, is that Elijah (and, through him, the hearer/reader of Israel's scripture) has to learn that such a journey is unnecessary. YHWH's repeated question to Elijah is the apparently uncomplimentary 'What are you doing here?' (verses 9b, 13b). The point of the theophany (verses 11–12) appears to be that, despite YHWH's appearing to Moses in earthquake, wind, and fire (Exodus 19) and passing before Moses (Exodus 33–4), this is not the sole or privileged mode of YHWH's appearing; rather it is implied that the 'sound of a fine silence' (which is probably a more accurate rendering than the time-honoured and resonant 'still, small voice') is to be the mode of YHWH's self-revelation to a prophet – at least, if one follows the LXX's gloss on the sound: 'and YHWH was there'. This is something intrinsically independent of potent public display or geographical restriction, being instead dependent for reception upon the kind of attentive disposition which can learn to hear such a divinely charged and diaphanous silence.

Thirdly, it follows from the previous point that this portrayal of Moses as prophet can be read (again, to anticipate aspects of our wider thesis) as an implicit critique of all suppositions that prophetic revelation requires the kind of abnormal psychological conditions (possession, ecstasy, trance, vision, locution, etc.) that are so well attested as regularly accompanying claims to encounter with the divine, not only in ancient Israel but also in countless other contexts both ancient and modern. The point, to which we will return, is that such psychological phenomena neither validate nor invalidate the supposed divine revelation – they are as it were optional extras – since it is the content of the encounter with the divine that is determinative of its validity and significance; that content is here understood in terms of that which enables fuller engagement with the will of YHWH as revealed in the Ten Commandments, through the Shema and all that follows.

Characteristic Christian extensions of the concept of prophetic speech

These Pauline and Mosaic texts concisely depict a claim that recurs constantly in the Bible, that human words can in reality be the word of God. Indeed, it has been characteristic of Christian faith to extend this claim, made primarily for prophets in the Old Testament and apostles in the New Testament – and, of course, supremely for Jesus Himself as the Word – in more than one way.

First and foremost, it has been extended to the words of the Bible as a whole. Although numerous Christians, especially in modern times, have expressed greater or lesser degrees of unease with this usage, usually on the grounds that it can encourage an undifferentiated and insufficiently critical handling of the text, the usage has nonetheless remained characteristic of Christian thought and practice.[25] From among the many accounts of this, both ancient and modern, I cite solely the words of Karl Rahner (1991:221–2):

> Scripture is a human word, a human product, insofar as in it human beings bear witness that God is no longer the mysterious ground of a history that presses on into the unforeseeable future, but that God hastens to meet history as its absolute future and introduces it into his own infinity and luminous sovereignty . . . But Scripture is also God's

25. For a theologically nuanced unease over too readily extending the prophetic notion of revelation and inspiration to the rest of Scripture, see Ricoeur 1981:75–7.

> word, and as God's word, it bears witness to God himself, as infinite gift to the world. Such an attestation is possible only if it is made by God himself, in a unique manner that goes beyond God's usual creative activity.
>
> If Scripture did not, through God himself (through what we call the light of faith), bear witness to God, as a gift that victoriously makes its way, it would speak only of realities that are distinct from God, even if it spoke of them in their relation to God. In that case the content of its statements would not differ basically from content that, in principle, might also be reached by unaided human words. And then that essential difference from other human words, which Scripture itself attests, would no longer exist. Of course, this essential difference between Scripture as God's word and human words can ultimately be conceived and defended only if we grasp Scripture's essential relation to the cross and the resurrection of Jesus. For only in these eschatological salvific events is the triumph of God's self-promise to the world presented historically and therefore in words. The words of Scripture are, when we read them with faith, once more animated by this self-communication of God. Thus they are not only words about God (although authorized by God) and thus only human words. They are indeed words of God.

Secondly, the prophetic conception has been extended to Christian preaching (which itself can include not only formal proclamation but faithful Christian witness in any situation). Karl Barth, who in his general context of discussion draws on Augustine, Luther, and Calvin (1956:743–58), speaks thus of Christian proclamation (pp. 745–6):

> We must begin with the affirmation that, by the grace of revelation and its witness, God commits Himself with His eternal Word to the preaching of the Christian Church in such a way that this preaching is not merely a proclamation of human ideas and convictions, but, like the existence of Jesus Christ Himself, like the testimony of the prophets and apostles on which it is founded and by which it lives, it is God's own proclamation. That it is men who speak here, men who are not themselves Jesus Christ or even prophets and apostles, does not in any way permit them, in an affirmation and assertion of their humanity, arrogantly to try to say something other than the Word of God. On the other hand, it does not permit them to be faint-hearted, as though in their humanity they were not able to speak the Word of God, but only their own human words. Again, it does not permit those who hear them, because of the humanity of those who speak, to adhere to

> their human word as such, to rejoice or not to rejoice in it, to accept it or to reject it, as though the word spoken was only this human word and not the Word of God. That it is men who speak must, of course, be taken into account with all its consequences. Nothing that this fact implies may be suppressed. But we can think meaningfully and practically about it only when we bear in mind first the prime consideration that these men speak and must be heard as members of the body of Christ and in the name of the Church, and that the Church is the assembly of those to whom, in all their humanity, the Word of God is entrusted. Above all criticism, even above self-criticism, the proclamation of this insight belongs to the Church's proclamation. It is only in the light of it that we can exercise the necessary criticism and self-criticism. This is what decides whether we do it in faith or lack of faith, and therefore profitably or otherwise.

The potential implications of the possibility that humans may speak for God are, therefore, enormous. Indeed, although prophecy itself does not constitute the central content of Christian faith in the kind of way that, say, christology and Trinity or election and grace or atonement and resurrection do, it is a *presupposition* of Christian faith. For Christians believe that the content of their faith is indeed given by God through human mediation. If, therefore, the notion of divine communication through human mediation cannot be sustained as coherent and valid, then the whole structure of historic Christian faith becomes untenable; 'revelation' becomes no more than imaginative and moving poetry (at best), and 'God' becomes the projection of deep human aspirations and longings.

A biblical depiction of the need for critical discernment

One should not, however, speak of the importance of the concept of prophecy without simultaneously recognizing that it also offers massive potential for abuse. The appeal to God may be not only deception of self (as, among others, those who care for the mentally ill can regularly testify) but also a potent tool for manipulation of others. It can be a means to validate human self-will and imposition upon others, with endless more or less subtle variations upon the theme of 'You must do what I say, because what I say is what God says', where the appeal to divine authority can serve to prevent or override legitimate question or objection.

The recognition of this difficulty is not, of course, novel. Indeed, one of the major contentions of this book is that the difficulty is addressed both more fully and more adequately within Scripture than is generally recognized. It will be appropriate, therefore, at this stage to set out one further keynote text, comparable to 1 Thess. 2:13, Exod. 7:1, and Deut. 5:22–33, a text that is probably the best known and most referred to in this context, that is 1 John 4:1:

> Beloved, do not believe every spirit, but test the spirits to see whether they are from God; for many false prophets have gone out into the world.

The context of this is a discussion of criteria for true knowledge of God, but, as with 1 Thess. 2:13, we will for the time being prescind from this context so as to focus directly on its twofold injunctions. 'Do not believe', which has the sense of 'do not be credulous', 'do not allow your faith to be misplaced', is accompanied by 'test', with the sense of 'be critical', 'be discerning'. It is a prime example of the kind of critical thought that the Bible itself encourages – not, as so often in modern biblical criticism, the development of various kinds of historically informed awareness about the genre of the text, the nature of its referents, and the processes of its composition (valid and useful though these can be), but rather the development of the kind of moral and spiritual awareness that enables its possessor to distinguish between the genuine and the counterfeit within human life in its moral and spiritual dimensions. This critical awareness is necessary for a simple reason: there are differing, indeed conflicting, claims on the part of those who speak for God. It is possible to claim to speak for God, and yet to do so falsely. The truth about God is contested, and may not be straightforwardly self-validating, and so those Christian believers whom John addresses must be prepared to tackle the conflict they face with appropriate resources.

As with 1 Thess. 2:13, the issues raised here are characteristic of the Bible more widely, even if, admittedly, injunctions as to the exercise of critical discernment are much less common than claims to speak for God. Concerns about critical discernment are also characteristic of much classic Christian theology and spirituality down the ages. So again, the potential ramifications of our text are considerable. It is, in effect, within the conceptual and existential space that is created when our keynote texts are taken together that our study will be focussed. The presupposition of both the Bible and classic faith is that speech (and action) on behalf of God is indeed a valid phenomenon but that the dangers of deception and malpractice are ever present; and so appropriate critical disciplines of discernment are needed.

2 Some modern approaches to the validity of prophecy

The claim that humans may speak for God has been extensively debated in the modern (as in the premodern) world. Generally speaking, the claim has become increasingly problematic for a variety of reasons. In terms of modern scholarship it would, I think, be difficult to disagree with William Abraham's words which form the epigraph for this chapter (Abraham 2002:254): 'If truth be told, the contemporary academy does not find the appeal to divine revelation at all attractive. Outside theology, and often within theology itself, the appeal to revelation is simply not permissible.'

As a preliminary introduction, I will first briefly note four general characteristics of modern biblical scholarship (and allow more specifics to emerge in the context of exegesis of the biblical text in subsequent chapters). Then I will look in a little more detail at the work of two scholars who between them interestingly open up some of the key issues with which a theologian must engage.

Four characteristics of modern biblical scholarship on the validity of prophecy

A first characteristic is that questions of discernment and authenticity have not featured prominently.[26] One looks in vain for 'discernment' in the indices of major Old and New Testament theologies. 'True and false prophecy' is an optional item in standard textbook treatments of prophecy: sometimes a section or chapter is devoted to it, sometimes not, and overall it is marginal rather than prominent.[27] Questions of 'authenticity' have overwhelmingly been addressed in historical-critical categories of identity of authorship and context of origin, not in the Bible's own preferred frame of reference.

Secondly, no major scholar, to the best of my knowledge, has attempted to engage this question in relation to Old and New Testaments together,[28] never mind in relation to practices of critical discernment in

26. Lange 2002:5, in his history of research, cites Matthes 1859 as the first modern monograph, with a short essay in 1895 as its successor. Given the general range and extent of biblical criticism since the late eighteenth century, this is indicative of our issue as a latecomer, of secondary significance, to the debates.

27. It is perhaps indicative that in one of the major recent works of reference, *The Anchor Bible Dictionary*, the lengthy four-part coverage of prophecy (Huffmon, Schmitt, Barton, Boring 1992) says nothing about this issue.

28. In the recent biblical theologies of Childs (1992) and Scobie (2003) there is no interest in discernment of prophetic or apostolic authenticity either within each testament respectively or within the testaments together.

classic Christian theology and spirituality (though some scholars, such as Quell 1952, do interestingly discuss aspects of post-biblical tradition).[29] To be sure, those whose primary focus is the Old Testament regularly have cross-references, notes, and excursus that refer to the New Testament; and vice versa. But in no work of which I am aware is comparable analytic attention given to both testaments. The notion that it might be fruitful to compare Jeremiah's criteria for prophetic discernment with Paul's criteria for apostolic discernment, indeed that they might be differing facets of one and the same issue, seems not to have been seriously entertained. This would appear to be indicative, among other things, of the way in which so much biblical study in the nineteenth and twentieth centuries became primarily a history of diverse religious thought and practice, in which synthetic and constructive theological thinking in relation to the totality of Christian Scripture tended to be a marginal phenomenon, of doubtful intellectual respectability.[30]

Thirdly, the overall tenor of such scholarly work as has been produced has been negative as to the possibility of valid criteria of discernment.[31] One significant and much-cited monograph has been James Crenshaw's *Prophetic Conflict* (1971). Crenshaw valuably surveys modern scholarly discussion up to his time of writing, and sees two tendencies at work (p. 13):

> If one were to isolate two tendencies of the literature on false prophecy from this [sc. the twentieth] century, it would have to be the trend toward a denial of valid criteria for distinguishing the false from the true prophet, and the attempt to understand reasons for the phenomenon of false prophecy, particularly the human ingredient of all prophecy.

29. There are, of course, various semi-popular accounts of discernment, eg. Dubay 1977, Gorringe 1990, Johnson 1996; and also the more formal Rahner 1963. These, while valuable and accessible, all have only minimal and piecemeal engagement with the OT, and usually (excepting Johnson) do not focus even on the characteristic voices of the NT in a sustained way.

30. The mid-twentieth-century Biblical Theology Movement and the biblical interpretations of Karl Barth, *inter alia*, are, however, a reminder of how perilous it can be to generalize.

31. It is perhaps indicative that in his major discussion of prophecy, his *Old Testament Theology*, vol. II, von Rad (1975:210, n. 27) devotes just one long footnote to the question of criteria for distinguishing between true and false prophets (though he had written an earlier essay on the subject, von Rad 1933). His brief survey reveals that there is 'no assured criterion' and he concludes (with supporting cross-reference to Quell 1952): 'The falsity [sc. of false prophets] . . . could only be seen by the person who had true insight into Jahweh's intentions for the time, and who, on the basis of this, was obliged to deny that the other had illumination.' Although von Rad is concerned with 'insight into Jahweh's intentions for the time', and so offers a form of the fourth characteristic scholarly emphasis that I mention below, he does not seem fully to appreciate that his conclusion, as it stands, has no real critical content and in effect just redescribes the initial problem.

Crenshaw's own discussion furthers each of these tendencies. On the one hand, he denies that there are valid criteria for distinguishing true prophecy from false: 'the Achilles-heel of ancient prophecy' is 'the absence of any validation for a prophetic word' (p. 38).[32] He lists the various criteria offered within the biblical text, comments on each in turn, and finds each wanting (pp. 46–61) – though the question of whether they might be combined synthetically in such a way that the whole might be greater than the sum of its parts is not addressed.[33] On the other hand, he primarily seeks to account for the phenomenon of 'false' prophecy through a mixture of social and cultural reasons; for example, he makes much of affinities between 'false' prophecy and 'popular' religiosity.[34] In general terms, what this means is that 'true and false prophecy' is transposed from an issue within theology to being instead a matter of religious sociology.[35] Crenshaw thereby fostered something of a trend no longer to speak of 'true and false prophecy', on the grounds that the evaluative epithets are no longer justifiable, and instead to speak of 'inner-prophetic conflict'. Crenshaw's overall view is that prophecy collapsed largely because the lack of 'an adequate means of self-validation' led to such an intolerable conflict of 'claim and counter-claim, self-assertion and inner turmoil' that Israel turned elsewhere for spiritual direction (p. 108).[36]

32. An excursus on the New Testament and early Christian literature is no more positive: 'the New Testament period bears witness to the continuing struggle to determine the genuine spokesman for God . . . and attests a simplistic approach to the setting up of criteria for distinguishing true from false prophets' (p. 115).

33. Similar to Crenshaw in both approach and conclusion (though fuller in textual discussion, and with greater attention to Jeremiah, diachronically analysed, en route) is Münderlein 1979. His conclusion (pp. 140–1) is that 'there are no criteria for discernment of prophets' because ultimately 'the substance of prophecy, the word of Jahweh, cannot be captured in rules' (though this latter point, somewhat differently construed, would in fact not be a bad starting point for serious discussion).

34. 'No longer will it be possible to view the religion of the people as unambiguously corrupt, thus constituting a handy foil against which to look at the pristine prophetic faith. Once this fact is grasped, it forces us to re-examine the theology of "false prophets", inasmuch as their orientation is frequently similar to the popular religion' (p. 38).

35. Crenshaw does also account for prophetic conflict in terms of 'the belief that Yahweh made use of men against their will or knowledge to accomplish his intentions, indeed on occasion sent deceptive visions to further the divine purpose for Israel', all of which he attempts (with some difficulty) to understand positively in terms of divine providence (p. 110).

36. According to Crenshaw, wisdom is the moral and spiritual resource to which Israel turned in its disillusion with prophecy. For himself he suggests that wisdom is the most enduringly valuable dimension of Israel's religion – which is presumably why, subsequent to this book, he is best known for work on wisdom in Israel and its neighbours.

The representative nature of Crenshaw's analysis[37] is perhaps best illustrated by its virtual replication (*in nuce*) thirty years later in a major work, *The New Interpreter's Bible*, whose aim, in its editors' words, is 'to bring the best in contemporary biblical scholarship into the service of the church to enhance preaching, teaching, and study of the Scriptures' (Keck 2001:xvii). Here David Petersen offers an introductory overview of prophetic literature, in which almost the whole of what little he has to say on 'true and false prophecy' is this (Petersen 2001:9):

> Prophecy, as such, may have a fatal flaw. Prophecy can work well if there is one prophet speaking to somebody who will take that prophet seriously. The situation becomes problematic when two prophets appear and say things that are contradictory, especially if both prophets use the standard language of an Israelite prophet. This problem has often been termed the conflict between true and false prophecy.
>
> [An intermediate paragraph offers a brief summary analysis of the story of Jeremiah and Hananiah in Jeremiah 28.]
>
> One can imagine the difficulties encountered by those who had witnessed the initial confrontation. They had no easy way of knowing which prophet was telling the truth. In fact, the deuteronomic rules that govern such a case (Deut 18:15–22) stipulate that one should wait and see which individual's words would turn out to be true. But when prophets' words require action, such inactivity would not be possible. Moreover, prophets could disagree about assessments of the present and the past, not just about pronouncements concerning the future. This potential for conflict between prophets may have provoked such difficulties that other forms of seeking information from the deity developed, forms such as priestly admonition or scribal intermediation, neither of which allowed for a direct public challenge.

Presumably the implicit moral for contemporary preachers and teachers is to leave the whole issue well alone, and just hope that they themselves are never confronted by 'direct public challenge'.[38]

37. The major monograph on the OT material since Crenshaw is Lange 2002. Lange propounds a religio-historical thesis in which he focusses on the putative traditio-historical and redactional processes involved in the formation of the prophetic literature, especially Jeremiah. Lange agrees with Crenshaw about inner-prophetic conflict in the pre-exilic period, but argues that prophecy did not die out in the way Crenshaw envisages (pp. 268, 316), for he sees it as transformed from living speech to written text and the interpretation thereof while still remaining prophecy.

38. Comparable for Crenshaw's significance is the approving citation of the contention that prophetic conflict is 'the Achilles heel of prophecy' in Preuss' major *Old Testament Theology* (Preuss 1996:85). Interestingly Preuss cites it from Hossfeld and Meyer 1973, where it is the

Fourthly, the main exception[39] to this generally negative tenor has been the attempt to understand prophetic conflict and discernment in terms of the difference between the well-timed and the mis-timed, the flexible and the inflexible; the true prophet is the one who aptly applies existing religious tradition to the present moment, while the false prophet is the one who appeals to existing religious tradition in a rigid and insensitive way (e.g. with varying emphases, Buber 1982 [1968/1942], Davidson 1964, Overholt 1970, Sanders 1977, Brueggemann 1991:23–9). As Overholt puts it (1970:94):

> Jeremiah's interpretations rest upon an affirmation of Yahweh's radical freedom to deal with his people in ways appropriate to their present situation, while those of his opponents are characterized by a tendency to accept the traditional patterns of the faith as normative for all of Yahweh's action, past and future. Both are attempts to remain faithful to the valued traditions of the past, yet in the conflict between them we have a striking example of the age-old tension between more or less rigid institutional expressions of the 'faith' and continuing attempts dynamically to appropriate this faith in terms relevant to the complexities of a contemporary historical situation.

There is an obvious prima facie appeal to such an approach. For a faith with such a richly diverse book as the Bible as its canonical text will always need to be open to issues of the discrimination of appropriate content, context, and timing in its use of the text (and although tradition, that is Christian living under God and with Scripture down the centuries, has made numerous such discriminations, many of which are taken for granted, fresh challenges often rightly lead to reassessment of the continuing appropriateness of past decisions).[40] Nonetheless, despite the undoubted general importance of supple understanding and of good timing, it should at least be noted that this is not the biblical text's own characteristic portrayal of what is at stake in prophetic authenticity

note with which their book begins; Hossfeld and Meyer make no reference to Crenshaw at that point, though I would be surprised if it was not his work (to which they refer elsewhere) which caused the phrase to enter the bloodstream.

39. One work that is difficult to categorize is Blank 1955. I find Blank's account of Jeremiah more thoughtful and moving than most, though not more persuasive; Blank unduly psychologizes the issue in terms of Jeremiah's attempt to assure the people that God had really sent him being a facet of Jeremiah's own quest for certainty, and thereby, in my judgment, misreads some of the key texts.

40. Aside from anguished contemporary debates about sex and sexuality, ecumenical discussions have profitably revisited the hugely contentious sixteenth-century debates about the nature of salvation. One might also note changes of mind in earlier periods on issues such as lending money at interest, slavery, or suicide.

(as will emerge in the exegesis). The appeal to flexibility and good timing seems to me on the whole to be a well-intentioned attempt to make positive sense of the relevant texts when the texts' own priorities are not understood (or, if understood, considered unacceptable).

Although much more would need to be said if a proper survey of modern scholarship on the subject were being attempted,[41] enough has been said to give some preliminary sense of some characteristic emphases within the literature. So I will turn directly to my two case studies, some of whose emphases will illuminate and extend concerns already noted.

Maxime Rodinson as an exemplar of psychological explanation

The first of my two selected scholars, Maxime Rodinson, I take as representative of scholars of religion who come to their subject in a way that brackets out the perspectives of faith and so shows limited or no interest in the classic disciplines of theology.[42] The fact that his work is not on the Bible but on Muhammad and the Qur'an has the added advantage for my purposes of being a reminder that what we are looking at primarily within a biblical and Christian context has important analogues in related religious traditions.

Very broadly speaking, one might say that it was in the nineteenth century that scholars began systematically to offer accounts of 'religion' which bracketed out reference to God or the traditional disciplines of theology and approached the subject in terms of its human motivations and aspirations, not least through the emerging social-scientific disciplines of anthropology, sociology, and psychology. (The ground had been

41. For example, Brenneman (1997) draws extensively on recent theory of interpretation and of the nature of canon to produce an account of biblical interpretation in relation to true and false prophecy which shifts the centre of gravity to the judgments of the interpretative community. His work is a useful reminder of the changing conceptual frame of reference within which biblical scholarship is taking place. Yet he offers no fresh exegesis of the well-known controverted texts; and, despite his emphasis on canon from a Christian perspective, he still focusses on Old Testament texts in effective isolation from engagement with comparable issues in the New Testament.

42. Another work which I considered for inclusion is Dodds 1951. Dodds' fine study of, among other things, claims to speak for the divine in ancient Greek religion, mainly from Homer to Plato, is closely comparable to Rodinson's work in approach. On the one hand he seeks to understand his texts in their own terms, while on the other hand he also offers a modern scientific explanation in sociological and psychological categories. Dodds' own personal 'credo', in terms of his work, comes at the end (1951:253–5), where the problems faced by a changing Western society, problems most sharply exemplified in the Second World War, constitute the context for reflection on how an improved understanding, and integration, of the irrational might enable contemporary civilization more constructively to face its problems.

prepared by seventeenth- and eighteenth-century philosophical accounts of God which either dismissed God altogether or relegated God to the margins in deist fashion.) Whatever the character of the non-theological accounts – and modern accounts of 'religion' have been many and varied – one strong and recurrent tendency has been to utilize them, singly or in combination, as comprehensive explanations. Many scholars have been confident that a sufficient explanation of the appeal to divine inspiration of human speech can be found without reference to 'God' or theology, but rather solely within the categories of sociology and psychology.[43]

Maxime Rodinson's fine, recently reissued, study of Muhammad[44] (1971 [2002]) is characteristic of such an approach. Rodinson writes as a self-confessed atheist[45] (as well as being a secular Marxist Jew), and right at the outset poses the key question of what to make of those who have believed 'that their message came from beyond our world, and that what they themselves represented was something more than merely human'. He makes two moves (p. xiii). First, unsurprisingly, he resists the claim to the divine, though in moderate and agnostic terms: 'The atheist can only say that this extra-human origin remains unproved'; and he gestures towards a psychological explanation: 'it may be rooted in functions of the human mind that we do not yet understand'. Secondly, he insists that this does not involve any pejorative assessment. On the one hand, 'he [sc. the atheist] may even place a higher value on [the religious message], as being an admirable effort to surpass the human condition';[46] on the other hand, distance can enable freshness of perspective: 'I believe that

43. This is the kind of explanation that theologians tend to label 'reductive'. However, while 'reductive' may be an appropriate label with regard to certain claims that religious experience and language are 'nothing but' a more or less mystifying form of psychological and sociological phenomena, it is important that theologians do not forget that their own accounts can sometimes be 'reductive' in a different kind of way – by so stressing God that complex, important, and influential human realities are not given the kind of consideration or intrinsic weight that they merit.

44. This is Rodinson's consistent spelling within his text, although, somewhat confusingly (presumably in deference to the publisher's desire for the content of the book to be readily recognizable through the familiar anglicized form of the name), the book's title is *Mohammed*.

45. He handles the problem of how far an atheist can understand a religious outlook with great care (1971:xiii): 'It may be objected that I, as an atheist, cannot possibly understand such a man [sc. Muhammad, who lived "with a keen sense of the direct presence of the divine"]. That may be so; after all, what actually constitutes understanding? However, I am convinced that, provided he takes enough trouble, and totally excludes any contempt, pharisaism or sense of superiority, an atheist can in fact understand a religious outlook – certainly as well as an art critic can understand a painter, an adult a child, a man of robust health an invalid (and vice versa) or a scholarly recluse a businessman. Certainly a religious man would understand my subject differently, but better? I am not so sure.'

46. Rodinson's 'higher value' needs some teasing out. I take it that his point is to do with an ability to admire and respect in a new way the quality of aspiration represented by religious

he [sc. the atheist] can sometimes capture the original excitement of it, and feel more at one with it than many of its conformist believers for whom that message has developed into something taken for granted.'

Within the body of the book Rodinson discusses the status of Muhammad's revelations from Allah, his visions and messages, which he presents as 'the question of his sincerity' (p. 75). He records various examples of eighteenth- and nineteenth-century rationalists who could only see Muhammad as a fraudulent liar, and comments that 'modern advances in psychology and psychiatry have made short work of such simplistic explanations of fraud, whether justifiable or otherwise' (p. 76). Indeed, it is psychology that now offers the most plausible account (p. 77):

> It is now generally understood and admitted that certain individuals can sincerely believe that they are the recipients of visual, auditory and mental messages from the Beyond; and also that their sincerity is no proof that these messages really come from where they are claimed to come. It is the concept of the unconscious which has enabled us to understand these things.

This enables Rodinson to offer a sympathetic account of the mystical experience and thought of Muhammad and others, both Muslim and Christian, but to be sure that the content of Muhammad's message is no more than the content of his unconscious (pp. 78–83).

Later, Rodinson reverts to the same issue, this time with reference to an evaluation of the Qur'an (pp. 218–20):

> For several centuries the explanation produced by Christians and rationalists has been that Muhammad was guilty of falsification, by deliberately attributing to Allah his own thoughts and instructions.
>
> We have seen that this theory is not tenable. The most likely one . . . is that Muhammad really did experience sensory phenomena translated into words and phrases and that he interpreted them as messages from the Supreme Being . . . His sincerity appears beyond a doubt, especially in Mecca when we see how Allah hustled, chastised and led him into steps that he was extremely unwilling to take.

claims, an admiration enabled by a certain distance and humane openness. Nonetheless, since the evaluation is necessarily 'admirable but mistaken' I am not sure how this can represent a higher evaluation than that of those who can say 'not only admirable but also true'. Or, in other words, Rodinson's point carries most weight in relation to the somewhat tired and conventional attitudes to religion that are often encountered among the faithful. But those who hold a fresh and robustly faithful understanding of their religion might need some persuading that there is more than rhetoric and diplomacy in an atheist's claim to place 'higher value' than they themselves place on what they, often at great cost, believe. Rodinson's claim, however (to be fair), is only about what 'may' be the case.

Thus far we have the sympathetic account utilizing Muhammad's own categories. But now comes the evaluation from the modern scientific perspective (which has the added merit for Rodinson of developing certain of Muhammad's own incipient intuitions):

> Men's capacity for self-deception is infinite. It is obvious to non-Muslims that the words which Muhammad heard, by which his experiences (in themselves almost inexpressible) were translated in so miraculously perfect a fashion, were dictated to him by his unconscious. He himself suspected it; he had doubted their source, he was afraid that human inspiration might have formed some part of it, and … he even admitted at a later stage that Satan himself had managed to insert his own orders.

But the incipient awareness of the problem within Muhammad himself was swamped by a success and a public acknowledgement which allowed the triumph of the noble illusion that Allah indeed spoke through him:

> There is plenty of evidence that, to the end, he remained convinced that what spoke within him was the voice of that implacable and omnipotent Master who directed him from above the seven skies, for whom he had dared and endured so much and for whom he was ready to endure again.

Several brief observations on this account are in order. First, Rodinson's account instantiates a generic approach to the study of religion in general. It is designed to enable sympathetic non-religious understanding of religious phenomena without conceding validity to the religious self-understanding. Accordingly, the assumptions whereby sense is made of Muhammad and the Qur'an would be (and are, in other contexts) used equally to make sense of all the biblical prophets, from Moses and Elijah to Jesus and Paul, and of the Bible itself. If one wishes to offer an account that does allow the intrinsic validity of the biblical claim – as in the thesis of this book – it seems clear that any such account must also be of a generic kind. That is, the account must offer a conceptuality that can allow reality to religious claims as such; for it is only within such a frame of reference that one could meaningfully advance grounds for ascribing greater truth to one claim in relation to another within the same tradition, or to privilege one tradition as a whole over another.

Thus the Christian cannot polemically dismiss Muhammad on the critical grounds offered by Rodinson, and yet exempt the Bible and

Christian faith from that critique. That would simply be special pleading, and would be no less special pleading if one tried to dignify it with descriptions such as 'the hermeneutical privilege of faith' or 'the need to see from a particular place'. A proper response to one generic/conceptual approach is to offer an alternative generic/conceptual approach. Within that alternative approach there can, and should, be space for making distinctions and for distinguishing the better from the worse, the valid from the invalid, the true from the false, i.e. there should be space for all the processes of discernment, and for articulating the resources made available by rootedness within a particular (albeit complex) tradition of faith and understanding. What is unacceptable is to formulate criteria which leave one simply saying (in effect) some form or other of 'Christian is valid; non-Christian is invalid.' For the criteria which allow one to discern valid and invalid speech for God within a Christian context must by their very nature (as will be seen) allow one to exercise discernment with respect to other religious and non-religious contexts with an openness to, and expectation of, finding that which is valid there also; to say which is not, of course, for a moment to concede to an 'anything goes' approach, which would be precisely to abandon the responsible exercise of discernment. In other words, the frame of reference within which one seeks to articulate an understanding of the biblical conception of prophecy cannot *a priori* exclude other comparable non-biblical (non-Jewish, non-Christian) phenomena, but must rather enable some kind of coherent account to be offered of *any* claims to speak for the divine.

Secondly, although this is not the place to engage substantively with the difficult question of the respective strengths and weaknesses of religious and non-religious approaches to religious phenomena, two possibly questionable implications of Rodinson's 'capturing the original excitement' and 'feeling more at one with it than many conformist believers' (a claim which is carefully qualified with a 'sometimes') may be worth mentioning. In general terms it is easy to see and to grant Rodinson's point. Yet on the one hand, his epithet 'conformist' is implicitly pejorative, depicting unthinking religious observance, without allowing for the possibility of reflective observance of traditional practice. That is, Rodinson is not offering an alternative to a good (lively, nuanced, sophisticated) religious account, but only to a second-rate one, and so is not really comparing like with like. On the other hand, one might observe that the 'excitement' and 'feeling' would remain solely at an intellectual and imaginative level, in that it would exclude the actual practice of those religious duties and observances which 'conformist believers' might still faithfully carry out. The possibility that such observances might themselves be intrinsically generative of insight would, I suspect, tend to be downplayed by Rodinson. Yet it is salutary to heed the critical comment of Jon Levenson (drawing on Leszek Kolakowski, Paul Mankowski, and Catherine Bell) on the frequent modern tendency to oppose thought and ritual action and to privilege the former (1993:115–16):

> It is no coincidence that in this model [sc. the identification of ritual as action in contradistinction to thought], it is the person whose life is *not* ritualized who has the clarity of vision: only as we break off from ritual communities and transcend their specific performances can we come to perceive the truth. The model does not allow for even the possibility that detachment from ritual performances may decrease one's insight and obscure one's vision. It definitively *and non-dialectically* [my italics] shifts the locus of truth from the practicing community to the nonpracticing and unaffiliated individual.

Yet the relation of practice to understanding is a key concern in any proper account of the hermeneutics of discernment, and so must not be pre-empted in an intellectualist way.

Thirdly, it is notable that Rodinson hardly seems to allow that a modern person could give an account other than the psychological, such as the theological. His point that the sincerity of recipients of visual, auditory, and mental messages 'is no proof that these messages really come from where they are claimed to come' should be completely granted by any reflective believer. As John Locke, for example, pointed out a good while ago when anatomizing seventeenth-century enthusiasm in the light of reason (1894 [1690]: 437): 'The strength of our persuasions is no evidence at all of their own rectitude: crooked things may be as stiff and inflexible as straight: and men may be as positive and peremptory in error as in truth. How come else the untractable zealots in different and opposite parties?' Yet it is precisely the recognition of this that called forth the classic theological practices of discernment. Rodinson continues that 'it is the concept of the unconscious which has enabled us to understand these things', in a way that implies that this is now the sole avenue to true understanding. There appears to be a clear implicit suggestion that there is no longer any need for theology, since psychology has solved the problem. This raises a major issue in the history of modern thought, to which we will return.

William McKane as Christian historical-critical exegete

My second exemplar, William McKane, I take as representative of biblical scholars who approach the text from the perspective of Christian faith and with corresponding interest, in one way or another, in the concerns of theology. I choose him for three reasons. First, his major two-volume commentary on Jeremiah (1986, 1996) and also his commentary on Micah (1998) have confirmed him as a substantial contributor to the interpretation of Old Testament prophecy. Secondly, the question of prophetic authenticity in relation to God is a recurrent interest not only in his commentaries but also in a significant monograph (1995).[47] Thirdly, McKane has extensive knowledge of Jewish and Christian biblical interpretation, ancient, medieval, and modern, and he draws on it valuably in his discussions of prophetic authenticity; his discussions have a depth lacking in some others. My treatment will focus primarily on the 1995 monograph.

One of McKane's primary concerns is the theological and philosophical question of the nature of human language in relation to God, which he regularly sums up as 'God does not speak Hebrew' (pp. x, 102–3, 145–8; cf. 1985:18–20; 1986:xcvii–xcix, 427–8). It is hardly fortuitous that he begins the monograph on prophecy with two chapters on Maimonides. Whatever his criticisms of Maimonides, McKane has deep sympathy with Maimonides' strong account of the limitations of human language and knowledge in relation to God. McKane includes discussion of Aquinas in this context, and approves of 'the conclusion to which Aquinas' discourse, like that of Maimonides, leads', which is that 'statements about God are not literal and his [sc. Aquinas'] emphasis on the metaphorical or analogical character of such statements is in general accord with this' (p. 6).

McKane's other primary, and closely related, concern is that any proper account of prophecy must fully respect, and in no way diminish, the humanity of the prophet. Again, he finds in Maimonides, and clearly considers correct, the understanding that 'the prophetic endowment is

47. There is also material in an essay (1985) which is mainly concerned with the larger issue of the relationship between exegesis and theology; the final section (pp. 18–20) focusses the larger issue in a discussion of the nature of the prophetic 'word of God', which McKane develops via a strong critique of Weiser's Jeremiah commentary.

special but it is located within the created order and "speech of God" has also to be contained within that order' (p. 30). As McKane says towards the end of the book (p. 151):

> An account of prophetic activity which holds that the prophet prophesies only when he is abnormal and never when he is wholly human is a disastrous dilution of his humanity. The canonical prophet is always both man and prophet.[48]

Language about God, language ascribed to God, is intrinsically and essentially human language spoken and written by human beings who were not somehow less human in so speaking and writing. Failure to understand and respect this – either by in any way 'dehumanizing' prophets or by in any way being 'literal' about the 'word of God' – is, for McKane, to fall at the first fence.

We get the feel of these related concerns in, for example, McKane's strong criticism of Austin Farrer's Gifford Lectures (1948) – whether or not it is entirely fair to Farrer is not my present concern – in which almost all his terms of disapproval are used (pp. 151–2; cf. 119–20):

> When we come to Farrar [*sic*], we have encountered one of the principal adversaries of the humanity of the canonical prophets. He has a zest for dehumanizing them and he takes aim at their humanity with a barrage of supernatural vocabulary. 'Word of God' receives a literal interpretation . . .
>
> What kind of men then were the canonical prophets? According to Farrar they were mouthpieces of God rather than men. When they speak only the voice is human, but otherwise they say what they must – a kind of automatic speech. They are witless men who have lost their own personalities, have been overwhelmed by a divine invasion and are God-possessed. They are overborne by a spate of supernatural, poetic eloquence over which they have no control. Farrar has done a thorough job demolishing the humanity of the canonical prophets. As the architect of a soaring supernaturalism he has worked with uncontained gusto and he has conjured up a theology of the prophets whose docetism will be difficult to surpass.

Within the context of these prime critical priorities, it is unsurprising that McKane also recurrently discusses the significance of a psychological

48. Compare 'It was to preserve the wholeness of man and prophet that I coined the dictum, "the prophet is always both a man and a prophet"' (p. ix). McKane's dictum has significant antecedents, as in John Locke's: 'God when he makes the prophet does not unmake the man' (1894 [1690]:438).

understanding of divine inspiration, for biblical scholars in the nineteenth and twentieth centuries have not been slow in utilizing psychology in this context, in ways analogous to Rodinson. McKane considers especially A. Kuenen (1877), H. Gunkel (1917), and J. Lindblom (1962). Kuenen spoke for many in the nineteenth century when he sought to explain not only prophecy but the whole of Israel's religious history without recourse to traditional theological categories such as 'inspiration' or 'revelation'. The conviction of prophets that they knew the will of YHWH is explicable in terms of extraordinary psychological states such as ecstasy or trance. McKane (p. 78) cites a representative and illuminating passage of Kuenen (1877:85–6):

> The certainty which the ecstasy could have given to a prophet was first of all purely subjective; he alone knew that he had witnessed a vision and that he proclaimed the revelation which had been made to him in that manner. We can have no control over the one or the other, but must accept both on his testimony. In the second place, a specific, supernatural character can in no wise be ascribed to the trance; its divine origin is not at all self-evident. Phenomena of that nature were far from uncommon in ancient times and in the middle ages, and occur even at this present day. It is true that for a long time people had no hesitation in ascribing them to supernatural influence. They seemed so singular and extraordinary that this explanation forced itself quite naturally on men's minds. What could not be derived from God was therefore regarded as a display of the power of evil. But we now no longer occupy this standpoint. Ecstasy is now accurately studied, compared with other affections allied to it, and is explained from the human organism itself, specifically from the nervous system. It may be – on that point I determine nothing at present – that the trances of the Israelitish prophets were of a nature altogether different: but that must be proved separately; for ecstasy in itself is no supernatural phenomenon. It does not therefore advance us a step in determining the origin of Old Testament prophecy.

As McKane observes, there are two distinct issues here. One is that 'ecstasy in itself is no supernatural phenomenon', or, in McKane's helpful paraphrase, 'unusual psychological phenomena cannot transcend the limits of the psychological domain and should not be confused with supernatural truth'.[49] The other is whether there is a different way in

49. It may be worth noting that McKane's denial that God speaks Hebrew should in no way be taken as a denial of the experiences of people, ancient and modern, who hear God speak to them in particular languages. McKane's concern is that such experiences cannot in themselves 'transcend the limits of the psychological domain'.

which prophetic truth can yet be discerned. For Kuenen this is not the case, except in general humanist terms, for his analysis leads to 'the disposal of the entire baggage of revelation and not [to] an alternative way of analysing and expressing the concept' (p. 78).

With regard to Gunkel and Lindblom, McKane's main concern is that, although they recognize in principle that one should not attach theological significance to unusual experiences (ecstasy, vision, etc.), in practice they lay such weight upon unusual psychological states as the context for prophetic utterances that they tend towards something of a Jekyll and Hyde view of the prophet in which the problem of 'dehumanizing' becomes apparent (pp. 133–47).

A few comments upon McKane's survey and analysis. First, although he usefully puts his finger on difficulties in those proposals about prophetic validity which he discusses, he has less than one might hope for by way of substantive positive proposals – some theological account of his own as to the nature of revelation or inspiration – to put in their place.[50] His two prime emphases, that God does not speak Hebrew and that prophecy should not be explained in ways that dehumanize the prophet, are indeed important critical concerns. Yet not only do they in themselves require further analysis, such as a probing of the inevitably linguistic dimension of a meaningful account of divine revelation (because of the role of language in shaping human experience), but they also need to be part of a larger positive construal – which never comes. To be sure, there are some clear indications as to the kind of answer that McKane thinks would be appropriate. For example, in the context of discussing Kuenen's approach and its limitations, McKane observes that (p. 78):

> Whether a prophet is true or false depends on the content of his utterance which is available to public scrutiny, whether as heard or read, and not on the interior psychological state associated with his utterance.

This is excellent as far as it goes, but it does not go very far, and it receives no further development.

50. It is disappointing that the seven essays which are primarily on the nature of prophecy in relation to the history of biblical criticism (1995:1–153) are not followed by a concluding essay in which McKane sets out his own positive proposals, as one would naturally expect at that point in the book. Instead there is a final essay on hermeneutics and Old Testament theology which, despite some clear commonality of concern with what precedes, feels a little out of place in relation to the book's dominant interest; and it continues with predominant criticism of others at the expense of McKane's own alternative construal.

Secondly, the lack of positive theological proposals seems to relate to McKane's view of what theology is, in connection with his view of the appropriate limits of biblical scholarship. Running right through the monograph, and also his other works, is an argument against the recurrent theological naivety which does not do justice to the humanist concerns which need to characterize the study of the Bible (and also other texts). If there is a revelation of God through human beings and in these human texts, then their human dimensions must be taken with full seriousness and not evaded at crucial moments – hence his rejection of any account of prophecy which 'dehumanizes' the prophet. Although this point must indeed be fully taken, one may yet query the way in which McKane formulates it. For his argument seems, to me at any rate, to be unduly locked into the standard (until recent years) self-understanding and master narrative of 'modern' biblical scholarship, in which it was only by disentangling the philological and historical concerns of textual study from the all-too-easily-distorting influences of theology that a clear and properly 'critical' understanding of the Bible could be gained. Yet this master narrative only grudgingly, if at all, allowed that the undoubted gains in understanding were accompanied by blind spots,[51] and also conceptual losses, not least as to how 'God' could still be an appropriate referent of biblical, or other human, discourse.[52] So when McKane himself wishes to make positive theological affirmations, he becomes remarkably tentative; and although he would no doubt justify this at least in part in terms of the intrinsic limitations of human language with reference to God (à la Maimonides), such legitimate concerns do not suffice to explain the thinness of what he feels able to say.

For example, in the context of discussing Lindblom and the need not to dehumanize prophets, McKane says (p. 145):

> I shall assume, without argument, that there is a transcendental dimension, an encounter of the prophet with God, though I am aware of the logical disadvantage of producing such an ultimate – an unanalysable – mystery out of the hat.

To sidestep the key issue at stake by appealing to encounter with God as an unargued assumption is deeply disappointing. Here the legitimate

51. Jewish and feminist scholars, among others, have regularly pointed out that the playing field was not as level as was usually claimed.

52. See further Moberly 2000:ch.1. There are, of course, exceptions to any such generalization; the work of Bultmann was, for better or worse, a sophisticated engagement with the question of God.

difficulties in speaking appropriately of God seem to be threatening to remove issues of faith and transcendence out of the realm of rational discourse altogether, and to make them into an arbitrary a priori about which all that can be said is 'either you have it or you don't' or 'take it or leave it' – which is, indeed, how much modern thought has characterized issues of faith in God, but which is a much-reduced account in relation to classic Christian understanding.

McKane in fact uses the above sentence to introduce the reuse of some of his own words from the introduction to his Jeremiah commentary (1986:xcviii – the second sentence of which is used verbatim also in 1985:20):

> Verbalization is a 'translation' or 'transmutation' of a prophet's meeting with God and we should not share Weiser's satisfaction with an external, talking God as the end of our understanding of 'revelation' and 'word of God'. The prophet absorbs the mysterious experience into his humanity, filtering it through human modes of apprehension and evaluation, and causing it to issue in a linguistic form which is human and not divine.

Here part of McKane's problem is apparent. He is so locked into fighting a mode of theology that does not do justice to the human that he cannot move beyond it towards offering an alternative account. For in the first sentence the initial point about prophetic speech is used negatively to underline the inadequacies of Weiser's 'literal' account; while the constructive thesis of the second sentence again ends in no more than a reaffirmation of his contention that prophetic language is 'human and not divine'. One can compare McKane's own summary of his concerns at the conclusion to the preface, whose train of thought exactly replicates this pattern (p. x):

> More may be said than I have attempted about the mystery of the divine–human encounter, of the converse between a prophet and God, and it may be urged that there is human language which can capture it. My contention is that God does not speak Hebrew, that the language of the Old Testament is human language and that, with this in mind, it must be studied like any other literature embedded in ancient documents.

The first sentence is the Christian scholar's recognition that his own theological account is rather thin. The second sentence, however, apart from the philosophically informed 'God does not speak Hebrew', is essentially the reassertion of one of the prime watchwords of emergent modern biblical scholarship – 'must be studied like any other literature' – which makes no attempt to indicate how a fuller theological account might be attempted.[53] In short, at the very point where one needs a positive account of the engagement of the divine with the human, one is left with the negative polemic of a biblical scholarship that has not ceased to believe in God, and still wishes to take seriously the truth content of the Bible in relation to God, but appears no longer to possess the language or conceptuality with which to do so.

Thirdly, although McKane makes good use of Maimonides and Aquinas for a general account of the nature of religious language, this is accompanied by a strangely unreflective use of key conceptual terms. McKane refers constantly to the perils of 'dehumanizing' – and also, throughout the book, uses related terms of disapproval, 'supernaturalism' or 'docetism' – but treats these as self-evident concepts which need no analysis in their own right. Since many of the difficulties in understanding prophecy relate to what it means to be human, what would count as 'normatively' or 'fully' human, and how the divine is to be conceptualized and articulated in relation to the human, the loose use of terminology in the very area where precision matters is disappointing (though again characteristic of much biblical scholarship which has perhaps too easily supposed that it could sit light to questions of conceptual analysis and adequacy).

53. The rhetoric of 'reading the Bible like other texts' is also rather less telling now than when it was first used in the eighteenth century by scholars as diverse as Ernesti (e.g. Minear 2002:27–8) or Herder (e.g. Boyle 2004:17–29), and it is dismaying that McKane apparently thinks that the developments of the nineteenth and twentieth centuries (secularization of society and universities; sociology of knowledge; Marxism; feminism; Holocaust; Wittgenstein and language games; recent hermeneutical theory; resurgent 'spirituality' largely divorced from the Bible and the institutional church and synagogue, etc., etc.) do not put contemporary biblical scholars who profess Christian faith in a rather different position with rather different challenges from those their eighteenth-century predecessors faced. The valid positive concern of the watchword, that the regular disciplines of philology, history, and literary criticism should be applied no less to the Bible than to other texts, and that there should be no forced exegesis under dogmatic constraint, has long since been absorbed into the bloodstream of academic biblical study, and none of the scholars whom McKane criticizes would have contested the principle. Moreover, in our contemporary context it has become clearer that the watchword is not as straightforward as it may sound. For example, its use has generally been combined with taking for granted the privileged status and expectations ascribed to the Bible by Jewish and Christian faith – in which McKane is no exception. This privileging means that, in important respects, the Bible is *not* studied like other ancient literature – a point neatly encapsulated in the convention, virtually unchallenged until recent years, of capitalizing the deity of the Bible ('God'), although the capitalization is not present in ancient Hebrew and Greek manuscripts, and it was not extended to other ancient religious literature, whose deities remain lower-case ('god'/'gods').

Identifying some problematic assumptions within Rodinson and McKane

Rodinson and McKane share significant common ground and also differ interestingly. On the one hand, both respect the terms within which the ancients gave their own account of divine inspiration, but both insist that today we must offer our own account in terms which may differ from those of the ancients. Rodinson effectively dismisses without further ado any possibility of speech for God except as a phenomenon of psychology. McKane is well aware of psychological explanation but resists it as a substantive account, for he remains open to the content of the ancient claim; however, he seems unable to offer an alternative modern account, for what he says is predominantly negative and reactive. I would like to try to make progress by identifying two problematic assumptions whose rethinking might be fruitful.

Within Rodinson's account, appeal to God is ruled out of court. Why? Obviously on one level because Rodinson is a self-confessed atheist. But on what grounds does the atheist feel confident in dismissing God and the content of theology? Here there are many possible reasons, but I will suggest that one in particular may be significant for the modern Western mind.

There is a rather long intellectual history, from the seventeenth century onwards, for the concept of what is crudely but not inaccurately called 'the god of the gaps'.[54] This is the mistaken tendency to 'find space for God' in what lies beyond the current scope of scientific explanation. It is not only mistaken for the obvious reason that what may be beyond the range of one generation of scientists becomes a challenge for the next generation, a challenge which regularly is successfully met; then as scientific explanation expands, 'space for God' correspondingly contracts and ultimately disappears.[55] The tendency is also conceptually confused in that it treats 'God' as an 'explanation' on the same level as the explanations offered by the empirical sciences. God is not an explanation but a mystery. But God is not a mystery in the sense of a conundrum or puzzle, something which leads ultimately, even though it may take time, to

54. Richard Dawkins (2003:149) refers to this as 'the Einstein/Hawking trick of letting "God" stand for "That which we don't understand" '.

55. A famous and paradigmatic moment came in 1802 when Pierre-Simon Laplace, in discussion with Napoleon, felt able confidently to pronounce, when asked about the significance of God for understanding the heavens, that 'I have no need of that hypothesis' (the episode is contextualized in Buckley 1987:325).

resolution, when there is no longer a puzzle any more for all is now clear; mysteries in that sense are indeed the sphere for scientific explanations. Rather the mystery of God in its true theological sense is a reality which for the human person is ever-expanding and ever-deepening, a reality whose existential dimensions engage one in his/her totality (sometimes neatly characterized as 'the more you know, the more you know you don't know'). Unfortunately Rodinson's strategy seems to presuppose, at least to some extent, a kind of 'god of the gaps' approach to theology, an approach which psychology renders superfluous.

By contrast, as is often pointed out, the theologian may properly insist that understanding in terms of God and explanations in the categories of scientific human understanding should not be set over against each other as their nature and purpose are different (though the familiar demarcation between 'why questions' and 'how questions', although convenient, is a potentially misleading oversimplification). The ability to account for a phenomenon in familiar human categories does not exclude the possibility that it may also be possible and appropriate to account for the same phenomenon in relation to God; in general terms, for the theologian the issue is 'both ... and' rather than 'either ... or'. The fact, therefore, that the phenomenon of speech on behalf of God is open to psychological explanation in terms of the unconscious (or anthropological explanation in terms of communal human practices) need not disqualify it from a legitimate theological account.

If this is so, however, it can raise a different problem for the theologian. If theological understanding can be predicated, in principle, of all human activities and explanations, then may it not become an ultimately vacuous exercise? That which 'explains' everything explains nothing. It may become the kind of optional intellectual activity which need not be missed by the ordinary person seeking constructive and useful understanding of the world. One still needs a frame of reference and criteria whereby appeal to God can be meaningful and make a *particular* difference in understanding and practice, without succumbing to a 'god of the gaps' approach. This is one of the issues which the following discussion will seek to illuminate.

The second issue I wish to identify relates to McKane's evident deep unease that appeals to the divine may 'dehumanize' a prophet. Although he appears not to hold that such dehumanizing necessarily follows from appeal to God, his failure to offer his own positive account of how this need not be so raises suspicions: at best, he finds himself unable to articulate what he intuitively believes to be correct, or, at worst, the danger of dehumanizing is simply more potent than traditional theology can allow itself to recognize and may not be answerable. Either way, McKane's unease seems to be part of a much more widespread modern suspicion that appeals to God may threaten in one way or other to devalue the human.

Alongside McKane's concerns as a Christian theologian one may set – as an example taken more or less at random – the concerns of a politician-turned-journalist who rather firmly does not profess faith in God, Matthew Parris. In a recent column in *The Times* (Parris 2003), Parris reflects on a trip to the Sahara where, among other things, he visited the mud-brick house in Tamanrasset where Charles de Foucauld had lived and witnessed as a Christian among the Muslim Tuareg tribesmen who, according to Foucauld, 'live[d] in the daily presence of God'. Parris tells the story of Foucauld and concludes with a reflection upon human goodness in relation to Foucauld ('Brother Charles'), the religious Sisters who now work in Tamanrasset, and the Tuareg tribesmen:

> From time to time one meets . . . people from whom goodness simply leaps. I may lack the theoretical foundations to explain it but the experience is too strong, too unmistakable to deny. These people have in common something extraordinary. What?
>
> Could it be God?, I asked myself. Was Brother Charles right? Is Islam right? Is God the explanation of human goodness? The answer struck me with unexpected clarity. There is no need to explain human goodness. It exists . . . It can be seen, and not only in the devout. Seek its source not externally but in the obvious place. Goodness is human, not divine, springing from us and not from anything, or anywhere, or Anyone, else . . . We do not need an outside explanation of human goodness. The very act of seeking another source is a denial of human goodness, a denial that we could be – in ourselves and on our own and for no other reason – good. The positing of God is a kind of insult, a blasphemy against humanity, a demeaning of ourselves. Brother Charles was looking for the right thing in the wrong place.

It is a nice irony for Christian, Jew, and Muslim that their respective faiths in the one God, which they have historically supposed to dignify and enrich human life, is now readily considered to do the opposite.

Two of Parris' assumptions merit comment. One is that the notion of God as a possible 'explanation' of human goodness is considered unproblematic, as though one does not need to consider whether there may not be valid modes of understanding quite distinct from 'explanation' when it comes to goodness and God.[56] The other is that God is 'external', 'outside' – not Jesus' Father who numbers the hairs of our heads, or Paul's One in whom we live and move and have our being,[57] or Augustine's One who is closer to us than we are to ourselves, but an intruder, and an unnecessary, because devaluing, intruder at that.[58]

It is probable that the supposition that appeal to God is likely to dehumanize is bound up with certain tacit assumptions, which are too rarely articulated and analysed. It is likely too that it is not unconnected to the difficulties in speaking meaningfully of God that are indicated by the sorry history of 'god of the gaps' arguments. Whatever exactly be the case here, my concern is that one is unlikely to make progress with understanding and evaluating the phenomenon of speech for God without recognizing, and successfully circumnavigating, the tips of some major icebergs that lurk in the sea of modern thought.

3 Conclusion: on relearning what is meant by 'God' and 'supernatural'

My proposed way ahead is to heed (selectively) those contemporary philosophers and theologians who speak of the need to rethink some of the assumptions most natural to us. If one premise of the 'postmodern' is the recognition that fundamental insights of the 'modern' do not necessarily have the significance sometimes ascribed to them, then the rethinking of modern assumptions about God that have come to be taken for granted may be no bad thing.

56. Compare the difference already noted, in relation to Rodinson, between the two senses of 'mystery'. Parris, in effect, understands mystery in possible relation to God as a puzzle requiring resolution; what is needed is explanation, and such explanation, if successful, is a limited activity in the sense that once the nature of the problem in terms of cause and effect is known, there is in principle nothing more to explain. However, the classic theological sense of 'mystery' as a reality whose unending dimensions are better appreciated the more one engages with them and knows about them requires the concept of *understanding*, a pattern of thinking that is always open to further development and enrichment (cf. Lash 2004:8–9). In other words, even if one holds strongly to the connection between goodness and God, God does not, indeed cannot, function as an explanation of goodness in the way Parris imagines.
57. In Luke's account of Paul in Athens (Acts 17:28), Paul uses these words in what appears to be an approving citation of what appears to be a sentiment of ancient Greek philosophy.
58. One might compare Robert Funk's colourful campaign for a new reformation on the basis of, among many other things, a strongly rhetorical misrepresentation of orthodox credal belief in Jesus as focussing on an 'external redeemer', who is 'not one of us', and who 'fulfills all our fantasies'; such a Jesus is (unsurprisingly) damaging 'religiously, socially and politically', and should accordingly be rejected in favour of 'a savior who understands my predicament' (1996:307–9). One must presumably suppose that the publicity given to Funk in the USA is indicative of widespread sharing of his misunderstandings.

Although numerous distinguished philosophers and theologians have argued the need to 'move on' from some of the characteristic assumptions of the Enlightenment, and in this context I cannot do more than gesture towards a way ahead, I would like to highlight the work of Nicholas Lash (1996), who addresses the specifically theological issues that are our concern.[59] Lash's general thesis is that too much contemporary theological thought is still unconsciously constrained by the deistic conceptions of God and the world that were introduced in the seventeenth century and that increasingly came to characterize modern religious thought in general. He argues that such conceptions of 'God' and 'religion' are part and parcel of a modernity whose characteristic assumptions are now significantly metamorphosing into unpredictable new forms. Instead of seeking to cling on to such notions of 'God' and 'religion' Lash argues that Christians should thankfully abandon them, recognizing the force of the modern critiques that rightly rejected both the existence of such a 'God' and the value of such 'religion'. Instead Christians should seek to relearn, downwind of modernity (and so not unlearning its lessons), older (biblical, patristic, medieval) conceptions which construe the nature of God and the world in ways many today find difficult to conceive (so deeply embedded are the seventeenth-century mental habits) but which must (for the sake of Christian truth) be freshly articulated and re-appropriated in our postmodern context.

Among the many specific issues that Lash addresses, his discussion of the term 'supernatural' directly engages with assumptions we have already noted to be important for our concerns. He says (1996:168–9):

> Consider, first, the case of 'supernatural'. Until the seventeenth century this term . . . had only been used adjectively or adverbially, to indicate the difference that is made when someone is enabled to behave in ways above their ordinary station. You come across a rabbit playing Mozart? That rabbit is performing supernaturally, is the beneficiary of supernatural gifts. So also (things being the way they are since we were barred from paradise) is the human being whom one finds behaving generously, justly, truthfully.[60] (And, of course, it is only *God* to whom

59. Lash draws on many specialist studies of the early modern period. One highly influential account is Buckley 1987, whose thesis is, in essence, that 'the origin of atheism in the intellectual culture of the West lies . . . with the self-alienation of religion itself' (1987:363). Other important sources for Lash include Funkenstein 1986, Harrison 1990, and Cavanaugh 1995.

60. Lash is here drawing on the ancient theological principle, which he cites in relation to understanding the work of Karl Rahner, that 'the possibility of experiencing grace and the possibility of experiencing grace *as* grace, are not the same thing' (1996:166).

> the term 'supernatural' could *never* be applied: who graces God? Who elevates the nature of divinity?)
>
> In the seventeenth century, for the first time, 'supernatural', the substantive, began to connote a realm of being, a territory of existence, 'outside' the world we know. With 'nature' now deemed single, homogeneous and self-contained, we labelled 'supernatural' that 'other' world inhabited (some said) by ghosts and poltergeists, by demons, angels and suchlike extraterrestrials – and by God.
>
> It is, I think, almost impossible to overestimate the importance of the massive shift in language and imagination that took place, in Europe, in the seventeenth century . . . One aspect of this shift was a transformation of the way in which relations with the Holy One, Creator and Redeemer of the world, were understood. For sixteen centuries, Christian discipleship had been understood as creaturely dependence transformed into friendship . . . By the end of the seventeenth century, 'believing in God', which, for Augustine and Aquinas, had been a matter of setting as our heart's desire the holy mystery disclosed in Christ towards whose blinding presence we walk in company on pilgrimage, had become a matter of supposing that there is, outside the world we know, a large and powerful entity called 'God'.

If Lash is at all on the right lines – and although his thesis is not beyond dispute, it has obvious contemporary resonance[61] – there is still of course much more to be said to fill out the map of modernity's theological thinking. But I want to use Lash heuristically, as a potentially fruitful way of articulating, in convenient shorthand, the perennial issue of the relationship between 'nature' and 'grace' with special reference to discernment. Thus the task is to conceptualize the relationship between the divine and the human in ways that will not turn the transcendence and immanence of God into the intrusion within the natural order of a large

61. The fit of Parris' assumptions within Lash's framework is evident. One might compare the associations of 'supernatural' in Richard Dawkins' passing remark (2003:17) that 'conjurors – professional illusionists – can persuade us, if we lack a sceptical foothold in reality, that something supernatural is going on'. Alternatively, in an interview in *The Times* (Morrison:2004) as a trailer for his new TV series *A Brief History of Disbelief*, Jonathan Miller ('avowed atheist') is quoted as saying: 'What I won't concede is that, skulking somewhere beyond the limits of what we know, there is this supernatural thing which *does* know everything . . . [There is] no "paranormal" or "supernatural" . . . Our capacity to behave generously is achievable without having to believe in the supernatural.' To which a Christian should probably just say 'Indeed', and 'Quite so'. There seems little doubt that much contemporary atheism displays both ignorance and misunderstanding with regard to Scripture and classic Christian theology, and does not understand the target it thinks it is aiming at. Or, in other terms, the kind of deity which Parris, Dawkins, and Miller reject ought no less to be rejected by Christians also. The real issues lie elsewhere.

supernatural being who does not belong there; and to be able to articulate how the fulfilment of human nature in God is to be differentiated from imposition upon, or diminution of, true humanity by something extraneous. In terms of our specific concern with prophetic speech, the need is to articulate how human speech may validly be ascribed to God in ways that fully respect human analyses of the world (not least psychological analyses of the mind, and sociological analyses of community conflicts), do not depend on literalist construals of religious language, and do not devalue the human integrity of the one who speaks for God; and to articulate how one can offer searching critical construals of claims to such speech in categories that are commensurate with those that enable its recognition in the first place.

On the heuristic assumption that it is appropriate to look to Scripture to see if such an understanding of God genuinely characterizes the Bible, and so should characterize also the faiths rooted in the Bible, it is time to turn to a detailed exegesis and interpretation of representative texts in both Old and New Testaments. However, since much of the scholarly engagement with the Bible in modern times has been carried out within a conceptual frame of reference which is, *ex hypothesi*, in certain ways questionable, it is likely that some significant misreadings of the text have become embedded in the standard literature of interpretation. For however much one observes the disciplines of philology and ancient history, attempts to 'make sense' of the content of the biblical text will necessarily draw on categories and assumptions that are unconsciously or self-critically brought to the study of the text from elsewhere (theology, philosophy, history, social sciences, etc.); and if the categories and assumptions, albeit used self-critically, are problematic, then so, in varying ways, will be the interpretations advanced. In what follows, therefore, although my prime concern will be to offer my own readings of the text, it will at times in the course of this be necessary simultaneously to try to show why certain widely favoured readings of the text may in fact be misreadings. My own readings, moreover, should not be understood as 'reading off the plain meaning' of Scripture (a notion which tends to smuggle in some doubtful positivist assumptions), but rather as disciplined attempts to construe the text with conceptual assumptions appropriate to a classic and renewed 'rule of faith'.[62]

62. For a brief account of what I do, and do not, mean by this, see Moberly 2000:39–44 (also republished in Ollenburger 2004:464–9). Perhaps I should add that I intend no exception whatever to the principle that any reading must be sustained or overturned by generally

Excursus 1: a curiosity – von Balthasar on Moses' prophetic office in Deut. 5:22–33

Israel's request for a mediator/prophet can easily excite a certain kind of 'Protestant' prejudice to the effect that Israel are surely settling for second best, in that they should really have been able to endure, indeed rejoice in, God's speaking to them face to face; to request a mediator is to lose spiritual nerve. A remarkable misreading of the deuteronomic text, along precisely these lines, comes – astonishingly – from one of the premier Roman Catholic theologians of the twentieth century, one noted for his creative fidelity to classic Roman Catholic thought – Hans Urs von Balthasar. In his suggestive study of Old Testament theology (unfortunately almost entirely ignored by biblical scholars – though I appreciate that an excursus such as this may not exactly encourage a rethink),[63] von Balthasar concludes a discussion of the concept of covenant with a lengthy paraphrastic exposition of Deut. 5:22–33 (1991:157–8):

> The immediate and absolute 'I–Thou' relationship between God and the people requires and justifies the concept of divine *jealousy* . . . Israel will not be able to sustain this 'I–Thou' relationship in the long term. It will break the covenant. The original intention is transposed *a priori*, in Deuteronomy's presentation, to Moses, the representative of the people. For the people, the voice of God rolls in waves that are too high and too dangerous, and the mediator is placed between God and the people as a breakwater: 'You, go near, and hear all that Yahweh our God will say; and speak to us all that Yahweh our God will speak to you; and we will hear and do it' (Deut. 5.27). Clericalism is something invented by the laity: even at the outset, at Sinai, the people takes up a position at a distance. The true history of the covenant will be the history of individuals, of representatives. Deuteronomy insists that

recognized canons of exegesis. Issues relating to a rule of faith properly arise at the level of the presuppositions one brings to exegesis, the nature of the questions one asks, the ways in which one contextualizes and synthesizes the exegesis, and the intended uses for one's work.

63. There have been a number of recent monographs devoted wholly to surveying work in Old Testament theology: Hasel 1991 [1972], Reventlow 1985, Hayes and Prussner 1985, Hogenhaven 1987, Perdue 1994, and especially Barr 1999. Yet none of them make any reference whatever to von Balthasar; and even if his work is self-confessedly dependent upon that of specialists within the field, it is by no means merely derivative. Despite numerous references to systematic theologians on the part of Reventlow and Barr, it is difficult not to feel that the ignorance of von Balthasar's work may be indicative of a tendency of would-be Old Testament theologians within the last generation to work in greater or lesser isolation from systematic theologians, in a way that was less true of von Rad and some of his contemporaries.

> God's voice with its commands for all the people sounded forth from the pure, formless fire of his glory. And thus the people themselves attest: 'Behold, Yahweh our god has shown us his glory and his greatness, and we have heard his voice out of the midst of the fire; we have this day seen God speak with man and man still live.' God is nothing other than a voice that calls out of the midst of the glory. And man, borne up by God's power, can hear the instruction without dying. For man is ultimately created, in a destiny that goes beyond himself, to support this voice. But the people continue, making mockery of all logic: 'Now therefore why should we die?' (And this, although they have just stated that they had seen and heard God without dying.) 'For this great voice will' (finally?) 'consume us; if we hear the voice of Yahweh our God any more, we shall die' (Deut. 5.24f). To stand fast is too great an exertion for them; they withdraw and send a representative to the front of their ranks. Moses, who communicates to them in Moab before his death the words of God which he alone has heard, has lost the game before he even begins.

Von Balthasar seems entirely unaware that this is the Old Testament's prime aetiology of Israelite prophecy, a phenomenon which elsewhere he treats positively. His negative comment on 5:27 is fascinating: 'Clericalism is something invented by the laity.' This may indeed be a valuable insight in its own right about some of the hidden dynamics within ecclesiastical hierarchies. Moreover, it is difficult not to suspect that von Balthasar's pejorative 'Protestant' depiction of the people's request for a prophet as constituting a desire for 'clericalism' was most likely written in the first flush of the Second Vatican Council. But somehow or other he manages to read the text as though the words of divine approval in verses 28–9 were absent or could just be ignored. With this crucial omission the text is transformed from a positive account of the nature and rationale of prophecy into a negative account of Israel's spiritual failing.

2

Jeremiah: the formulation of criteria for discernment

In our world, the truth seldom goes uncontested. We have seen it before. Let a Jeremiah appear; on the moment there springs up a coven of opposition, peddling other versions of God, of community, or moral behavior. The Jeremiahs are rare, that strong unmistakeable presence, a veritable field of force. Then the opposition proliferates and bears down implacable, over and against the truth-teller.

— DANIEL BERRIGAN, SJ (BERRIGAN 1999:96)

Introduction

This quest for criteria for critical discernment of prophetic authenticity will start in what is arguably the only book in the Old Testament to engage with the issue in a focussed and explicit rather than *ad hoc* way – Jeremiah. The general reason for the presence of such criteria within the book would appear to be the particular context within which Jeremiah's prophetic ministry was situated. The final years of the kingdom of Judah (late seventh and early sixth centuries) raised in an unprecedentedly disputed way the question of what kind of future, if any, the kingdom was to have, especially in relation to the growing power of Babylon. Jeremiah's witness[1] in this context was contested by other prophets in a

1. My focus will be on the received portrait of Jeremiah in the MT, without prejudice to questions of possible sources, tradition history, and redaction (though I am not unaware of likely historical depth in the received portrait). Differences between MT and LXX will only be noted where significant. The principle underlying this is that the book itself is the fruit of a process of discernment designed to present a portrait of Jeremiah in such a way as to make his significance accessible to subsequent generations (see Moberly 2004b); its heuristic value will also, I hope, be justified by its fruitfulness for moral-theological understanding and appropriation. Since recent monographs on prophetic conflict in Jeremiah (Meyer 1977, Sharp 2003; largely, Lange 2002), analyse and utilize the text in stratified, diachronically constructed categories, and also tend to pose issues in a way rather different from mine

way that is not evidenced in the books associated with Hosea, Amos, Isaiah, or Micah, or the post-exilic prophets. It is not that the words of these other prophets do not encounter their own opposition, but such opposition is predominantly expressed in terms of a reluctance to take their challenge seriously rather than in terms of alternative Yahwistic prophetic messages. There is also nothing comparable within the narrative accounts of Elijah and Elisha, where the opposition is famously depicted as arising from an alternative allegiance, i.e. to Baal (1 Kgs. 18, 2 Kgs. 10:18–27), rather than from within a shared acknowledgement of YHWH.[2]

Because Jeremiah's context was in certain ways shared with Ezekiel, the problems of conflicting Yahwistic prophecies arise within the book of Ezekiel also (13:1–14:11). There, however, they play a smaller role, probably because Ezekiel's ministry only begins when exile in Babylon is no longer a disputed possibility but rather a given. For reasons of space, the focus of this chapter will be restricted to Jeremiah.

My approach will be cumulatively to build up an understanding of Jeremiah's construal of the nature of prophecy, within the context of his moral theology as a whole. The explicit discussion of criteria for critical discernment of prophetic authenticity is Jer. 23:9–32, a section with a special heading 'Concerning the prophets' (23:9). However, this section is, in my judgment, easily misunderstood; so I wish to place it within the wider context of Jeremiah's moral and theological concerns so that one may be better able to see what Jeremiah is, and is not, saying – for the pattern of thought in 23:9–32 is foundational for the thesis of this book as a whole. A discussion of 23:9–32 will therefore be the climax of this chapter, for which the exegesis of other passages is the necessary preparation. I should also mention that the encounter between Jeremiah and Hananiah (Jeremiah 28), which many take to be the key to what Jeremiah has to say about discernment, does not, in my judgment, fulfil this role; consideration of this episode will therefore be postponed until the following chapter.

(e.g. Meyer hardly moves beyond description of the theological problem; Sharp focusses on putative ideological conflicts as mirrored in the text; Lange considers criteria for discernment to be a marginal concern in the text of Jeremiah), my interaction with them will be oblique.

2. Jeremiah does, to be sure, repeatedly charge Judah with faithlessness to YHWH and a corresponding turning to Baal (2:8, 23, 7:9, etc). Yet this plays a marginal role in the discernment of authenticity.

Prophecy and moral theology in Jeremiah: an outline

Jer. 1:1–10. YHWH's word in Jeremiah's words

> 1 The words of Jeremiah son of Hilkiah, of the priests who were in
> Anathoth in the land of Benjamin, 2 to whom the word of the LORD
> came in the days of King Josiah son of Amon of Judah, in the thirteenth
> year of his reign. 3 It came also in the days of King Jehoiakim son of
> Josiah of Judah, and until the end of the eleventh year of King Zedekiah
> son of Josiah of Judah, until the captivity of Jerusalem in the fifth
> month.

The book begins with an editorial superscription (1:1–3) which sets out the general historical context and chronology for Jeremiah's ministry. It also states as clearly as could be the theological issue which is our concern: human words, those of Jeremiah, which constitute the book that follows,[3] also convey a divine word, the word of YHWH.[4]

The singular form, 'word of YHWH', is noteworthy.[5] A plural reference to divine speech, i.e. 'words', not infrequently occurs within Jeremiah, and would seem a natural, perhaps prima facie more obvious, form to use; and such usage probably means that the singular had not yet come to have the significance it acquired in classic Jewish and Christian parlance, and so it is difficult to know how much weight it is right to ascribe to it within the context of Jeremiah.[6] Nonetheless, the singular 'word of YHWH' is already the predominant form, and the exclusive form as active

3. This is clearly a general introduction, whose point should not be lost to the perfectly proper qualifications both that portions of the book are narratives about Jeremiah (with a concluding chapter that does not mention him at all) and that some of the content ascribed to Jeremiah has been (in all likelihood) developed by others whose names, apart from that of Baruch, have not been preserved.

4. The LXX keeps the point but lacks the pattern of MT in that it begins 'The word of God which came to Jeremiah'. Since in verse 2 LXX corresponds to MT, the LXX reads awkwardly and repetitively, and its wording in verse 1 is most probably a secondary accommodation to the superscriptions of other prophetic books.

5. I am not unmindful of a general difficulty, articulated by von Rad 1965:80: 'A critical account of the prophetic concept is needed all the more urgently to-day in that we simply cannot assume that our conception of "the word of God" or of the function of words in general is identical with that held by the prophets.' The problem is heightened by the fact that von Rad's own account (1965:80–98) is in important ways rendered invalid by more recent work on the nature of language, e.g. Thiselton 1974; for a suggestive possible way ahead, see Schneiders 1999:27–63.

6. Commentators tend to deny significance here. So, e.g., Rendtorff, 'there is no coherent theory of the "word of God" . . . no fundamental distinction is made between statements about the "word" and "the words" of God' (2005:205).

subject of a verb,[7] and it creates an implicit contrast with the plural 'words of Jeremiah', in a way that suggests that the 'word of YHWH' is not the same sort of thing as Jeremiah's words. YHWH does not speak to Jeremiah in the way that Jeremiah speaks to others; where human words are many and varied, the active divine word is singular. Such singularity encourages the reader to understand 'word' in relation to YHWH as in some way metaphorical, in that YHWH does not endlessly utter one particular sound or group of syllables. Rather the prophet responds to an active divine reality which is such that the fruit of the encounter is appropriately conceived in terms of something meaningful and communicable. The singularity of the divine word may also suggest a communication that is intrinsically simple, in the sense of being a wholistic reality of a kind that involves the total range of human awareness in the task of comprehension.

At this point our text shows no interest in offering any account of how the divine word and the human words should be understood to interrelate. A simple juxtaposition, with its correlative implication of the fundamental significance of the human words that follow, suffices to set the stage. We should also note, however, that the divine word is encountered in a specific historical context. On the one hand, Jeremiah comes from a family with a long and religiously involved history.[8] On the other hand, what he says arises within a period of time, labelled conveniently by its Judahite kings (1:2–3), which led up to the exile of Jerusalem (i.e. its destruction and the deportation of many of its inhabitants by the Babylonians).[9] In an obvious sense what Jeremiah says is not

7. When the text does speak of 'the words of YHWH', *divrē yhwh* (or with suffixes, 'my words/your words', 1:9, 5:14, 15:16, 18:2, 23:22), it is always as object, never as subject, and the phrase is mainly used to depict the written content of the scroll that was read to Jehoiakim (36:4, 6, 11; but also the general 37:2). This suggests that passing or general reference to what YHWH says can readily be expressed in the plural, but that a formal introduction, when what YHWH says is active subject, is appropriately expressed in the singular.

8. The priests resident at Anathoth are most likely to be seen as descendants of Abiathar, who had served King David but who was rusticated by Solomon for having supported Adonijah's claims to the throne (1 Kgs. 2:26); and Abiathar is descended from an ancient priestly family known as the house of Eli (1 Kgs. 2:27, 1 Sam. 2:27–36, 3:11–14), which was based in the temple at Shiloh (cf. below on Jeremiah 7). This priestly family's possible involvements in the religious politics of Jerusalem, and the possible impact of such involvements upon Jeremiah, are a potentially fascinating issue – though almost entirely of a speculative kind, given the lack of evidence.

9. This is another general point, which should not be obscured either by the unarguable fact that the book itself contains material that extends beyond the fall of Jerusalem (esp. Jeremiah 40–4) or by modern puzzling as to whether Jeremiah's ministry could really have begun as early as the thirteenth year of Josiah (627/6 BC) when most of his dated oracles are dated to the reigns of Jehoiakim (609–598) and Zedekiah (597–587).

'timeless' but rather embedded in a particular time; and even if Jeremiah's words have an enduring significance beyond that of their originating context – which is already the tacit implication of this editorial superscription, quite apart from the implications of the recognition and reception of the book of Jeremiah within the collection of Israel's scriptures – the particularities of Jeremiah's own context have been preserved as integral to the comprehension of his message.

The narrative now gets underway with a first-person account of YHWH's speaking to Jeremiah and commissioning him:

> [4] Now the word of the LORD came to me saying,
>   [5] 'Before I formed you in the womb I knew you,
>   and before you were born I consecrated you;
>   I appointed you a prophet to the nations.'
> [6] Then I said, 'Ah Lord GOD! Truly I do not know how to speak, for I am only a boy.'
> [7] But the LORD said to me,
>   'Do not say, "I am only a boy";
>   for you shall go to all to whom I send you,
>   and you shall speak whatever I command you.
>   [8] Do not be afraid of them,
>   for I am with you to deliver you, says the LORD.'[10]
> [9] Then the LORD put out his hand and touched my mouth; and the LORD said to me,
>   'Now I have put my words[11] in your mouth.
>   [10] See, today I appoint you over nations and over kingdoms,
>   to pluck up and to pull down,
>   to destroy and to overthrow,
>   to build and to plant.'

YHWH's initial words are astonishing in their scope (verse 5b): Jeremiah is to be 'prophet to the nations'. One might have expected a narrower scope, since Jeremiah's own people, the inhabitants of Jerusalem and Judah, are the specified addressees of most of what he says. To be sure, Jeremiah does also address other peoples – Egypt, Philistia, Moab, Ammon, Edom,

10. Although this rendering of the common idiom *ne'ūm yhwh* is not incorrect, McKane 1986:6 freshly renders the idiom with 'you have my word'.
11. Rudolph 1968:4 notes, though does not follow, Budde's proposal to conform this usage to the norm by repointing as a singular. The emendation would make good sense, but is unsupported in the ancient versions and is unnecessary (cf. the singular object 'my word' in verse 12b).

Damascus, Kedar, Elam, and Babylon all receive oracles from him (Jeremiah 46–51; cf. 25:15–38); but one would not expect this group of oracles to characterize Jeremiah's ministry as a whole, since most of the time he is not addressing these recipients. Nonetheless, the point would appear to be that what Jeremiah will say applies not only to Israel and Judah but to other nations as well, in that the dynamics of YHWH's message through Jeremiah do not solely apply to God's chosen people but rather characterize the relationship of the Creator with created humanity generally.[12] Perhaps this also implicitly envisages the preservation of Jeremiah's words in written form, so that their scope can best be realized.

Because of the demanding nature of such a commission, it is prefaced with words of both challenge and reassurance (verse 5a): Jeremiah's identity as a human is to be understood in terms of God's purposes as articulated in this commission. On the one hand, it means that if being a prophet to the nations is the *raison d'être* of Jeremiah's existence, then this is not a vocation that could be declined or evaded without doing violence to his very being. On the other hand, if Jeremiah's vocation is an outworking of God's purposes, then what he says and does will necessarily have meaning and value – even if that meaning and value is not readily apparent in terms of Jeremiah's immediate reception.

Jeremiah's sense of inadequacy for so demanding a task (verse 6) is overruled by God (verses 7–8) with a classic articulation of what prophecy is. YHWH *sends* (*shālah*) Jeremiah, to underline that the initiative lies with God rather than human choice; and likewise what Jeremiah *speaks* on God's behalf is to accord with divine directing (verse 7b). Further, Jeremiah is not to fear, for God will be present to deliver (*nātsal*) him from his enemies. This is not a promise that Jeremiah will not encounter opposition, but that the opposition will not be permitted by God to silence or destroy him. This is tacitly demonstrated in two narratives of acute, life-threatening conflict: first, in the temple precincts, where Ahikam successfully protects Jeremiah from murderous temple officials (26:24), and secondly, when Jeremiah's hiding from an irate Jehoiakim is made successful by God (36:19, 26).

YHWH's words are now reinforced by an action, whose symbolic meaning is spelled out so that there can be no doubt about the divine

12. See further below on Jer. 18:7–10.

origin of Jeremiah's words (verse 9).[13] YHWH's commission in verse 5b is now, in characteristic Hebrew idiom, repeated with expansion (verse 10). Jeremiah's appointment to/for (*le*) the nations now becomes a position of authority over (*'al*) nations and kingdoms. This authority will be evidenced by the searching purpose of his prophecy: extensive demolition and destruction of what is presently in place, but also a building and planting which indicates a new start and fresh hope. The nature of Jeremiah's authority as 'moral' and 'spiritual' is made clear. His destruction and building could not be further from the kind of destruction of property regularly visited by the militarily powerful on those weaker than, or defeated by, them,[14] for Jeremiah's instrument is explicitly words, not sledgehammers; and yet the word of YHWH faithfully transmitted may be exactly like a sledgehammer in terms of its impact upon human life ('Is not my word ... like a hammer that breaks a rock in pieces?', 23:29). It is particularly ironic that such extensive and devastating authority is given to someone who as a person is vulnerable emotionally, socially, and militarily. The kind of reconstrual of authority and power that is deeply characteristic of the Jewish and Christian faiths (a reconfiguring of human priorities as a whole in terms that Jeremiah will spell out to do with public justice and integrity before God) is already clear within this text.

Jeremiah's commissioning thus sets out in paradigmatic form the phenomenon of the word of God in human words: the initiative for, and the content of, the human words lies with God.[15] It is important to see that at this stage, when as yet there is no contesting of Jeremiah's credentials, there is no concern to validate the testimony beyond presenting it as an authentic commissioning by YHWH. We are given a depiction fraught with implication. Criteria of authenticity will only emerge in due course.

13. The language of the text is almost identical to that of Deut. 18:19, tacitly portraying Jeremiah as one of those successors to Moses envisaged by Deut. 18:9–22, esp. 15.

14. In modern times, the 'cultural revolution' inflicted by Mao upon China stands out as a prime example of fundamental misunderstanding of the kind of clearing away necessary to enable a fresh start.

15. A strange misreading of this passage, which indicates how deeply rooted in some interpreters is the conception of God as an alien 'other' whose presence might diminish rather than enhance the prophet's humanity, is Berquist 1989:131: 'Jeremiah claims that the source of his prophecy is not himself but Yahweh. This validates his message by grounding its origins in the divine realm, and it removes Jeremiah from criticism by denying his responsibility for the content of his messages.'

Jer. 18:1–12. The nature and purpose of Jeremiah's prophetic speech

> [1] The word that came to Jeremiah from the LORD: [2] 'Come, go down to the potter's house, and there I will let you hear my words.' [3] So I went down to the potter's house, and there he was working at his wheel. [4] The vessel he was making of clay was spoiled in the potter's hand, and he reworked it into another vessel, as seemed good to him.

The scene within the potter's house is swiftly set. YHWH implictly requires an appropriate particular context for the message that is to be communicated; his word[16] will be an extended exploration of the analogical implications of a potter at work. Jeremiah obediently complies (verse 3a) and depicts what he sees there,[17] initially in general terms (verse 3b), but then with a specific instance of the potter's actions (verse 4).

It is not quite clear how much significance one should find in the details of what the potter does, for more than one detail is suggestive, but not all details are picked up in the interpretations that will follow. The fact that (a) the vessel is *spoiled* could be probed, as could the fact that (b) the potter *remakes* it, as could the fact that (c) *the new vessel appears to be a remaking of the original vessel which is not discarded as it might have been*, as could the fact that (d) the potter does what he does *as seems good to him*. But whatever the potential of the picture for fuller exploration of its details, it is points (b) and (d) that are developed in the word of YHWH that follows:

> [5] Then the word of the LORD came to me: [6] Can I not do with you, O house of Israel, just as this potter has done? says the LORD. Just like the clay in the potter's hand, so are you in my hand, O house of Israel.

Although Jeremiah is (presumably) in Jerusalem, the capital of Judah, God's address is to the people of God in general, 'house of Israel'; the address relates to God's dealings with his chosen people as a whole. The prime emphasis appears to be YHWH's power, to do as he likes just as a

16. As in 1:9 YHWH speaks of 'my words' (verse 2), but this is contextualized by the narrator's use of the singular 'the word' (verse 1) and the comparable subsequent use of 'the word of YHWH' in verse 5.

17. The Hebrew introduces verse 3b with *hinneh* (with an unusual form in the *ketib* replaced by a more common form in the *qere*), a common narrative device, with analogies to the modern use of the camera within films, to shift the point of view from the narrator's overview to the particular viewpoint of the character within the text.

potter does. Here it is worth pausing to reflect on the symbolic logic of the imagery of potter and clay as an analogy for God.[18]

The logic of the imagery is not that of interpersonal relationships, which are the characteristic and predominant mode of depicting God and His dealings within Israel's scripture: king and subjects, master and slave, husband and wife, father and son are perhaps the most common images. However unequal all such relationships were, they were always nonetheless in principle mutual; they engage the stronger party no less than, although differently from, the weaker party. Moreover, sheer pity and compassion might renew the relationship at times when it was in danger of breaking down – as, famously, God cannot restrain compassion towards his errant son Israel (Hos. 11:1–9, esp. 8–9). But with a lump of clay a potter has no relationship, no responsibilities, no feelings (other than the aesthetic, which is significant on a different plane) – the clay is an object to be used. When applied to God, therefore, the imagery of potter (*yōtser*) does not evoke mutuality, but rather unilateral power. Thus it is an idiom which is readily used in the context of God's work of creation (Gen. 2:7, 19, *ytsr*), as in God's creation of Jeremiah himself (Jer. 1:5a, *ytsr*). It is in keeping with such a sense of the intrinsic meaning of the imagery that it is used elsewhere in Scripture in two contexts: either to emphasize divine strength in contrast to human weakness,[19] or to discourage, indeed disallow, dissent from a divine decision that appears problematic and open to objection.[20] So when Jeremiah hears the word of YHWH at the potter's house saying that Israel in God's hand is like clay in the potter's hand, the primary thrust would appear to be that God can shape Israel in whatever way he will; power, not accountability or mercy, is the point of the imagery.

The sequel is therefore unexpected, not least because it does not develop the image of the potter (*yōtser*) other than in a rather general sense that change and alteration is implied in the potter's reworking of his vessel:

> [7] At one moment I may declare concerning a nation or a kingdom, that I will pluck up and break down and destroy it, [8] but if that nation, concerning which I have spoken, turns (*shūv*) from its evil, I will change

18. I draw here on my earlier discussion, Moberly 1998. **19.** Isa. 64:8–9, 2 Cor. 4:7.
20. Isa. 45:9–13 in relation to the depiction of Cyrus the Gentile as YHWH's 'anointed' in the mode of the Davidic king (45:1–7); Rom. 9:19–21 in relation to God's not only having mercy but also hardening whom He wills (9:16–18).

my mind (*niham*)[21] about the disaster that I intended to bring on it. [9] And at another moment I may declare concerning a nation or a kingdom that I will build and plant it, [10] but if it does evil in my sight, not listening to my voice, then I will change my mind (*niham*) about the good that I had intended to do to it.

Several combined factors give this passage its force. First is its clear reference to the terms of Jeremiah's commissioning in 1:10.

See, today I appoint you over nations and over kingdoms,
to pluck up and to pull down,
to destroy and to overthrow,
to build and to plant.

There is the same concern as in 1:10 with nations and kingdoms, to pluck up and break down and destroy (18:7),[22] as well as to build and to plant (18:9). Also we see that while Jeremiah 1 specified what Jeremiah was to say and do, Jeremiah 18 speaks of what God will say and do. Thus the pattern of God's word in the human words of Jeremiah is fully presupposed. This suggests that Jer. 18:7–10, and by extension the whole episode at the potter's house, functions as a kind of commentary on the purpose of Jeremiah's commissioning.

Secondly, there is the transition from the clear address to the 'house of Israel' (verse 6), indicating the totality of God's people, to a concern for nations and kingdoms generally. This gives a clue to understanding Jeremiah's overall commission to 'the nations' (1:5, 10). The underlying implication is that God's dealings with his chosen people are not different in kind, in their moral and spiritual dynamics, from his dealings with any and every people – as indeed is appropriate for the God who has formed (*ytsr*) all creatures.[23] The principles of prophetic speech apply not just to the people of God, but everywhere.

21. There is no difficulty-free translation of *niham*, but preferable is 'rescind' or perhaps 'repeal' or 'revoke'; the point is not YHWH's psychology, but rather his responsiveness whereby he will authoritatively reverse a previous equally authoritative pronouncement (I am indebted to Rob Barrett for discussion and suggestions here).

22. The fourth term in 1:10, 'overthrow' (*harōs*), is omitted in 18:7, but this makes no substantive difference. Both here and in 1:10 the LXX has one less verb than MT, but again this does not alter the sense of the text, though its idiom becomes a little less emphatic.

23. The evenhandedness of God is also a major concern in the analogous presentation of God's dealings with the world in general and with Israel in particular in the stories of the flood (Genesis 6–9) and of the golden calf (Exodus 32–4). See Moberly 1983:91–3 for the prime textual indicators, though the list could be extended. A Christian naturally thinks also of Paul's 'there is no partiality with God' (Rom. 2:11) and Luke's portrayal of Peter, 'I truly

Thirdly, the content of these words is remarkable, so striking that some commentators have found fault with it; for how could God allow His freedom to be in some way dependent upon His creatures?[24] Yet there is a simple, and surely deliberate, paradoxical logic. In a context whose imagery and explicit statement strongly emphasize divine power (verses 1–6), we have a strong statement of divine responsiveness to human attitude and action (verses 7–10).[25] The point of verses 7–10 is not to deny God's freedom, but rather to specify the moral and responsive nature of that freedom. Where God is free to act ('most' free, in terms of the text's potter imagery), God binds Himself ('strongly', in terms of the text's language) in that acting. YHWH's sovereignty is not exercised arbitrarily, but responsibly and responsively, taking into account the moral, or immoral, actions of human beings. This episode of the potter's house becomes a striking formulation of the relationship between divine sovereignty and human responsibility.

The theological principle thus enunciated is regularly exemplified elsewhere in Israel's scriptures. While Jeremiah formulates the principle with regard to nations, Ezekiel expresses much the same conceptuality in different terminology in terms of particular people (Ezek. 33:10–16, esp. 12–16),[26] which further underlines the wide applicability of the principle; though the OT tends to use Jeremiah's terminology. So, for example, God's responsiveness (*niḥam*) to human turning from evil (*shūv*, in classic terminology, 'repentance') is most famously displayed in the story of Jonah (Jonah 3:1–10), but is also appealed to in the narrative of Jeremiah's temple address (Jer. 26, esp. 26:16–19). Conversely, and no

understand that God shows no partiality' (Acts 10:34; related nominal forms of *prosōpolēmpteō* are used in each passage), and comparable sentiments elsewhere in the NT. It should be noted that neither in OT nor in NT does such lack of partiality deny a doctrine of election; rather it constitutes one of the crucial factors for understanding what election does, and does not, mean.

24. Von Rad 1965:198–9, for example, comments on 18:7–10 that it 'is meant to indicate Jahweh's freedom as he directs history, but it does this in an oddly theoretical way by giving imaginary examples which are quite contrary to the sense of the passage, for they almost make Jahweh's power dependent on law rather than on freedom', and he concludes, in a time-honoured way of dealing with a difficult biblical passage, that it 'should probably be regarded as a theological expansion'. When a Lutheran theologian speaks of a depiction of divine power as 'almost dependent on law', this evidences a high level of unease with the text.

25. This point may be missed if one puts all the interpretative weight on verse 6. Thus Stulman 1999:55 comments on verses 5–11: 'Like the potter, Yahweh is utterly at liberty to shape or remold the clay at his discretion . . . Yahweh enjoys the utter freedom to reverse the good fortune of a nation . . . on account of its "evil".'

26. Interestingly, Ezekiel's account of divine responsiveness in relation to the righteous and the wicked follows on immediately from the portrayal of Ezekiel's prophetic ministry as that of a watchman/sentinel (33:1–9). It thus interprets Ezekiel's prophetic ministry in a way analogous to the interpretation of Jeremiah's prophetic ministry in the potter episode.

less importantly,[27] God's responsiveness (*niham*) to human complacency and corruption in terms of withdrawing promised good is equally illustrated, both for the world in general (Gen. 6:5–8) and for particular people, the house of Eli (1 Sam. 2:27–30)[28] and Saul (1 Sam. 15:11, 35).[29]

We are thus presented with a fundamental axiom about prophecy.[30] On the one hand, what a prophet says on behalf of God with reference to the future of those addressed will not be realized in isolation from the response that is given. This means that whatever the precise words of the prophet, that which will take place cannot be predicted *tout court*; human attitude and action are integral to the divine unfolding of history. On the other hand, what a prophet says on behalf of God seeks a particular kind of response – turning from sin, or avoiding a turn to sin, as the case may be. Admittedly the text of Jer. 18:7–10 speaks in terms of consequence ('X then Y then Z') rather than purpose ('X in order that Y in order that Z'), yet in the wider context of Jeremiah, and much other prophetic literature, it is difficult not to conclude that purpose is indeed the sense of the words.[31] For elsewhere the appeal to turn (*shūv*) is the explicit point of what the prophet says (e.g. Jer. 3:7–10, 12, 14, 22), so that turning cannot be seen as a 'mere' consequence which is not integral to the intentionality, or purpose, of the prophetic address.[32] Prophetic speech is response-seeking speech – in the first instance the purpose of pronouncing impending disaster is that the sinful respond by turning to God,[33]

27. Elias Bickerman (1967:39) once sharply observed, 'Few among us care to remember, however, the other part of Jeremiah's startling theory: that God's promises no less than His threats are conditioned on man's conduct. We like to believe . . . that every favorable word issued from the mouth of God, even if it was given conditionally, was never withdrawn.'
28. This example displays the conceptuality without using *niham*.
29. For the construal of God's relenting in 1 Sam. 15:11, 35 in relation to the story's categorical assertion that 'God does not relent [*niham*]' (15:29), see Moberly 1998.
30. There is a difficult debate as to how far Jeremiah is innovating in relation to his prophetic predecessors, who may not have understood their message as intrinsically conditional; Bickerman (1967:38), typical of many, says that Jeremiah at this point 'offered a new perspective in theology'.
31. This view of prophecy is sometimes depicted in terms of the prophet as a 'preacher of repentance'. So, for example, McKane 1979:177 characterizes Buber's understanding of the prophets (1997:19–21), even though Buber himself prefers to speak of 'turning' rather than 'repentance'. But whatever the merits of such a characterization for depicting the primary thrust of most of the content of, say, Jeremiah and Ezekiel, it is incapable of capturing the dynamic of the warning that promised good may be forfeited through complacency and corruption.
32. See further Excursus 1 on Jer. 23:22.
33. Similarly, promised good ('to build and to plant') seeks a response of enhanced faithfulness and hope (somewhat as declarations of love between lovers seek to enhance mutual responsiveness).

but there is also the further prospect that God may then respond by withholding the disaster.

The word of YHWH to Jeremiah at the potter's house continues, however, somewhat unexpectedly:

> 11 Now, therefore, say to the people of Judah and the inhabitants of Jerusalem: Thus says the LORD: Look, I am a potter shaping evil[34] against you and devising a plan against you. Turn now, all of you from your evil way, and amend your ways and your doings.

Jeremiah is now given a specific message for those who hear him speak, the people of Judah in and around Jerusalem. This has the striking effect of strongly implying that what has been said to Jeremiah so far is *not* what he is to proclaim.[35] Rather it is for his own understanding,[36] and through him – presumably especially in his written presentation – for the understanding of Israel and other nations: they are to be able to know how the sovereign God is morally bound and responsive and how his pronouncements through his prophet are to be construed.

What Jeremiah *is* to say to his contemporaries goes back to the original image of the potter (verse 4), which is now developed in a way different from, and perhaps less intuitive than, that of verse 6. This new interpretation fixes on the specific word 'potter' (*yōtser*) which is now reinterpreted as an active participle (*yōtser*). As in the first interpretation YHWH is still the potter, but the clay is no longer Israel. Rather it is now taken to be YHWH's plan for his people, which is being fashioned and refashioned so as to bring disaster. The point would be that just as a potter can rework a vessel until it is to his liking, so YHWH can rework his impending judgment so that it will most surely come upon his people in the most appropriate and inescapable way. Yet if this use of the potter image implies the inescapable nature of impending disaster, the second part of the verse opens a way of escape (for it presupposes the understanding

34. A better translation of *rāʻāh* is 'disaster' as in verse 8, and as regularly in prophetic announcements of impending judgment (e.g. Gen. 19:19, Amos 3:6b, Jonah 3:10). What is envisaged is not 'evil' in a moral sense – and it is difficult to use 'evil' in contemporary English without a moral sense – but rather trouble or hardship, the affliction or overthrow of a city, usually through an assault by its enemies.

35. Lundbom 1999:817 comments: 'We are not told that Jeremiah delivered this oracle [sc. 18:6–10], but it can be assumed that he did.' It is not just that we are not told of Jeremiah's delivering the oracle, but we are not even told of his being required to deliver it in his public ministry.

36. Perhaps it is analogous to the interplay between Jeremiah and YHWH in Jeremiah's 'confessions'.

of prophetic speech articulated in verses 7–10): the people must turn (*shūv*), they must reform; when the prophet announces impending disaster, what he seeks is a response of turning to God. Interestingly, the possibility of divine relenting (*niham*) is not included in what Jeremiah is to say. This is not because it is not integral to an understanding of prophecy, but because it may not be necessary or appropriate on the practical level: the moral and spiritual challenge to turn requires response on its own terms.

> 12 But they say, 'It is no use![37] We will follow our own plans, and each of us will act according to the stubbornness of our evil will.'

This appears to be a kind of comment upon what has preceded, though it is also an introduction to what follows (verse 13 begins with 'therefore . . .'). The identity of the initial speaker who cites what Judah says is not entirely clear. The words could be ascribed to YHWH as a continuation of verses 6–11, or to the voice of the narrator who introduced the section (verse 1a), or to Jeremiah himself. Whichever way, the thrust of the words is clear: Jeremiah's prophetic warning and challenge is not going to elicit the kind of response that it seeks, i.e. turning (*shūv*). Rather, instead of attending to YHWH's plan (*mahashāvāh*), the people are fully resolved to pursue their own plans (*mahashāvāh*) and go their own way.[38]

Contextually this signifies a refusal to engage with the implications of the potter and clay imagery. Although the preceding explication has predominantly emphasized the possibilities of change – in effect, YHWH can reshape the vessel into something better (stronger, more beautiful, more serviceable) if the people are responsive to the prophetic message – the people will have none of it. They wish only to be the kind of vessel

37. The Heb. *no'ash* appears to be an expressive one-word response, whose idiomatic equivalent in English would be a comparable single word, e.g. 'Hopeless', 'Useless'. Its sense is indicated by its use in 2:25b, where, as in 18:12, it introduces a statement of determination to resist Jeremiah's appeal and to persist in a course already chosen.

38. The people are here imagined to speak about themselves in the kind of pejorative terminology that is elsewhere used by YHWH when speaking about them (Jer. 3:17, 7:24, 9:13 (ET 14), 11:8, 13:10, 16:12, 23:17); and there is a comparable occurrence in Deut. 29:18 (ET 19). It is imaginatively suggestive if one thinks of the people as taking to themselves these pejorative terms and being willing to use them contemptuously ('You call us stubborn and evil? Fine, that's how we'll be'). Against this it can be argued that one should not press the significance of the people's sentiment being transposed into a Jeremianic idiom, because it may simply be the way in which the author thinks. But even if one cannot press the point in authorial terms, it may nonetheless be a legitimate point in terms of the narrative dynamics within the text.

they are already are, with no fresh possibilities opened up. They are not malleable, but unchanging, rigid. It thus comes as no surprise when the narrative resumes in ch. 19 that Jeremiah is told to take a jug, which is explicitly said to be a 'potter's jug' (*baqbūq yōtser*, 19:1),[39] and to smash it with the accompanying interpretation: 'Thus says the LORD of hosts: So will I break this people and this city, as one breaks a potter's vessel (*keli hayyōtser*), so that it can never be mended' (19:11). Jeremiah's words enunciate what the context of ch. 18 has already established: the earthenware jug represents the people of Judah and Jerusalem. If the pot will not allow itself to be the kind of vessel that its maker requires, then the potter will do away with it by smashing it to pieces; and the final irony of the refusal to change is that the smashing will be one that is beyond change through mending. Even if this will not represent the ultimate decision on the part of the potter, who will not be as inflexible as the clay (Jeremiah 30–3),[40] it represents a real decision whose dire outworking is narrated elsewhere within the book of Jeremiah.

Jer. 3:6–11, 4:3–4. The difficulty of repentance

It is one thing to recognize that prophetic warnings seek a response of turning to God. It is another thing to be able to discern when that response of turning is genuinely being made. Many writers in the OT are well aware that it is all too easy to make a claim of engaging with God while in fact lacking the reality.[41] So also within Jeremiah there is a recurrent awareness that claims to turn to God may in reality be less than they appear to be. Thus I move now from passages which explicitly speak of Jeremiah as prophet to the first of a number of passages which illuminate aspects of wider prophetic conceptuality.

One of the dominant concerns in an early section of the book, 3:1–4:4, is 'turning'. The section is structured around the verb 'turn' (*shūv*), with numerous plays upon this verbal root. A good example is 3:6–11:

> 6 The LORD said to me in the days of King Josiah: Have you seen what she did, that faithless one ['turning away', from *shūv*], Israel, how she went up on every high hill and under every green tree, and played the

39. *BHS* ad loc. notes the linkage with 18:2ff., and suggests that this may be a reason for deleting *yōtser*. Quite apart from the fact that this is not a text-critical judgment, and so does not belong in a text-critical apparatus, it illustrates rather well how the quest for a putative original form of the tradition can impede rather than assist an understanding of the text in its received form.

40. See further Excursus 3.

41. Two famous examples are Isa. 29:13 and Josh. 24:16–24.

> whore there? [7] And I thought, 'After she has done all this she will
> return [*shūv*] to me'; but she did not return [*shūv*], and her false sister
> Judah saw it. [8] She saw that for all her adulteries of that faithless one
> [*shūv*], Israel, I had sent her away with a decree of divorce; yet her false
> sister Judah did not fear, but she too went and played the whore.
> [9] Because she took her whoredom so lightly, she polluted the land,
> committing adultery with stone and tree. [10] Yet for all this her false
> sister Judah did not return [*shūv*] to me with her whole heart, but only
> in pretence [*sheqer*], says the LORD. [11] Then the LORD said to me:
> Faithless [*shūv*] Israel has shown herself less guilty than false Judah.

Whether or not one can identify a particular historical allusion in verse 10,[42] the important point for our concerns is the juxtaposition of two of the key terms within Jeremiah, 'turn' (*shūv*) and 'pretence/falsehood' (*sheqer*). Claims, even attempts, to turn to YHWH, whether in response to Jeremiah or someone else, may be vitiated by superficiality. As we will see, *sheqer* in the context of moral and spiritual language and practice denotes a fundamentally self-serving attitude which lacks integrity ('a whole heart', verse 10).[43] Even a moving, and genuine-sounding, expression of turning to YHWH (3:22b–25) receives only a cautious response which emphasizes that turning to YHWH must be genuine (4:1–2), and the section concludes with a restatement of what turning to YHWH entails (4:3–4):

> [3] For thus says the LORD to the people of Judah and to the inhabitants of Jerusalem:
>
> Break up your fallow ground,
> and do not sow among thorns.
> [4] Circumcise yourselves to the LORD,
> remove the foreskin of your hearts,
> O people of Judah and inhabitants of Jerusalem,
> or else my wrath will go forth like fire,
> and burn with no one to quench it,
> because of the evil of your doings.

The initial image is that of a field which has suffered neglect – its ground has become hard and given over to weeds. If it is to become fruitful again with a crop that a farmer may want, then the sowing of seeds requires

42. Probably the most common option among modern commentators has been to find a reference to Josiah's reform.

43. Indicative for the sense of *sheqer* is Jer. 5:2–3, where it appears as the opposite of *'emunāh* ('faithfulness', 'trustworthiness'); *sheqer* is comparably contrasted to *'emeth* in 9:4 (ET 5); also in 6:13 being greedy for gain (*bōtsēa' betsa'*) is closely linked with practising *sheqer*.

thorough preparation: the removal of the weeds and the tilling of the earth. The second image, circumcision, recognizes the way in which any ritual practice may become so externalized that it fails to symbolize a reality larger and deeper than itself. The prescription for this is twofold: first, to have a renewed sense of the purpose of the ritual not as sufficient in itself but as directed towards God ('circumcise yourselves *to the* LORD'); secondly, so to internalize and appropriate the ritual that it represents a purifying of the very springs of thought and action ('remove the foreskin *of your hearts*').[44] Each image seeks to overcome likely superficiality by requiring depth and thoroughness in turning to God; the temptation to try to turn to God, only 'not with a whole heart', must be recognized as a fraud (*sheqer*).

Jer. 7:1–15. The temple sermon and religious complacency

Jeremiah's address in the temple precincts in Jerusalem comes twice within the book (for reasons that are not entirely clear). In ch. 7 there is mainly speech, with a brief narrative introduction, while in ch. 26 there is mainly narrative, with a brief speech summary at the outset. Our focus will be upon ch. 7, which further amplifies some of the key moral and theological concerns within Jeremiah.

> 1 The word that came to Jeremiah from the LORD: 2 Stand in the gate
> of the LORD's house, and proclaim there this word, and say, Hear the
> word of the LORD, all you people of Judah, you that enter these
> gates to worship the LORD. 3 Thus says the LORD of hosts, the God
> of Israel: Amend your ways and your doings, and I will let you dwell
> in this place.[45] 4 Do not trust in these deceptive [*sheqer*] words:

44. There is comparable language in Deut. 10:16. Moses has reviewed Israel's history as continuously stiff-necked and rebellious, not only at the very mountain of God but elsewhere in the desert (9:7, 8, 22, 24) and is climaxing this part of his address with a challenge to Israel to respond more faithfully in future (10:12–22); within this context there is an appropriate emphasis that Israel's response must be as searching and fundamental as possible.

45. NRSV margin, adopted here, which follows the vocalization of MT (*sh-k-n, pi'el*), is preferable to NRSV text (*sh-k-n, qal*, 'and let me dwell with you'), because the threat of exile is the note on which the sermon culminates (verse 15), and so the possibility of averting exile is the appropriate note to sound at the outset (*contra*, e.g., Ehrlich 1968:259, 261; Rudolph 1968:50, 54). The issue is whether YHWH will permit Judah to remain in and around Jerusalem or else send them into exile, rather than whether YHWH's presence will remain in the temple or else depart – which is indeed the content of Ezekiel's powerful vision (Ezek. 8–11); but Jeremiah should not be conflated with Ezekiel. Jeremiah's point is not that Judah's sin will cause YHWH to distance Himself from Judah, but that Judah's sin will cause YHWH to distance Judah from Himself. These are not just two sides of the same coin, for Jeremiah's point is that the divine presence can become a positive danger to a sinful people – in offending God, they endanger themselves.

> 'This is[46] the temple of the LORD, the temple of the LORD, the temple of the LORD.'

A position in the entrance, with people coming and going, would give Jeremiah's words maximum exposure to the would-be worshippers of YHWH. Two things are proclaimed initially (verse 3). First, there is a call to 'amend' (*heytiv*) their ways. We have seen that elsewhere Jeremiah's prime call is to 'turn' (*shūv*). Why that word is not used here is unclear, but the difference is only one of terminology, not of substance,[47] for with each term a change towards greater integrity under God is the goal.

Secondly, there is a promised consequence of amendment, continued dwelling in Jerusalem and Judah around the temple as the heart of the land. The presuppositions here are twofold. On the one hand, warfare was a regular part of life, and deportation into slavery was a regular consequence for failing to withstand a powerful aggressor. The possibility that enemies might come and overthrow Judah and take the most significant of its surviving inhabitants into exile was never far away; especially when Jeremiah had regularly spoken of YHWH raising up an enemy against Judah as an instrument of divine judgment upon their faithlessness.[48] On the other hand, YHWH can protect his people, and keep them from overthrow and deportation. However, this protection is not unconditional, as it requires appropriate human conduct. Moreover, there is an implicit warning, which will soon become explicit, that YHWH's presence may in fact become the prime reason for an unresponsive people to be taken into captivity and exile.

It is the thought of divine protection that leads into verse 4. For the natural assumption would be that in the place where YHWH is in some way specially present – which is how all strands of the OT in their various ways understand the Jerusalem temple – His power to deliver would be most likely to be realized. If therefore the people wish to reassure themselves in time of threat, then the most natural thing to do would be to invoke the fact of the divine presence in that place. Thus the repeated assertion that 'this is the temple of YHWH' is clearly envisaged as a ground

46. There is a textual problem noted by NRSV margin: 'Heb *They are*'. For the Hebrew has the plural pronoun *hēmmah* instead of the expected singular *hū'* or *zeh*. Amidst various proposals – one thinks perhaps of a cluster of buildings in the area – the most apt comment is McKane 1986:161: 'The puzzle of *h-m-h* is unsolved.'

47. The wording of 7:3aβ, *heytivū darkeykem uma'aleleykem*, is identical to that of Jeremiah's challenge to Judah in 18:11bβ, where it is immediately preceded by *shūv*.

48. So important is this within Jeremiah's message that it constitutes the content of the second of the visions which immediately follow Jeremiah's commissioning (1:13–16).

for confidence and trust. One naturally thinks of those psalms that celebrate YHWH's presence in Zion: 'The LORD of hosts is with us; the God of Jacob is our refuge' (Ps. 46:12 ET 11).[49]

Jeremiah, however, pronounces such a trust in YHWH's protecting presence to be a falsehood or deception (*sheqer*). If one can understand this, then much else within Jeremiah, not least to do with prophetic authenticity, will also make sense.

It is important initially to see that what Jeremiah pronounces to be deceptive or false is, on one level, undoubtedly true. For, as a matter of fact, the building in question was a temple and it was dedicated to YHWH. Nor is Jeremiah implying that the dedication is empty or meaningless, either in the sense that it should really be called 'temple of Baal', or in the sense that YHWH was not there but somewhere else; as the address continues, YHWH emphatically acknowledges the temple as his own, both in that it is called by his name (verses 10, 11, 14) and in that when people come to worship they stand 'before me [YHWH]' (verse 10). Thus words may be factually true and yet, in the way that they are understood and used, be false. How and why this is the case is spelled out in what follows.

> [5] For if you truly amend your ways and your doings, if you truly act justly one with another, [6] if you do not oppress the alien, the orphan, and the widow, or shed innocent blood in this place, and if you do not go after other gods to your own hurt, [7] then I will let you dwell[50] in this place, in the land that I gave to your ancestors for ever and ever.

49. Commentators regularly suggest that the tradition of Jerusalem's deliverance in the time of Hezekiah and Isaiah (Isaiah 36–7) underlies the confidence that is here called in question. Some such background awareness is certainly conceivable. However, a strong thesis that differing attitudes to the Isaian tradition is the key to understanding prophetic conflict in Jeremiah as a whole has recently been put forward by Sweeney 2003. In discussing the temple sermon he comments (p. 17): 'The presumption that the Jerusalem Temple signaled YHWH's guarantee of security for the city of Jerusalem and the house of David is a basic tenant [*sic*] of Isaiah's prophetic message approximately a century before. The book of Isaiah is clear throughout, i.e., if the Davidic monarchs would put their trust in YHWH, YHWH would protect Jerusalem and the Davidic line . . . From the standpoint of late-seventh/early-sixth century Jerusalem, Isaiah's prophecies were understood to support the notion that YHWH would protect Jerusalem and the house of David.' Yet the confident assertion about how Isaiah was understood is a hypothesis, and one which says nothing about the significance of Isaiah's precondition of putting trust in YHWH, and what would count as its realization. From a theological perspective the appeal to Isaiah hardly furthers understanding if there is no clear distinction between genuine trust, which brings with it an openness to YHWH and obedience to his will, and complacency, which uses religious language uncomprehendingly, not least to buttress self-will.

50. The Hebrew verb is identical to that in verse 3. NRSV fails to repeat its marginal note as in verse 3.

The succinct formulation of verse 3 is now resumed and expanded. The content of amendment (or turning) is spelled out. First and foremost, the content is the practice of justice (*mishpāt*) in public dealings.[51] This general thrust is then given detailed specification (characteristic of the OT) in terms of refraining from taking advantage of those of whom advantage could most easily be taken; first the resident foreigner, who is away from the protection and support of family and kin and so easily victimized; secondly, the orphan and widow, who have lost the protection and support of their man in a male-dominated society. Shedding of innocent blood envisages manipulation of the processes of law to condemn and execute those who, like Naboth, had done nothing to deserve it. The going after other gods represents fundamental disloyalty to YHWH (as in the first of the Ten Commandments), and a denial of the heart of Israel's identity as the people of YHWH, in the kind of way that would lead to their own disintegration. The moral and spiritual demands articulated by Jeremiah are to do with the practices, priorities, and allegiance of Judah's public life. Finally, the fact that the land was given of old as a gift in perpetuity gives no reason for a complacent assumption that residence in the land is assured; only if there is amendment of living will continued dwelling in Jerusalem and Judah be permitted.

> 8 Here you are, trusting in deceptive [*sheqer*] words to no avail. 9 Will
> you steal, murder, commit adultery, swear falsely, make offerings to
> Baal, and go after other gods that you have not known, 10 and then
> come and stand before me in this house, which is called by my name,
> and say, 'We are safe!' [*nātsal*] – only to go on doing all these
> abominations?

The formulation of verse 4 is now, like that of verse 3 in verses 5–7, resumed and expanded. The earlier repetition of 'This is the temple of YHWH' is now clarified by the declaration 'We are safe.' The verb in question, *nātsal*, is one that is used for deliverance from one's enemies, as in YHWH's opening assurance to Jeremiah (1:8). So the people are clearly proclaiming YHWH's (anticipated) deliverance of Jerusalem from its enemies.

This, says Jeremiah, is false, *sheqer* – because of the people's behaviour, their self-seeking exploitation of others, and their failure to be true to

51. The emphatic form of the verbs 'amend' and 'act/practise' (prepositive infinitive absolute) contributes to Jeremiah's wider concern that response should be genuine and not superficial. NRSV 'truly' well captures the idiomatic sense.

their basic allegiance to YHWH. The fundamental nature of this failure is highlighted by the fact that each of the transgressions mentioned here is prohibited in the Ten Commandments, the prime charter of Israel's existence as the people of YHWH.[52] Jeremiah thus spells out a basic contradiction between corrupt living and expectations of God's protection. To speak of YHWH and His presence and protection is self-involving language, which commits those who would speak thus to live in accordance with YHWH's own priorities. To suppose that one can use the language and yet detach oneself from its intrinsic moral and spiritual dimensions is to empty the language of its content and indeed to abuse it – which is why claims about YHWH's temple, which may be factually true, can become essentially untrue, *sheqer*. But not only is it the case that YHWH's presence in the temple does not guarantee protection for the corrupt; the thrust of Jeremiah's indictment and warning is that the divine presence will actually ensure the very thing that the people fear and from which they seek deliverance.

> 11 Has this house, which is called by my name, become a den[53] of
> robbers in your sight? You know, I too am watching, says the LORD.
> 12 Go now to my place that was in Shiloh, where I made my name dwell
> at first, and see what I did to it for the wickedness of my people Israel.
> 13 And now, because you have done all these things, says the LORD, and
> when I spoke to you persistently, you did not listen, and when I called
> to you, you did not answer, 14 therefore I will do to the house that is
> called by my name, in which you trust, and to the place that I gave to
> you and to your ancestors, just what I did to Shiloh. 15 And I will cast
> you out of my sight, just as I cast out all your kinsfolk, all the offspring
> of Ephraim.

The point of the ironic reference to a den/cave of robbers appears to be that the temple has become a place where corruption can flourish and its perpetrators can consider themselves secure. Yet although a cave is an enclosed space where those inside might think that they are out of sight, the temple, though indeed an enclosed space, is where YHWH is present and all that goes on is transparent to his sight. YHWH's response to what he sees can be learned from a precedent, the former temple at Shiloh.

52. The OT's presentation distinguishes the Ten Commandments from all other laws, not only by setting them first, but also by presenting them as uniquely spoken and written by YHWH without the mediation of Moses. Deut. 4:13 even identifies the Ten Commandments with the covenant itself.

53. Heb. *me'ārāh* means 'cave'.

At the time of Jeremiah's speaking, this temple was in ruins and had been abandoned. The temple in Jerusalem is no more privileged than the one in Shiloh, even though each is a place of YHWH's name. If the corruption of Israel led to the overthrow of Shiloh – presumably envisaged in terms of YHWH's using the Philistines whose victory over Israel is recounted in 1 Samuel 4 (even though that narrative focusses on the fate of the ark and the priests of Shiloh, and does not mention the destruction of the temple)[54] – then the corruption of Judah can similarly lead to Jerusalem's overthrow at the hands of an enemy, operating at YHWH's behest. The result will be that Judah will no longer be 'allowed to dwell in this place', but they will suffer the deportation that is the fate of the vanquished.

The point, therefore, of Jeremiah's warning is not only that the failure to display moral and spiritual integrity (*mishpāt*) transforms any kind of claim to YHWH's presence and protection into a falsehood (*sheqer*), such that without amendment (in effect, *shūv*) destruction and exile will happen. For the very divine presence that was looked to for protection will become the decisive factor in the people of Judah losing everything as they become slaves in a foreign land – 'I will cast you out of my sight.' Complacency and corruption can transform the divine presence from blessing to bane.[55]

Jer. 6:13–15//8:10b–12.[56] Superficial words

13 For from the least to the greatest of them,
  everyone is greedy for unjust gain;
and from prophet to priest,
  everyone deals falsely [*sheqer*].

54. There are strong theological resonances between Jeremiah 7 and 1 Samuel 4. The complacent, indeed superstitious, attitude of the Israelites, who suppose that the presence of the ark will guarantee victory over the Philistines, is confounded by the fact that the presence of the ark leads to a defeat far more crushing than that suffered previously. The words of Israel's elders in 1 Sam. 4:3, 'Let us bring the ark of the covenant of the LORD here from Shiloh, so that he may come among us and save us from the power of our enemies', are a close functional equivalent to 'This is the temple of YHWH' and 'We are safe' (Jer. 7:4, 10); and YHWH's response, implicit in the narrative of 1 Sam. 4–6, and explicit in Jeremiah's warning, is closely comparable.

55. There are strong theological resonances between Jeremiah's temple sermon and Micah's 'temple sermon' in Mic. 3:9–12. Micah denounces Israel's leadership: they are corrupt and venal, and yet they claim YHWH's protection, 'Surely the LORD is with us! No harm shall come upon us.' As a result of this (*lākēn*, 'therefore') both temple and city will be destroyed; that is, the very divine presence to which they complacently appeal will bring about the disaster they fear. The fascinating use of this passage in Jer. 26:17–19 illustrates, among other things, the intrinsically response-seeking and contingent nature of prophecy as articulated in 18:7–10.

56. The following passage occurs in almost identical form in the two contexts noted. The translation given is of 6:13–15. The repetition in ch. 8 is only in MT and not LXX.

14 They have treated the wound of my people carelessly,
saying, 'Peace, peace',[57]
when there is no peace.
15 They acted shamefully, they committed abomination;
yet they were not ashamed,
they did not know how to blush.
Therefore they shall fall among those who fall;
at the time that I punish them, they shall be overthrown,
says the LORD.

Jeremiah's indictment begins with a general complaint about widespread venality, that people seek to profit at the expense of others (verse 13a). This leads into the more specific complaint that religious leaders, those with special responsibility to lead and guide others, have fallen into falsehood and deception (*sheqer*). This is given content by what immediately follows. The wound of the people is probably a metaphor for their moral corruption (of a kind addressed in the temple sermon). The pronouncement not just of 'peace' but of 'certain peace' is presumably a reassurance, at a time of national unease about security, perhaps especially about the possible predation of the Babylonians, that security is not endangered. Such reassurance is no doubt what the people of Judah deeply longed to hear and believe in such a context.[58] Yet to tell people what they want to hear, when it is not what they ought to hear, is to speak in a way that is basically self-serving. Jeremiah labels such reassurance 'light'/'careless', i.e. inadequate (in effect, *sheqer*) for the reasons that are spelled out in 7:1–15. The pronouncement of 'certain peace' is an exact functional equivalent of 'this is the temple of YHWH' and 'we are safe', which complacently presumes YHWH's protection when in reality the wound of the people needs to be confronted by a challenge of genuine

57. The familiar English replication of the Hebrew repetition tends to obscure the idiomatic force of the repetition, which Hebrew uses for emphasis. For example, in the case of adjectives: *ra' ra'*, 'quite worthless' (Prov. 20:14), *'āmōq 'āmōq*, 'extremely deep' (Eccles. 7:24); or with nouns, *be'ērōt be'ērōt*, 'full of pits' (Gen. 14:10). In Isa. 26:3 *shālōm shālōm* is often rendered 'perfect peace', and that should presumably be the tenor in our passage, which might perhaps be rendered 'certain peace'.

58. It is difficult not to think of Neville Chamberlain when he returned from Munich in 1938 and proclaimed 'Peace in our time', in the vain hope that the corrupt and brutal ambitions of Hitler's Nazism could be appeased without having to be confronted. At the time his words were widely welcomed within England, because they articulated what people longed to hear (not least, because of memories of the war of 1914–18 and because of Hitler's opposition to communism). To criticize Chamberlain is not simply to indulge in the wisdom of hindsight, for Churchill had long since discerned the nature of the threat that Hitler's Germany posed, even though he had been 'a voice crying in the wilderness'. Churchill spoke as a true prophet (though he himself would not have put it in those terms), who was also vindicated by events.

amendment of life, without which there will be calamity for both leaders and led.

Jer. 22:13–19. The criteria for 'knowing YHWH'

The last few passages have illuminated the meaning of key terms in Jeremiah's vocabulary, especially *shūv* and *sheqer*, and the concern with the searching integrity that God seeks of His people. The last passage to be considered before an analysis of the material 'Concerning the prophets' in Jer. 23:9ff. is an indictment of a particular king. As will be seen, Jeremiah's critiques of king and of prophets have deep affinities between them.

13 Woe to him who builds his house by unrighteousness,
and his upper rooms by injustice;
who makes his neighbours work for nothing,
and does not give them their wages;
14 who says, 'I will build myself a spacious house
with large upper rooms',
and who cuts out windows for it,
panelling it with cedar,
and painting it with vermilion.
15 Are you a king
because you compete in cedar?
Did not your father eat and drink
and do justice[59] and righteousness?
Then it was well with him.[60]
16 He judged the cause of the poor and needy;
then it was well.[61]
Is not this to know me?
says the LORD.
17 But your eyes and heart
are only on your dishonest gain,
for shedding innocent blood,
and for practising oppression and violence.
18 Therefore thus says the LORD concerning King Jehoiakim son of
Josiah of Judah:
They shall not lament for him, saying,

59. A translation which brought out the idiomatic sense would be: 'practise justice and righteousness as naturally as eating and drinking'. See further below.

60. A likely idiomatic rendering would be 'then he was a true king'. See further below.

61. A likely idiomatic rendering would be 'then kingship was true'. See further below.

'Alas, my brother!' or 'Alas, sister!'
They shall not lament for him, saying,
'Alas, lord!' or 'Alas, his majesty!'
19 With the burial of a donkey he shall be buried –
dragged off and thrown out beyond the gates of Jerusalem.

The context of this material is a lengthy section devoted to the kings of Judah (Jer. 21:1–23:8). The identity of this particular corrupt king, who is compared unfavourably with his father, is not specified at the outset, but it becomes clear in verse 18 that Jeremiah's target is Jehoiakim and the praiseworthy father is Josiah. Jehoiakim is the king of Judah most strongly criticized by Jeremiah. Significantly, Jehoiakim is never specifically criticized for worshipping a deity other than YHWH, such as Baal, and so one may presume that in formal terms his Yahwistic allegiance was not in question; the problem was on another level. Jeremiah's message made no headway with Jehoiakim, however, whose attitude to Jeremiah is most memorably portrayed in Jeremiah 36, where an unheeding king steadily slices up the scroll which contains Jeremiah's message as it is read to him, and throws it bit by bit into his wintertime brazier.

Jeremiah's criticism focusses on a lavish building project[62] – for a perennial temptation for rulers who do not rightly understand their responsibilities is to indulge in prestige building projects so as to enhance the image of their authority.[63] His criticism is initially focussed on the exploitation of those involved in the building work, the reduction of Jehoiakim's fellow people[64] to mere sweated labour (verse 13). But pretension as well as

62. It may be that the appropriate level of the impressive structures excavated at Ramat Rahel between Jerusalem and Bethlehem is the lasting remains of Jehoiakim's project (so Aharoni 1978:1000, 1006), though the text could envisage an extension of the royal palace complex in Jerusalem (so Clements 1988:133), none of which now remains (or is accessible for excavation).

63. In recent history more than one such corrupt ruler comes to mind. President Félix Houphouët-Boigny of the Ivory Coast managed to divert substantial resources of his poor country into building the world's biggest basilica at Yamoussoukro, when there was no substantial popular desire for such a building as a focus of national faith and identity. The basilica was then offered to the Vatican, which presumably felt that it could not refuse. However, the prize must surely go to Saddam Hussein. A 1999 State Department report estimated that since 1991, forty-eight palaces had been built in Iraq, at a cost of approx. $2.2 billion, in addition to the twenty or so palaces already there before the Gulf War. Some estimates put the total number of palaces at over a hundred; but there is disagreement as to what counts as a 'palace'.

64. The Heb. *rēʿa* ('neighbour', NRSV), where one might perhaps have expected *ʿam* ('people'), is noteworthy, for it depicts a person with whom one stands in a reciprocal relationship. The use of this word may be an implicit critique of royal pretension. Thompson 1980:478 makes a similar point about *rēʿa* with a delightful anachronism: 'there is a strong democratic note here'.

oppression is attacked, that is the assumption that what shows a king to be a king is the grandeur of his building work. Jehoiakim's imaginings of architectural splendour and luxury (verse 14) are confronted with a withering 'Are you a king because you compete in cedar?' Over against this are set the priorities of Josiah, which are summed up in the fundamental OT word-pair 'justice and righteousness' (*mishpāt ūtsedāqāh*), which were as regular and natural to Josiah as eating and drinking,[65] and which were appropriately expressed in judicial integrity for the poor and vulnerable who could not 'afford' justice; *that* is the proper image of kingship.[66]

Jeremiah's commendation of Josiah's judicial integrity is now strikingly transposed into a different, more explicitly 'religious', idiom: '"Is not this to know me?" says the LORD.' Although the passages chosen for consideration in this chapter have not yet included the language of 'knowing YHWH', it is another recurrent term in Jeremiah's moral theology, so that its use here is not surprising. Here we are given a quasi-definition[67] of a term which, at least in part because of its use within

65. Various different proposals have been offered for the initially puzzling reference to eating and drinking, but they generally struggle to express a relevant sentiment. So, for example, while it may be pleasing to contemplate the image of Josiah as an 'earnest, God-fearing man' who is also 'enjoying in measure the pleasures of the table (in this resembling Charlemagne, and William the Silent, and other distinguished personages), but resolute in administering justice ...' (Skinner 1930:248), or as a man who 'enjoyed a balanced life of aesthetic pleasure and the practice of justice' (Carroll 1986:428), such thoughts are extraneous to Jeremiah's concerns, whose problem with Jehoiakim was neither gluttony nor immoderation. The construal which I offer here, that 'eat and drink' indicates that which is natural and regular (so also Ehrlich 1968:298–9 who makes the case more fully), makes excellent contextual sense by emphasizing that the practice of justice was intrinsic to Josiah's character.

66. Again, there is difference of opinion as to the sense of the repeated *'āz tōv (lō)* ('then it was well (with him)', NRSV). The issue is precisely what is being pronounced as 'good'. Commentators tend to think in terms of either Josiah's or the kingdom's condition, the point then being that justice makes for personal and/or social well-being. My suggestion is that, in context, where the nature of what constitutes true kingship is the immediate issue at hand, kingship itself is the implied antecedent. The text is a commendation of Josiah as the model of a king; so its sense, if paraphrased, is: 'that was how he showed the right pattern of kingship', 'that was how he got it right'. Michael Sadgrove has interestingly suggested a possible parallel between *tōv lō* here and *wayyahshevēhāh lō tsedāqāh* in Gen. 15:6, which would also support a sense of divine approval of Josiah's construal of kingship.

67. I say 'quasi-definition' rather than simply 'definition' because of the strongly rhetorical and polemical context. To recognize the polemical rhetoric is not in any way to undermine or fail to take seriously what is said, for what is said is clearly meant. It is to allow that this is not the kind of definition which would exclude questions of analytical precision or the specifying of further content to 'knowing YHWH' in other contexts. Unfortunately scholars who have seen the importance of the text have not always allowed for this. For example, Miranda 1977:44–5 (who has influenced Brueggemann 1988:193, 1997:613) observes: 'Here we have the explicit definition of what it is to know Yahweh. To know Yahweh is to achieve justice for the poor. Nothing authorizes us to introduce a cause–effect relationship between "to know Yahweh" and "to practice justice". Nor are we authorized to introduce categories like "sign" or "manifestation of". The Bible is well acquainted with these categories, and when it means them, it says so. A fundamental hermeneutical principle is at stake here: What possibility are

Jeremiah, has received a prominent position in Jewish and Christian theology and spirituality. A contemporary context offers many ways in which knowledge of God might be construed, but few would be likely to use Jeremiah's category of the consistent and heartfelt[68] practice of public integrity and justice.

A brief look at some of the prior usage within Jeremiah of 'know' (*yāda'*) with YHWH as object will underline the nature of the moral content ascribed to knowledge of YHWH in 22:16. The examples are predominantly negative, specifying how Judah fails to know YHWH, and they well illustrate the interpretative value of poetic parallelism:

> 'For my people are foolish,
>   they do not know [*yāda'*] me;
> they are stupid children,
>   they have no understanding.
> They are skilled in doing evil,
>   but do not know [*yāda'*] how to do good.'
>   (4:22)
>
> They bend their tongues like bows;
>   they have grown strong in the land for falsehood [*sheqer*], and not for truth;
> for they proceed from evil to evil,
>   and they do not know [*yāda'*] me, says the LORD.
>   (9:2, ET 3)
>
> They all deceive their neighbours,
>   and no one speaks the truth;
> they have taught their tongues to speak lies [*sheqer*];
>   they commit iniquity and are too weary to repent.
> Oppression upon oppression, deceit upon deceit!
>   They refuse to know [*yāda'*] me, says the LORD.
>   (9:4–5, ET 5–6)

we leaving to the sacred authors of affirming a strict identification if, whenever they attempt it, we "interpretatively" put in our categories of "sign of" or "cause" or "manifestation", which imply duality? If we were to use this procedure the biblical authors could never tell us anything which our theology did not already know.' On this account, one must presumably conclude that since Jeremiah himself did not achieve justice for the poor (the text makes no mention, nor was it his task), Jeremiah did not know YHWH. Miranda's passionate rhetoric seems somehow tone-deaf to Jeremiah's passionate rhetoric. Alternatively Volz's contention (1928:224), that verse 16 is a generalizing gloss by a pious reader of the prophetic corpus, also arrives at a decontextualizing construal by a different route.

68. This is a further paraphrase of the sense of 'Did not [he] eat and drink . . .?'

These texts all ring the changes on one basic insight – the practice of oppression, falsehood, and evil in one form or other is a disqualification from knowing YHWH. The fundamental theological rationale underlying this is articulated positively in a famous passage in the same general context:

> Thus says the LORD: Do not let the wise boast in their wisdom, do not let the mighty boast in their might, do not let the wealthy boast in their wealth; but let those who boast boast in this, that they understand and know [*yāda'*] me, that I am the LORD; I act with steadfast love, justice, and righteousness in the earth, for in these things[69] I delight, says the LORD.
>
> (9:22–3, ET 23–4)

The obvious and common grounds for human assurance[70] are here relativized in favour of a different kind of good, one which most fully and appropriately grounds human confidence and assurance: knowing YHWH.[71] Why is this the supreme good? Because of YHWH's qualities, which are not theoretical or ethereal but which are demonstrated and realized in the known realms of human life ('in the earth'). In addition to the already familiar word-pair 'justice and righteousness' there is also the quality of 'steadfast love' (*hesed*), a term which, among other things, expresses YHWH's gracious initiative and unfailing commitment towards his covenant people.[72]

However, the point of the words is missed if they are thought solely to depict YHWH in Himself, for they implicitly presuppose a human

69. It is preferable to see the final clause as a reference to those people who boast appropriately and to translate 'for in such people I delight' (cf. Duhm 1901:97). The Hebrew just has 'these' (*'ēlleh*), which could refer either to people or to things. Contextually, to say that YHWH delights in the qualities He practises would be somewhat redundant, for His practising them necessarily implies His delight in them. The point of the text is what kind of person most meets with divine approval.

70. Although being wise, a strong soldier, and wealthy are all conditions which may become problematic, and so are sometimes criticized in the OT, there is no reason to suppose that Jeremiah here views these categories pejoratively. His point is the relativization of that which usually would give acceptable grounds for self-esteem.

71. The usual *yāda' yhwh* is strengthened by an additional verb *haskēl* (and the combination is also used of the qualities of good shepherds of YHWH's people, 3:15). If there is significance in this, it may perhaps be to add the dimension of an 'intellectual' understanding of YHWH's ways, in addition to the more moral and existential dimensions of *yada'* (see further Holladay 1986:318).

72. Within the canonical structure of the OT, the weightiest presentation of the nature of YHWH is Exod. 34:6–7, YHWH's self-revelation to Moses on Sinai in the context of response to Moses' intercession for the renewal of the covenant after Israel's paradigmatic sin with the golden calf. Here *hesed* is said to characterize not only YHWH's intrinsic nature (verse 6) but also His actions (verse 7).

dimension also. The reason a person can supremely 'boast' in knowing YHWH is that such a person will have imitated and appropriated YHWH's own qualities of steadfast love, justice, and righteousness. The realization of these divine characteristics as human characteristics enables an appropriate sense of human assurance, for they make the most important and fundamental difference to life in the world that can be made, and such people receive unqualified divine approval ('in these/such people I delight'). Thus the vision of right human life is a corollary of the vision of God.[73]

However – to return to Jehoiakim in Jeremiah 22 – the problem is that the Davidic king, who has the greatest responsibility to display qualities appropriate to God,[74] may construe his power not in terms of responsible service ('judging the cause of the poor and needy') but in terms of self-aggrandizement at the expense of others. Thus Jeremiah's initial critique of oppression and pretension is renewed by an attack on Jehoiakim's venal self-seeking and generally oppressive practices (22:17). The result of these will be that when Jehoiakim dies people will not lament him with the usual expressions of grief heard at funerals; rather his end will be that of an animal, unlamented, unceremonious, and uninterred (22:18–19).[75] One might perhaps paraphrase the sense of the passage by saying that because Jehoiakim has denied the humanity of others, treating people as mere objects for oppression and exploitation, so at his

73. Compare Berrigan 1999:54: 'Here Jeremiah touches on the apogee of the religion of Israel: true "knowledge" of God . . . In these three graces the self-revelation of Yahweh is complete – and the people are granted their full humanity.'

74. Compare, for example, Psalm 72, where the portrayal of the king's priorities in terms of justice and righteousness is presented not only as a prayer, for such priorities cannot be taken for granted, but also as implicit guidance by Israel's greatest king David (72:20) for his son Solomon (I take *lishelōmōh*, 72:1, to mean 'for Solomon'), and thus as fundamental as could be within Israel's royal traditions.

75. There is a similar prophecy of Jehoiakim's unburied end in 36:30. There has been much discussion about the relationship between these Jeremiah passages and the account of Jehoiakim's death in 2 Kings. Does 'he slept with his fathers' (2 Kgs. 24:6) imply normal burial, or is it a routine formula compatible with lack of burial? The formula generally (though with some exceptions) is used for national leaders who die peacefully (Johnston 2002:34–5), and so one might expect the Kings writer, if aware of an ignominious end in line with Jeremiah's words, to choose different wording. In general terms, however, the question of what actually happened to Jehoiakim is unanswerable because of a lack of evidence beyond the texts already mentioned. The underlying issue is: what difference might possible non-fulfilment make to an understanding of Jeremiah's prophetic words? There are, however, numerous imponderables. On the one hand, whether or not Jehoiakim at any time or in any way turned to YHWH, and the difference this could have made to the outworking of the prophecy, is unknown. On the other hand, the moral vision of Jehoiakim's final loss of humanity because of his treatment of others would retain imaginative moral power as the depiction of an appropriate fate of a cruel tyrant even if its details were not realized in the history of an impenitent Jehoiakim.

dying his humanity too will be denied, and he will be treated as a mere object of heedless neglect.

Jer. 23:9–22.[76] Setting out criteria for discernment of prophetic authenticity

I have so far offered an outline of some key concepts within Jeremiah's moral theology and his construal of prophecy. YHWH's word through Jeremiah has potent authority to transform human life; prophetic speech instrinsically seeks a response of serious engagement with God (predominantly through turning to YHWH, *shūv*), such that a prophesied future is contingent upon that response; turning to God is easier to say than to do, and apparent turning may be superficial, that is false (*sheqer*); popular complacency and corruption can transform otherwise true claims about YHWH into falsehood (*sheqer*), because corrupt practice and self-serving language transform YHWH's presence from blessing to threat; religious leaders easily encourage this popular complacency and self-deception by speaking in comparably self-serving (*sheqer*) ways; lack of knowledge of YHWH is displayed by the absence in life of YHWH's moral priorities. Against this background, it is at last appropriate to consider Jeremiah's specific account of criteria for prophetic authenticity.

> 9 Concerning the prophets:
> My heart is crushed within me,
> all my bones shake;
> I have become like a drunkard,
> like one overcome by wine,
> because of the LORD
> and because of his holy words.

Most interpreters, surely rightly, construe the opening word (*lannevi'im*) as a heading for the section, separating it from the oracles about the kings of Judah that have preceded.[77] But before Jeremiah says anything about other prophets, he says something first about himself. It is a striking picture of a man overwhelmed: mentally incapacitated[78] and trembling,

76. The full unit is 23:9–32 (33–40 are a distinctive supplement). My reason for going only as far as verse 22 is pragmatic, on the grounds that the basic logic and pattern of Jeremiah's critique are already apparent by that point.

77. Comparable is 21:11, which heads the preceding collection of admonitions to the house of David.

78. I am assuming that 'heart' (*lēv*) here, as so often in the OT (e.g. Ps. 14:1, Isa. 10:7), indicates the seat of thought.

one whose behaviour is beyond his own control in the way that those who are drunk can no longer control themselves. The reason for this is 'YHWH and his holy words'. It is quite likely that the 'holy words', rather than having general and unspecified reference, are referring to all of what follows,[79] so that verse 9 is Jeremiah's response to everything that is said about the other prophets. Jeremiah's feelings are not those of superiority or triumphalism, but rather an acute anguish, discomfort, and disorientation that words and deeds that are incompatible with YHWH's holiness should be ascribed to YHWH.

> [10] For the land is full of adulterers;
> because of the curse the land mourns,
> and the pastures of the wilderness are dried up.
> Their course has been evil,
> and their might is not right.
> [11] Both prophet and priest are ungodly;
> even in my house I have found their wickedness, says the LORD.
> [12] Therefore their way shall be to them
> like slippery paths in the darkness,
> into which they shall be driven and fall;
> for I will bring disaster upon them
> in the year of their punishment, says the LORD.

This opening section focusses not on prophets alone but on prophets and priests together, as commonly elsewhere (cf. 6:13//8:10). It is a general characterization of leaders with special responsibilities to YHWH and his people who are faithless[80] and corrupt. This corruption extends even to the place of greatest sanctity, the temple. As a result, any security and stability which they think they have achieved by their corrupt ways will become the opposite – precariousness, darkness, and falling, as disaster

79. Some commentators see verse 9 as part of a unit comprising verses 9–12, with a new unit beginning at verse 13 with the specific reference to 'prophets' (e.g. McKane 1986:569). In compositional terms this may be correct. Since, however, the divine address is more or less consistent throughout the chapter after verse 9, it is probably more appropriate, in terms of reading the text in its received form, to construe 'YHWH's words' as the totality of what follows.

80. Here and subsequently it is unclear whether the primary sense of 'adulterers' is moral (faithlessness within marriages) or, more metaphorically, spiritual (faithlessness to YHWH). Although either sense is appropriate, we should note that when Ahab and Zedekiah are condemned as prophets who speak *sheqer* (Jer. 29:21–3), their conduct is sexually immoral ('folly'/'outrage', *nevālāh*, a term which seems to be used for various kinds of non-adulterous sexual malpractice, cf. Gen. 34:7, 2 Sam. 13:20; Judg. 20:6,10), and they also commit adultery explicitly 'with their neighbours' wives'.

overtakes them. It seems to be implied, as in Jeremiah 7, that it is the very proximity of corruption to YHWH's presence in the temple that makes YHWH into an agent of overthrow.

> [13] In the prophets of Samaria
> I saw a disgusting thing:
> They prophesied by Baal
> and led my people Israel astray.
> [14] But in the prophets of Jerusalem
> I have seen a more shocking thing:
> they commit adultery and walk in lies [*sheqer*];
> they strengthen the hands of evildoers,
> so that no one turns [*shūv*] from wickedness;
> all of them have become like Sodom to me,
> and its inhabitants like Gomorrah.
> [15] Therefore thus says the LORD of hosts concerning the prophets:
> 'I am going to make them eat wormwood,
> and give them poisoned water to drink;
> for from the prophets of Jerusalem
> ungodliness has spread throughout the land.'

The comparison of Samaria with Jerusalem, to the detriment of the latter, is a rhetorical device we have already encountered (3:6–11). If the prophets of the northern kingdom had generally failed to speak and lead faithfully, the prophets of Jerusalem had not only acted faithlessly and deceptively (*sheqer*) in their own right, but they had positively encouraged evildoers to persist in their course of action, with the result that any turning to YHWH (*shūv*) was out of the question. This point (which anticipates the climactic verse 22) is at the very heart of Jeremiah's critique. The consequence of all this is that ways of life estranged from YHWH's character and priorities had flourished and spread. Jerusalem has thus become like the paragons of sin (cf. Gen. 13:13). And as the undrinkable water of the Dead Sea and the blasted character of its environment are a symbol of YHWH's judgment on sin, so too the self-serving prophets will have to consume that which is bitter and life-destroying as a symbol of what they have done to the land.

> [16] Thus says the LORD of hosts: Do not listen to the words of the prophets who prophesy to you; they are deluding you. They speak visions of their own minds, not from the mouth of the LORD. [17] They keep saying to those who despise the word of the

> LORD,[81] 'It shall be well [*shālōm*] with you'; and to all who stubbornly follow their own stubborn hearts, they say, 'No calamity shall come upon you.'

After the appraisal of the character of the prophets and the nature of their impact upon others, the focus now shifts to those who are addressed by the prophets: they are warned to beware. In terms of the reader of the text, it encourages an existential awareness of the need to engage with and evaluate all purported messages from God, beginning with those in the text of Jeremiah. The prophets are 'deluding' people,[82] because what they say is merely the product of their own imagination and does not convey the realities of YHWH. Their message that things will be well, presumably in the sense that there will be national peace and security (*shālōm*),[83] is vacuous for reasons already made clear, especially in the temple sermon. Their message is detached from serious moral content, since it is supposed that national well-being and peace, which presuppose divine protection, can be expected on the part of those who are heedless of the will of YHWH. Jeremiah has reiterated that moral complacency and carelessness are incompatible with divine blessing. In other words, the absence of a challenge to the morally corrupt or heedless that they should turn (*shūv*) qualifies a prophetic promise of security (*shālōm*) as falsehood (*sheqer*).[84]

> 18 For who has stood in the council [*sōd*] of the LORD
> so as to see and to hear his word?
> Who has given heed to his word so as to proclaim it?
> 19 Look, the storm of the LORD!
> Wrath has gone forth,
> a whirling tempest;
> it will burst upon the head of the wicked.
> 20 The anger of the LORD will not turn back
> until he has executed and accomplished

81. Here and elsewhere in this section there are difficulties in the MT both in itself and in relation to the Versions. If the difficulties make no difference to the tenor of Jeremiah's words, and do not pose any specific problem for my use of the text, then I will not enter into the text-critical debate and will simply follow NRSV.
82. The verb is cognate with the noun *hevel* ('emptiness', 'vanity'), which is most famously used as the keynote of Ecclesiastes (Eccles. 1:2, etc). The point is the vacuousness of the hopes which these prophets engender.
83. Compare 14:13, 'Here are the prophets saying to them, "You shall not see the sword, nor shall you have famine, but I will give you true peace in this place."'
84. For an interesting generalization of the issue of true and false prophecy in Jeremiah 23 in relation to human attempts to establish security (*shālōm*) in the wrong ways, see Niebuhr 1938.

the intents of his mind.
In the latter days you will understand it clearly.

The point that what the prophets say represents only their own imaginings and is not from YHWH is now put in a different way: they have not had that access to the mind of God which would come from their standing in His presence, as someone who is privy to the divine deliberation and decision-making. The Hebrew term *sōd*, multi-nuanced and difficult to translate,[85] here probably means 'council', and so may imaginatively depict YHWH as a monarch surrounded by advisers and messengers, the kind of picture that is utilized by Micaiah ben Imlah (1 Kgs. 22:19–22). But *sōd* also more generally indicates a gathering of people (Jer. 15:17), and by extension the kind of understanding that characterizes those who are intimate with one another (Prov. 25:9); so it can be used to depict that knowledge of YHWH's will that is the hallmark of authentic prophets, those who stand close to YHWH, as in the axiomatic formulation of Amos 3:7: 'Surely the Lord GOD does nothing without revealing his secret [*sōd*, better is "counsel" or "purpose"] to his servants the prophets.' This depiction is not in essence different from the deuteronomic picture of Moses as the paradigmatic prophet who stands in YHWH's presence, and is thereby able to hear YHWH's word and convey it to others (Deut. 5:23–33)[86] – or indeed from the comparable portrayal of Abraham in Gen. 18:17–19, where the famous dialogue between YHWH and Abraham about the fate of Sodom is prefaced by YHWH's explicitly speaking of admitting Abraham to a knowledge of his purposes, which is with a view to furthering obedience to God's will among Abraham's descendants.[87]

The absence of the prophets from this intimacy with YHWH is evidenced by the fact that what is coming upon the people of Judah is the opposite of the *shālōm* of which they speak; rather it is a violent storm which will bring YHWH's judgment upon the wicked. However, YHWH's wrath is not random and is to fulfil his own (sc. moral) purposes, at which point it will

85. See, e.g., Fabry 1999 or McKane 1986:581–2. 86. See Chapter 1, pp. 4–10.
87. Significant also is the succinct formulation in Ps. 25:14, *sōd yhwh liyrē'āyw*, which is better translated 'the LORD confides his purposes to those who fear him' (REB) than 'the friendship of the LORD is for those who fear him' (NRSV). The basic thought is that intimacy with YHWH, in terms of access to an understanding of his will and ways, is for those who 'fear him', which is the prime OT term for appropriate human responsiveness to God (cf. Moberly 2000:78–88, 96–7). Since Abraham is a prime exemplar of fear of God (Gen. 22:12), it is a natural intertextual move to relate the principle of Ps. 25:14 to Abraham and the depiction of his privileged access to YHWH in Gen. 18:17–19 – a move interestingly made, for example, in *Gen. Rab.* 49:2.

cease. Yet it is only in the aftermath of the disaster that represents YHWH's judgment that those addressed will understand the nature of YHWH's intent (where the 'you' of the persons in danger of being deluded by the prophets readily transposes to the reader of the text).

> 21 I did not send [*shālah*] the prophets,
> yet they ran;
> I did not speak to them,
> yet they prophesied.
> 22 But if they had stood in my council,
> then they would have proclaimed my words to my people,
> and they would have turned them[88] from their evil way,
> and from the evil of their doings.

The problem with the prophets is summarized. The prophet who would speak for God must, as a corollary of standing in God's council, be sent [*shālah*] by God.[89] Only the speaker whose initiative is from God speaks for God. Yet these prophets have eagerly spoken in YHWH's name without his authorization, with the result that they 'prophesy lies [*sheqer*] . . . and the deceit of their own heart' (23:26); they speak self-servingly, telling people what they want to hear. The absence of these prophets from YHWH's council is shown by their failure to proclaim a message whose purpose was to turn [*shūv*] people from evil into ways that would be more in keeping with YHWH's will and character.[90]

Conclusion: discerning the criteria for discernment in Jer. 23:9–22

How should the argument of this key section, Jer. 23:9–22, be evaluated as a whole? There are clearly three main emphases. First, there is a lack of

88. Better is 'and they would have sought to turn them . . .', or perhaps simply 'so as to turn them . . .'. See the discussion in Excursus 1.
89. See above, p. 4.
90. I offer no detailed discussion of verses 23–32 because these verses do not, in my judgment, break fresh ground but rather develop variations on the theme of the conceptuality already established. The two prime issues that are raised in verses 23–32 are dreaming and stealing. The dreaming in particular should not be decontextualized as though it were an independent discussion of appropriate channels of divine revelation (as, for example, verse 28 might appear if taken out of context). The dreaming of verses 25, 27, 28 is rhetorically interpreted by reference to *sheqer* and 'their own heart' in verse 26, thus linking the unacceptability of dreams to the moral critique of the earlier verses, while the dreaming of verse 32 is comparably construed in terms of corrupt guidance of YHWH's people. The stealing of verse 30 underscores the derivative, merely human origin of pronouncements made in YHWH's name (verse 31). The theme of 'the burden of YHWH' in verses 33–40 develops a different and distinct facet of the problem posed by the prophets whom Jeremiah critiques.

integrity in the character and conduct of the prophets (verses 10, 11, 14a). Secondly, they fail to try to turn evildoers from their ways, indeed they positively encourage them to be morally complacent (verses 14b, 17, 22). Thirdly, their message originates within themselves and is not from YHWH, for they have not stood in the divine council (verses 16, 18, 21, 22).

The first two points, and the implied relationship between lifestyle and message, are not difficult to grasp, especially in a book where attention is paid to Jeremiah's own life as well as his prophetic words. It is the third point, and its relationship with the other two points, that has caused most difficulty to modern interpreters. This is because comprehension of Jeremiah's meaning raises the issue of the adequacy of the conceptual categories with which one seeks to construe the text. For this reason I will change the mode of argument in this section, so as to engage explicitly in my main text with the interpretations, and implied conceptual categories, of significant interpreters, in the hope that this will illuminate most clearly what the biblical text does, and does not, mean.

The claim that someone has, or has not, stood in the divine council may easily appear to be an empty claim,[91] empty because incapable of meaningful adjudication.[92] To Robert Carroll, for example (1981:164), the claim to speak for YHWH is only meaningful as an exercise in partisan hindsight, in this case that of the deuteronomistic editors responsible for the portrayal of Jeremiah:

> That is the problem with this analysis [sc. that some prophets speak out of their own minds] – it does not help determine which prophet is true and which false at the time when both are speaking in the divine name but offering different visions of the future . . . Because it is *not* obvious to the audience which prophet is speaking lies from the

91. Alternatively, it may be a puzzle to be circumvented. Overholt 1970:61 says, 'The problem, then, is whether Jeremiah is denying the validity of his opponents' message on the grounds that they had received no call. My contention is that he is not doing this, but is instead centring his attack on the content of their message.' Yet patently Jeremiah is doing both, and Overholt misses the sense in which there are distinct but related dimensions to the reality of prophetic inauthenticity (because of his own thesis, which is shared by others also, that the only real fault of the criticized prophets is their failure to read their contemporary historical circumstances with a sufficiently flexible construal of past tradition).

92. Typical is the comment of Grabbe 1995:84: 'This is not very helpful, though, since we do not know who did this. We cannot assume that other prophets did not see themselves as called by God or standing in Yhwh's council.' Unhelpful in a different way is Sweeney 2003:11, who says: 'Such a contention cannot be demonstrated by absolute standards of empirical observation.' For whatever exactly 'demonstrated by absolute standards of empirical observation' means, it sounds like a yardstick of the natural sciences by which not just theological claims but a substantial proportion of work in the humanities generally would be found wanting.

> deceit of his own mind, and which prophet is really speaking the divine word (assuming one is and the other is not, rather than that both are not), the judgment made by the redactors (through hindsight and out of their own ideology) is not available to the audience.

Yet even seasoned and sympathetic theological interpreters of Israel's scriptures can find themselves in difficulty here. If we go back to John Calvin (n.d.:3753–5), we find that he is rather unhelpful on this material. He seeks a resolution in terms of the classic understanding of prophets as interpreters of the law.[93] Calvin construes 'standing in the divine council' in terms of 'knowing the content of God's revealed Law', and interprets God's 'my words' which the true prophet would have spoken to people as 'the word of the Law'. Thus the distinction between true and false prophet is the distinction between faithful and faithless interpreters of God's Law. As he puts it later in a summary way, in the context of Jeremiah 28 (n.d.:3858):

> But as our state now is different from that of the ancient people, we must observe that sent by the Lord is he only whose doctrine is according to the rule of the Law, and of the Prophets, and of the Gospel. If, then, we desire to know whom the Lord has sent, and whom he approves as his servants, let us come to the Scripture, and let there be a thorough examination; he who speaks according to the Law, the Prophets, and the Gospel, has a sure and an indubitable evidence of his divine call; but he who cannot prove that he draws what he advances from these fountains, whatever his pretences may be, ought to be repudiated as a false prophet.

Unfortunately this is more a transposition into a different frame of reference than it is a substantive engagement with the subject matter of the text.[94] And as long as the notions of 'thorough examination' and 'prove' in relation to Scripture are considered apparently unproblematic, the genuine problems of discernment in this different frame of reference are also being sidestepped.

93. McKane (1995:48) sees Calvin's conception of the prophets as 'no more than teachers of the Law' as the reason for a lack of interest in certain critical questions surrounding prophecy. Because prophecy is derivative, 'there is no agonizing over the theological problems of inspiration and revelation'.

94. McKane (1995:48) points out that Calvin's working analogy between biblical prophet and Christian minister underestimates the differences between them and 'reduces' the prophetic office.

More recent commentators have the benefit of a sharper historical frame of reference and more nuanced religio-historical conceptualities than were available to Calvin, but these of themselves do not resolve the problems. Walter Brueggemann (1997:631, 632), for example, says in a general way that:

> Prophetic mediation makes a claim of authority that is impossible to verify. That is, all of these claims and uses are reports of a quite personal, subjective experience. No objective evidence can be given that one has been in the divine council. No objective support can be given to a messenger formula. No verification of a call experience is possible. These are all formulations that seek to confirm a hidden experience of transcendence . . . The prophets provide only tenuous, highly subjective grounds for their disturbing utterances.

It is surprising that, in a book which consistently seeks to reconfigure the task of theological interpretation of the Old Testament within a contemporary pluralist (postmodern) context, Brueggemann at this point lapses into characteristically 'modern' categories of a sharp antithesis between the 'objective' and the 'subjective' in which speech on behalf of God, and talk of the divine council, is entirely relegated to the latter. The basic biblical and theological notion that the given (objective) knowledge of God may be intrinsically self-involving (subjective) is strangely absent. To be sure, Brueggemann does not want to abandon the notion of prophetic truth, and so formulates how it may still be conceived (1997:631):

> In the end the canonizing process has accepted certain prophets as genuine, even though these prophets were not readily accepted in the context of their utterance. We must not imagine, however, that a decision in such a canonizing process is necessarily an innocent or neutral one. Undoubtedly the process of determining who speaks a true word of Yahweh is decisively controlled by larger, albeit not disinterested, notions of what constitutes genuine Yahwism in any particular moment of crisis. The canonizing process, which produced and authenticated the voices now accepted by Israel as 'true prophets', is surely an ideological struggle, both to define Yahwism and to determine who would define it.

But again Brueggemann's categories are surprising, as though the only choice were between an 'innocent or neutral process' or an 'ideological struggle'. I cannot imagine that any informed interpreter today would envisage the canonizing process as 'innocent or neutral', while 'ideological struggle' is too amorphous and all-embracing to lend analytical precision in this context. Neither alternative captures well the kind of particular moral and spiritual vision of God and humanity that underlies the canonizing of a book such as Jeremiah, or the way in which the content of this vision implies particular kinds of struggle on the part of those biblically rooted communities of faith for whom the text becomes normative. Ultimately, it is hard to see how, in substance, Brueggemann differs from Carroll, since for each the bottom line appears to be an ideological struggle that has embodied the wisdom of hindsight in the biblical text but appears otherwise to be intrinsically beyond the realm of meaningful arbitration;[95] the difference is that Brueggemann is favourably disposed towards the ideology of the canonizing process while Carroll is not.

Alternatively, Terence Fretheim (2002:342) summarizes his analysis of Jeremiah 23 thus:

> Various criteria were apparently used to try to distinguish truth from falsehood, and some of these efforts may be evident in this text. Examples include: their worship of false gods, including Baal; promising good news rather than judgment; false claims to have received a word from God or to have had visions or dreams; immorality; absence from the council of the Lord. Yet, these are not sure-fire criteria, not least because these claims cannot be publicly demonstrated . . . finally, one is stuck with a 'Wait and see' approach to such matters.

Fretheim simply lists the various apparent criteria mentioned in the text, and makes no attempt to analyse their intrinsic logic and interrelatedness. It is hardly surprising, then, that he can find no genuine value in them – his 'not sure-fire' seems to be a disarming euphemism for 'effectively unworkable in practice'. He makes no progress beyond Carroll and Brueggemann, since he too finds hindsight to be the only real criterion of discernment.

95. In his earlier commentary (1988:205), when discussing Jer. 23:18–22, Brueggemann ascribes a positive role to the content of the prophetic message: 'Against this background of the divine council, the final adjudication among these various voices is made on the actual substance of the message.' Since, however, he also (1988:201) speaks of 'no objective criteria by which to adjudicate the various claims' and depicts Jeremiah being legitimated by the canonical process through the benefit of hindsight, there does not appear to be any significant shift within Brueggemann's thinking, for his consistent point appears to be that the content is only validated in hindsight.

Finally, Patrick Miller (2001:752, 754), sees two prime criteria of discernment in Jer. 23:9–40: access to the council of YHWH, and speaking a challenging message. These he discusses in isolation from each other, as though there were no intrinsic relationship between them. With regard to the divine council he says:

> It is difficult for the interpreter to determine how it was that the prophet gained access to the council of the Lord. Isaiah 6 and 1 Kings 22 suggest the likelihood of some kind of visionary experience that may have belonged to the ecstatic dimensions of prophecy. Contemporary language for this would be an 'out-of-body experience'. From a number of texts, we know that the prophets had visions ... Such a revelatory medium is not accessible to rational analysis or objectification, but the authority of such a vision was profound and clearly part of the credentials of the true prophet. The only problem, of course, was that any prophet could claim to have a vision of the council of the Lord.

Miller makes two assumptions, each of which is characteristic of a peculiarly 'modern' construal of religious experience.[96] First, claims about the divine council must be based upon unusual or abnormal states of consciousness;[97] secondly, they are non-rational and subjective in a privatizing kind of way. In the light of these, however, the claim that 'the authority of such a vision was profound' is hard to credit with much content, as it is immediately undercut by the problem that anyone could make such a claim.

The problem is that certain widely held, but in fact deeply questionable, assumptions about the nature of religious experience and language make it difficult to appreciate the logic of the biblical text in its appeal to the divine council. Within the Old Testament, however, the deuteronomic account of Moses' standing in YHWH's presence (5:23–33), or the

96. The classic formulation is William James 1960 [1902]. Yet recent work in the philosophy of religion has revealed deep conceptual confusion within James' work, and has proposed alternative models for envisaging encounter with God, models both conceptually more coherent and also more deeply rooted in biblical and historical Christian theology and spirituality. See especially Lash 1988. The essence of Lash's approach is succinctly spelled out in Lash 1996:93–111.

97. To be sure, unusual experiences and times of heightened consciousness, even out-of-body experiences, do happen and are well attested. The most famous biblical example is probably Paul's being taken up to the third heaven, though whether in or out of the body he was unsure (2 Cor. 12:1–4). The key question, however, is what kind of significance should be attributed to such experiences. We will discuss this later, pp. 201–6.

comparable account of Abraham's standing in YHWH's presence (Gen. 18:17–19), may provide a more helpful heuristic guide. In these accounts there is no interest whatever in 'ecstasy' or in content whose validity would require hindsight, but rather in a moral and spiritual proximity to YHWH whose purpose is explicitly to convey a content to Israel for their benefit.[98] In the light of this, the logic of Jeremiah's argument becomes, in principle, simple: the all-important claim to be from God – to have stood in the divine council, to be sent, to speak YHWH's word(s) – is to speak of a divine realm that is not vacuous, for the reason that it is the prophet's lifestyle and message, whose moral character are open to scrutiny in the present, which give content to the claim about God. The 'spiritual' nature of the prophetic message, whether or not it is from God, is determined by its 'moral' content and accompaniment.[99] Claims about the invisible spiritual realm are validated (or not) by the content of the visible and accessible realm of character, conduct, and priorities. Standing in the council of YHWH is not a matter of some unusual 'experience' but of having a disposition that is open to, engaged with, and responsive to YHWH's will for his people when YHWH calls; such a person's consciousness is indeed altered, but not through transitory or induced states of 'exaltation' but through appropriation of God's will in such a way that one's vision of the world and of life within it, and one's conduct correspondingly, is transformed. The trouble with the prophets whom Jeremiah denounces is that the character of their conduct and message show all too clearly that what they say is self-willed and people-pleasing and does not convey the will of YHWH.

This critique of the prophets is not fundamentally different from the critique of the kings, however much the specifics and the details vary. If one sets alongside each other the culmination of the critique of Jehoiakim and the culmination of the critique of the prophets, the point should be clear:

> Did not your father [Josiah] practise justice and righteousness
> as naturally as eating and drinking?
> Then he was a true king.
> He judged the cause of the poor and the needy;

98. The linkage between divinity and the practice of justice upon earth in Psalm 82 could also be fruitfully developed in this context.
99. As in Chapter 1, the inverted commas are reminders of the ease with which these generalizing categories may be narrowed and misconstrued.

then kingship was true.
Is not this to know me? says YHWH.
(22:15b–16, my translation)

For who has stood in YHWH's council
so as to see and to hear his word? . . .
I did not send the prophets,
but they for their part went eagerly to the task;
I did not speak to them,
but they for their part delivered prophecies.
But if they had stood in my council,
then they would have proclaimed my words to my people,
and they would have sought to turn them from their wicked way,
and from their evil deeds.
(23:18a, 21–2, my translation)

The reality of YHWH may be discerned in public life when His character and priorities are appropriately enacted in the words and deeds of His human representatives. By this criterion either prophets or kings – or, by extension, others also – may be discerned as demonstrating, or lacking, genuine engagement with the God they profess to serve. As Nicholas Lash (1996:179) has well put it in a more generalizing way:

> The search for God is not the search for comfort or tranquillity, but for truth, for justice, faithfulness, integrity: these, as the prophets tirelessly reiterated, are the forms of God's appearance in the world.[100]

To be sure, the right application of this criterion will itself be a demanding matter, not susceptible of reduction to any kind of moralistic check-list.[101] But if it is demanding to discern as well as to be discerned, that is no argument against the validity of the enterprise; as will, I hope, become clear in the next two chapters.[102]

100. At a time when much 'spirituality' is concerned with a quest for inner peace, this point is crucial for discerning the authenticity of spirituality generally. Compare Lonsdale 1992:60: 'A person whose heart is basically set on satisfying his or her own desires and interests without much regard for others, for the reign of God or for living the gospel, can experience a form of "inner peace" when those fundamentally self-centred desires are being satisfied. In this case the "inner peace" may be more akin to complacency, a sense of satisfaction with oneself, than to "the peace which the world cannot give".'

101. See further Excursus 2.

102. One particular difficulty for my thesis, the relationship of Jeremiah's moral theology to certain other emphases in the book, is discussed in Excursus 3.

Excursus 1: Jer. 23:22 and Robert Carroll's construal of a criterion of prophetic authenticity

The interpretation of Jer. 23:22 deserves fuller attention. This is partly because of its intrinsic interest, but also because Robert Carroll clearly regarded it as a test case within his approach to prophetic authenticity; Carroll singled the verse out in an early (1976) and a late (1995:41–6) article, not to mention giving space and emphasis to it in a commentary (1986:461–3) and also in monographs (1979:191; 1981:171–3, 193) in between the articles, and in one of his last essays on Jeremiah (1999a:77–8).[103] In his view the verse clearly demonstrates the vacuousness of the criteria within Jeremiah for distinguishing between true and false prophets. It is appropriate, therefore, in the context of this account of prophetic authenticity, to take seriously the detailed exegesis and understanding which played a key role in Carroll's different construal.[104]

The essence of Carroll's construal is stated succinctly in his Jeremiah commentary (1986:463). He bases his remarks upon the RSV translation of 23:22, which is identical to that of the NRSV:

> [22] But if they had stood in my council,
> then they would have proclaimed my words to my people,
> and they would have turned them from their evil way,
> and from the evil of their doings.

He comments:

> The claim in verse 22 cannot be substantiated because there is no inherent connection between preaching the divine words and turning the people from the evil of their doings. A simple *tu quoque* argument will demonstrate this. The holistic approach to the tradition makes Jeremiah the speaker of these oracles, yet in the summary of Jeremiah's twenty-three years of preaching it is quite clear that he failed to turn the people or to persuade them to turn (25.1–7). If failure to turn the people is evidence of not having stood in the council then Jeremiah had no more stood in the council than had the other prophets. The argument of verse 22 lacks cogency as well as coherence.

103. In this latest essay Carroll says with reference to his earlier treatment: 'I cannot think of a convincing argument which would make me dissent from that judgment made then.'

104. Carroll had kindly agreed to debate with me the interpretation of Jer. 23:22 at the January 2001 meeting of the Society for Old Testament Study in Leeds. Unfortunately this was prevented by his premature death. The content of this excursus is what I would have presented on that occasion.

This incoherence of this particular text then serves a generalized observation about the nature of Jeremiah's attempts to discern the genuineness of prophetic speech:

> The arguments used against the prophets are ideological ones and, like all ideological argumentation, only achieve what is already believed to be the case. If they are reversed in a *tu quoque* manner they undermine the ideologists as effectively as their opponents.

All the biblical text provides is 'mere' ideology, a clatter of contradictory claims.

In his later essay (1995:42) Carroll raises one obvious objection to his construal, only to dismiss it summarily as apologetic rationalization and poor philology:

> Readers of Jeremiah usually can avoid this reading of the texts [sc. Jer. 23:22 and 25:3–7] together by modifying the sense of 'turn' in 23:22 to mean 'try to turn', so that the quarrel is between prophets who make no effort to change people's ways and prophets who try to turn the people even though they fail with their efforts. To me that looks like some form of rationalization driven by the need to 'save the appearances' and rescue the prophet from failure.[105] I do not believe that the Hebrew word *shuv* includes the sense 'try to turn', nor would it have to if the problem of implicating Jeremiah in a failure similar to the other prophets was not entailed by the conjunction of the two sets of texts.[106]

Carroll then considers two reading strategies to try to cope with the contradiction between 23:22 and 25:3–7 and concludes (1995:44, 46) that either Jeremiah is shown as incapable of learning from his experiences of failure or Jeremiah must be exempted from what is said about other prophets in a way that is forced. Carroll's underlying thesis in the essay

105. Compare his earlier (1981:172): 'Some would modify it [Jer. 23:22] to mean: the genuine prophet is the one who preaches repentance and *tries* to turn the nation from its evil ways. This is the slippery slope down to the death by a thousand qualifications, but it is necessary to slide down it a little if the criterion is to be retained in any sense as a criterion.'

106. Similarly, in the earlier essay (1976:46–7) Carroll comments: 'Perhaps his [sc. Jeremiah's] principle could be saved by insisting that all he meant was that the genuine prophet would have preached against the people and challenged them to change their way of life. Thus "turning from evil" would simply mean "preaching against evil". But such an attenuated position, while distinguishing between Jeremiah and the other prophets, has really suffered from that form of attack known among philosophers as "death by a thousand qualifications".' And he concludes that the most likely construal of 23:22 is 'that at this stage of the argument Jeremiah had lost his grip on rationality and simply accused them [sc. other prophets] of failing to do what he had failed to do'.

is that 'treating these texts as contradictory . . . is a much more interesting approach which generates greater interpretative possibilities than the conventional approaches' (1995:41);[107] but despite this rhetoric about the value of being unconventional, the actual yield seems to me rather less than is promised.

How should this construal be evaluated? In general terms, Carroll's handling of the text appears distinctly wooden. To suppose that success in eliciting response should be a mark of verification of prophecy would be a strange assumption both within the book of Jeremiah and within the Bible more generally. As we have seen, Jeremiah is portrayed as constantly urging the people of Israel/Judah to turn/repent (*shūv*, e.g. 3:1–4:4), yet most of those to whom he speaks refuse to heed his message (e.g. 5:3b, 'they have refused to turn back [*shūv*]'), the paradigmatic example being King Jehoiakim, for whom Jeremiah's words are merely an irritant which provoke contemptuous destruction of Jeremiah's written scroll and a desire to arrest and punish their author (Jeremiah 36); or if there is some expression of turning, it may be a superficial expression which does not touch the wellspring of people's thoughts and deeds (3:10, 4:3–4). Within such a context, if Jer. 23:22 really does mean that the proof of prophetic authenticity is the hearers' positive responsiveness, then it conflicts not only with 25:1–7 but with the rest of the book as a whole. Within the wider biblical context *no* prophet who is portrayed as speaking genuinely for YHWH is also portrayed as eliciting consistent or even regular responsiveness[108] – with the sole exception of Jonah, where the point of depicting unparalleled prophetic success is not to hold Jonah up as a model of authenticity to admire or emulate but rather to set an ironic context for probing and exposing Jonah's failure to understand God's mercy and his sullen reluctance to allow others than himself to benefit from that mercy.[109]

107. Compare his: 'having read so many theological readings of Jeremiah, especially Christianized theological readings, I felt I desperately needed to escape from the throttling suffocation of piety and its domestication of the text' (1999b:436).

108. Within the OT even Moses can elicit no more than a vacillating response from Israel, while a Micaiah (see Chapter 3 below) meets solely resistance and imprisonment. Within the NT Jesus' ministry meets with very mixed responses which culminate in his betrayal, abandonment, torture, mockery, and execution. To be sure, with respect to most of the canonical writing prophets, and the apostolic letter writers of the NT, we simply are not told in any detail what kind of response they encountered, though references to resistance to their messages are not uncommon (e.g. Isa. 6–8, 30:8–11, Ezek. 3:4–11, 1–2 Corinthians). Generally speaking, responsive recipients are not to be equated with original or intended recipients, but rather with 'ideal readers'.

109. On the interpretation of Jonah see Moberly 2003a.

Carroll would presumably respond to the above point along the lines he adopts in his essays by insistently pointing to what the text actually appears to be saying – no apologetic smoother of the rough text was he;[110] yet his exegetical discussion is strangely truncated. Carroll says that the only alternative to taking 'turn' at its face value is to make it mean 'try to turn' – where the fact that this appears to be poor philology in terms of the meaning of the verbal root *shūv* seems intended to serve to discredit any such attempt to 'evade' the face value of the text. But he makes no attempt to explore either semantic or possible rhetorical factors of the sort that one would expect a commentator at least to consider.

If Hebrew has a verb for 'try', it is probably *biqqēsh* (as in Exod. 4:24). Although this is not very common, it might have been used in Jer. 23:22b, and it is not. This in itself could favour Carroll's construal. However, from a semantic perspective one should bear in mind the well-known point that Hebrew is not well provided with modal forms of verbs, i.e. what is usually expressed in other languages either by specific conjugations such as subjunctive and optative or by auxiliary terms ('can', 'may', 'must', 'want'; 'could', 'might', 'would', 'should', etc.). Hebrew does indeed have some verbs for modal nuance, such as 'can' (*yākōl*) or 'want' (*hāphēts*). Yet it also uses the imperfect/*yiqtol* form of the verb, which is the form used in 23:22b, to express modal nuances.

Particularly significant here is the possible nuance of desire/volition. A recent Hebrew grammar (JM #113n) lists nine examples where the sense of 'want' may appropriately be found in a *yiqtol* form. Perhaps the clearest example is Ruth 3:13, Boaz's words to Ruth about there being a next-of-kin/redeemer with a claim upon Ruth prior to his own, who thus must have first refusal: 'if he wants to act as next-of-kin for you [*'im-yig'ālek*], good, let him do so; if he is not willing to act as next-of-kin [*we'im lō' yahpōts lego'olēk*] . . .'. Here the simple *yiqtol* form in the first clause is balanced by the explicit auxiliary use of 'want' (*yahpōts* from *hāphēts*)

110. Carroll repeatedly portrays himself as one of the few scholars who really take seriously the difficulties within Jeremiah which other scholars are inclined to smooth over: 'Whatever the more sanguine commentators on Jeremiah may say and think, I am still of the opinion that the book of Jeremiah is a very difficult, confused and confusing text . . . I do not think it is the contemporary commentator's task to make the text conform to our own values or to protect the text from critique . . . It is not part of my remit to save the appearances of the text, to make it conform to my expectations or to yield comfort to my prejudices' (1999a:75, 78). One can entirely agree with the need to be intelligently attentive to the text and to recognize that it may not conform to expectations, and yet still think that Carroll is offering a distinctly limited account of what is necessary for good interpretation.

in the parallel negative in the second clause.[111] Although the sentence structure of Jer. 23:22b differs from that of Ruth 3:13, it nonetheless becomes clear that in terms of Hebrew idiom a good case can be made for the *yiqtol* of *shūv* having a volitional sense if appropriate to the context.[112] Thus we may quite properly translate 23:22bβ: 'they would have sought to turn them from their wicked way and from their evil deeds'.[113]

From a rhetorical perspective one must consider extensive recent work on the nature of religious (and other) language, not least in relation to speech-act theory in development of the work of J. L. Austin (1975).[114] Here a basic and helpful distinction is between (a) that which is done intrinsically *in* an utterance, in terms of its meaning or significance according to the conventions of the speaker and the context – its 'illocutionary' force, and (b) that which is done *through* an utterance, in terms of the effect or impact it has upon its audience – its 'perlocutionary' force. So Austin (1975:102), for example, distinguished between 'the illocutionary act "he argued that . . ." [i.e. what the speaker is intentionally doing] and the perlocutionary act "he convinced me that . . ." [i.e. the effect achieved by what the speaker said]'.

The possible implications of this distinction for the construal of prophetic speech in general, and Jer. 23:22 in particular, are not hard to see. As Walter Houston 1993:177 has well put it:

> the successful performance of an illocutionary act does not in general depend upon the appropriate response of the hearers. It is necessary to distinguish, as Carroll has failed to do, between the illocutionary and the perlocutionary effects of an utterance. For example, if an officer gives an order to a mutinous army, the order may or may not be obeyed, but there can be no question that he has given an order . . . The *illocutionary* act of giving an order has been successfully performed,

111. Other good examples of a volitional nuance in a *yiqtol* form of a verb are: Deut. 18:6, 'And if a Levite wants to come [*weki yāvō' hallēwi*] from one of your towns . . . he may come whenever he desires [*ūvā' bekol 'awwat napshō*] . . .'; 1 Sam. 21:10 (ET 9), '[Ahimelech speaking to David at Nob about the sword of Goliath] If you want to take it [*'im 'ōtāh tiqqah lekā*], take [*qah*] it'; Ruth 1:11, '[Naomi to Ruth and Orpah] Why do you want to come [*lāmmāh tēlaknāh*] with me?'.

112. Compare McKane's more general observation on Carroll's construal, that 'to understand verse 22b . . . as "exerting themselves to turn them from their wicked ways and evil deeds" is not straining after sense to a greater degree than is often demanded in the interpretation of the Hebrew Bible' (1986:584).

113. There is a good Greek parallel in 2 Cor. 5:11 where Paul's 'we persuade people' is routinely taken to have a conative sense, 'we seek/try to persuade people'. See pp. 188–9 below.

114. Carroll was, of course, well aware of J. L. Austin's work, and he offers his own account (1979:69–77) of the distinction between illocutionary and perlocutionary acts, and the importance of all this for understanding prophetic discourse; though here too he shows a tendency to assume that perlocutionary failure undermines the convention-constituted legitimacy of the illocutionary act.

> even though the *perlocutionary* effect of getting them to obey has not... In these terms, as long as the prophet's hearers understood that they were warning them, calling for repentance or whatever the particular speech act might be, then the prophets had *done* what they set out to do, even if they had not achieved the effect they had hoped for.

It should be readily apparent that the semantic point about the modal expression of desire and the rhetorical distinctions of speech-act theory converge in their implications for the interpretation of Jer. 23:22. For both point to ways of understanding the significance of prophetic speech that distinguish clearly between the determinate intentionality of a prophet's message of repentance (a desire that people should turn is intrinsic to the sense of the words and the conventions they embody) and the consequences that may or may not follow from that message according to how people respond. Carroll's failure to make such a distinction leads him to suppose that the text is saying that failure of responsiveness negates the genuineness and meaningfulness of a challenge to respond, when in fact the text is saying that it is constitutive of genuine prophetic speech that its intrinsic meaning and purpose should be such as to confront sinful people with their need to turn to God.

Excursus 2: is the moral-theological criterion of discernment workable? An engagement with Robert Carroll

The viability of the biblical criteria for discernment is an issue I will address in the final chapter. Nonetheless, it is appropriate at this stage briefly to note some broad and basic objections that are often raised by OT scholars. As in the previous excursus, I will focus on the work of Robert Carroll, who wrote extensively on prophecy in general and Jeremiah in particular, and who took seriously the changing nature of contemporary biblical studies; his work therefore constitutes a significant contribution, requiring serious response. Although, as is apparent, I regularly disagree with his approach to and construal of the biblical text, Carroll usually saw more clearly than many other scholars what were the fundamental issues at stake underneath all the surface noise of scholarly debate, and he tended to formulate the issues with refreshing sharpness.[115]

115. I will draw on a number of Carroll's writings. As with his views on Jer. 23:22, I can find no significant shift of outlook within his writings over time.

Carroll's general view of discernment of prophetic authenticity is well spelled out in a general book on biblical interpretation (1991:44):

> No one can distinguish between words spoken under the influence of Yahweh and words spoken out of a prophet's own mind. If the two activities could be differentiated the Hebrew Bible would not be so full of lengthy tirades against the prophets (e.g. Jer. 23.9–40; 27–29; Ezek.13.1–14.9; Mic. 3.5–8). The claim to speak for the gods is easily made, but testing the truth of the claim has so far defeated the wit of human communities.

Discernment simply cannot be done in a way that is valid and meaningful. In this Carroll no doubt speaks for many a modern agnostic, who finds the religious certainties of former ages both puzzling and inaccessible. Nonetheless, the way in which he puts things is open to obvious question. On the one hand, his first two sentences are surely a *non sequitur*. For why should the fact that a problem recurs mean that it is incapable of any kind of meaningful resolution? One might compare: 'No one can distinguish between honest government and corrupt government. If the two activities could be differentiated, human history would not be so full of lengthy tirades against corrupt government.' The well-known corrupting effects of power do not mean that an uncorrupt, or relatively uncorrupt, exercise of power is impossible, but only that it is an always-to-be-sought goal that can only be achieved through high levels of discipline, self-denial, and vigilance.

On the other hand, Carroll's confident assertion that 'testing the truth of the claim has so far defeated the wit of human communities' is simply an assertion. It receives no warrant or substantiation, presumably because Carroll considered it a self-evident truth. But what I miss (here and in all the places where he discusses prophetic authenticity) is any acknowledgement of, let alone engagement with, the substantial literature in classic Christian theology and spirituality which deals precisely with such issues and offers criteria of discernment which many have found, and still find, meaningful and valid.[116] Carroll's sweeping dismissal of the possibility of testing is more revealing about Carroll than about possible testing.

116. At the very least, when one of the major theologians of the twentieth century has written explicitly on the subject – Rahner 1963 – one might reasonably expect some acknowledgement and engagement. And this is quite apart from the voluminous literature on discernment, especially in the searching contexts of Carmelite and Jesuit spirituality.

In terms of Carroll's overall approach to the moral theological criterion that is advanced within Jeremiah (and elsewhere), one can find remarks of a generally pejorative nature liberally sprinkled through his various writings (1979:190, 192):

> The general charges of immorality and idolatry may have been the standard form of abuse directed at opponents which was characteristic of all the prophets . . . The polemic against the prophets had here a certain hysterical note of desperation induced by the frustration experienced by Jeremiah as he tried to make a coherent and cogent case against the prophets. The unsatisfactory nature of his criteria against them was part of the difficulty of producing a criteriology for distinguishing one prophet from another as the authentic spokesman of Yahweh.

Alternatively (1981:176):

> Fierce struggles, abusive onslaughts, *ad hominem* arguments and the hurling of whatever functioned in those days as the Hebrew equivalent of *Anathema sit* – such were (and always have been) the stock-in-trade of the accomplished polemicist. Given this structuring factor behind the oracles, the small details of the argument should not be too closely examined.

If what the text really offers is variations on the theme of more or less hysterical abuse, then it may indeed follow that the specifics of the text ('the small details of the argument') do not need too much careful thought. Indeed, one wonders why it is worth bothering with such material at all, except for the purpose of disabusing those who misguidedly suppose that it contains truth about God and human life. But such an approach to the text, which Carroll himself consistently maintains is 'liberating',[117] is by no means the only possible or responsible approach. Indeed, Carroll's lack of sympathy for the perspectives within the text may obstruct rather than enable an accurate understanding of what the text does, and does not, mean.

With regard to the practical viability of the kind of moral theological criteria of authenticity that emerge in Jeremiah, Carroll offers various main arguments (1979:192–3). First, he draws on the work of James Crenshaw (1971:56–61) to argue that the charge of immorality is open to a *tu quoque*; for it is possible to find examples of canonically approved

117. See, for example, 1991:7–33.

prophets behaving in ways that are open to moral question. He recognizes, of course, that actions that look immoral to us may not have looked so within ancient Israel, but still thinks that the examples given 'sufficiently muddy the waters' to 'indicate that, as a criterion of genuine prophecy, Jeremiah's charge of immorality against the prophets was inadequate'. I do not propose here to examine all the suggested examples of immorality on the part of canonical prophets, though I find most of them less than compelling,[118] but solely to focus on the one example given from the book of Jeremiah: 'Jeremiah was guilty of telling a lie to protect King Zedekiah' (Jer. 38.24–7).[119]

The context of Jeremiah's words is this (to précis Jeremiah 38): Jeremiah's message that the only future hope lies in surrender to the Babylonians is resented as defeatist by senior officials. Although King Zedekiah in some way thinks well of Jeremiah (Jeremiah 37), he weakly does not try to resist his officials (he even says 'the king is powerless against you', verse 5), but hands Jeremiah over to them. Jeremiah is lowered into a muddy cistern, where he is left (to die?). Ebed-melech, a junior official ('eunuch'), makes representations to Zedekiah, who orders that Jeremiah be rescued from the cistern; which he is, though he is still detained. Zedekiah, who again wants to hear what Jeremiah has to say, then arranges a clandestine meeting with Jeremiah. Jeremiah does not want to speak, but Zedekiah swears to preserve his life, even from his officials. Jeremiah repeats his message that the only hope for future life lies in surrender. When Zedekiah expresses the fear that if he surrenders he will be handed over to Judaeans, who have already defected to the Babylonians and who will treat him badly, Jeremiah reassures him that this will not be the case, and renews his warning of the dangers of not surrendering. At this point Zedekiah tells Jeremiah to keep their conversation secret, on pain of death; and should his officials hear of it and press Jeremiah to tell, he should just say that he was making a plea to the king for merciful treatment. The officials do question Jeremiah, and Jeremiah responds 'in the very words the king had commanded', which satisfies them, and Jeremiah is just left in general detention.

118. One of the examples is Micaiah deceiving King Ahab (1 Kgs. 22:16). We will see in the following chapter that this is a superficial misreading of the text. Moreover, I cannot see why Isaiah's symbolic 'wandering about half-naked' (Isa. 20.2) should be classified as 'immoral' rather than 'shocking', which is what it is clearly meant to be.

119. Others also, e.g. Osswald 1962:16, have found Jeremiah's 'lie' problematic for moral evaluation of prophetic authenticity.

Indeed, Jeremiah told a lie. However, the situation is readily recognizable as the kind of difficult situation in which people often find themselves, in which there is no entirely satisfactory course of action – if Jeremiah did not lie to the officials, he would have had to ignore not only the royal instructions (which could be represented as disobedient to legitimate authority and so in some way morally questionable) but also the feelings and fears of a weak man who was clearly afraid of his power-broking officials. To find fault with this at all is surely astonishing. I suppose that one might conceivably argue that Carroll displays a Kantian concern for truth-telling as a categorical imperative; but the criticism more naturally suggests a small-minded moralism which I am sure Carroll would have been the first to denounce if he had encountered it in any other context. Carroll not only finds fault but implicitly[120] suggests that Jeremiah's minor lie to the officials is somehow comparable to the systematically self-serving use of language that elsewhere is designated *sheqer*, in the kind of way that Jeremiah's lie to the officials could in part counterbalance, and so at least in part cancel out in any moral calculus, the other kind of lie. This suggests a worrying failure to distinguish between (a) a healthily and robustly moral view of life, in which compromises and failures are more or less inevitable but signify little unless they get out of control and are not set within a context of humility and self-examination, and (b) a rigid and legalistic moralism which is so preoccupied with small trees that it never even realizes that there is a wood. Again, in other contexts I have no doubt that Carroll would have been quick to make just such a distinction, and to distance himself from the latter option. So why handle the biblical text here so flatly?

Interestingly, Carroll backtracked somewhat, but only somewhat, when he had to discuss the passage in its own right in his commentary on Jeremiah (1986:689–90). For in the dialogue between Zedekiah, Jeremiah, and the officials he recognizes 'conscious irony', and comments:

> It would be inadvisable to take Jeremiah's 'white' lie in verses 24–27 too seriously, though recent writers on prophetic conflict have noted it

120. In his discussion of prophetic conflict and authenticity, Carroll (following Crenshaw) does not really discuss Jeremiah's lie on its own in relationship to the rest of the book of Jeremiah, but rather uses it as part of a cumulative portfolio of immorality on the part of canonical prophets. It is the portfolio which is then used to counterbalance Jeremiah's account of moral criteria for prophetic authenticity (and the focus is primarily Jeremiah, for it is Jeremiah who makes the case most fully).

> carefully (e.g. Crenshaw 1971, 59). If moral issues are to be imported into the scrutiny of prophecy then it may be of some importance, but in the context of a story variation it is only an element used by a storytelling technique to explain how Jeremiah overcame the hostility of king and princes . . . It is hardly the intention of the writers to present Jeremiah as a liar by their development of the theme of his interview with the king.

His recognition that the lie is trivial, and that the narrative portrayal of Jeremiah is not that of a liar, is clearly right. Is it indicative of a slight unease that when he notes the use of the episode by 'recent writers on prophetic conflict' he cites only Crenshaw and omits any reference to his own use of Crenshaw? Yet he does not distance himself from his earlier view. Indeed, his comment that 'if moral issues are to be imported into the scrutiny of prophecy then it may be of some importance' is a weaker statement than in his previous work, but suggests no basic change of mind. His position seems to be: Jeremiah is not a liar here, and the lie is trivial – but if you want to assess prophetic authenticity in moral categories, then this passage still counts as a counter-example to Jeremiah's main thesis. But is this really different from 'heads I win, tails you lose'?

A second issue that Carroll raises (1979:193) is to suggest that finding fault with prophets on moral grounds may be a kind of category mistake.

> Further difficulties are involved in the argument that morality so validates a message that immorality would invalidate it. This is the old problem of 'would a good man make a better pair of shoes than a good cobbler?' . . . The complicated arguments involved in determining the relation between morality of speaker and speaker's utterance (in terms of its truth value) indicate that the matter is a good deal more complex than Jeremiah's easy equation of life style and falsity of message.

Carroll is indeed correct that the issues are complex, but is wrong on a point of detail and a point of substance. The point of detail is his 'Jeremiah's easy equation', for 'easy' is a trivializing and dismissive epithet, which makes Jeremiah sound like a complacent moralist. This does justice neither to Jeremiah's searching exposure of moral and spiritual complacency and self-serving (e.g. Jer. 7:1–15, 6:13–15)[121] nor to the

121. Another aspect of Jeremiah's thought in this regard, which has not yet featured in our exposition, is a recognition of the unfathomability of so much human thought and action,

prefacing of his indictment of the prophets with an account of the disturbing impact it makes upon himself (23:9).

The point of substance is the supposition that moral concerns in relation to a prophet are not essentially different from moral concerns in relation to a cobbler. Since Carroll is clearly (and not unreasonably) doubtful that a cobbler need be a good person to make a good pair of shoes (and similar issues are regularly and cogently raised about artists and their work), he extends this also to prophets. But this is to fail to recognize the distinctive nature of the vocation of a prophet, which is not to do with the creation of material objects (which may have moral implications but are not primarily or intrinsically moral) but rather to do with the formation of human lives. If human life is intrinsically moral and spiritual, which is a premise of biblical prophecy, then prophets must necessarily partake of those qualities of life that they seek to engender in others. A better analogy than that of the cobbler would be whether someone can teach well without first having mastered their subject. The issue at stake, for teacher or prophet, is whether the person up front does or does not know what they are talking about.

Finally, we may note Carroll's handling of a closely related issue, the significance of appropriately moral conduct on the part of those who hear a prophet. In the course of discussing Jeremiah's temple sermon Carroll says (1986:211–12):

> Jerusalem fell, but those who survived that fall, and their descendants, needed to be taught the lessons of that fall. Wherein lay security? Not in false beliefs about cultic security but in following a certain ethical way of life. If that conviction also appears false (*šeqer*) to the modern reader, then it is not because of the hermeneutics of suspicion but because Job, Qoheleth and the lament psalms (e.g. Ps. 44.17–22) have exposed it, too, as being ideologically based and therefore capable of becoming *šeqer*.

If Carroll's point were solely that Jeremiah's words are *capable* of becoming false, one could not disagree. For there is nothing – certainly no moral or spiritual truth – which is not susceptible of misunderstanding and misuse in the kind of way that makes it, in practice, false. But his real concern seems to be the stronger one that Jeremiah's moral understanding *is* false, and that for the (apparently unarguable) reason that other

except ultimately *coram deo*: 'The heart is devious above all else; it is perverse – who can understand it? I the LORD test the mind and search the heart, to give to all according to their ways, according to the fruit of their doings' (Jer. 17:9–10).

voices in the canon have revealed its intrinsic inadequacy. This is obviously not the place to discuss Job, Qoheleth, or the lament psalms,[122] but on any reckoning Carroll's appeal to these texts is odd. For if Job and his comforters in their respective ways show the inadequacy of a moralistic understanding of God, if Qoheleth stresses the apparent indeterminacy of so much of life, and if the Psalms recognize the pain and puzzlement that are intrinsic to following YHWH faithfully, none of these emphases show that a profound moral dimension is not still intrinsic to a right understanding of YHWH and of human life. The mainstream of Jews and Christians down the ages, following the compilers of the biblical canon, has not had undue difficulty in holding together both the moral and the imponderable in their knowledge of God.

Here as elsewhere, Carroll narrows a substantive moral understanding into a rigid moralism, and treats this moralism as a kind of Aunt Sally target to be knocked down. This is a disappointing and unpersuasive handling of the biblical text.

Excursus 3: divine freedom and responsiveness: some further reflections on the potter and the clay

One difficulty with my thesis that must be addressed relates to the role within the book as a whole of Jeremiah's moral theology as outlined. For there are two emphases within the book which stand in some tension with this moral theology.

On the one hand, the shape of the book as a whole conveys the message that national disaster for Judah is inevitable. Thus, for example, the prime section of the temple sermon (7:1–15), which seems to envisage as a real possiblity both amendment and aversion of destruction, is directly followed by material which emphasizes the inevitability of coming judgment upon an unresponsive people, for whom Jeremiah is forbidden to intercede (7:16–8:3).[123] Alternatively, one genuine-sounding expression of repentance (14:7–9) meets with a rebuff (14:10), while another genuine-sounding expression of repentance (14:19–22) meets a further rebuff and a

122. Carroll's appeal to Ps. 44:17–22 is, however, a decontextualized misreading of that portion of the psalm. For the overall sense of Psalm 44, and the related Psalm 89, see Moberly 1997:880–2.

123. It is interesting that most commentators are inclined to take this prohibition at face value, even though they are equally inclined to take YHWH's prohibition to Moses in Exod. 32:10 in the opposite way as, in effect, an invitation to intercede. I hope to discuss this issue in another context.

further prohibition of intercession (15:1–4, cf. 14:11). One could, of course, classify such expressions of repentance as superficial – to a greater or lesser extent *sheqer* – and that could be right. But another possibility is that the expressed turning may be genuine in intention, but it can no longer make any difference. Jeremiah is required to say that a lifetime's subjugation to the Babylonians is God's will for Judah, and attempts to play this down are necessarily mistaken, that is false (*sheqer*) – so the narrative sequence in Jeremiah 27–9. Even if once there was a time when human turning (*shūv*) might have elicited a divine rescinding (*niham*), that time has now passed, and disaster is inevitable. If there is hope for the future, it is hope only on the far side of judgment; Judah must pass through the valley of deep darkness, and cannot go around it.

On the other hand, corresponding to this emphasis that turning to God cannot avert the coming national disaster is an emphasis that turning to God is not a precondition of national restoration. On the contrary, the initiative lies entirely with God. In the oracles of hope for the future, Jeremiah 30–3, there is only marginal reference to human turning, and overwhelming emphasis upon divine initiative in a way that seems to bypass human action. This is the point of the famous 'new covenant' passage (31:31–4), where YHWH says: 'I will put my law within them, and I will write it on their hearts . . . I will forgive their iniquity, and remember their sin no more.' The consequence, or corollary, of this divine initiative is that normal human processes of formation and growth will no longer be needed: 'No longer shall they teach one another, or say to each other, "Know the LORD", for they shall all know me, from the least of them to the greatest, says the LORD.' In a comparable way Jeremiah's symbolic purchase of a field that expresses hope for the future (32:1–15) is interpreted by a prayer that expresses astonishment that YHWH should act thus for a disobedient people (32:16–25). This prayer receives an answer (32:26–44) that underlines the evil of Israel and Judah and says nothing of their turning (other than that they have failed to do it), but again speaks of divine initiative in restoration under the general principle, 'See, I am the LORD, the God of all flesh; is anything too hard for me?' (32:27).

If disaster cannot be averted by repentance, and if restoration does not presuppose repentance, then what role is played by Jeremiah's moral theology with its repeated insistence upon the necessity of repentance, knowing YHWH, practising justice and righteousness, and avoiding falsehood? We are faced by the fundamental issue of the relationship of divine sovereignty and initiative with human moral responsibility and accountability. Can one articulate the one without misrepresenting or downplaying the other? Or, to use Jeremiah's own terms, how are we to understand the relationship between the potter and the clay?

As already noted, the image of the potter working with the clay is, like all good images, open to more than one way of having its implications developed. The prime move within the text is to stress the power of the potter (18:6), but then immediately to complement this with an account of the moral and responsive nature of that power as channelled through prophetic witness, which leaves the future open and contingent (18:7–10). It is this upon which I have laid emphasis, not least because the language of the text explicitly relates it in an interpretative way to the nature of Jeremiah's comissioning as a prophet. The wider context of the book, however, necessitates a more precise articulation of the bearing of verses 7–10 upon verse 6. A first reading might perhaps suggest that verses 7–10 represent a comprehensive construal of divine sovereignty, as only and always exercised in a moral and responsive way. However, a second reading in the light of the wider context strongly suggests that verses 7–10 are to be understood as a general or normative construal, that is a rule, but a rule that admits of exceptions which 'prove' (i.e. test) it: although as a rule YHWH the potter handles the clay in the responsive way specified (which accords with the frequency of the language and conceptuality elsewhere in the Old Testament), there may be times, of which the fall and restoration of the kingdom of Judah becomes a prime example, when this cannot account for YHWH's actions.

The second move within the text is to see the potter as shaping disaster, in a way that constitutes the warning that Jeremiah is to give to the people of Judah (18:11). Although this is explicitly a challenge to turn, with an implicit possibility of the disaster being averted, the refusal of the people to respond appropriately (18:12) means that the disaster that is in the process of being formed will surely be brought to completion.

The third move is that, because of the utter unresponsiveness of Judah to YHWH, Judah is the vessel which YHWH the potter will smash so thoroughly that it is beyond repair (19:1–15, esp. 11). This seems to symbolize and enact the point that disaster and exile have become inevitable.

However, a fourth move is latent in the initial depiction of the potter at work (18:4). As noted above, one implication of the depiction that is open to development, though not actually developed in the immediate context, is that the new vessel appears to be a remaking of the original vessel, which is not discarded as it might have been. This can be taken as a picture of a fresh start that is entirely dependent upon the will of the potter ('as seemed good to him') to work with recalcitrant material rather than start afresh with new clay.[124] Although the images of future restoration in chs. 30–3 do not use the imagery of the potter refashioning spoiled clay 'as seemed good to him',[125] the consistent tenor of these chapters could undoubtedly be expressed in terms of a potter reworking unresponsive clay into a fine new vessel.

Thus all the dimensions of our problem are capable of being expressed in terms of the image of the potter with the clay. Three conclusions may be drawn from this. First, the openness of the imagery to different construals suggests that one may be unwise to seek some particular theological formula to express both YHWH's moral responsiveness and His freedom to act irrespective of the responsiveness of His people; it may be preferable, and less likely to lead to reductiveness or one-sidedness, to stay with the image, for the image has a dynamic and an imaginative power that could be lost in the transposition to a different mode of theological thought.[126]

Secondly, the juxtaposition of accounts of YHWH's responsiveness with accounts of His independent initiative and the resultant tension between them is an important guide to the understanding of the language that is used – in essence, that although the language is to be taken seriously, it must not be taken woodenly. For example, Christians historically have shown a tendency to fix upon the wording of Jer. 31:31–4 as

124. This dimension of the text has, of course, regularly been noted. Nicholson 1973:155, for example, comments: 'verses 1–6 alone look like the original saying of the prophet. The message of this original saying was one of judgement and renewal after judgement, a theme which is found frequently elsewhere in the book. As a potter remoulds a spoilt vessel on his wheel, so God would remould his people who had been "spoilt" by their sinfulness; he would destroy what they had been and reconstitute them to conform to the original purpose he intended for them.' My only quibble is that Nicholson suggests that this is the explicit meaning of verses 4–6 (taken on their own), while in fact it is entirely implicit, one possible reading of the imagery.

125. There is a passing use of *ytsr* in 33:2, in parallel with *'āsāh*. Interestingly, each verb has an unspecifed object, a pronominal suffix 'it'. Although most commentators, following the lead of the LXX, suppose that 'earth'/'world' is the implied referent, in accord with the usage of Isaiah 40–55, it may be that Israel/Judah should be understood as the referent. However, the Hebrew reads awkwardly and the text may be corrupt, so it would be unwise to lay weight upon it.

126. Compare Calvin's comment (n.d.:3652) on the significance of the potter's house as the context for God's speaking to Jeremiah: 'Naked doctrine would have been frigid to slothful and careless men; but when a symbol was added, it had much greater effect.'

depicting the radical newness of God's redemption through Christ in ways that have not been fair to the text; the emphasis upon newness and 'not like the old' has been prioritized, while the text's equal emphasis upon the needlessness of teaching and learning faith in God, which of course does not correspond to Christian experience, is passed over in some embarrassment. Rather than turning one's reading of this text into a matter of, in effect, picking and choosing, it would be better to take the picture of 31:31–4 as a whole as a strong portrayal of divine initiative and commitment (in which human action is downplayed) which is to be held in constructive tension with other passages such as, say, 18:7–10 with its strong portrayal of divine and human responsiveness (in which what people do matters). Theological thinking that is attuned to Scripture requires a richness which, while not anti-systematic, resists any easy transposition into any systematic formulation which would diminish those tensions that are intrinisic to life.

Thirdly (notwithstanding the first point), the text's portrayal of disaster and restoration points to an understanding of divine action which is characterized in Hebrew as *hesed* (Jer. 9:23 (ET 24), 31:3) or *hēn* (31:2) and in Christian theology as 'grace'. To be sure, the language of grace looks more applicable to the promise of restoration than it does to the warning of inevitable judgment, and yet these are two facets of a single whole (analogous to the inseparability of the death and resurrection of Jesus in the New Testament). For all the text's emphasis upon the fact that what people do matters to God and makes a difference to God, there is a corresponding concern both with human self-will which cannot bring itself to live rightly and respond to God's will and also with God's refusal to be bound by that failure. Among other things, this is perhaps the clearest guidance within the text that its strong moral emphasis is not to be reduced to any kind of moralism, least of all a moralism that excludes the unfathomable divine dimension of grace.

3

Micaiah ben Imlah: the costs of authenticity and discernment

'Azarias', I said: 'You told me once I may find out who or what you worshipped when we got to Ecbatana. Might you tell me now?' . . .

'How would courage and truth and mercy and right action strike you?'

'But those are not gods!' I protested . . .

'Tobias, for heaven's sake, what do you think a god looks like when he works in men?'

And to that I had no answer, so we hurried on without more talk towards Nineveh.

– Tobias and Azarias in SALLEY VICKERS' *Miss Garnet's Angel* (VICKERS 2000:327–8)[1]

Introduction

Thus far I have sought to set out the criteria for discernment of prophetic authenticity as found in Jer. 23:9–22 within the wider context of Jeremiah 1–23. The appropriate next stage is to consider a narrative exemplification of these criteria. For many biblical narratives are constructed around the articulation of central theological issues, and a narrative can explore elements of the issue that may be less visible in other genres. An appropriate narrative should usefully test the thesis so far, and perhaps qualify and/or extend it in various ways.

The question is: Which narrative? At this point almost all biblical scholars, with a rare unanimity, opt for the story of Jeremiah and Hananiah (Jeremiah 28), as a story whose concern is 'how could one tell

1. I am indebted to Lash 2004:2 for making me aware of this novel.

a true prophet from a false one?' (Bright 1965:202).[2] Indeed, not a few scholars hardly move beyond it on the grounds that this is the heart of the question of prophetic discernment within Jeremiah.

There are, of course, obvious reasons for attention to this story. The narrative develops the theme of Jeremiah's conflict with other prophets who contest his message, which appears to be the concern of Jeremiah 26–9 as a whole, a section of the book not far removed from Jer. 23:9–40;[3] Jeremiah appears to articulate two criteria of discernment (28:8, 9); and at the end Hananiah is said by Jeremiah not to be 'sent' (*shālah*) by YHWH, and to be making the people trust in a lie (*sheqer*, 28:15), language reminiscent of 23:9–22. Therefore, so the common assumption goes, this must be a prime narrative articulation of the dynamics of discernment.

I believe that this is a mistake. Although I wish primarily to develop my own positive proposal with reference to another narrative, 1 Kings 22, it is necessary briefly to justify my position on Jeremiah 28. This will best be done by quickly setting out the story and the kind of interpretation that usually attaches to it, and equally quickly indicating my reasons for dissent.

1 Jeremiah 28: the conflict between Jeremiah and Hananiah

A conventional exposition

[1] In that same year, at the beginning of the reign of King Zedekiah of Judah, in the fifth month of the fourth year, the prophet Hananiah son of Azzur, from Gibeon, spoke to me in the house of the LORD, in the presence of the priests and all the people, saying, [2] 'Thus says the LORD of hosts, the God of Israel: I have broken the yoke of the king of Babylon. [3] Within two years I will bring back to this place all the vessels of the LORD's house, which King Nebuchadnezzar of Babylon took away from this place and carried to Babylon. [4] I will also bring back to this place King Jeconiah son of Jehoiakim of Judah, and all the exiles from Judah who went to Babylon, says the LORD, for I will break the yoke of the king of Babylon.'

2. Cf., e.g., Hoffman 1997:230: 'The pivotal point of the plot is the question: which of the two contenders delivering contradictory messages in the name of God will prove his genuineness as a real *nabi*"?

3. 'There is general agreement that both chapters [sc. Jeremiah 27, 28] are part of a larger editorial unit which begins in 23.9 with the superscription "concerning the prophets", and extends through ch. 29' (Childs 1985:137).

An initial blow, defeat and deportation, has fallen on Judah. But although Jeremiah has said that Judah's subjugation will be lengthy – expressed either as a whole lifetime, seventy years (25:11–12), or as three generations of rulers (27:7) – Hananiah proclaims that the blow will be of short duration and restoration will be speedy.[4] So how will Jeremiah handle this challenge which contradicts his message?

> [5] Then the prophet Jeremiah spoke to the prophet Hananiah in
> the presence of the priests and all the people who were standing in the
> house of the LORD; [6] and the prophet Jeremiah said, 'Amen! May the
> LORD do so; may the LORD fulfil the words that you have prophesied,
> and bring back to this place from Babylon the vessels of the house of
> the LORD, and all the exiles. [7] But listen now to this word that I speak in
> your hearing and in the hearing of all the people. [8] The prophets who
> preceded you and me from ancient times prophesied war, famine, and
> pestilence against many countries and great kingdoms. [9] As for the
> prophet who prophesies peace, when the word of that prophet comes
> true, then it will be known that the LORD has truly sent the prophet.'

Initially Jeremiah is ironic. He would like to believe what Hananiah says, but he cannot. Why? He gives two reasons, both of them criteria for discerning that what Hananiah says is not to be believed. First, there is a strong precedent of prophets (implicitly, those who have been recognized as true) speaking a message of impending disaster (verse 8). Secondly, one can know that a prophet who goes against the precedent by speaking of peace is truly sent (*shālah*) by YHWH when the message 'comes true' (verse 9), in apparent use of the principle articulated in Deut. 18:21–2.

The trouble is, neither of these criteria is much use. As to the first, even if there is a general precedent, it must be possible to recognize exceptions. Jeremiah's canonical predecessors, especially Isaiah, sound strong notes of hope and restoration as well as of disaster. Indeed, Jeremiah's own prophetic commissioning includes the charge 'to build and to plant' as well as 'to pluck up and pull down' (1:10), and Jeremiah speaks extensively along these lines in chs. 30–3. As to the second, 'wait and see' gives one no guidance when it is most needed, in the present moment when conflicting visions are proclaimed and one needs to be able to recognize

4. If Hananiah had said 'in three years', this would naturally be taken as the conventional Hebrew idiom for an indefinite short period of time, i.e. a non-specific 'in a few years'. His 'two years' is specific about the proximity of YHWH's action.

which (if either) to heed – quite apart from further difficulties as to what would count as a message of peace 'coming true' in relation to the dynamics of human responsiveness (cf. 18:9–10).

> [10] Then the prophet Hananiah took the yoke from the neck of the prophet Jeremiah, and broke it. [11] And Hananiah spoke in the presence of all the people, saying, 'Thus says the LORD: This is how I will break the yoke of King Nebuchadnezzar of Babylon from the neck of all the nations within two years.' At this, the prophet Jeremiah went his way.

Hananiah's response shows that he is unimpressed by Jeremiah. He performs his own symbolic action in breaking Jeremiah's yoke. His message has as much right to be considered as from YHWH as does Jeremiah's. We then expect a counterblast from Jeremiah. But the fact that Jeremiah says nothing and just withdraws in silence shows that he had nothing that he could say. His criteria of discernment in this context were hollow, in effect a bluff that has been called.

> [12] Some time after the prophet Hananiah had broken the yoke from the neck of the prophet Jeremiah, the word of the LORD came to Jeremiah: [13] Go, tell Hananiah, Thus says the LORD: You have broken wooden bars only to forge iron bars in place of them! [14] For thus says the LORD of hosts, the God of Israel: I have put an iron yoke on the neck of all these nations so that they may serve King Nebuchadnezzar of Babylon, and they shall indeed serve him; I have even given him the wild animals. [15] And the prophet Jeremiah said to the prophet Hananiah, 'Listen, Hananiah, the LORD has not sent you, and you made this people trust in a lie. [16] Therefore thus says the LORD: I am going to send you off the face of the earth. Within this year you will be dead, because you have spoken rebellion against the LORD.'
> [17] In that same year, in the seventh month, the prophet Hananiah died.

Only later, and in private, does Jeremiah receive a fresh word from YHWH. Then, and only then, does Jeremiah know that Hananiah was not sent by YHWH and was speaking a lie (just as in another context Jeremiah only knows how to respond to Johanan after awaiting a word from YHWH, Jer. 42:4, 7). Hananiah is then condemned in language deriving from the deuteronomic portrayal of a false prophet ('speak rebellion', *dibber sārāh*, Deut. 13:6 (ET 5)), and he suffers accordingly.

Even on a sympathetic construal, the criteria of discernment look tenuous; as von Rad (1975:209–10) put it, 'It is surprising to see a prophet so much at sea with a problem. At times in his famous encounter with

Hananiah Jeremiah's arguments are almost groping.' If Hananiah, whom recent commentators tend to see as an honest broker,[5] was wrong, it was probably because of his inability to relate the past traditions of YHWH's deliverance of Jerusalem to the present situation. Many have supposed that the past prophecies of Isaiah are being reappropriated by Hananiah; for even though the text does not mention Isaiah, appeal to Isaiah would appear plausible in that historical context.[6] Thus poor timing and a misreading of the historical situation, not malice or genuine deceptiveness, were Hananiah's problem.[7] And anyway, who can be confident that they are not misreading their situation without the benefit of hindsight? Jeremiah's inability to gainsay Hananiah at the time, together with the private nature of Jeremiah's own fresh word from YHWH, suggests that the concept and practice of discernment are only tenuously, if at all, a matter for the contested public arena.

At best, then, the story may make a contribution through recognition of the possibility that 'yesterday's certitude has become today's distorting ideology' (Brueggemann 1991:25), or 'Whenever the freedom of God as creator is forgotten or denied in adapting traditional "text" to a given context, there is the threat of falsehood' (Sanders 1977:38); thus the point is that one needs to hold all religious traditions with appropriate openness to changing circumstances[8] – a point which indeed is valid, as far as it goes. At worst, however, the story shows that all claims to be able to discern prophetic authenticity are 'mere' ideology – 'The redaction is

5. 'Whether Hananiah appeals primarily to the David–Zion traditions or to the memory of Isaiah, we may imagine that he spoke in good faith and believed that he was articulating a serious form of bold and responsible faith. He is likely not a charlatan or a huckster' (Brueggemann 1991:25); 'It is not said, probably because it could not be said, of Hananiah that he was immoral like the prophets of Jerusalem castigated in 23.14 . . . It was precisely the exemplary character of Hananiah which makes this the classic confrontation of prophecy with prophecy' (Jones 1992:355). The move to a widespread positive evaluation of Hananiah appears to be the contribution of Gottfried Quell (1952:50–5, 65–6; Quell was not the first to suggest it, but the first to argue it); he surveys at length the bad press given to Hananiah since the LXX, deprecates it as unfeeling and dogmatic ('to understand him [Hananiah] you must love him'), and proposes a favourable assessment – for which scholars writing subsequently no longer feel they need to argue.

6. Osswald 1962:20 traces back to Stade 1881 the supposition that Hananiah is drawing on Isaiah. The supposition is now so widespread that many interpreters, e.g. Lange 2002:84, take it as established and needing no argument.

7. Osswald 1962:21 is typical in seeing this as the key issue: '*the inability to orientate himself in the historical situation*, i.e. to recognize the will of Jahweh at a certain time and in a certain place'.

8. This appears to be the dominant view among recent Christian interpreters; compare Goldingay 2001:116: 'He [sc. Hananiah] would have sounded very like Isaiah, promising that Yahweh would in the end deliver Jerusalem from its attackers. There was nothing wrong with Hananiah except that he was living in the wrong century. Time had moved on, and Yahweh was no longer saying the things that Isaiah had said.'

committed to Jeremiah, *therefore Hananiah is false*' (Carroll 1986:550); such ideology represents the imposition of a perspective that is eloquent about human conflicts but silent with regard to any deity other than the 'tribal' deity who symbolizes and reinforces partisan allegiances.

A rereading

What is wrong with the above? Jeremiah 28 is undoubtedly a narrative of prophetic conflict. The mistake is to assume that a narrative about prophetic conflict must also be about prophetic discernment.[9] Just as the narrative of Amos and Amaziah (Amos 7:10–17) is about conflict but not about discernment, as is also the strange story of the prophets of Judah and Bethel (1 Kings 13) which appears to be a symbolic portrayal of the history of the divided kingdoms at whose outset it stands,[10] so Jeremiah 28 is a conflict story. Its purpose is to portray the opposition to, and consequent suffering of, the faithful prophet, but also to show his vindication.

If a narrative of prophetic conflict were supposed to be about discernment, then a prime question should be: Who is supposed to be doing the discerning? The most natural candidates would presumably be third-party hearers/onlookers within the story who have to decide which of the prophets to believe. Yet although there are references to 'the priests and all the people' or just 'all the people' who hear Hananiah and Jeremiah (28:1, 5; 7b, 11a), there is no mention whatever of their response to the encounter or of their being in any uncertainty or difficulty as to which prophet to believe. Even though the preceding narrative about Jeremiah's temple sermon, which is also set in the house of YHWH (26:2, 7, 10, 28:1, 5) has the people deciding that Jeremiah does not deserve to die, there is no significant constituency either in Jeremiah 26 or in Jeremiah 28 that believes that Jeremiah may be speaking truly for YHWH. On the contrary, Jeremiah's words to Hananiah, that he has 'made this people

9. Childs 1985:135–9 expounds and critiques the conventional approach with many sharp insights. But because he does not break with the assumption that at least part of the story is about discernment – in 28:5–9 'Jeremiah is uncertain regarding God's plan' and 'sets up a criterion for determining the truth of Hananiah's claim' – he still struggles to make good sense of the text; his critique of psychologizing Jeremiah is well taken, but his redescription of the issue about God's will as 'theocentric' does not properly engage the epistemological issue which *ex hypothesi* is at stake. Sheppard 1988 interestingly develops Childs' concerns through social-scientific insights, but he too retains the debilitating assumption that Jeremiah 28 is about discernment.

10. Karl Barth 1957:393–409 seems to have been the first in modern times to recognize something of the true significance of an otherwise baffling narrative (see also Bosworth 2002).

trust in a lie', underline that the people do not appear to be in doubt as to whom they believe. Jeremiah 28, like Jeremiah 26, shows the suffering of a prophet whose word is not considered even a serious option for belief; but each narrative portrays also his defence (ch. 26) or vindication (ch. 28).

Is it then Jeremiah who has difficulties with discerning Hananiah's veracity? Or perhaps the ideal reader, who would be in much the same position as Jeremiah? This would be an odd reading in the context of the wider book, which has presented the consistency of Jeremiah's message of judgment in the teeth of alternative, and more attractive, pronouncements of 'peace'. Indeed, it looks even odder in the light of the immediately preceding Jeremiah 27, which is integrally related to Jeremiah 28,[11] as it is the context where Jeremiah puts on the symbolic yoke which Hananiah breaks (27:2–7, 28:10) and speaks of the temple vessels whose return Hananiah promises (27:16, 28:3).[12] Here Jeremiah explicitly says 'to the priests and all the people' (27:16–17):

> Thus says the LORD: Do not listen to the words of the prophets who are prophesying to you, saying, 'The vessels of the LORD's house will soon be brought back from Babylon', for they are prophesying a lie (*sheqer*) to you. Do not listen to them; serve the king of Babylon and live. Why should this city become a desolation?

The natural contextual inference, when Hananiah speaks as he does a few verses later, is that Hananiah is an example of the lie against which Jeremiah warns.[13] Why on earth should one suppose that Jeremiah is

11. The methodological decision to read ch. 28 in relative isolation from ch. 27 is basic to a 'conventional exposition', and has usually been buttressed by a variety of compositional and traditio-historical arguments about the relative independence of ch. 28 in relation to ch. 27. To be sure, the flow both within ch. 27 and from ch. 27 to ch. 28 is not entirely smooth, and so the numerous proposals to rearrange the text in one way or another are unsurprising. Nonetheless, and notwithstanding difficulties in the LXX, the text in its received form is by no means so difficult as to lack intelligibility of sequence.

12. One might also note that Jer. 27:18 proposes a different kind of marker of prophetic authenticity, that is intercession (compare Gen. 20:7, where even Abraham is called a *nāvi'*, specifically because he will intercede for Abimelech; also 1 Sam. 12:19, 23, Jer. 15:1, etc.). It is unclear whether, or how far, intercession might be appealed to in a context of public discernment, for the practice of intercession might not be publicly knowable. Nonetheless, intercession is a criterion fully in keeping with what Jeremiah says elsewhere, for in general it presupposes a longing that people should turn to God or in some area of need receive God's mercy.

13. So the LXX introductory depiction of Hananiah in verse 1 as *pseudoprophētēs* is fully in keeping with the tenor of the presentation. (Although there are considerable textual variations in the preceding chapter, Jeremiah's words about the falsity of those speaking of a speedy return of the temple vessels from Babylon are present in LXX as in MT.)

suddenly filled with uncertainty when someone actually says what he has just warned against?[14]

How, then, should Jeremiah's response to Hananiah be understood? His words are both ironic and *ad hominem*, and might be paraphrased: 'Fine. May YHWH indeed bring peace/restoration (*shālōm*), which I as well as you hope for (27:22). But the precedent of true prophecy speaks of judgments which are so searching that speedy restoration is hardly possible. When a message goes against precedent, it invites suspicion such that one should only believe it when one sees it.' Although Jeremiah is prima facie offering a criterion of discernment, its prime contextual thrust is as a rhetorical gesture in a situation where nobody is heeding him anyway – not a criterion but a caveat (cf. Lange 2002:87, 173). Since no positive response is recorded to Jeremiah's words in ch. 27, and since there is no turning to God (*shūv*) of the kind of which he has spoken so extensively, there is no reason for him to suppose that God might for some reason have rescinded his former pronouncement (*niham*) and now be delivering a different message to Hananiah.[15] The real point of Jeremiah's words is simple: it is a reminder that the fact that one would *like* something to be the case is no guarantee that it actually *will be* the case.

The rhetorical *ad hominem* nature of Jeremiah's criterion is also clearly shown by his own complete disregard for it in the sequel (verses 15–17). If he meant it, why should he ignore it? Although McKane (1996:719) finds fault with Jeremiah for being impatiently 'high-handed' with Hananiah

14. It is, of course, possible to psychologize Jeremiah's words and behaviour, not least since psychological complexity within the portrayal of Jeremiah is indicated by his famous 'confessions' (primarily 11:18–12:6, 15:10–21, 17:12–18, 18:18–23, 20:7–18). This could suggest a reading of Jeremiah in Jeremiah 27–8 in terms of his confident public pronouncements being accompanied by inward self-doubt or uncertainty, which could lead to genuine vacillation in the face of Hananiah's opposition. However, it should at least be noted that the issues articulated in the laments concern the pain and anguish that has come about because of Jeremiah's vocation, and his desire for vindication; uncertainty as to what he is proclaiming is not his problem.

15. Thus Buber's moving interpretation (1982 [1968/1942]:167) is a misreading: 'Jeremiah had heard him [sc. Hananiah] speak like a man who "knows it all", but there were still things Jeremiah himself did not know. God had, indeed, spoken to him only an hour before. But this was another hour. History is a dynamic process, and history means that one hour is never like the one that has gone before. God operates in history, and God is not a machine which, once it has been wound up, keeps on running until it runs down. He is a living God. Even the word God speaks at a certain hour, the word one obeys by laying a yoke on one's neck, must not be hung up like a placard. God has truth, but He does not have a system.' Buber's strong point is the recognition of the need for constant attentiveness to God. His weakness is an effective denial of the consistency of moral and spiritual content in Jeremiah's knowledge of God – a denial which was congenial to Buber himself in terms of his own larger, and idiosyncratic, theological frame of reference.

in disregarding the criterion of discernment he has just established, the simpler explanation is that Jeremiah did not intend his words as a criterion rather than a caveat in the first place. Jeremiah provides his own construal of the significance of his antecedent words.

When Hananiah reinforces his version of things with a symbolic action and Jeremiah goes his way with no further word, this is not because Jeremiah is uncertain of what is going on or of what to say,[16] but because he has already made his position clear and there is no point in saying anything further.[17]

When the word of YHWH subsequently comes to Jeremiah, there are two new elements which are ascribed to YHWH. First, YHWH gives Jeremiah a construal of Hananiah's symbolic action which inverts its intended meaning, for it will intensify servitude to Nebuchadnezzar rather than alleviate it (verses 13–14). The content of 27:2–7 is restated more forcefully: an ordinary wooden yoke that could be broken by Hananiah will be replaced by an iron yoke that will resist all breaking.[18] Secondly, Jeremiah, in the name of YHWH, announces to Hananiah his coming death (verse 16).[19] It is noteworthy, however, that when Jeremiah tells Hananiah that he is (in effect) a false prophet (verse 15), this is *not* something said to be communicated to Jeremiah by YHWH. Indeed, there would have been no point, for Jeremiah would never have been in doubt. His charge that Hananiah has 'made this people trust in a lie' so exactly recalls the content, and precise wording, of the temple sermon (7:4, 8)

16. An analogy with the time Jeremiah needed to await a word from YHWH so as to answer Johanan (42:4, 7) is misleading; for in that context Johanan raises a fresh issue about what the remnant in Judah should do (42:3), about which Jeremiah had not yet thought or sought the will of YHWH.

17. Compare Calvin n.d.:3856: 'When there is no hope of doing good, it is better sometimes to be silent than to excite a great multitude without any profit . . . Had he [sc. Jeremiah] contended longer with Hananiah, contentions would have been kindled on every side, there would have been no hearing in a tumult, and the Jews would have wholly disregarded anything he might have then spoken'; or, more recently, Lundbom 2004:337: 'might not leaving the scene be the better part of wisdom?'.

18. The symbolism of the yoke within the wider context of the book merits further thought. I am inclined towards a suggestion by Rob Barrett that the figure of Hananiah may be parabolic of the people of Judah in the reign of Zedekiah; the desire to rebel against God's appointment of Nebuchadnezzar was enacted with initial success and yet led to a worse and more destructive servitude.

19. There is a small puzzle, in that YHWH tells Jeremiah to say one thing to Hananiah (verses 13–14), but what Jeremiah says is another thing (verses 15–16). One presumes that both are to be seen as YHWH's word to Jeremiah, and that there is an ellipsis within the narrative (for a comparable ellipsis see 1 Kgs. 21:17–24, where YHWH's words to Elijah lead into a response from Ahab, and Elijah's subsequent words to Ahab go beyond YHWH's initial words to him). The ellipsis is presumably for reasons of narrative economy and so as to make Jeremiah's unanticipated words to Hananiah into a dramatic climax.

that it aligns Hananiah with those who complacently encourage claims upon YHWH's delivering power without a corresponding seeking to turn (*shūv*) people to YHWH; thus the falsity of Hananiah is entirely of a piece with what has consistently been depicted elsewhere. The content of verse 15 is something Jeremiah has known all along, but he articulates it here to ground the specific announcement of judgment upon Hananiah that follows.

In short, therefore, the narrative consistently presupposes that Hananiah does not speak for YHWH; he appears so as to personify the kind of opposition faced by Jeremiah, and to exemplify the possible fate of spurious prophesying (and perhaps also symbolically to anticipate the fate that will come on Judah as a whole: cf. 27:15). Since the narrative is not about prophetic discernment, despite Jeremiah's rhetorical flourish, it is unsurprising that attempts to construe it as though it were about discernment have led to such unsatisfactory results.

2 1 Kgs. 22:1–38: the conflict between Ahab, Micaiah ben Imlah, and 400 prophets

I turn instead to a story where prophets are summoned to provide guidance for the kings of Israel and Judah with regard to a military campaign, and where different messages from different prophets unambiguously pose the problem for the kings of needing to discern the voice to which they should pay heed.[20]

The location of the story is in a sequence of narratives which otherwise depict Elijah in his confrontations with Ahab. Why Micaiah (who appears nowhere else in the Old Testament) should appear in this cameo instead of Elijah is not entirely clear. Nonetheless, the story has contextual weight as a climactic portrayal of Israel's most notorious king, Ahab, in a situation where all – his life and that of many of his subjects – depends on the decision that he makes in response to the differing prophetic voices.

20. Unlike my exposition of Jeremiah, I will expound this text with only limited engagement with scholarly literature. This is for two reasons. First, I have discussed issues of compositional integrity, tradition-history, and redactional significance within the deuteronomistic history elsewhere (Moberly 2003b). Secondly, prolonged working with the text and its interpreters has led me to the conviction that almost all the disagreements about particular parts of the story relate to disagreements about its meaning as a whole. A piecemeal discussion of all detailed disagreements would risk being tediously argumentative; a better strategy is to concentrate on a comprehensive understanding of the whole.

> [1] For three years Aram and Israel continued without war. [2] But in the third year King Jehoshaphat of Judah came down to the king of Israel. [3] The king of Israel said to his servants, 'Do you know that Ramoth-gilead belongs to us, yet we are doing nothing to take it out of the hand of the king of Aram?' [4] He said to Jehoshaphat, 'Will you go with me to battle at Ramoth-gilead?' Jehoshaphat replied to the king of Israel, 'I am as you are; my people are your people, my horses are your horses.'

The issue for going to war is the perennial problem of disputed frontier territory (Ramoth-gilead is close to that part of the Golan which is still in dispute between Syria and Israel today). Although, according to other texts, Ramoth-gilead was part of Israel under Solomon (1 Kgs. 4:13) and was assigned to the tribe of Gad as a city of refuge (Deut. 4:43, Josh. 20:2), the text does not specify whether or not the king's claim to the territory should be seen as a good one. Territorial integrity is a legitimate concern for a king. The peace between Aram and Israel, however, had only been a short one,[21] and the king is willing to sacrifice peace for the arguable benefit of regaining disputed territory; arguable, because no benefit is specified for anyone, except, implicitly, the king in his reputation and power. Moreover, if one allows the placement of this story next to the preceding story of Naboth's vineyard to bear upon its interpretation, then the reader will be less inclined to see territorial responsibility as the prime royal motive. Thus the king may implicitly be abusing royal prerogative in lightly sacrificing peace and greedily undertaking war.

The fact that the king lets what he has in mind be known publicly in his court (verse 3) implies that his mind is already made up. His question is not a genuine question (as it is, at least in form, in verse 6), but a leading question. Since people do not like changing publicly adopted positions, for fear of loss of face, they do not ask for support for a position unless the decision is already taken. That the king knows what he wants to do, and is resolved to do it, is basic to the dynamic of the story. So Jehoshaphat consents to the king's request (verse 4) in the deferential language of diplomacy.

> [5] But Jehoshaphat also said to the king of Israel, 'Inquire first for the word of the LORD.' [6] Then the king of Israel gathered the prophets together, about four hundred of them, and said to them, 'Shall I go to

21. As noted above, three years/days is the Hebrew idiom for an indefinite short period of time, as opposed to forty years/days for an indefinite long period of time.

> battle against Ramoth-gilead, or shall I refrain?' They said, 'Go up; for the LORD will give it into the hand of the king.'

But Jehoshaphat, who is a man of religious principle as well as a diplomat, does not in fact want simply to rubberstamp the king's decision. So he requests that proper practice be observed, and that God's will be sought before such an undertaking begins. To this the king consents. The prophets, religious functionaries whose livelihood depends on the king, know which way the wind is blowing and what the king wants – for the king had made his wishes public (verse 3); so they duly oblige by telling the king what he wants to hear.

> 7 But Jehoshaphat said, 'Is there no other prophet of the LORD here of whom we may inquire?' 8 The king of Israel said to Jehoshaphat, 'There is still one other by whom we may inquire of the LORD, Micaiah son of Imlah; but I hate him, for he never prophesies anything favourable about me, but only disaster.'[22] Jeshoshaphat said, 'Let the king not say such a thing.'

The assumption that the prophets are telling the king what he wants to hear is confirmed by Jehoshaphat's response. He smells a rat. We are not told how. Maybe it is simply as obvious to Jehoshaphat as to the 400 which way the royal wind is blowing, and he wants his request for the seeking of God's will to be taken more seriously.

Even before Micaiah has appeared, discernment of whether the prophets truly speak for YHWH is beginning to be an issue. One false start in this context is to suppose that Jehoshaphat thinks that the 400 are not truly prophets of YHWH at all, but are prophets of Baal or Asherah like the prophets of the contest on Mt Carmel (1 Kgs. 18:19). Although the 450 prophets of Baal are killed at the end of the story, the 400 prophets of Asherah play no active role in the story and their fate is not mentioned; could the 400 prophets here be those prophets of Asherah?[23] This

22. Preferable is 'bad' or 'unfavourable'. The king's words use in contrast the two basic Hebrew words for 'good' (*tōv*) and 'bad' (*ra'*). The point is that Micaiah does not tell the king what he would like to hear ('good' in the sense of 'favourable', 'positive'), but rather what he does not want to hear ('bad', in the sense of 'unfavourable', 'negative'). When the sense is not generally 'bad' but specifically 'disaster', Hebrew usually uses the feminine/neuter form *rā'āh*, as in verse 23 (cf. Amos 3:6b, and the use of *rā'āh* in Jeremiah's axiom, Jer. 18:8, and in the adoption of Jeremiah's axiom in Jonah 3:10, 4:2).

23. The reference to 400 prophets of Asherah in 1 Kgs. 18:19b (and 18:22 LXX), who otherwise play no role in the Carmel narrative, seems odd and out of place. I suggest that it may well be an early interpretative gloss that sought to 'locate' the prophets of 1 Kgs. 22 'appropriately', i.e. in proximity to the prophets of Baal. If so, it nicely illustrates that reading the text in its

typological linkage with the Elijah story has the venerable precedent of the Septuagint translators (followed recently by the NIV), but depends on omitting one Hebrew word (*'ōd*, 'other') and goes against the fact that Zedekiah and the 400 prophesy in the name of Israel's God (*'adōnay*, verse 6,[24] cf. *yhwh*, verses 11, 12, 24). That is, the issue is not as simple as just distinguishing the one who speaks for YHWH from those who speak for another deity such as Baal or Asherah, as though it were a matter of formal, public allegiance, the prophets being suspect simply because they do not adhere to YHWH. The problem of the text is the harder one, as in the book of Jeremiah – when prophets indeed speak in the name of the acknowledged God, and yet there is reason to doubt what they say.

The king knows of another prophet, Micaiah ben Imlah, but he is unwelcome for a simple reason. Micaiah is known by the king as someone who does not tell him what he wants to hear, but rather what he does not want to hear; Micaiah says things which the king dislikes.

However, as Jehoshaphat diplomatically puts it, the fact that the king does not like Micaiah does not mean that Micaiah may not have something to say which needs to be heard. Jehoshaphat still wants a second opinion, and if Micaiah is the only other prophet around, then he must be heard; to which the king again agrees.

> 9 Then the king of Israel summoned an officer and said, 'Bring quickly Micaiah son of Imlah.' 10 Now the king of Israel and King Jehoshaphat of Judah were sitting on their thrones, arrayed in their robes, at the threshing-floor at the entrance of the gate of Samaria; and all the prophets were prophesying before them. 11 Zedekiah son of Chenaanah made for himself horns of iron, and he said, 'Thus says the LORD: With these you shall gore the Arameans until they are destroyed.' 12 All the prophets were prophesying the same and saying, 'Go up to Ramoth-gilead and triumph; the LORD will give it into the hand of the king.'

As Micaiah is summoned, the narrator pauses to fill out the context in which all this is happening, which so far has been passed over in favour of

received form should retain diachronic nuance. That is, if there is such a link between the 400 of 1 Kings 18 and 1 Kings 22, then it is a gloss that not only is isolated but also goes against the clear grain of 1 Kings 22 in itself. As such it is illuminating for a certain kind of inner-biblical exegesis which is less constrained by the narrative's own logic than I wish myself, and my readers, to be.

24. NRSV follows numerous manuscripts in reading the tetragrammaton in the words of the prophets in verse 6, though the L text in *BHS* reads *'adōnay*. Walsh 1996:345, 347 makes much of the absence of the tetragrammaton here to suggest that these prophets are 'equally at the service of Yahweh and of Baal or Asherah' depending on the exigencies of the moment. Yet in terms of the narrative flow of 1 Kings 22, allegiance to Asherah is not an issue.

focussing on the content of the dialogue (verses 6–8). An impressive scene it is – the kings of Israel and Judah, wearing the special clothes (robes) and sitting on the special chairs (thrones) which symbolize the dignity and authority of their position. And they are at the gate of the city, the formal gathering place where those with public responsibility administered justice (cf. Ruth 4:1–12, Job 29:7–17). In the presence of these kings, the prophets are performing their accredited religious function of speaking on God's behalf to the leaders of God's people. Zedekiah, presumably the leader of the prophets, performs a symbolic action such as Hebrew prophets characteristically performed (e.g. Jer. 13:1–11, 19:1–15),[25] while the rest prophesy similarly, supporting their leader. The temporal and spiritual authorities of God's people are gathered together in their official capacity in the place of justice. Here surely one can expect God to be present and his will to be done.

Why does the narrator take the trouble thus to depict the setting? It is not, I think, that he likes grand occasions (of a sort still to be found today, *mutatis mutandis*, in Westminster, Washington, or the Kremlin). There are, I suggest, at least three reasons in terms of his story. First, because the story has already raised as a possibility that the 400 prophets are speaking less than the truth, we are invited to contemplate the possibility that such a formal and symbolically resonant gathering of religiously responsible leaders may in fact be a sham, an elaborate fraud. Secondly, related to this, the scene of the earthly court prepares for Micaiah's vision of a heavenly court (verses 19–23), at which the true nature of the earthly court will be revealed. Thirdly, we are given to know exactly what Micaiah has to face – not a private meeting with the king, where the privacy of the occasion and the not unfriendly presence of Jehoshaphat might perhaps allow Micaiah space and confidence. Rather, he must face a meeting in a formal, public, symbolically charged context whose every dimension underlines the authority of the hostile king and so will bring pressure on Micaiah to conform to the will of that king.

> [13] The messenger who had gone to summon Micaiah said to him, 'Look, the words of the prophets with one accord are favourable to the king; let your word be like the word of one of them, and speak favourably.'

25. It is often suggested that Zedekiah is symbolically enacting Moses' blessing on Joseph: 'A firstborn bull – majesty is his! His horns are the horns of a wild ox; with them he gores the peoples, driving them to the ends of the earth' (Deut. 33:17). This is entirely plausible (in historical-critical as well as canonical terms), and enriches the likely resonances of Zedekiah's action.

> [14] But Micaiah said, 'As the LORD lives, whatever the LORD says to me, that I will speak.'

We are not told of special instructions from the king to the messenger, but that is because he needs such instructions no more than do the 400 prophets. The messenger, like the prophets, lives and works at court, and he knows what is going on. So he already starts to bring pressure to bear on Micaiah. Micaiah must tell the king what he wants to hear, something that will sound 'favourable' (*tōv*) to him – that which the king has already complained he never got from Micaiah (verse 8). Micaiah, not surprisingly, given what the king has already said about him, refuses to do any such thing, but rather formulates his responsibility to speak truly for God. By his invocation of YHWH, Micaiah makes clear that it is to YHWH that he is accountable.

> [15] When he had come to the king, the king said to him, 'Micaiah, shall we go to Ramoth-gilead to battle, or shall we refrain?' He answered him, 'Go up and triumph; the LORD will give it into the hand of the king.' [16] But the king said to him, 'How many times must I make you swear to tell me nothing but the truth in the name of the LORD?'

A surprise! Micaiah says what the other prophets say, when we expected him to say something different. But the surprise is shortlived, for the king's indignant response shows what is happening. Micaiah is a skilled communicator who understands the dynamics of the situation. If what the kings wants is a favourable message, then that is what Micaiah, his loyal subject, will give him. Micaiah repeats verbatim the words of the other prophets (verse 12b). But as he does so, he mimics them so sarcastically that the king instantly gets the point – he, the king, is being mocked by Micaiah. This provokes from the king a protestation of delicious irony. The man who hitherto has wanted nothing but confirmation of his own will now claims the moral high ground and says that he wants nothing less than the truth of God, and implies that Micaiah is the one who has problems with being truthful.

In thus provoking the king, Micaiah has thrown him off guard, and has at least got him to express how important it is that he, Micaiah, truly speaks the word of YHWH to him. Such an expostulation is, of course, no guarantee that that is what he really wants, but it at least might lead to a greater openness. Moreover, the king's recognition that the promise of victory on Micaiah's lips is empty words, mere mockery of himself, perhaps indicates that the king himself knows (or at least suspects) that his prophets are toadies whose word is not to be relied upon. But can Micaiah make the king openly acknowledge this?

> [17] Then Micaiah said, 'I saw all Israel scattered on the mountains, like sheep that have no shepherd; and the LORD said, "These have no master; let each one go home in peace".' [18] The king of Israel said to Jehoshaphat, 'Did I not tell you that he would not prophesy anything favourable about me, but only disaster?'[26]

Micaiah's message from YHWH initially takes the form of a vision, a vision of the future and its interpretation by YHWH. The king instantly thinks that he understands it and pronounces accordingly. His prejudices about Micaiah have been confirmed: Micaiah just makes unpleasant threats against the king.

But has the king understood the vision? Only in part. He has seen, rightly, that it is a vision which implies his death in battle. What he has not seen is that it is not primarily a vision about him at all. It is a vision about Israel, the people for whom he has responsibility; they are scattered and leaderless. YHWH's concern is for them and their safe return home. But the king is concerned only with the implications for himself. Micaiah's words, in essence a challenge to the king to remember his responsibilities as shepherd to his people before it is too late, evoke no response. Or rather, they evoke the wrong response.

The story here presupposes some of the basic dynamics of Hebrew prophecy, as in the episode of Jeremiah at the potter's house (Jer. 18:1–12). As articulated there, prophecy is relational, engaging language that seeks a response. As has been seen, it is typically a warning of 'disaster' (*rā'āh*) which seeks a response of fundamental change of heart and action ('turn'/'repent', *shūv*) so that the disaster may be averted because YHWH himself responds to such response (he may 'rescind'/'revoke', *niham*).[27] This means that Micaiah's vision of Israel's distress, and their loss of a leader, is a warning designed to avert its taking place. It is a challenge to the king to turn/repent, i.e. to abandon his self-willed

26. There is the same translation problem here as in verse 8.
27. Compare the depiction of Ezekiel's prophetic ministry in terms of his being a watchman or sentinel (Ezek. 33:1–20, esp. 10–16), where prophetic speech is a warning whose purpose is to get the delinquent person (*rasha'*) to respond and avert death (as well as to warn the righteous, *tsaddiq*, not to become complacent and corrupt and forfeit life). If the person responds, the words fulfil their purpose of bringing life. If the person does not respond, and if they die in their sin, there is no satisfaction in the literal fulfilment and correctness of the warning; there is only the knowledge that the prophet who gave the warning is not at fault for having failed to do so.

ambitions for Ramoth-gilead and in so doing both to save his own life and to benefit his people. But the king is not moved. Rather, in the language of classical Hebrew idiom, he 'hardens his heart'/'stiffens his neck',[28] simply seeing in Micaiah's words a confirmation of his prejudices.

At this point it might seem that Micaiah has failed. After skilfully mocking the king into requesting a true message, he has delivered his message from YHWH. But he has not been heeded. Micaiah, however, is not intimidated and does not give up. Rather, he speaks again with words of such keen sharpness that they will surely cut through even the hardest of hearts.

> [19] Then Micaiah said, 'Therefore hear the word of the LORD: I saw the LORD sitting on his throne, with all the host of heaven standing beside him to the right and to the left of him. [20] And the LORD said, "Who will entice [*pittāh*][29] Ahab, so that he may go up and fall at Ramoth-gilead?" Then one said one thing, and another said another, [21] until a spirit came forward and stood before the LORD, saying, "I will entice [*pittāh*] him." [22] "How?" the LORD asked him. He replied, "I will go out and be a lying [*sheqer*] spirit in the mouth of all his prophets." Then the LORD said, "You are to entice [*pittāh*] him, and you shall succeed; go out and do it." [23] So you see, the LORD has put a lying [*sheqer*] spirit in the mouth of all these your prophets; the LORD has decreed disaster [*rāʿāh*] for you.'

The dynamics of the encounter between Ahab and Micaiah are crucial – Micaiah begins with 'therefore'. This vision of the heavenly court is not the initial or primary message of Micaiah, which has already been delivered (verse 17). But Micaiah is faced by the king's refusal to respond positively to his warning. The issue at stake is, in the proper sense, one of life and death. But how do you get through to someone who does not want to hear? This is Micaiah's supreme attempt to engage with the king.[30]

Micaiah has a communicative strategy similar to that of Nathan in his famous confrontation with David (2 Sam. 12:1–7). The golden rule is simple: Don't state the obvious. If you simply tell reluctant people what they think they already know, using categories that they already accept, then they will ignore you; you are at best a bore, and more probably an

28. Hebrew uses a number of related terms: *hizzēq/hiqshāh/hikbīdh lēv/ʿōreph*.
29. Here and in verses 21, 22 preferable is 'deceive'. See below.
30. Numerous commentators have considered verses 19–23 a secondary insertion, which is in various ways at odds with the rest of the story (e.g. Hossfeld and Meyer 1973:32–6). At root, the issue is exegetical. My construal, like Micaiah's warning, must be its own justification.

irritating nuisance. So Micaiah cannot just repeat what he has already said, or baldly say 'your prophets are lying to you' or 'your prophets are telling you what you want to hear', but must find some other way of expressing his warning to the king so that it brings home to the king the reality of his situation.[31] Micaiah does not resort to right-sounding religious rhetoric (he does not use the familiar formula 'Thus says YHWH'). Rather, he paints a picture and tells a story of such imaginative starkness that the king must surely be moved by it.

The purpose of the vision (verses 19–22) is made crystal clear by Micaiah in his closing words (verse 23), in which he interprets the vision to the king. His conclusion, that 'YHWH has decreed disaster (*rā'āh*) for you', makes the vision into a classic prophetic warning, the logic of which we have already seen in relation to Micaiah's first vision – it is a warning whose purpose is fulfilled if it moves the person addressed to respond in such a way (turn/repent, *shūv*) that what is envisaged need not actually happen. The second vision has the same purpose as the first vision. If the message is that the king will die, it is given so that the king may not die.

The narrator has told in some detail of the court scene in Samaria to which Micaiah has been summoned: the kings on their thrones and their religious courtiers speaking in their presence. Micaiah now tells of another court scene, of a king on his throne surrounded by his courtiers. But now the king is YHWH and the setting is 'heaven'. But 'heaven' does not mean somewhere else – another place, another time – but rather represents and depicts the spiritual reality of what is happening in the here and now on earth, at the entrance of the gate of Samaria. That is, the relationship between the court of YHWH and the court of Ahab is not that of a causal relationship between two different times and two different places: i.e. first, YHWH makes a decision at his court, and subsequently this is enacted upon a luckless Ahab; first, a decision is made somewhere else (wherever heaven might be supposed to be), and subsequently it is enacted in Samaria. Rather, God is both *now* and *here*. The court of YHWH is the spiritual counterpart to the court of Ahab; it is the other side of one and the same coin. The scene of YHWH's court interprets to Ahab the reality of his court.

31. Francis Dewar has drawn to my attention some words of Emily Dickinson which well capture the kind of strategy that Micaiah adopts: 'Tell all the truth but tell it slant, Success in circuit lies.'

How, then, should we understand Micaiah's vision? There are three different levels or dimensions within Micaiah's words, though these are all interrelated facets of the one vision, and to take any one element in isolation may lead to misunderstanding.

First, there is the ('psychological') level of the communicative dynamics of Micaiah's trying to get through to Ahab. Here the issue focusses on the word used to initiate the plot within the vision, that is YHWH's proposal that someone should 'deceive' (*pittāh*, verses 20, 21, 22) Ahab. The meaning of the Hebrew word is a little controverted, but is sufficiently clarified by parallel usage.[32] The basic verbal root means 'simple-minded/foolish', i.e. the sort of person who is easily put upon by others. The *piel* form of the verb here means 'make a fool out of', that is to make someone act unwisely against their own best interests;[33] and so is probably best rendered in English with 'deceive'. Thus in God's proposal, 'Who will deceive Ahab?', Micaiah is in effect saying to Ahab 'You are letting your prophets make a dupe of you.' The point is that nobody likes being told that they are being duped, and nobody willingly goes along with it. If you think that you are being duped, you do something different. In this sense, the difference it makes that it is not just the court prophets (whom Ahab may hold in contempt) but God himself who is behind the prophets who are duping Ahab is that it greatly sharpens the challenge – it is a real and serious deception, in which the stakes are as high as they could be, and the results will be permanent. All the more reason, then, not to acquiesce in being duped. To tell someone that they are being deceived has a similar logic and dynamic to that of warning someone of coming disaster.

The second ('moral') level within Micaiah's vision arises once the deception has been agreed on, with reference to the means by which it is to be carried out. The issue here focusses again on one particular Hebrew word, that which the spirit says it will be in the mouths of Ahab's 400 prophets, which YHWH commends as sure to succeed, and

32. The problem tends to be which other usage is considered the best parallel. Recent scholarship has often made much of overtones of sexual manipulation (what the Philistines want Samson's women to do to him, so that he reveals his secrets, Judg. 14:15, 16:5) or seduction/rape (Exod. 22:15 (ET16)), and has found such overtones in the famous lament of Jeremiah (Jer. 20:7). This may underlie the NRSV's preference for 'entice' in 1 Kgs. 22:20–2 as in Jer. 20:7. Yet overtones of seduction are 'extremely unlikely' (Mosis 2003:171) in Jer. 20:7, and the point of the deception in 1 Kgs. 22 is that the king should be 'incapable of seeing and doing what is necessary to avoid defeat' (Mosis 2003:169–70).

33. For example, Joab accuses Abner before David of 'deceiving' David in his apparent peace mission (2 Sam. 3:25).

which Micaiah confirms in his explanation of the vision. The word is *sheqer* ('lie', 'falsehood', 'deception'), another fundamental term of Hebrew prophetic language, especially, as we have already seen, within the book of Jeremiah. There *sheqer* is that which prophets speak when they are not sent by YHWH and when they tell people the things that they want to hear – in that context an assurance of peace (*shālōm*), in this context something 'favourable' (*tōv*). It is at heart a self-serving use of religious language, whose lack of engagement with God is demonstrated by its lack of integrity.

If the message of Ahab's prophets is designated as *sheqer*, Micaiah means that what the prophets say lacks integrity. It is self-serving because the prophets are telling the king what he wants to hear. But in speaking thus the prophets are reflecting back to the king his own self-will. Here is the implicit moral point of Micaiah's vision. The deceptive message of the prophets is the counterpart to the king's self-seeking. Thus Micaiah complements the psychological challenge to the king not to let himself be duped ('don't be a fool') with the moral challenge to recognize a lack of integrity about the proposal to fight at Ramoth-gilead ('don't be so self-seeking').

The third ('theological') level in Micaiah's vision is the God-centred dimension – that the proposal to deceive Ahab through putting a self-serving message in the mouth of his prophets be ascribed to YHWH. Micaiah's clear concern is that Ahab should recognize *his* message (and not the message of the 400 prophets) as none other than the message of their God. It is not just that he, Micaiah, has 'decreed disaster' for Ahab, but that YHWH (verse 23b emphasizes YHWH as subject; cf. Job 1:21) has spoken thus. A divinely ordained disaster is the (admonitory) meaning of the visionary scene. It is God whom Ahab is confronting.

What sort of God is YHWH as spoken of by Micaiah? As already seen, one whose purpose in sending the prophets to announce 'disaster' (*rā ʿāh*) is a compassionate one, to reach out to and reclaim those who are going astray, so that they may turn to God (*shūv*) and so that the disaster may possibly never take place, because YHWH may mercifully respond (*niham*) to genuine response. But how is the compassionate concern of God to be communicated to someone resolved on morally questionable self-will? The announcement of compassion in such a context – 'Although you are pursuing your own course, God will be merciful to you' – is hardly capable of conveying, or being understood as, true compassion. Rather, it will invariably sound to the addressee like ultimate indifference and consequent licence, that is acquiescence in, or even encouragement of, the self-willed course of action, with no fundamental change of direction required because God will be merciful come what may (one might compare the famously complacent dictum ascribed to Heine on his deathbed, 'Dieu me pardonnera, c'est son métier'). Such a message would lack genuine engagement with the moral and spiritual realities of human resolve. This means that the message of divine compassion must be expressed in other terms which do engage with, and challenge, the human will. In other words, the message of divine compassion must be formulated as a challenge. The message of God must be presented as, in one way or other, confrontational and adversarial, so that its moral character may be genuinely represented.

What is at stake is the 'I–thou' dynamics of encounter. In encounter with God, the compassionate but demanding engagement of God with the human may be unwelcome and even threatening unless and until appropriate response is made. Moreover, such engagement does not, and cannot, leave the human person where they were previously, for response of some kind to God is inevitable. The one who does not respond positively is thereby driven further away from a positive response. In Hebrew terminology, when the initiative of God does not engender 'turning' (*shūv*), it engenders 'hardening of heart'/'stiffening of neck'. This is not just a description of the subsequent state of a person, but also a description of what is happening in the moment of encounter. In short, Micaiah's depiction of God's mercy as hostility towards Ahab cannot be understood if abstracted from the dynamics of Micaiah's encounter with Ahab.

Once Micaiah's vision is seen for what it is, a supreme attempt to touch the king's heart and mind, one may feel that surely it cannot leave the king unmoved.

> [24] Then Zedekiah son of Chenaanah came up to Micaiah, slapped
> him on the cheek, and said, 'Which way did the spirit of the LORD pass
> from me to speak to you?' [25] Micaiah replied, 'You will find out on
> that day when you go in to hide in an inner chamber.' [26] The king of
> Israel then ordered, 'Take Micaiah, and return him to Amon the
> governor of the city and to Joash the king's son, [27] and say, "Thus says
> the king: Put this fellow in prison, and feed him on reduced rations of
> bread and water until I come in peace." ' [28] Micaiah said, 'If you return
> in peace, the LORD has not spoken by me.' And he said, 'Hear, you
> peoples, all of you!'

At this point Zedekiah intervenes. Zedekiah, as leader of the court prophets, is the person who stands to lose the most if the king heeds Micaiah. If publicly exposed as one who self-servingly deceives the king, he would face at least public shame and probably more – loss of his position, perhaps loss of his life. So at the moment of truth he decides (not consciously, but in effect) fully to embody the lying spirit of Micaiah's vision. He intervenes to ensure that a possibly wavering king remembers who his real friends and advisers are.

Zedekiah performs another action, as much a symbolic action as was his previous wielding of iron horns (verse 11). He hits Micaiah, to hurt and humiliate him. At the same time he asks a clever rhetorical question, which seeks to change the whole dynamics of the moment. For if Micaiah tried to answer such a question on its own terms, i.e. to justify or explain what he has said, Zedekiah would hold the initiative in interrogating a defensive Micaiah; and ultimately Micaiah has no justification beyond that contained in what he has already said. Micaiah, therefore, does not waver but responds with a challenge to Zedekiah.

The point of Micaiah's utterance at first seems obscure. Is it another vision? Is it a riddle? It is neither. Its point can be seen in the logic of his wording in his context. Why might Zedekiah 'go to hide in an inner room'? The 'inner room' is not a place of piety (for prayer) or modesty (a privy), but the most obscure place possible within a building (a cubby hole of some kind or other), the place where you hide when you are trying to escape from people who want to kill you (the Hebrew idiom for 'inner room' is used to depict where Ben-Hadad escapes to when he is fleeing for his life (1 Kgs. 20:30)). When you are hiding in fear for your life, you are vulnerable; the time when you are fearful of discovery and death is the time when you pray to God for safety. The meaning of Micaiah's words, then, is this. At the present moment Zedekiah is deflecting any possible danger to his own fraudulent position by abusing Micaiah. Accordingly, the reality before God of what he is saying and doing is hidden from him, for in abusing Micaiah he is hardening his heart. But if a time comes when Zedekiah seeks God in his own hour of need, a time when Zedekiah's own life is threatened, his future hangs by a thread, and he genuinely cries out to God – then the truth will searingly become clear to him and he will know the genuineness of what God has said through Micaiah.

For the present, however, Zedekiah's action and words are decisive. The king does not heed Micaiah, but arrests him and orders him to be detained. One may wonder whether placing Micaiah in the charge of two such significant figures as the city governor and one of the king's sons may not imply some kind of VIP treatment, a tacit recognition of Micaiah's stature. But certainly the instruction that Micaiah be given only meagre amounts of bread and water makes no concessions. The king's final words, that Micaiah be held in prison on minimum subsistence 'until I return in peace' – which, in terms of what Micaiah has said, will not happen, and so anticipates a possible life sentence for Micaiah – may even be one last attempt by the king to get Micaiah to change his message to one of 'peace'/ 'good' (*shālōm/tōv*), so that Micaiah may escape incarceration.

Micaiah does not flinch. Although he may be signing his own death warrant, he reaffirms the content of his message and warning. If the king is indeed successful at Ramoth-gilead, then Micaiah is prepared to recognize that his own words – as conveyed by his initial vision and challenge, verse 17 – have been empty and have not conveyed the will of God to Ahab.

There is then a postscript, a summons to 'all peoples' to hear Micaiah's message (verse 28b). The wording is in fact identical to that of the opening words of the message of the canonical prophet Micah (Mic. 1:2).[34] The precise significance of this parallel is unclear. It is initially striking that Micaiah appears to speak suddenly to an audience different from that within the story – different inasmuch as there has been no previous reference to the presence of 'peoples' (*'ammim*) in Samaria, even if some wider public gathering may be presupposed.[35] He appears now to be addressing a wider audience of those who will read his story. Therefore Micaiah's words function in the same kind of way that one is familiar with today when a character within a film suddenly turns to address the camera/viewer. If such a shift of mode is successful, it can draw (or jolt)

34. The wording may well, of course, be a gloss of unknown date. Interestingly, although it is not in the LXX of 1 Kgs. 22:28, it is in the LXX of the parallel account in 2 Chr. 18:27 (see further Ball 1977). As a gloss it might indicate some typological identification of Micaiah with the canonical Micah, perhaps on the part of the early compilers and interpreters of Israel's scriptures.

35. There is some awkwardness in the Hebrew which has a third-person plural suffix, i.e. strictly 'all of them' (*kūllām*) rather than the expected second-person suffix, 'all of you' (*kūllekem*). However, this awkwardness is equally present in Mic. 1:2, which is clearly a second-person address. In fact the form *kūllekem* is not attested in the OT, and usage of *kol* with a third-person suffix indicating the totality of what is referred to is not uncommon (GKC #135r, JM #146j).

the audience into a more immediate engagement with the issues of the story.[36]

If one takes the wording at face value in its present context, it indicates that the kind of conflict between king and prophet which has just preceded is not something peculiar to the history of Israel, but is rather, in one form or other, recurrent in the history of every nation. What the story of Micaiah does is to illuminate the fundamental issues within the conflict in the light of God's desire for truth and integrity in public human life.

> 29 So the king of Israel and King Jehoshaphat of Judah went up to
> Ramoth-gilead. 30 The king of Israel said to Jehoshaphat, 'I will
> disguise myself and go into battle, but you wear your robes.' So the
> king of Israel disguised himself and went into battle. 31 Now the king of
> Aram had commanded the thirty-two captains of his chariots, 'Fight
> with no one small or great, but only with the king of Israel.' 32 When
> the captains of the chariots saw Jehoshaphat, they said, 'It is surely the
> king of Israel.' So they turned to fight against him; and Jehoshaphat
> cried out. 33 When the captains of the chariots saw that it was not the
> king of Israel, they turned back from pursuing him.

The king has decided to seek his moment of glory at Ramoth-gilead. What would a confident king do, who trusted his own judgment that the campaign was a good idea, who took seriously the divine reassurance from a large and unanimous group of prophets, and who genuinely dismissed the unwelcome words of Micaiah? He would surely go in all his splendour, prepared to celebrate a great victory. Within English history I think of Edward II in June 1314, who marched on Scotland with an unprecedentedly large English army to relieve the castle of Stirling and deal once and for all with the troublesome Scottish king, Robert the Bruce. The English forces outnumbered the Scottish by three or four to one, and Edward took with him the royal wardrobe with a large amount of jewels and ecclesiastical vestments in order to be able fully to celebrate the anticipated victory. Edward acted with confidence and took with him the visible signs of royal splendour and victory – since the idea that he might lose it all at the Bannock Burn clearly never entered his mind.

36. The 'so what would *you* have done?' look (if that is the right construal of a defiant but enigmatic expression) that the compromised cardinal gives to the viewer at the very end of the credits in *The Mission* is a good, visual rather than verbal, example of the technique.

But for Ahab something has gone wrong. At the very moment that his glory and power should be demonstrated in anticipation of victory, the king puts on a disguise, so that nobody will recognize him as king. He cannot savour his longed-for battle, because when it comes he is too afraid. Why? Presumably because the king recognizes in his heart what he cannot bring himself to acknowledge publicly or act upon – that Micaiah was probably speaking the truth. But he thinks that he can get round Micaiah's words by a deception of his own. If he is a 'marked man' because of Micaiah's warning – and perhaps aware that the king of Aram regards him as the cause of the warfare and so wants to single him out – then he will remove his public markings and become, as it were, invisible. If he can survive, he may yet triumph. The Aramaeans are initially taken in by this ruse and think that Jehoshaphat in his robes must be Ahab. Jehoshaphat – who after his early initiative (verses 5, 8) has been a passive figure throughout the story, strangely compliant with Ahab, and apparently rather slow on the uptake – now realizes what is happening and makes sure that they discover their error. But if Ahab remains indistinguishable, can the Aramaeans do anything about it?

> [34] But a certain man drew his bow and unknowingly struck the king of Israel between the scale-armour and the breastplate; so he said to the driver of his chariot, 'Turn around, and carry me out of the battle, for I am wounded.' [35] The battle grew hot that day, and the king was propped up in his chariot facing the Arameans, until at evening he died; the blood from the wound had flowed into the bottom of the chariot. [36] Then about sunset a shout went through the army, 'Every man to his city, and every man to his country!' [37] So the king died, and was brought to Samaria; they buried the king in Samaria. [38] They washed the chariot by the pool of Samaria; the dogs licked up his blood, and the prostitutes washed themselves in it, according to the word of the LORD that he had spoken.

The end comes simply. Ahab's device works, in that he remains unrecognized. Nobody points him out, not even God, who might perhaps have given specific instructions to a particular Aramaean. Rather, an archer acts unknowingly, that is not specifically targeting Ahab, and his arrow finds not just Ahab but also the chink in his armour, so as to give a fatal wound. Ahab lives a little longer, but only to see his army defeated. And so it becomes apparent that the message of Zedekiah and the 400 prophets was indeed a falsehood. Micaiah's words receive the fulfilment that they never sought (as earlier words of Elijah are also fulfilled, 22:38, cf. 21:19),[37] and even in unintentional human action God's purposes are fulfilled.

3 Conclusion: the cost and challenge of discernment

The story of Micaiah is a good example of much that is characteristic of biblical prophecy. Although it contains an inseparable element of future prediction on which Micaiah is willing to stake his credibility, its prime focus is a conflict between self-will and integrity, understood in terms of responsiveness to the moral character and will of God – an issue central to the religious faiths rooted in the biblical literature. Moreover, message and life are interwoven. The person who speaks for God, even – or, rather, especially – when faithfully, cannot necessarily expect a ready reception. Challenging the complacencies and self-deceptions of the human heart and mind with the searching truth of God will regularly provoke a hostility whose consequences may be devastating. Trying to avoid this by being more accommodating risks becoming a prophet whose message is ultimately self-serving.

The appropriateness of this story, rather than that of Jeremiah and Hananiah, to illustrate the construal of prophetic authenticity articulated within the book of Jeremiah will, I hope, be apparent. For the similarities of both presentation and content between Jeremiah and Micaiah are striking. Jeremiah, like Micaiah, is presented as a lone voice in the midst of numerous other prophets who speak a more palatable message (*shālōm*/*tōv*). Consequently problems of falsehood and deception (*sheqer*) play a major role in each text. Jeremiah, like Micaiah, fulfils his vocation only at the cost of considerable personal suffering, including imprisonment. Although both Jeremiah and Micaiah are primarily concerned with the dynamics of moral responsiveness to YHWH (*shūv*), each also offers a prediction of future events which is so integral that his credibility is tied up with it – for Jeremiah, the fall of Jerusalem to the Babylonians, for Micaiah, the king's death in battle. It is Jeremiah who spells out the axiom that human turning to God (*shūv*) is the explicit goal of prophetic warning (Jer. 18:7–8, 23:21–2), even though there is a corresponding awareness of how costly and difficult true turning to God may be

37. A certain looseness of detail (Jezreel/Samaria) between Elijah's prophecy and its fulfilment is not uncharacteristic of Hebrew prophecy, though in this particular instance there may be certain other difficulties under the surface (see Moberly 2003b:18–21).

(Jer. 3:10, 3:19–4:4); and it has been seen how the application of this axiom makes sense of everything Micaiah says.[38]

The story unambiguously raises the fundamental issue of how one might be able to differentiate between conflicting voices, when all speak in the name of the same God. The king has to choose between rival accounts of what is good for him, in which he must decide who is speaking the truth. What the king has to choose between is, in essence, his own self-seeking desire, as expressed and represented by his prophets (verses 6, 12), and Micaiah's warning that he is neglecting his duty and jeopardizing his life (verse 17). Even before Micaiah has spoken, a certain kind of integrity is what the king grudgingly recognizes as characterizing Micaiah (verse 8). Micaiah challenges the king about the integrity of his proposed action, and in his climactic appeal he is most explicit. There is no integrity about the prophetic encouragement to fight at Ramoth-gilead. It is a message which only a fool will heed, because it is deceit, and it is deceit because it represents an outworking of Ahab's heedless self-will. Thus integrity is, in essence, the key to discernment. Micaiah demonstrates an integrity that is lacking in Zedekiah and the 400. But the recognition of Micaiah as speaking the truth also requires a certain kind of integrity (a degree of honesty, openness) on the part of those who need to do the recognizing – in particular, a willingness to relinquish self-will and admit error. That makes integrity a demanding key to use, too demanding for Ahab and Zedekiah.

Finally, the story of Micaiah and Ahab illustrates well an important dimension of the moral and spiritual nature of prophecy, inasmuch as here the moral and spiritual is in no way narrow or privatized, but set rather at the heart of the public arena, where Micaiah's prophetic responsibility (which devolves onto those Jewish and Christian communities which canonize the story) is to 'speak truth to power' (Lash 1997:130).[39] The story does not, of course, deny that military campaigns may have an appropriate political/military rationale, but it does show how a military campaign may raise hard, and generally unwelcome, issues at the core of the human will.

38. I became aware, through presenting early versions of this interpretation in several universities, that many of my colleagues were resistant to my reading of Micaiah's visions in terms of divine concern for Ahab, apparently on the grounds that it represents some kind of pious smoothing of the rough-hewn texture of the ancient narrative. However, no one has yet cogently argued the inappropriateness of using the book of Jeremiah as a theological template. Indeed, the likely proximity in time of the editing of the books of Jeremiah and of Kings, with some relation to the perspectives of Deuteronomy within each, gives my proposal credibility in historical-critical terms as well as in terms of reading strategy.

39. There are some interesting reflections and caveats as to how this responsibility may, and may not, apply to contemporary preachers in Brueggemann 2003.

Moreover, there is no support for any notion that political decisions with public effect could have little or nothing to do with responsiveness, conscious or unconscious, to the will of God for human integrity and flourishing. As suggested in Chapter 1, the modern tendency to conceptualize 'God' as some kind of 'external' explanation of an optional (and problematic) kind results from thoroughly questionable theological convictions. The Micaiah story suggests rather that God is the searching presence who seeks to penetrate human self-will and thereby transform human life through the purifying processes of grace and goodness. As in the book of Jeremiah, this is the dimension where prophetic authenticity is to be discovered.

Excursus 1: the status of Micaiah's prediction of the future

In the context of considering prophetic authenticity, one question which may reasonably be raised concerns the status of Micaiah's vision of Ahab's death in battle (22:17). So important is this that Micaiah is willing to stake the credibility of the divine source of all he says upon it (22:28a). The way in which he puts this resonates with the principle of prophetic discernment specified in Deut. 18:21–2:

> You may say to yourself, 'How can we recognize a word that the LORD has not spoken?' If a prophet speaks in the name of the LORD but the thing does not take place or prove true, it is a word that the LORD has not spoken. The prophet has spoken it presumptuously; do not be frightened by it.

In each context the point is made negatively, that non-fulfilment would be a criterion of inauthenticity. So are Micaiah's words perhaps a utilization of Deut. 18:22 as a kind of principle of falsification (perhaps anticipating Karl Popper)?[40] Even if this is the case, the interesting issue within the narrative is the relationship of this criterion to everything else Micaiah says. One way of posing this would be for the modern interpreter

40. I realize that I have said little about Deut. 18:21–2, which scholars not infrequently use as a starting point for discussion. The text is intrinsically somewhat puzzling, both in its isolation in relation to the concerns of Deuteronomy, and in its apparent distance from the contingent and response-seeking nature of prophecy elsewhere in the OT, not least in Jeremiah (a puzzle only exacerbated by the interrelationships between Deuteronomy and Jeremiah). I hope to return to this text in another context, and so only offer two brief comments here. First, in general terms, some issues undoubtedly only become finally clarified by living with them and discerning them over time (compare the reception of the ordination of women within the Anglican communion); the counsel of Gamaliel (Acts 5:34–9), often praised for its wisdom, can be read as a restatement of Deut. 18:21–2 in some

to make a distinction that Micaiah in the biblical text apparently will not make – that is, to ask whether the predominant moral dimension of Micaiah's message could still be considered valid even if the prediction were falsified.[41]

Much, of course, depends on the precise angle of the question. If it is primarily a hypothetical in relation to the biblical story ('What if Ahab had survived?'), then the answer must surely be that there would be no story in the first place; for it is the story that presents the prediction that displays also its fulfilment, and the two belong together. If it is primarily a general question about moral validity even when prediction is disappointed, then some distinction is helpful and hardly inappropriate – the biblical text itself notes Ahab's death in a place other than that predicted, without posing this as a problem. As was observed in relation to the issue of what happened to Jehoiakim's corpse, a prophetic prediction could still have value in terms of moral vision even if its specifics were not realized and it did not lead to repentance on the part of the addressee.

Perhaps, however, given our wider concern with human mediation of the word of God (the nature of 'revelation'), a slightly different question may also be put to Micaiah's prediction: Does Micaiah's prediction of the king's death, like Jeremiah's prediction of the fall of Jerusalem to the Babylonians, constitute the privileged disclosure from God of knowledge otherwise unattainable? That is, does the divine revelation in this context involve the communication of something beyond the unaided capacity of human reason?

On one level this is indeed the case. Both Micaiah and Jeremiah are clearly portrayed as having received an insight from God about the future, and both have complete confidence in this and speak accordingly. On another level, however, the privileged information is not something esoteric or supra-rational but concerns rather the regular sphere of life.

such terms. Secondly, if one common reading of the text – in terms of alluding to those prophetic books which have been considered vindicated and have become canonical – is at all on the right lines, then an analogy for the individual prophet would perhaps lie in the traditional practice of the Catholic Church of considering canonization for a person only when their life can be viewed retrospectively as a whole after their death.

41. The preservation of the moral dimensions of prophecy, and of the biblical text more generally, even while the conventional pre-modern understanding of its predictive qualities and of its relatedness to Christian doctrines was set aside, was a strong characteristic of nineteenth-century scholarship. The self-sufficiency and desirability of these moral dimensions became much less self-evident over the course of the twentieth century, and it is now apparent that their continuing validity depends to a significant extent on their location within some larger, overarching account (not predictive, but certainly related to Christian doctrine) of the nature and purpose of human life.

Moreover, it is initially a *possible* future, not a necessary future, of which they speak – even if the failure of response, alike from Ahab and from the people of Judah, increasingly erodes the contingency. In other words (and without necessarily generalizing from the two particular instances of Micaiah and Jeremiah), the story of Micaiah, like that of Jeremiah, does support an understanding of revelation as the communication of content by God to a receptive human person, but does not support an understanding of revelation as access to unusual or esoteric information. It is the heightened perception of, and engagement with, the mundane – the natural supernaturally transformed – that is the consequence of the word from God.

4

Elisha and Balaam: the enabling and disabling of discernment

> We must now go back a bit and explain what the whole scene had looked like from Uncle Andrew's point of view. It had not made at all the same impression on him as on the Cabby and the children. For what you see and hear depends a good deal on where you are standing: it also depends on what sort of person you are.
>
> – The narrator in C. S. LEWIS' *The Magician's Nephew* (LEWIS 1963:116)

Introduction

In the two preceding chapters I have considered criteria for the discernment of prophetic authenticity in contexts where the prophetic message was contested. The prime emphasis has been on the related issues of the character of the prophet (integrity and lack of self-seeking) and the nature of the message (its challenge to complacency and self-will) as constituting the 'accessible' factors by which the apparently 'inaccessible' realm of God is rendered evident and potent within the human sphere. What is necessary for the activity of discerning has also been touched upon in relation to Ahab and Zedekiah, but with less emphasis, and so it is that issue on which I wish to focus in this chapter.

My texts will be two further prophetic narratives, both imaginatively rich and resonant, which portray the ability of Elisha and Balaam to discern God (2 Kgs. 2:1–18, Num. 22:1–35). In these narratives Elisha and Balaam, although particular figures with distinctive characteristics, seem clearly to function to a significant degree as symbolic images ('types' in traditional parlance), the stories of whom constitute portrayals of the nature and consequences of those dispositions which they embody.

At the outset, however, it must be recognized that there are prima facie difficulties with the relevance of these narratives to my developing thesis. For my concerns are with (a) how God may be discerned and heard specifically in human speech (and action) and (b) how those who are not necessarily prophets might be able to discern those who are prophets; and neither of the two narratives addresses either of these two issues. Nonetheless, I wish to argue that what enables, or disables, prophetic vision of God is not different in kind, but only in degree, from what enables, or disables, anyone's vision; and that the discernment of God in Himself does not take place on a basis different from the discernment of God in a human person. If the most illuminating material in the Old Testament for what is involved in discerning is found in stories about prophetic discerning, then that is where we must take our bearings.

In many ways, what is at stake here is well summed up in the words of Jesus, 'Blessed are the pure in heart, for they will see God' (Matt. 5:8). This pithy formulation of an axiom about humans and God was adopted by the Fathers as central to theology and spirituality. It also represents the kind of concern that tended to fall by the wayside in the reconceptualizing of 'God', 'religion', and 'theology' from the seventeenth century onwards, the recovery of which is essential in our contemporary context.[1]

The precise meaning and scope of Jesus' words has, of course, been extensively debated. On the one hand, there is a strong, and surely correct, consensus that 'pure in heart'[2] denotes not only moral integrity but also consistency of focus upon God, a kind of recovery of fundamental simplicity in the midst of complexity.[3] On the other hand, there is a perhaps more questionable consensus, based primarily upon a judgment

1. There is at least some renewed awareness of the possible significance of disposition and qualities of character for biblical interpretation generally: 'the interpretation of Scripture is a difficult task *not* because of the technical demands of biblical scholarship but because of the importance of character for wise readings' (Fowl and Jones 1991:49). Or, with a more theocentric emphasis, Webster 2003:254: 'The reader's will needs not simply to be called to redirect itself to appropriate ends, but to be reborn. Reading Scripture is inescapably bound to regeneration.' For a suggestive account of a hermeneutics of love for reading and interpretation generally, see Jacobs 2001.

2. The language resonates strongly with, and may well be derived from, the psalms, e.g. Ps. 24:3–4 [23:3–4, LXX, where there is the same language as in the Gospel, *katharos tē kardiā*], Ps. 73:1 [72:1, LXX].

3. 'So purity of heart must involve integrity, a correspondence between outward action and inward thought . . . a lack of duplicity, singleness of intention (cf. Augustine, *De serm. mont.* 1:8: *cor simplex*), and the desire to please God above all else. More succinctly, purity of heart is to will one thing, God's will, with all of one's being' (Davies and Allison 1988:456); '*Pure in heart* should not be restricted to moral, still less sexual, purity; it denotes one who loves God with all his heart (Dt. 6:5), with an undivided loyalty, and whose inward nature

about the nature of the beatitudes as a whole, that the intended sense of the promise of 'seeing God' is 'eschatological'. The consensus is questionable not for finding reference to the eschaton, but only inasmuch as it seeks to limit the realization of the promise to the eschaton.[4] For one of the most characteristic emphases of the gospels is that the eschatological realities of God are already breaking in and are open to realization and appropriation already in this life; the reality that God grants beyond this life is continuous with the reality that has already begun to be lived in this life through faith in Christ. Moreover, however valuable it is to look for original determinate meaning as a critical control in the understanding and use of the biblical text, many a pithy and epigrammatic saying (beatitude, proverb, or similar) is intrinsically open to be validly understood and used in a wide variety of contexts.

In any case, what matters for present purposes is the principle that when it comes to 'seeing' God – which is in essence the nature of discernment – the condition and qualities of the person who would see may be crucial in either enabling or disabling the act of seeing.

1 What enables Elisha to succeed Elijah? 2 Kgs. 2:1–18

My first story represents the conclusion of the Elijah narratives. As with certain other of the Elijah narratives, especially Elijah at Horeb (1 Kgs. 19), there are strong resonances with the Mosaic narratives of the Pentateuch,[5] and any thorough interpretation would need to take these

corresponds with his outward profession (*cf.* Is. 29:13)' (France 1985:110). So also the fine popular exposition of Jim Forest (1999:96): 'Purification of the heart is the endless struggle of seeking a more God-centred life.'

4. So Luz 1989:239 says without more ado of the words in their gospel context: 'The promise is meant eschatologically, just as in the other beatitudes.' He does, however, recognize that in Christian interpretation: 'the distinction between the present and the eschaton, in which the viewing of God will be granted, often is broken through just a little; the viewing of God is now already realized, in the radiance of the image of God in the perfected Christian [Gregory of Nyssa]'; and he also affirms the openness of the biblical text 'to disclose new dimensions in new people' (1989:240). However, Davies and Allison 1988:457 solely say: 'Mt 5.8 has to do with the eschatological future; the possibility of attaining the beatific vision in the present life – something taken for granted by medieval theologians – is not implied'; while Eugene Boring 1995:180 similarly says: '"Seeing God" refers not to mystical vision in this world, but to the eschatological hope (1 Cor 13:12; Rev 22:4)'; curiously, at this point these scholars seem still to be unduly locked into the mode of biblical scholarship where the important thing is to show that the biblical text, understood in its original context, may/does not mean what Christian tradition came to take it to mean, without feeling obliged freshly to engage with the meaning of the text and to ask whether something within this present life other than the beatific vision might yet come within the scope of the words.

5. The succession from Moses to Joshua is the only comparable 'prophetic succession narrative' in the OT.

into account. For the present, the focus will be solely upon what enables Elisha to succeed Elijah.

> 1 Now when the LORD was about to take Elijah up to heaven by a
> whirlwind, Elijah and Elisha were on their way from Gilgal. 2 Elijah
> said to Elisha, 'Stay here; for the LORD has sent me as far as Bethel.' But
> Elisha said, 'As the LORD lives, and as you yourself live, I will not leave
> you.' So they went down to Bethel. 3 The company of prophets who
> were in Bethel came out to Elisha, and said to him, 'Do you know that
> today the LORD will take your master away from you?' And he said,
> 'Yes, I know; keep silent.'
>
> 4 Elijah said to him, 'Elisha, stay here; for the LORD has sent me
> to Jericho.' But he said, 'As the LORD lives, and as you yourself live,
> I will not leave you.' So they came to Jericho. 5 The company of
> prophets who were at Jericho drew near to Elisha, and said to him, 'Do
> you know that today the LORD will take your master away from you?'
> And he answered, 'Yes, I know; be silent.'
>
> 6 Then Elijah said to him, 'Stay here; for the LORD has sent me to
> the Jordan.' But he said, 'As the LORD lives, and as you yourself live,
> I will not leave you.' So the two of them went on.

It is a strange and mysterious sequence. For some unspecified reason Elijah three times tells Elisha to do something which he emphatically refuses to do; yet Elijah in no way demurs. The two companies of prophets speak only to Elisha and not to Elijah, even though one might perhaps imagine that their knowledge that YHWH will 'take' Elijah would make them want to speak some final words to, or seek some final blessing from, Elijah. This strangeness is only intensified, not dispelled, as the story proceeds.

The sole insight the reader is given is the introductory narratory comment, which reveals in advance the main thing that is to happen within the story. Then the perspective instantly shifts to the characters within the story, whose knowledge of what is to happen is less clearcut. Each participant – Elijah, Elisha, the respective companies of prophets – knows something about what YHWH purposes for Elijah, and their knowledge appears more definite than a foreboding (there is some kind of analogy with Jeremiah's and Micaiah's knowledge of YHWH's future purposes). But precisely what they know, how they know it, and why they find it difficult to speak of what they know is left entirely to our imagination.

Elisha appears to be the key figure in the sequence. He is the one addressed by both Elijah and the companies of prophets, and so is the only person who is party to all the dialogues. It seems, moreover, that in some way Elisha is being tested.[6] He is implicitly right to resist Elijah's bidding to stay in Gilgal, Bethel, or Jericho, just as he is apparently right to know what YHWH is going to do and yet not to speak of it either to Elijah or to the companies of prophets. Unquestioning persistence in accompanying his master seems to be the correct mode of conduct.

> 7 Fifty men of the company of prophets also went, and stood at some distance from them, as they both were standing by the Jordan. 8 Then Elijah took his mantle and rolled it up, and struck the water; the water was parted to the one side and to the other, until the two of them crossed on dry ground. 9 When they had crossed, Elijah said to Elisha, 'Tell me what I may do for you, before I am taken from you.' Elisha said, 'Please let me inherit a double share of your spirit.' 10 He responded, 'You have asked a hard thing; yet, if you see me as I am being taken from you, it will be granted you;[7] if not, it will not.'

The fifty prophets, who are indeed prophets but of a lesser stature than Elijah or Elisha, keep their distance. Like a Moses or Joshua, Elijah parts the waters so that he and Elisha may cross. Why they need to cross is not specified. Two possible factors are that Elijah is now east of the Jordan, as was Moses when he died, and that the parting of the waters is an act that displays the power of the Mosaic prophet. In any case, the key moment comes when Elisha's persistence in staying with Elijah is vindicated. Elijah's initial offer to Elisha could be read simply as an offer of a final blessing, but may better be taken as a further testing question, which seeks to draw out Elisha: will he ask for the right thing? Elisha's response is almost always, and surely rightly, understood by reference to Deut. 21:17,[8] which indicates that the request for a 'double portion' is not

6. That Elisha is being tested is regularly (e.g. Nelson 1987:159) but not always (e.g. Fretheim 1999:137) recognized.

7. The verb is a jussive, *yehi* ('let it be'), as in Gen. 1:3, not an indicative, *yihyeh* ('it will be'). So a better rendering is 'let it be granted you'. It is odd that most modern translations opt for an indicative here (AV, RV, RSV, JB, NIV, REB, ESV). The only translation on my shelf that gets it right is NEB; why REB should have backtracked at this point is a puzzle. Gray 1977:473 translates 'then may it be so', but offers no commentary on its possible significance. However, the difficulty appears to be ancient, since LXX has *estai* (future indicative) rather than *estō* (third-person imperative), and Vg similarly has *erit* rather than *fiat*; although Targum follows MT.

8. A law in Deut. 21:15–17 discusses the problem of inheritance in a situation, resonant of Jacob with Leah and Rachel, when a man has two wives, of whom one is favoured over the other, and the firstborn son is the son of the unfavoured wife. When it comes to inheritance, 'He [the man with two wives] must acknowledge as firstborn the son of the one who is disliked, giving him a double portion of all that he has.' The same idiom for 'double portion' (*pi shenayim*) is used in both 2 Kgs. 2:9 and Deut. 21:17.

greedy but rather the mark of the firstborn son and thus legitimate heir. Thus Elisha rises to the challenge and requests the highest privilege and most demanding responsibility – to continue the prophetic ministry of Elijah as '*the* successor, not *a* successor' (Brichto 1992:162).

Elijah replies by noting that this is a 'hard' request,[9] and sets a further, now explicit, test in terms of whether or not Elisha sees his departure. Three things are significant here. First is the logic of the test. Why specify that Elisha must see Elijah being taken if he is to become Elijah's heir? Because it is the responsibility of the prophet to be able to see God, and if Elisha cannot see God in this critical instance, then he is not able to take on the role of one who sees God in other instances;[10] Elisha cannot be a prophet like Elijah unless he has the requisite spiritual capacity.[11] Secondly, the nature of the test clarifies the 'hardness' of the request (if that is the right construal of the Hebrew). Elijah's point would be not just that Elisha's request is (appropriately but demandingly) ambitious, but that the issue at stake, prophetic vocation which implies the ability to discern God in the world, is intrinsically demanding; it is an area where nothing can be taken for granted and where failure is common. Thirdly, although Elijah can definitively pronounce that if Elisha does not see what he needs to see then he will not be his successor, the converse does not hold. If Elisha does see, then this of itself does not guarantee the succession, for such succession remains a gift from God. That is why Elijah uses the jussive, 'let it be granted you', and not the indicative, 'it will be granted to you' (even though, as noted, many translations, both ancient and modern, render the Hebrew as though it were an indicative). Elisha's succession, if he displays appropriate capacity by passing the test of seeing, is indeed Elijah's desire, but prophetic succession is only God's, not Elijah's, to bestow.[12]

9. There is no close parallel for this idiomatic use of *qāshāh*. In Exod. 13:15 *hiqshāh* qualifies Pharaoh's act of sending (i.e. releasing) Israel so as to mean that he was reluctant to send and put obstacles in the way of sending; in Gen. 35:17 *hiqshāh* qualifies Rachel's giving birth to Benjamin, a birth so difficult that it killed her. These parallels would suggest a sense of 'You have found it difficult to ask this question.' Although a meaning that Elisha struggled to formulate or put the question seems prima facie less likely than the conventional interpretation (as in NRSV), it would not be impossible if it meant something like: 'Your perseverance when being tested until now has enabled you at last to make this request.'

10. The prime term for prophetic seeing is *ḥāzāh*, while this narrative uses the most common word for seeing, *rā'āh* (verses 10b, 12a). Nonetheless, the conceptual point is unaffected.

11. 'What Elijah implies is that Elisha's status as successor depends on his ability to see and comprehend the spiritual world' (Jones 1984:385).

12. Another possible dimension of the 'hardness' of Elisha's request may be that, despite Elijah's offer to do something for Elisha, what is involved takes matters beyond Elijah's say-so; he can set up the appropriate test, but cannot pre-empt God's response even to a successful outcome.

> [11] As they continued walking and talking, a chariot of fire and horses of fire separated the two of them, and Elijah ascended in a whirlwind into heaven. [12] Elisha kept watching and crying out,[13] 'Father, father! The chariots of Israel and its horsemen!' But when he could no longer see him, he grasped his own clothes and tore them in two pieces. [13] He picked up the mantle of Elijah that had fallen from him, and went back and stood on the bank of the Jordan. [14] He took the mantle of Elijah that had fallen from him, and struck the water, saying, 'Where is the LORD, the God of Elijah?' When he had struck the water, the water was parted to the one side and to the other, and Elisha went over.

Fire is the prime symbol of the presence of YHWH, both when YHWH appears to Moses in the burning bush and when YHWH appears to all Israel at Sinai (Exod. 19:18, Deut. 4:12, etc.). So the chariots and horses of fire in some way represent YHWH's presence and action. This, presumably, is the main thing that Elisha must see, and does see.

The closeness of the connection between verse 11 and verse 12, which in the Hebrew are one continuing sentence, is often missed.[14] The phrase which mentions Elisha's seeing is a circumstantial clause, which in this form (where the verb is participial) is used in Hebrew to depict concomitant rather than sequential action (as in verse 18a);[15] hence my preferred rendering 'while Elisha saw …'.[16] The point is that all the while the symbols of YHWH were present as Elijah was taken up to heaven, Elisha was able to see what was there.[17] Thus he shows that he has the capacity to be the true successor to Elijah, for he can discern God.

The wider symbolic significance of verses 11, 12 can be construed in many ways. I would suggest that the chariots and horses of fire – which appear not to be needed to transport Elijah to heaven, which is what the

13. This captures the idiomatic sense in relation to Elisha's test. But I would prefer: 'while Elisha saw and cried out'. See below.

14. For example, the *BHS* editor (A. Jepsen) inserts a space, indicating a paragraph marker, between verse 11 and verse 12.

15. See GKC #141e, JM #159d, Gibson 1994:#137b. Unfortunately 2 Kgs. 2:12 has not been included in the grammarian's list of standard examples of this idiom.

16. Some translations miss the point by rendering '(And/when) Elisha saw it' (RSV, JB, NEB, NIV, ESV, Hobbs 1985:17), as though the Hebrew were the sequential *wayyar' 'elishā'* instead of the text's circumstantial clause.

17. It is, I think, a mistake, or at least potentially misleading, to pose the issue in terms of worth rather than capacity, as do, e.g., Montgomery and Gehman 1951:354, '[Elisha] must be found worthy of the sight of the *mysterium*.'

whirlwind does[18] – are a divine honour for Elijah. They are symbols of divine power expressed in military images, which reveal something of Elijah's significance.[19] Elisha's cry at the critical moment can be read as his seeing the meaning of these symbols for Elijah; so he predicates the symbols of Israel's military strength of Elijah,[20] in a reconstrual of the nature of power that is characteristic of the prophetic literature and of the faiths rooted in the Bible – we have already noted something similar in the context of Jeremiah's authority over nations and kingdoms (Jer. 1:10). Here, in the person who speaks and acts for God in such a way as to mediate the divine will and power, is Israel's true strength to be found.

Elisha then acts as the true successor of Elijah, able to do what Elijah could do, with the mantle acting as a symbol of continuity.

> 15 When the company of prophets who were at Jericho saw him at a distance, they declared, 'The spirit of Elijah rests on Elisha.' They came to meet him and bowed to the ground before him. 16 They said to him, 'See now, we have fifty strong men among your servants; please let them go and seek your master; it may be that the spirit of the LORD has caught him up and thrown him down on some mountain or into some valley.' He responded, 'No, do not send them.' 17 But when they urged him until he was ashamed, he said, 'Send them.' So they sent fifty men who searched for three days but did not find him. 18 When they came back to him (he had remained at Jericho), he said to them, 'Did I not say to you, Do not go?'

The company of prophets has in some way seen Elijah's departure, though precisely what they have seen is unclear. Maybe they thought of Elijah coming and going by the spirit of YHWH (as Obadiah thought, 1 Kgs. 18:12), or perhaps one might infer that they saw the whirlwind, though not the chariots and horses of fire. Either way, they have clearly not understood the significance of what has happened to Elijah in the way Elisha understands it; hence their insistence upon a futile search (perhaps simply for a corpse to bury? (Provan 1995:174)). The point, for

18. Some interpreters unsurprisingly assume otherwise, e.g. Montgomery and Gehman 1951:353, 'his ascent in a fiery chariot with fiery steeds'. This construal is at least as ancient as Sirach 48:9, 'You [Elijah] who were taken up by a whirlwind of fire, in a chariot with horses of fire.'

19. 'The images of fire and wind are emblematic for the presence of God and the chariot and horses for the character of the prophetic task' (Fretheim 1999:138).

20. Comparable is Joash's subsequent ascription of these predicates to Elisha (2 Kgs. 13:14). I see no reason to restrict the primary significance of the phrase to Elijah's being Israel's 'defense' against aggression (e.g. Nelson 1987:160, 162).

our purposes, is the implicit gradation of capacity to see. They are prophets, and they have seen something of YHWH's action, just as they knew something about it in advance; yet they have seen less than Elisha, who is shown by the story to stand above them as did Elijah. Seeing God is not only a capacity to be tested, but something that exists unequally among those called to serve God.

2 Balaam: the loss and regaining of ability to see God, Num. 22:1–35

My second story is the first part of the 'Book of Balaam',[21] an extended narrative sequence – chapters 22–4 – within the book of Numbers which has always been somewhat puzzling on account of its apparent lack of links with the concerns that otherwise characterize Numbers, apart from its situating Israel in that same context of place and time where Numbers situates them. The overall concern of this 'Book of Balaam' is to display YHWH's irrevocable commitment to Israel as His people, which stands in sharp counterpoint to the depiction of a murmuring and rebellious Israel, with whom YHWH is frequently displeased, elsewhere within the narratives of Numbers. For the present I will focus on the opening section of this material, which famously explores the issue of discerning God.[22]

> [1] The Israelites set out, and camped in the plains of Moab across the Jordan from Jericho. [2] Now Balak son of Zippor saw all that Israel had done to the Amorites. [3] Moab was in great dread of the people, because they were so numerous; Moab was overcome with fear of the people of Israel. [4] And Moab said to the elders of Midian, 'This horde will now lick up all that is around us, as an ox licks up the grass of the field.' Now Balak son of Zippor was king of Moab at that time. [5] He sent messengers to Balaam son of Beor at Pethor, which is on the Euphrates, in the land of Amaw, to summon him, saying, 'A people has come out of Egypt; they have spread over the face of the earth, and they have settled next to me. [6] Come now, curse this people for me, since they are stronger than I; perhaps I shall be able to drive them from the land; for I know that whomsoever you bless is blessed, and whomsoever you curse is cursed.'

The Israelites are encamped east of the Jordan in the general region of Moab. Balak, king of Moab, knows of other peoples east of the Jordan

21. This is a traditional rabbinic name for the material.
22. I have written a more extended exposition of this text in Moberly 1999a.

whom Israel has already dispossessed, and is fearful lest a similar fate befall himself and his people. He therefore summons assistance in the form of Balaam, the power of whose curse may enable Balak to overcome the otherwise superior numbers and strength of Israel; for blessings and curses pronounced by Balaam are, in Balak's view, definitive and determinative.

> [7] So the elders of Moab and the elders of Midian departed with the fees for divination[23] in their hand; and they came to Balaam, and gave him Balak's message. [8] He said to them, 'Stay here tonight, and I will bring back word to you, just as the LORD speaks to me'; so the officials of Moab stayed with Balaam. [9] God came to Balaam and said, 'Who are these men with you?' [10] Balaam said to God, 'King Balak son of Zippor of Moab has sent me this message: [11] "A people has come out of Egypt and has spread over the face of the earth; now come, curse them for me; perhaps I shall be able to fight against them and drive them out."'
> [12] God said to Balaam, 'You shall not go with them; you shall not curse the people, for they are blessed.' [13] So Balaam rose in the morning, and said to the officials of Balak, 'Go to your own land, for the LORD has refused to let me go with you.' [14] So the officials of Moab rose and went to Balak, and said, 'Balaam refuses to come with us.'

Officials travel on Balak's behalf, to carry out the necessary negotiations to secure Balaam's assistance. Balaam responds as one who speaks for God should respond.[24] He says that he must respond as directed by God (rather than, implicitly, in terms of his own preferences). He also speaks of God with the proper name revealed to Israel, YHWH (verses 8, 13, cf. verse 18, 'YHWH my God'; although the narrator uses the generic term

23. The meaning of the Hebrew *qsmym* ('divinations') is unclear, though I think that it probably means 'tools of divination' rather than 'fees for divination' (Moberly 1999a:3–4).

24. It is difficult to know which term/category is most appropriate to depict Balaam in this narrative. Although the implication of *qsmym* (verse 7, whatever exactly it means) is that Balak regards Balaam as a 'diviner' (*qōsēm*), the narrator does not depict him thus; nor, despite the later (isolated) reference to his use of 'omens' (*nehāshim*, 24:1), is Balaam depicted as practising divination, for he converses with YHWH as does many a psalmist or prophet. The depiction of Balaam elsewhere as a *qōsēm* (Josh. 13:22) must not be taken in isolation from the larger problem posed by the consistently negative depiction of Balaam everywhere else in the Old Testament, even though the overall depiction in Numbers 22–4 is positive. Within Numbers the narrator's implicit category might be 'seer' (*rō'eh*), given the centrality of 'seeing' in 22:22–35, the emphasis on Balaam's ability to 'see' (*hāzāh*) at the outset of his third and fourth oracles (24:3–4, 15–16), and his climactic 'seeing' (*rā'āh*) of Israel's future conqueror of Moab (24:17). However, the interesting terminological note in 1 Sam. 9:9b indicates that within standard Hebrew parlance the term 'prophet' (*nāvi'*) has displaced the previously popular term 'seer' (*rō'eh*). Thus it may be appropriate to call Balaam a 'prophet', as long as the complexities of such a generic category in this context are recognized.

'God', verses 9, 10, 12).[25] That night God speaks to Balaam. When Balaam explains the situation, God's directive is crisp and clear. In an emphatic negative (*lōʼ* rather than *ʼal*), Balaam is not to accompany Balak's officials. He is not to curse the people for a basic, indeed axiomatic, reason: 'for they are blessed'. So next day, Balaam dismisses Balak's officials, on the grounds that he has been refused permission to go with them,[26] and they return to their master to report their failure.

> 15 Once again Balak sent officials, more numerous and more
> distinguished than these. 16 They came to Balaam and said to him,
> 'Thus says Balak son of Zippor: "Do not let anything hinder you from
> coming to me; 17 for I will surely do you great honour, and whatever
> you say to me I will do; come, curse this people for me." '

When does 'no' really mean 'no'? Often in life it is difficult to tell. Balak, for his part, is sure that Balaam's 'no' is not really meant; rather, it is a negotiating stance, and what Balaam's refusal really means is 'I'm playing hard to get' and 'You must offer me more.' So Balak acts accordingly with a more prestigious, honorific embassy, whose message is so mouthwatering that Balaam will surely accede. For the offer this time is 'Name your price, and I will meet it.'

> 18 But Balaam replied to the servants of Balak, 'Although Balak were to
> give me his house full of silver and gold, I could not go beyond the
> command of the LORD my God, to do less or more. 19 You remain here,
> as the others did, so that I may learn what more the LORD may say to
> me.' 20 That night God came to Balaam and said to him, 'If the men
> have come to summon you, get up and go with them; but do only what
> I tell you to do.' 21 So Balaam got up in the morning, saddled his
> donkey, and went with the officials of Moab. 22 God's anger was
> kindled[27] because he was going . . .

25. The narrator's assumption is that, since Balaam is ultimately to pronounce YHWH's blessing upon Israel, it is YHWH whom Balaam knows and on whose behalf he speaks, even though Balaam is not an Israelite. This may be related to another characteristic assumption of OT writers – whatever reality is allowed to gods other than YHWH, the possibility that any deity other than YHWH should be operative in a prophet is never entertained.

26. 'The Hebrew verb *mēʼēn* "to refuse" implies, although this is never stated explicitly, that a request had been made by Balaam of the God of Israel to allow him to accept Balak's offer' (Levine 2000:152).

27. Preferable is 'but God was angry'. The Hebrew connective *waw* is omitted by NRSV on the assumption that verse 22 begins a new paragraph (underlying which is most likely the common assumption that verses 22–35 is an originally independent story only poorly integrated into its present context). The exposition will seek to demonstrate the interconnections within the narrative.

At first sight, Balaam's response is the impeccable response of a true prophet: obedience to God in terms of what he says for God is non-negotiable, no matter what the inducement to personal gain (verse 18). So his proposal to repeat his nocturnal encounter with God (verse 19) would also appear to be a repetition of the proper practice of seeking God's will displayed earlier.

Yet all may not be what it appears, and there are reasons for the reader to be wary of Balaam's words. First, if Balaam means to stand by his earlier 'no' as a genuine 'no', why does he not simply dismiss the men? Balaam already knows YHWH's mind with regard to Balak's request (verse 12); what YHWH said was not a contingent matter dependent on time or circumstance but a theological principle – 'they are blessed'. If that was the case previously, Balak's renewed offer of honour and unlimited riches should make no difference whatever – what YHWH said then still stands.

An alert reading would then see the right-sounding words of verse 18 as a pious smokescreen.[28] Comparably, within Jeremiah we saw that there may be a gap between right-sounding language and the realities of the human will; one only knows that the language is genuine when it is accompanied by appropriate action (as in countless situations in life generally). If Balaam is in fact acceding to Balak's construal of his earlier refusal as a negotiating ploy (whether or not it was initially meant that way), then he is hardly going to announce that he wants to compromise his faithfulness to his God for the sake of an offer of fame and profit; rather, he will quite naturally protest his integrity and hope that people will not see through him but take him at his word.[29]

Secondly, Balaam's going to learn 'what more' YHWH may say has dubious resonances within a wider OT context. The Hebrew idiom signifies not simply that God will speak again but that He will say

28. There is also the question of why the narrator should give such space to the summoning of Balaam, if there is not within it some subtlety of development crucial to the story overall (cf. Noth 1968:175 for a recognition of the problem, though Noth can only resolve it via the conceptuality of sources and apologetic redaction).

29. Some interpreters are happy to oblige: 'Nothing suffices to seduce him from carrying out the will of Yahweh' (Gray 1903:318); 'No amount of money could make him act contrary to the command of Yahweh, his God' (Dozeman 1998:183); 'Balaam's resistance to these blandishments remains firm' (Budd 2003:148). Knierim and Coats explicitly reject the interpretation I propose: 'It should be clear that this renewal of the enquiry is not a violation of faith, an effort to find a way to accept a big honorarium despite the previous assertion of God that Israel was blessed' (2005:254); yet the basis for this supposed clarity is simply taking Balaam's words in verse 18 at face value, on the (hardly argued) assumption that the story is about a prophet only saying what YHWH tells him to say (and that the ass episode, which indicates otherwise, is poorly integrated).

something additional to what was said previously.[30] There are strong resonances with the Mosaic prohibition on 'adding to [*yāsaph*] the word which I am commanding you' (Deut. 4:2). In the context of Deuteronomy, this is hardly a quantitative concern – that all possibly desirable laws are already promulgated and contained within Deuteronomy – for that would have little point within the rhetoric and logic of Moses' admonitions in 4:1–40;[31] an appropriate contextual sense would be that of moral challenge, of not seeking expedients which in some way qualify or diminish a whole-hearted response of obedience. Balaam's desire that God should 'say more' can be read as a prime example of a desire to find some way of evading the cost of obedience to God's previous words that Israel 'is blessed' and so not to be cursed – since now obedience would mean turning down the offer of a lifetime.

Thirdly, God's response gives the reader pause. If God's initial words (verse 20) are taken on their own, they can of course be read as straightforward permission (with a renewed reminder of obedience). Yet God's anger at Balaam's going (verse 22a) suggests otherwise,[32] and indicates a more complex and ironic tone to God's words of permission. God tells Balaam the very thing he wants to hear, but it is not going to mean for Balaam what he may want and expect it to mean (i.e. that he will be able to curse Israel and so gain what he has been offered), for God intends something quite different, even though at this stage He gives nothing away ('do only what I tell you to do').[33]

We can see, then, that in the crucial development of the story in verses 18–20 neither the words of Balaam nor the corresponding response of God should be taken superficially, at face value – just as, of course, Balak did not take Balaam's refusal at face value. On the one hand, Balaam preserves the language of divine vocation and obedience as used in his

30. The idiom is *yāsaph* ('add') with *dibbēr* ('speak'). For the general idiomatic use of *yāsaph* (and also *shūv*) to express the adverbial sense 'do X again', see JM #177 b, c. They observe that '*ysph* expresses continuation . . . or augmentation'. In the context of Num. 22:19 for God to continue is for God to augment what has already been said.

31. Compare the discussion in Tigay 1996:43–4. One presumes also that the wording was not understood in a quantitative sense by the compilers of the Pentateuch with its multiplicity of laws in Exodus, Leviticus, and Numbers in addition to those in Deuteronomy.

32. On the place of the she-ass episode within the story, see Excursus 1.

33. An obvious scriptural analogue would be Ps. 106:15, 'He gave them what they asked, but sent a wasting disease among them.' Milgrom (1990:189) conveniently summarizes rabbinic construal of the tension within the received form of the text thus: 'The rabbis . . . see in this tale the source of the doctrine of human responsibility and free will: "From this you learn that a man is led in the way he desires to go" [Mak. 10b, Num. R. 20:18]; "If one comes to defile himself, he is given an opening", that is, he is given the opportunity [Shab. 104a, Yoma 38b].'

initial response to Balak, where it is possible that what was said was meant; only now the language is becoming a tool of self-interested financial negotiation. In the terminology of Jeremiah for prophets whose message is false (6:13, 8:10), Balaam is now *bōtsēa‘ betsa‘* ('greedy for gain').[34] Similarly, in the terminology of ancient Jewish and Christian interpretation of the story, Balaam is succumbing to greed.[35] On the other hand, YHWH's permission to accept a commission to curse Israel could in no way be expected to lead to the commission's fulfilment in such a way that Balaam could be able to receive what Balak is offering. The point is that if Balaam wants, for reasons of self-interest, to evade YHWH's affirmation that Israel is blessed, then he must learn the hard way that this is not possible. In short, God wishes to teach Balaam a lesson:

> 22 . . . and the angel of the LORD took his stand in the road as his adversary
> (*sātān*).[36] Now he was riding on his donkey, and his two servants were
> with him. 23 The donkey saw the angel of the LORD standing in the
> road, with a drawn sword in his hand; so the donkey turned off the
> road, and went into the field; and Balaam struck the donkey, to turn
> it back into the road. 24 Then the angel of the LORD stood in a narrow
> path between the vineyards, with a wall on either side. 25 When the
> donkey saw the angel of the LORD, it scraped against the wall, and
> scraped Balaam's foot against the wall; so he struck it again. 26 Then the
> angel of the LORD went ahead, and stood in a narrow place, where there
> was no way to turn either to the right or to the left. 27 When the donkey
> saw the angel of the LORD, it lay down under Balaam; and Balaam's anger
> was kindled, and he struck the donkey with his staff.

34. Compare Mic. 3:11 for the way in which venality can turn religious language into falsehood.

35. In the interpretation incorporated in the New Testament, the Greek keyword for Balaam's failing is *misthos*, 'profit' (Jude 11; 2 Pet. 2:15 is fuller: *misthon adikias ēgapēsen*, which I would render 'he set his heart on profit gained wrongly'). In St Augustine's interpretation (*Quaest. in Hept: Num.* XLVIII) the Latin keyword is *cupiditas*, 'greed/desire' (*se victum cupiditate monstravit*). One important difference, however, between my interpretation and that common among pre-moderns is that pre-moderns tended to see Balaam as a negative character throughout, largely because of their reading the story in the light of negative references to Balaam elsewhere (Num. 31:8, 16, Josh. 13:22, etc.). When Numbers 22–4 is read on its own terms, Balaam is a positive figure, who only temporarily succumbs to greed and who, after rebuke and repentance, speaks powerfully for YHWH.

36. The most illuminating parallel usage of *sātān* is the story of Solomon in 1 Kings 11. Because of Solomon's unfaithfulness (verse 9), God raises up Hadad and Rezon, each to be an adversary (*sātān*) to Solomon (verses 14, 23), and so remove the previously given divine rest which was marked by the lack of an adversary (*sātān*, 5:18 (ET 5:4)). They are figures who oppose and cause trouble, whose opposition symbolizes divine disfavour with the failure in faithfulness of someone who should know better.

The form that the divine anger takes is unexpected and surprising, though appropriate to the situation. One might naturally expect it to take the form of direct action against the offender (just as Balaam's anger leads directly to violent action against his beast, verse 27), perhaps through affliction with disease, blinding the eyes, or attack by a lion (all actions of divine judgment attested elsewhere in the Old Testament); and in whatever form it came, the action would be immediate and inescapable. Yet the angel with the sword, although clearly deadly if encountered directly, is not like this, for the angel can, initially at least, be avoided. Instead of the angel coming at Balaam, the angel is a stationary object able to be circumvented – except that each time the angel appears the circumvention becomes more difficult, until finally the ass can circumvent no longer and so adopts the sensible alternative expedient of lying down and so making herself incapable of going a step further. The point is that something deadly does not assault Balaam. Rather it awaits him if he continues to take the path that he has embarked on, and it becomes more inescapable the further he proceeds. That is, a journey motivated by corrupt self-seeking is not immediately disastrous, yet its end is not gain but destruction, and the destruction looms larger and closer the further one goes.

The obvious, and humorous, concern of the story at this stage, however, is to do with ability to see God and the things of God, here in the form of the angel of YHWH. On the one hand, Balaam is a prophet of renown, known for his potency in the divine realm. He is, as it were, the Top Man from North-East Aram, the best religious hit-man that money can buy. On the other hand, the ass on which he rides is proverbially the dullest of animals.[37] Yet the ass can see clearly what Balaam cannot see. In the light of the drawn sword that the angel holds, the importance of being able to see in this instance is no less than a matter of life and death; yet Balaam is entirely unaware that the ass's action is saving his life and responds solely with uncomprehending violence and anger. Indeed, his total incomprehension is what his faithful beast is enabled to point out to him.

> [28] Then the LORD opened the mouth of the donkey, and it said to
> Balaam, 'What have I done to you, that you have struck me these three
> times?' [29] Balaam said to the donkey, 'Because you have made a fool

37. Admittedly, it is difficult to find evidence elsewhere within the Old Testament for the dullness of the ass as a commonplace; nonetheless, this narrative at least suggests its heuristic usefulness in terms of sharpening the contrast with Balaam.

> of me! I wish I had a sword in my hand! I would kill you right now!'
> 30 But the donkey said to Balaam, 'Am I not your donkey, which you
> have ridden all your life to this day? Have I been in the habit of treating
> you in this way?' And he said, 'No'.

The ass's first question simply elicits from Balaam a self-interested and ridiculous concern about looking stupid,[38] and a threat to inflict on the ass the very fate from which she had just saved him – although, as the angel will point out, the ass herself was not at risk (verse 33). So her second question is more focussed. The ass points to the wholly unprecedented nature of her behaviour. Balaam has had the ass and ridden on her for as long as he can remember, so his familiarity with her patterns of behaviour is as thorough as it could possibly be. So when she asks whether there is any precedent for her present behaviour, the ass knows that he knows that the answer is negative – which he duly acknowledges. The point is that unusual behaviour should have caught his attention and signified to him that all was not well, particularly when repeated twice more even in the face of his immediate and painful displeasure. Such unusual behaviour was obvious both to see and interpret in terms of its general tenor: *something must be wrong*. And underlying the ass's question appears to be the implicit logic which the rabbis called *qal wāḥōmer*, which is that what applies in a less important case applies also in a more important case: how can the man who cannot interpret the obvious actions of his ass interpret the more difficult actions of God? Balaam's failure to carry out even the simplest exercise of discernment, an exercise accessible to any ordinary person, serves to underline his total failure in that very area where he should excel other people. If he gets the point of his ass's prompting, Balaam can now indeed see something – that his humiliation is complete.

> 31 Then the LORD opened the eyes of Balaam, and he saw the angel of
> the LORD standing in the road, with his drawn sword in his hand;
> and he bowed down, falling on his face. 32 The angel of the LORD said to
> him, 'Why have you struck your donkey these three times? I have come
> out as an adversary, because your way is perverse before me. 33 The

38. 'The wonderful absurdity of this response is that Balaam doesn't miss a beat. Confronted with the articulated speech of his ass's eminently justified complaint, he answers irascibly as though he were thoroughly accustomed to conducting debates with his beast' (Alter 2004:800). Compare 'Nothing here indeed appears more wondrous (*mirabilius*) than that when the ass speaks he is not terrified but rather, as though accustomed to such portents [*monstris*], he continues to reply angrily to it' (Augustine, *Quaest. in Hept: Num.* XLVIII). I doubt that Alter has read St Augustine on this passage, but there is a remarkable similarity between them, only in interestingly different registers.

> donkey saw me, and turned away from me these three times. If it had not turned away from me, surely I would by now have killed you and let it live.' [34] Then Balaam said to the angel of the LORD, 'I have sinned, for I did not know that you were standing in the road to oppose me. Now therefore, if it is displeasing to you, I will return home.' [35] The angel of the LORD said to Balaam, 'Go with the men; but speak only what I tell you to speak.' So Balaam went on with the officials of Balak.

If the ass highlighted Balaam's failure, the angel of YHWH now makes it possible to do something about it. When YHWH opens Balaam's eyes, and so enables him to see that danger to which he had been blind, Balaam responds by prostrating himself; whether this represents cowed evasiveness or genuine responsiveness will only become apparent by what further he says and does. The angel does not specify why Balaam's course is unacceptable, for Balaam knows the reason all too well, and the angel's words achieve what true prophetic speech seeks to achieve – Balaam repents/turns to God (i.e. *shūv*, though the term is not used). First, he unconditionally acknowledges his wrongdoing: 'I have sinned.' Secondly, he acknowledges his uncomprehending inability to see what he should have seen. Thirdly, he expresses willingness to abandon the enterprise that is causing offence – he will relinquish all hopes of honour and wealth from Balak and go home; he will change his course of action appropriately.

Now, however, that Balaam has turned from that which was corrupting his vocation, the angel says that he should indeed continue to go with Balak's envoys. What was a deadly error when undertaken in self-seeking greed becomes a fruitful course to pursue if done in obedience to God. The reason for God's direction to Balaam to go on becomes abundantly clear as the story continues to unfold, and has already been hinted at in Balak's initial summons to Balaam (verse 6): Balaam's ability to pronounce blessings as well as curses. Thus YHWH directs Balaam to speak on his behalf, i.e. as a prophet – now with the prospect that Balaam will genuinely fulfil his mandate, even though the emphatic blessing of Israel that ensues will not be what Balak wants or will pay for.[39]

39. How is one to explain the divergence between the positive portrayal of Balaam in Numbers 22–4, where his fall is followed by repentance, restoration, and exemplary fulfilment of YHWH's will, and the consistently (even if varying in details) negative portrayal of Balaam elsewhere in the Old Testament? There is no easy or satisfying answer. Perhaps what we really need is another story about Balaam, in which he sought to curse or seduce Israel, a story whose imaginative location might be between the end of Numbers 24 and the beginning of Numbers 25. But there is no such story.

In conclusion, there remains one question to put to the text. Why should Balaam be so blind? If Balaam conversed so readily with YHWH, how could he fail to see the angel of YHWH? The answer should, by now, be clear – though this clarity has generally been more apparent to pre-modern than modern interpreters.[40] Balaam is allowing his vocation to be corrupted by greed, and this greed has made him blind to the presence of the God with whom, and for whom, he speaks. As Calvin (1882:272–3, my translation) put it:

> Whence came such blindness, but from the greed [*avaritia*] by which he had been rendered so senseless, that he preferred filthy lucre [*turpe lucrum*] to the holy calling of God? Finally there was fulfilled in him that which Scripture often declares to the reprobate, that struck by a spirit of giddy madness he should see nothing.[41]

Moral failure induces spiritual blindness. Avaricious self-seeking obscures the reality of the Other. The impure in heart fail to see God. The reason for Balaam's failure to see the angel of YHWH is fully comparable to the reasons for Ahab's and Zedekiah's failure to see that Micaiah was speaking YHWH's truth. No understanding of the dynamics of discernment can afford to neglect the fact that seeing what is before one's eyes can depend as much upon the condition of the person seeing as upon the nature of that which is seen.

Excursus 1: the place of the she-ass episode (Num. 22:22–35) within the Balaam narrative

My concern in this book is consistently to try to make sense of the biblical text in its received form, without as such engaging with the debates of

40. The reluctance of many modern interpreters to see Balaam as succumbing to greed is to some extent a consequence of treating verses 22–35 as not being integral to the narrative, but this is not a sufficient explanation. An early-twentieth-century commentator such as Gray (1903:318–19, 330–1) is still clearly to a degree reacting against the common pre-modern approach which could see no good in Balaam at all, though Gray is inclined simply to see the writer as indifferent to the question of Balaam's character. More recently, there has been a tendency to view the text as a cipher for ideological party politics within ancient Israel, in the kind of way that would not encourage one to say much about its moral implications; so, fairly conventionally, John Van Seters (1997:132): 'the talking ass story is the final degradation of the faithful prophet into a buffoon who must be instructed by his own humble donkey', or, more ingeniously, Mary Douglas (2001:233): 'Balaam works well as a skit on Nehemiah, stupidly berating and beating the ass on which he rides . . . [which] stands for Israel.' Amidst these diverse readings, and difficult accompanying questions of appropriate method in interpretation, my construal stands or falls by its ability to do justice at every point to the specifics of the Hebrew text.

41. Compare Matthew Henry (1662–1714) as representative of a pre-modern consensus: 'the ass he rode on saw more than he did, his eyes being blinded with covetousness and ambition' (1960:166).

historical-critical analysis (while still accepting their validity). Nonetheless, it may be important on occasion to address a particular issue. Although, to be sure, reading the text in its received form is a different kind of exercise from analysing it for its possible antecedents, there can be times when a renewed appreciation of the text's logic can call in question at least some of the traditio-historical and redactional analyses insofar as these are based upon supposed lacunae and relative incoherence in the text's received form. So I offer some brief and heuristic comments upon the scholarly consensus that the ass episode sits loosely and not very coherently within its present narrative setting.

There is an obvious prima facie puzzle in the narrative, when God says 'go' to Balaam and then gets angry with him for going (22:20, 22). Although I have argued that there are sufficient internal indicators within the story for the reader to suspect that there is some lack of fit between what is said and what is meant both by Balaam and by God (although of course the dynamics are different for each speaker), the common modern approach has been to redescribe the tension between verse 20 and verse 22 in terms of sources, tradition-history and redaction. Although at one time the tension was understood in terms of the editorial conflation of J and E narratives, the story of Balaam and his she-ass tends now to be seen as an independent unit of tradition (i.e. neither J nor E), probably a tale in mockery of diviners, which has been rather loosely appended to its present context.[42] On its own terms, however, this hypothesis faces at least three difficulties.

First, if one distinguishes on the basis of differing divine attitude between the main narrative, in which God is happy for Balaam to go with Balak's envoys (verse 20), and the story of the ass, in which God is angry with Balaam for going (verse 22), then what is one to make of the conclusion of the ass episode (verse 35)? If Balaam's journey is displeasing to God, he ought to be told to return home, in the expectation that, now his eyes have been opened and he has confessed his sin, he would do so. Yet the conclusion of the ass episode (verse 35) renews, in similar wording, the permission of God in the main narrative (verse 20). To be sure, one can argue that the wording in verse 35 is redactional; but the argument is then circular (and also fails to explain why the editor should have felt it important to smooth the narrative sequence at the end of the

42. Levine 2000:138–9, 154 seems to me representative of the consensus.

episode without feeling any comparable need to do the same at its beginning).

Secondly, the view that the episode serves to mock diviners usually only attends to the humorous and ironic dimension of Balaam's failure to see, and tends to leave other features of the storyline unexplained (sometimes even, apparently, unnoticed). Neither the unusual form of divine anger together with its intrinsic symbolism nor its appropriateness to a situation in which Balaam is being blinded by greed receives convincing explanation in standard arguments for the independence of the episode (at least, those that I have read).

Thirdly, the episode of Balaam with his ass serves with witty irony to introduce and interpret the encounter between Balak and Balaam.[43] Just as an unseeing Balaam three times urges on his seeing and uncompliant ass, so an unseeing Balak three times urges on a now-seeing and uncompliant Balaam; and as the angel's opposition to Balaam becomes harder to circumvent each time, so Balaam's oracles become more expansive and emphatic about God's blessing each time. The fact that Balaam pronounces four oracles in all has sometimes obscured this three:three pattern. But the logic is that Balaam gives three solicited oracles in response to Balak's threefold urging, for which he is then dismissed without remuneration, 24:10–11. He then gives a fourth, unsolicited oracle, a parting shot, which contains the final sting of Moab's subjugation to a coming Israelite ruler (24:17).

43. See Daube 1973:14–16, Alter 1981:104–7.

5

John: God's incarnate love as the key to discernment

> The soul of a saint receives light from the Sun of Righteousness, in such a manner, that its nature is changed, and it becomes properly a luminous thing: not only does the sun shine in the saints, but they also become little suns, partaking of the nature of the fountain of their light . . . Christians are Christlike: none deserve the name of Christians that are not so, in their prevailing character.
>
> – JONATHAN EDWARDS (1959 [1746]:343, 346–7)

Introduction

Although thus far I have sought to outline an understanding of critical discernment of prophecy within an Old Testament context, no Christian reflection upon the understanding and possible appropriation of this material would be complete without some account of how this issue is handled within the New Testament.

Broadly speaking, what one would expect to find in the New Testament is what one does find. That is, there are two main strands to the New Testament's engagement with critical discernment. On the one hand, the account within the Old Testament is presupposed, taken as read, and used accordingly. Indeed, so thoroughly is it presupposed within the bloodstream of faith that none of the New Testament writers, when engaging with this issue, ever cite any of the Old Testament material we have considered; yet, as will be seen, their pattern of understanding replicates the basic contours of the Old Testament understanding. Thus the New Testament writers *continue* the Old Testament tradition.

On the other hand, the New Testament writers consistently address the question of what kind of difference the life, death, and resurrection of

Jesus makes to their inherited understanding of God, Israel, and life in the world. Unsurprisingly, their general answer is that the difference is not optional or marginal but rather integral and central. Critical discernment of speech on God's behalf is no exception to this general rule, and so the New Testament writers characteristically *transform* the Old Testament criteria into a pattern that is both Christ-centred and cruciform. Some prime examples of the ways in which these two strands are present in the New Testament will be the focus of this and the next chapter.

Continuing Israel's tradition: Jesus in the Synoptic Gospels

One famous passage in which Jesus[1] addresses the issue of critical discernment, and indeed uses the specific term 'false prophet' (*pseudoprophētēs*), whose first biblical appearance is in the Septuagint rendering of the Old Testament, comes towards the end of the Sermon on the Mount (Matt. 7:15–23):[2]

> 15 'Beware of false prophets, who come to you in sheep's clothing but
> inwardly are ravenous wolves. 16 You will know them by their fruits.
> Are grapes gathered from thorns, or figs from thistles? 17 In the same
> way, every good tree bears good fruit, but the bad tree bears bad fruit.
> 18 A good tree cannot bear bad fruit, nor can a bad tree bear good fruit.
> 19 Every tree that does not bear good fruit is cut down and thrown into
> the fire. 20 Thus you will know them by their fruits.
>
> 21 'Not everyone who says to me, "Lord, Lord", will enter the
> kingdom of heaven, but only one who does the will of my Father in
> heaven. 22 On that day many will say to me, "Lord, Lord, did we not
> prophesy in your name, and cast out demons in your name, and do
> many deeds of power in your name?" 23 Then I will declare to them,
> "I never knew you; go away from me, you evildoers." '

The mention of false prophets seems abrupt, so the context is important. The positive teaching of the Sermon concludes with the Golden Rule in 7:12. Thereafter the Sermon is a series of warnings and challenges about

1. By 'Jesus' I mean Jesus as interpreted and portrayed by the evangelist and received by the Church, without prejudice to questions about the origins, tradition-history, and composition of the Gospel text.

2. Although the primary literary unit is 7:15–20, it seems clear that 7:21–3 is to be read as its continuation, since the issue of spurious prophesying is explicit in 7:22 (for fuller arguments, see Davies and Allison 1988:693–4, Luz 1989:439–40).

the need to embrace the way of life/the kingdom (i.e. the way of Jesus) and avoid the way of death.[3] The first such challenge is to 'enter through the narrow gate; for the gate is wide and the road is easy that leads to destruction, and there are many who take it. For the gate is narrow and the road is hard that leads to life, and there are few who find it' (7:13–14). Since reference to false prophets follows this directly, it suggests that what is envisaged is people who offer an easier, less demanding version of the way to life; their message is designed to be more readily appealing to those they address. This, of course, resonates strongly with the opposition faced by Jeremiah and Micaiah, those whose message (peace/good, *shālōm*/*tōv*) is false (*sheqer*) because ultimately it is insufficiently demanding and too readily pleasing, telling people what they want to believe to be the case.

The difficulty posed by false prophets, however, is that they may have the perfect disguise. The polarity of wolf and sheep is traditional (though there are, of course, added resonances in a biblical context where the image of sheep/flock is commonly used to depict God's people). The one is rapacious and deadly, the other peaceful and defenceless. Yet if those who come to ravage are seen for what they are, then at least some of their prospective victims may run away and escape. So the most deadly approach is the most insidious one – to be in appearance indistinguishable from those who are to be ravaged, so that the prospective ravager can be welcomed by the innocent prospective victims as 'one of us'. In contextual terms, this would seem to indicate a prophet whose message sounds entirely plausible, even if with diminished moral challenge (and, in some contexts, the perfect disguise could presumably include the formulating of undiminished moral challenge). In fact a contextual portrayal of plausibility is offered in verse 22, where the plausibility includes both words ('prophesy in your name') and actions ('do many deeds of power in your name').

So how is such plausibility to be penetrated, if the inward reality is at odds with the outwardly accessible appearance? Jesus offers a simple-sounding axiom (verse 16a), whose importance is further indicated by its repetition (verse 20) so that it frames the elaboration of its meaning: 'You will know them by their fruits.' The logic of the image appears to be that although many trees[4] have much in common – roots, trunk, bark,

3. There is a strong resonance with Moses' summative challenge in Deut. 30:15–20, 'See I have set before you today life and prosperity, death and adversity . . . Choose life . . .'
4. *Dendron* appears to be used broadly here to include also shrubs and bushes.

branches, leaves – so that the untrained eye might not know how to distinguish between them, there is nonetheless a clear means of distinguishing, in terms of that which grows on the tree and is the thing most readily available to people to take from the tree: its fruit.[5] The kind of fruit indicates the specific nature of the tree (verse 16b), in a way that enables a generalizing point that fruit which nourishes comes only from nourishing trees (verses 17–18). There is then a warning about the fate of unnourishing trees (verse 19), analogous to other warnings about final judgment (Matt. 13:30, 41–2, 49–50), before a reiteration of the basic principle (verse 20).[6]

The imagery of tree and fruit is intrinsically suggestive and resonant. For example, one further possible generalizing implication could be that although the life of a tree, if thought of in terms of its sap that makes it moist and alive rather than dry and dead, is invisible to one who looks at the outward bark of a tree, it becomes visible in terms of the fruit that grows; the inward and invisible becomes discernible through that which is outward and visible. Whether or not that is envisaged in this Matthean context, some such understanding of the imagery seems presupposed by Paul's famous account of the 'fruit of the Spirit' (Gal. 5:22–3). Paul's language applies to every Christian the principle articulated elsewhere specifically with reference to prophets, that it is the visible ('moral') conduct of a person that gives access to that person's invisible ('spiritual') state.

Given that the test of a prophet is that what comes from them should be nourishing for others (and so analogous to Paul's critical principle of 'building up', 1 Cor. 12–14), the question of what constitutes nourishing fruit now receives further specification. First, verse 21 spells out a basic principle, which is not so much 'deeds, not words' but rather that what one does gives content to what one says (or reveals its absence).[7] Words,

5. Compare Matt. 12:33–7. Here the explicit principle that 'the tree is known by its fruit' is directly applied to an appraisal of human speech in relation to the human heart.
6. The repetition of the principle after the reference to final judgment could perhaps imply that even if the false prophets are not discerned in this life, their final fate will nonetheless be evident and they will be known then for what they were; but the prime thrust of the text seems to be discernment in the present.
7. The distinction may sound nitpicking, but I do not think it is. This is not just for the exegetical reason that the text itself focusses on the validity or otherwise of an invocation of 'Lord', for Matthew's Gospel can certainly envisage the importance of actions performed in ignorance of their true significance (Matt. 25:31–46). It is rather that 'deeds, not words' can all too easily become a kind of slogan that leads to an ethicizing of faith which diminishes its fullness, by potentially making engaged recognition of the nature of God's reality, with corresponding prayer and worship, less than central. For example, Luz 1989:446, n. 48 cites

not least right-sounding religious words ('Lord, Lord'), can be cheap and easy; only when there is obedience to God's will that is commensurate with invoking Him can the words be considered genuine. Again, this has already been seen to be a recurrent issue within Jeremiah, most famously in the appeal to 'This is the temple of YHWH ...' (Jer. 7:4). Although the principle of Matt. 7:21 is formulated in a generalizing way, the context suggests that its primary application here is to the false prophets against whom Jesus is giving warning;[8] those whose prophetic words are not matched by appropriate obedience to God's will are not prospective members of God's kingdom, and so should not be heeded.

However, the question of what counts as obedience to God's will is itself not straightforward. The plausibility of pseudo-prophets is envisaged in terms of their being able to appeal on the day of judgment not only to performing exorcisms in Jesus' name but also, more generally, to 'doing many deeds of power in your name' (verse 22). This indeed sounds like the mark of authenticity; yet it is not.[9] The reason such pseudo-prophets will be dismissed is curt: they are 'evildoers' (which is the NRSV's idiomatic rendering of 'those who practise lawlessness', *hoi ergazomenoi tēn anomian*).

The keyword here is clearly 'lawlessness' (*anomia*), whose precise scope is open to debate. Probably the best commentary is a related passage within the same Gospel (Matt. 24:11–12):

> [11] And many false prophets will arise and lead many astray. [12] And because of the increase of lawlessness (*anomia*), the love (*agapē*) of many will grow cold.

Jesus apparently presumes that likely plausibility of appearance and acceptability of message on the part of 'prophets' will ensure widespread reception (verse 11) and that this will result in an increase of lawlessness (verse 12a). Thus the linkage between 'false prophet' and 'lawlessness' is clear and

as 'impressive' the comment on prophetic authenticity of Marguerat 1981:192, ' "La vérité chrétienne est éthique" ' (Christian truth is ethics).' Although one can appreciate the evident force and truth within such an affirmation, it seems to me an affirmation that can readily become problematic, for it can sever the nerve of Christian (or, relatedly, Jewish or Muslim) resistance to the idolatries of the age which depends upon the vision of the one God.

8. The unavailing appeal of the foolish bridesmaids (Matt. 25:11–12) is also a strong intertextual linkage, which shows that what is at stake is applicable to all.

9. An important comparable passage in the Old Testament is Deut. 13:2–6 (ET 1–5). This denies any kind of probative value to the prediction and realization of 'omens or portents' if they are in any way used by prophets to undermine Israel's exclusive allegiance and obedience to YHWH; such phenomena should not be marvelled at but rather construed as tests of Israel's commitment as daily recited in the Shema (13:4 (ET 3), cf. 6:4–5). This passage is drawn on in the warning about false prophets in Matt. 24:24, and its principle has played an important role in the history of Christian discernment.

emphatic. Illuminating, however, is the gloss on the increase of lawlessness, that is the decrease of 'love'. Within the context of Matthew's Gospel, the primary resonance is with 22:34–40, the hermeneutical key to the law and the prophets in terms of the commandments to love God (i.e. the Shema) and love neighbour. The purpose of the law is not mere adherence for its own sake, but rather the transformation of life into what it should be through deeper, self-giving engagement with God and other people of a kind regularly spelled out elsewhere in the Gospel (perhaps most famously in the scenario of the sheep and goats, where the reality of the service of Jesus is construed in terms of the service of the needy, Matt. 25:31–46). Thus the meaning of the 'lawlessness' which false prophets promote is not primarily the non-observance of this or that commandment; rather it depicts a failure to embrace a way of life which would seek to penetrate, and so live out, the true meaning and purpose of the law – with the kind of self-giving love that Jesus himself demonstrates in his ministry and passion.

In all this, and notwithstanding characteristic Matthean emphases, Jesus speaks in the mode of a Jeremiah. The conceptuality here for dealing with spurious prophets is none other than that articulated in the Old Testament, and it does not move beyond it – except in the sense that it is now the teaching of Jesus that determines the meaning of the law and so faithfulness to God's revealed will. The reality of purported prophets can be discerned through the consistency of what they say and what they do in relation to God's searching will for integrity and faithfulness on the part of His people. On its own terms this is clearly itself a demanding criterion of discernment, and its usability will be discussed more fully in the final chapter. For the present, it illustrates well how the New Testament continues the understanding of discernment articulated in the Old Testament.

Critical discernment in 1 John

Introduction to 1 John

We come now to the central discussion of this chapter, an analysis of how an apostolic letter tackles the issue of discernment in the light of a post-Easter understanding of the overall significance of Jesus. Before I look in detail at the key passage, it is appropriate briefly to set out my overall understanding of the nature and purpose of John's letter.[10]

10. Here as elsewhere I use a conventional designation without prejudice to discussions of historical authorship.

First, although John's purpose in writing has been much debated and characterized in many ways, I suggest that it may best be characterized as *articulating a critical theological epistemology* – or, in John's own, more straightforward, terminology, the key issue is: how can we know that we know God?[11] As John puts it at an early stage (2:3), 'By this we know that we know him . . .', and his criterion is a demanding one, 'by keeping his commandments'. The criteria for knowledge of God are, however, easily misrepresented ('I write this to you about those who would lead you astray', 2:26), and so towards the end John states his positive overall purpose, 'I write these things to you who believe in the name of the Son of God, so that you may know that you have eternal life' (5:13).[12] John's concern is intrinsic to any form of Christian faith. For where notions of divine self-revelation and corresponding human knowledge of God play a crucial role, possibilities of error and the deception of either self or others abound. If faith in God in and through Jesus is in some way the key to human existence – as the prologue to John's Gospel puts it – then there is a need for criteria not only to specify the content of this faith but also for determining when it is, and is not, truly present. This critical concern is not primarily focussed upon claims to speak for God as such; but, as we will see, this is one of the issues which is addressed in the course of the exposition.

Secondly, the need to articulate such an epistemology is urgent since clearly some kind of schism had recently taken place within the community John addresses (2:18–19).[13] Yet although we would like to know more about the stance of John's 'opponents', and although interpreters would be unwise to turn their backs on any source of illumination, in the case of 1 John we simply do not have any knowledge of context other than what may be gleaned from the letter itself – which is minimal. Whatever may

11. The overall structure of the document clearly indicates this concern: 'the structure of the letter itself reproduces the process of self-analysis and testing' (Lieu 1991:50). After the introduction (1:1–4), an affirmation about God (1:5) leads instantly into a series of denials and affirmations as to what human engagement with God entails (1:6–2:2), which then leads into the explicit statement of 'knowing that we know him' (2:3–6). The letter concludes with a series of 'we know' affirmations (5:18, 19, 20), which culminate in 'We know that the Son of God has come and has given us understanding so that we may know him who is true; and we are in him who is true, in his Son Jesus Christ. He is the true God and eternal life' and a corresponding warning to shun what is counterfeit and deceptive with regard to God, 'Little children, keep yourselves from idols' (5:21).

12. The verbs *ginōskō* (2:3) and *oida* (5:13) are used interchangeably in the Gospel of John and 1 John. Likewise, 'having eternal life' is not different from 'knowing God' (cf. John 17:3).

13. Standard contextual proposals are conveniently set out with some preliminary evaluation in Edwards 1996:ch. 5.

have been affirmed or denied by others in John's context of writing, an understanding of the letter requires above all else a grasp of the intrinsic logic of John's thought.[14]

Thirdly, John's pattern of thinking does not involve sequential logic in the manner of a conventional argument so much as the literary equivalent of musical variations on a theme – a constant circling round the basic issue, coming at it from a variety of angles, developing now this aspect and now that aspect, balancing one statement with another to clarify what is and is not entailed, returning to a point already made so that it may be seen afresh in the light of what has been said subsequently, and generally amplifying a basic conceptuality until he considers his exposition to be sufficient for conclusion to be appropriate.[15] Thus the parts and the whole need to be read in constant conjunction with each other. It also means that any proposed interpretation of John is likely to be persuasive to the extent that it operates in a way not dissimilar to John – enabling the reader to 'see it like this', with a heuristic ability to make better sense than alternatives of both parts and whole.

'Test the spirits': 1 John 4

Our detailed study begins with the text that we noted in Chapter 1, possibly the best-known biblical injunction to critical discernment.[16] I will seek to understand it first in its own context, so that there will be appropriate critical discipline when it is utilized in more wide-ranging synthetic thinking about the task of discernment.

> [1] Beloved, do not believe every spirit, but test the spirits to see whether they are from God; for many false prophets have gone out into the world. [2] By this you know the Spirit[17] of God: every spirit that confesses that Jesus Christ has come in the flesh is from God, [3] and every spirit that does not confess Jesus is not from God. And this is the spirit of the antichrist, of which you have heard that it is coming; and now it

14. Schmid 2002 relativizes the significance of John's 'opponents' rather differently, for theoretical reasons to do with the nature of reading and intertextuality.

15. Thus seeming repetitiveness and lacunae need not give rise to the complex theories of composition that are sometimes proposed, even though compositional complexity cannot be ruled out.

16. This exposition draws on Moberly 2004a.

17. Perhaps better is lower case, 'spirit'. The question as to when a Christian interpreter might appropriately capitalize 'Spirit' in 1 John is difficult. My preference would be for lower case as much as possible, for John is not speaking of the Holy Spirit in the mode of Luke or Paul – [*to*] *hagion pneuma* does not appear in 1 John – but rather of that realm which is both life-giving and destructive, whose accurate discernment is crucial.

> is already in the world. 4 Little children, you are from God, and you have conquered[18] them; for the one who is in you is greater than the one who is in the world. 5 They are from the world; therefore what they say is from the world, and the world listens to them. 6 We are from God. Whoever knows God listens to us, and whoever is not from God does not listen to us. From this we know the spirit of truth and the spirit of error.

John's concern is with the discernment of that which purports to belong to the realm of God, i.e. 'spirit(s)'. So his basic injunction is clear: 'Do not believe every spirit', i.e. do not be gullible, credulous, or unthinking in the spiritual realm, but rather 'test the spirits', to see whether claims to be 'from God' are indeed justified; they may well not be, for those who proclaim messages that purport to be from God but are not in fact from God are not isolated or occasional but rather numerous ('many false prophets').

The language of being 'from God' (4:1, 2, 3, 4, 6) is contrasted with being 'from the world' (4:5), and expresses a fundamental Johannine polarity between life responsive to and expressive of, and life estranged from and antipathetic towards, its Creator.[19] As in the Gospel,[20] this polarity can be expressed in a number of ways,[21] and its significance is best articulated in the Gospel prologue. John's premise is not only that humanity is created by God and for God, so that the true nature of being human is realized when people are rightly responsive to God, but that this creation has been enacted through the Logos/Word: 'all things came into being through him, and without him not one thing came into being' (John 1:3). This means that in appropriate responsiveness to Jesus, the Logos/Word made flesh, people discover that for which they are made. The problem, however, is the darkness of the world, which means that people are not responsive as they should be and struggle to know what constitutes true response to the Creator; so John offers criteria.

18. Perhaps a rendering such as 'you have enduring victory over them' might bring out more clearly the likely significance of the perfect tense in *nenikēkate*.
19. This polarity has a heuristic value analogous to that of sociological ideal types.
20. The Gospel contrasts that which is 'from God', 'from above', 'from heaven', 'from the Spirit', 'not from this world' with that which is 'from the world/earth', 'from the flesh', 'from oneself' (see, e.g., John 1:12–13, 3:1–8, 31–2, 8:23, 28, 18:36–7).
21. In 1 John, for example, those who are 'in the light', 'in/have life', 'in Him', 'of God', 'of the truth', 'have overcome the evil one/the world', 'do the will of God', are contrasted with those who are 'in darkness', 'in death', 'love the world', 'are of the world', 'of/in the devil/evil one' (1:5–7, 2:5, 9–11, 14, 15–17, 3:8, 12, 19, 5:4–5, 12–13, 19).

In our passage the parallelisms in 4:6a are illuminating:

> We are from God;
> Whoever knows God listens to us,
> Whoever is not from God does not listen to us.

The second clause could presumably be equally well expressed as 'Whoever is from God listens to us.' Being 'from God' is inseparable from, or another facet of, 'knowing God', though context and nuance may make difference of formulation appropriate. Thus the original injunction to 'test the spirits to see whether they are from God' could be re-expressed as 'test those who speak as prophets to see whether they know God'.

The logic of 4:6, that it is those who know God who heed those who are from (who know) God, makes knowing God a condition for knowing whether others know God – it takes one to know one. Such a circularity, which is characteristic of John, could appear to be vicious. Yet John regards the context within which the knowing person is located not only as open (people may leave or enter, 2:19, 3:14), but also as involving qualities capable of growth and diminution (love must grow to fullness, 4:12, 17–18). So the circle is not something fixed but involves the dynamics of responsiveness and growth, and is more akin to a spiral.

Since John has made clear that claims to know God are testable, he specifies the communicable content of the knowledge of God and so enables testing to be carried out: every spirit which confesses that Jesus Christ has come in the flesh (*en sarki elēluthota*) is from God. This poses three related interpretative problems (apart from that of the best textual reading).[22] First, what is the precise meaning of this confession? Secondly, how does this confession relate to other confessions and statements of belief in the Johannine letters? Thirdly, how does this confession relate to John's wider argument?

In terms of meaning, the perfect tense of 'come' (*elēluthota*) suggests 'the enduring result of a past coming' (Brown 1982:493). How far this should be pressed is open to dispute.[23] If it is given full weight (as I am inclined to think it should), it suggests the continuing presence of Jesus

22. Textually (see, e.g., Metzger 1971), the variants mainly affect verse 3a, and seem to be expansions of its summary restatement of verse 2. The variant *luei* in place of *mē homologei* makes no real difference to the overall sense. Likewise, the Codex Vaticanus variant in verse 2, the perfect infinitive *elēluthenai* in place of the perfect participle *elēluthota*, makes no difference in sense.

23. For example, Raymond Brown (1982:493) regards this as a temptation to be resisted, on the basis of 2 John 7, where a similar formula is used without the perfect, while Georg

in the (Johannine) community of believers, along the lines expressed elsewhere the letter,[24] i.e. the presence of God spiritually mediated – the very issue whose critical testing John is expounding.

The most controverted phrase, however, is 'in the flesh' (*en sarki*). It is usually supposed that the precise force of *en sarki* is best illuminated by positing a supposed alternative which is being denied. The most common form of this thesis is that John is opposing some docetic idea of the (mere) 'appearance' of Jesus which envisages less than his full humanity; as Dunn (1980:31) puts it, 'I John contests a docetic-like christology whose closest parallels are the earliest forms of Gnosticism proper which probably emerged round about the turn of the first century AD.' But although this is plausible and, given the lack of evidence, impossible to disprove (or prove), it is also possible that 'anti-docetism' may well be a distraction, which imposes a seemingly appropriate religio-historical category upon what could be, in essence, a convenient Johannine shorthand for the coming of Jesus on earth. That is, John may be succinctly articulating his understanding of the importance of the foundational figure towards whom he looks and directs his fellow believers, with no implicit polemical alternative other than what he mentions. In short, John's concern, I suggest, is not that Jesus' mission on earth is *real* as opposed to *apparent*, but rather that it is, quite simply, *definitive* for knowledge of God; the crucial distinction among people is between those who recognize and affirm the definitive significance of Jesus and those who deny it.

Comparable confessions and affirmations of belief abound in the Johannine letters (1 John 2:22–3, 3:23, 4:14–16, 5:1, 5, 13, 2 John 7). All the formulations look to be variations on one theme – that in Jesus, God's salvation/gift of life has come to the world, and this life is appropriated through responding to Jesus as the Son in whom God's nature and action are known.[25] The precise wording of 1 John 4:2 is not making a different affirmation, but expressing a particular variation of the one core belief.

The fuller significance of this confession of 4:2 is not immediately spelled out, because John's initial move is to stress the definitive nature of the confession as that which embodies the power of God to overcome the

Strecker (1996:134, 133, n. 12) considers the choice of tense meaningful on the basis of comparable variations elsewhere. I incline towards Strecker, for one can regard 2 John 7 simply as a less precise formulation than 1 John 4:2.

24. For example, 3:24: 'All who obey his commandments abide in him, and he abides in them. And by this we know that he abides in us, by the Spirit/spirit that he has given us'; or 4:13: 'By this we know that we abide in him and he in us, because he has given us of his Spirit/spirit.'

25. A passage such as John 5:19–24 spells out the underlying thought in a characteristic way.

world and divides between the true spirit and the spirit which leads astray (4:4–6). But John has not finished with it yet.

> 7 Beloved, let us love one another, because love is from God; everyone who loves is born of God and knows God. 8 Whoever does not love does not know God, for God is love.

Crucial to the understanding of what John is saying is the recognition that in 4:7 John is (a) still addressing the issue of discernment posed in 4:1, and (b) resuming and continuing his treatment of the significance of the confession in 4:2. To be sure, this goes against the consensus of recent commentators, who consistently, in one way or another, see 4:1–6 as a discrete section and 4:7 as the beginning of a new topic.[26] However, it is to further his treatment of critical discernment that John now reintroduces the topic of love (*agapē*), which has already been a concern earlier in the letter. John has not long since spoken of believing and loving together – 'and this is his commandment, that we should believe in the name of his Son Jesus Christ and love one another' (3:23) – and both there and here these are not two different matters which happen to be juxtaposed ('doctrine and ethics'), but interrelated facets of the one reality of knowing God through Jesus.

John's procedure is to reintroduce a key term in the context of reiterating terms and concerns just used. We have just seen that 'being from God' and 'knowing God' mutually express different angles on one and the same reality (verse 6). Now John specifies that love is also 'from God', in such a way that the person who embodies love can be said to be 'born from God' (a fuller formulation, applicable to persons, of the more common 'from God'). At the end of verse 7 love is also linked to the existing motifs: 'loving God' is thus added to 'being from God' and 'knowing God' as another variant facet of the same core reality.

26. For example, Brown (1982:542–3) lists numerous scholars who see no real link between 4:1–6 and 4:7ff., dissents from them, but himself sees the linkage in terms of 4:1–6 as an exposition of 3:23a while 4:7–5:4a expounds 3:23b and 'praises' those who love. Strecker (1996:xliv) classifies 4:1–6 as 'dogmatic exposition' and 4:7–5:4a as 'paraenesis'. Marshall (1978:210) comments: 'Somewhat abruptly John turns from his discussion of true and false spirits to present his readers with a further appeal to love one another.' Smalley (1984:232, 235) sees 4:1–6 as about doctrine and 4:7–5:4 as about ethics, and although these are 'closely related', the transition is still 'somewhat abrupt'. Dodd (1946:107) sees 4:1–6 as 'in the nature of a parenthesis'. Schmid (2002:183–5) sees 4:1–6 as an excursus in John's argument. Thomas (2004) sees 4:1–6 as about discernment (pp. 197–214) while 4:7–5:5 is about love, which he discusses at some length with not one reference to discernment (pp. 214–49).

The relationship of this to the task of critical discernment is instantly spelled out (4:8): 'Whoever does not love does not know God, for God is love.' This is the negative aspect of discernment, the importance of being able to know how to disqualify, and so not heed, those who might unjustifiably claim to know God (be from God, speak for God as prophets), since to credit unjustified claims could entail being led astray from what is true. The criterion is the absence of love. For just as the Father is seen and known in the Son, who displays the qualities of the Father, so too believers, who become children of God (3:1–2), display the qualities of God their Father – supremely love (cf. 3:14, 'We know that we have passed from death to life because we love one another. Whoever does not love abides in death'). From this one may infer that the absence of love shows the absence of knowing God (being a child of God, being from God). The principle of 4:8 thus restates the negative aspect of discernment spelled out in confessional terms in 4:3. This suggests that the meaning of 4:8 is an 'applied' way of looking at the confession of 4:2–3; John's concern with displaying love is not a different matter from confessing Jesus 'come in the flesh', but a related facet of one and the same reality – i.e. the difference that Jesus makes – which enables one to discern those who are 'from God'/'speak for God' and those who are/do not.

> [9] God's love was revealed among us in this way: God sent his only Son into the world so that we might live through him. [10] In this is love, not that we loved God but that he loved us and sent his Son to be the atoning sacrifice for our sins. [11] Beloved, since God loved us so much, we also ought to love one another.

That 4:8 should be seen as a practical re-expression of 4:2–3 is indicated also by the specific form of the developing exposition. For John gives content to that love which God is (verse 8b) by spelling out its revelation in Jesus, and the form this takes is the recitation of a summary account of the meaning of the life of Jesus (4:9–10). This quasi-credal recitation is an amplification of the earlier, summary formulation 'Jesus Christ has come in the flesh', spelling out in slightly more extended (though still summary) form what is the significance of Jesus (and not requiring a denial of, e.g., gnosticism to be fully meaningful). The fact that John is not thinking of his immediately preceding affirmation, 'God is love', in generalizing or definitional terms is evident not least in the use of the aorist 'God loved' (verse 10b) as distinct from a present-tense 'God loves'; God's love is spoken of in specific terms, in relation to the particular person and mission of Jesus.[27] The consequence is that followers of Jesus, to be true to their calling, must reciprocate and replicate in their lives and their dealings with each other that same mode of being that characterizes God in the sending of Jesus, i.e. love (4:11).

> [12] No one has ever seen God; if we love one another, God lives in us, and his love is perfected in us.

This love enables critical discernment to take place. This is the logic of 4:12a, which easily seems puzzling: why specify that 'No one has ever seen God'? The point may be that God is not a person or object within the world, of the kind where questions to do with verification of claims to knowledge could in principle be resolved by conventional criteria.[28] God is intrinsically Other (which John would most likely express in terms of *pneuma*, 'spirit', as in John 4:24), in that God entirely eludes that sense of sight by which people generally establish their understanding of the reality of what there is in the world. Hence the problem of verification and validity with reference to claims about (or on behalf of) God. Yet for John this Otherness of God in no way leads to undecidability (and ultimate meaninglessness) with reference to claims to know God as a reality.[29] Rather, John reworks (in a brief way, to be expanded later in 4:20–1) his principle that the presence of God's qualities in those who would know God/be of God demonstrates the validity of their claim (4:12b).

> [13] By this we know that we abide in him and he in us, because he has given us of his Spirit.[30] [14] And we have seen and do testify that the Father has sent his Son as the Saviour of the world. [15] God abides in those who confess that Jesus is the Son of God, and they abide in God. [16] So we have known and believe the love that God has for us. God is love, and those who abide in love abide in God, and God abides in them.

The concern for critical discernment is directly restated. Mutual abiding (another mode of knowing God) can be known through God's gift of His

27. Compare the famous John 3:16.
28. It may be, however, as Marianne Meye Thompson has suggested to me in correspondence, that John's point is that God is not *presently* seen, though seeing God remains a future hope for the children of God (1 John 3:2). Either way, human knowledge of God under the conditions of normal life poses particular problems of validation.
29. Compare John 1:18 for the centrality of Jesus' role in making known the unseeable God.
30. Or 'spirit', as in the comment on verse 2.

own spirit. This reiterates the earlier affirmation about God's gift of spirit (3:24: 'And by this we know that he abides in us, by the Spirit that he has given us'). Just as that earlier affirmation led directly into the question of critical discernment (4:1 is the verse following 3:24) and a christological specification, so here too (4:14–15) John complements the affirmation about the spirit with an affirmation about Jesus, comparable to 4:2. Knowing that one abides in God has as its corollary the presence of the spirit given by God. It equally has as its corollary that one affirms God's action in making Jesus the saviour of the world and that one confesses Jesus to be Son of God. Then in 4:16a the language of knowing and believing would most naturally be followed by some propositional content about Jesus in summary form. Instead the expressed object of knowledge and belief is love – the nature and meaning of which is to be found in the mission of Jesus to the world, as spelled out in 4:9–10. This love which is encountered in the mission of Jesus is constitutive of God in a way that enables critical discernment to take place (here expressed in a positive formulation that balances the negative formulation of verse 8): 'God is love, and those who abide in love abide in God, and God abides in them.' One can know that one abides in God because of the spirit; one can know that one abides in God because of one's confession of Jesus; one can know that one abides in God because one shows that quality of love that is constitutive of God (and continues the presence of Jesus in the world). John rings the changes on his one theme: that one can only know that one knows God if the loving reality of God in Jesus is appropriated and demonstrated. The presence of God's spirit, confession of Jesus, and the enacting of love are different facets, or modes of expressing, the one rich reality of the knowledge of God.

> [17] Love has been perfected among us in this: that we may have boldness on the day of judgment, because as he is, so are we in this world.
> [18] There is no fear in love, but perfect love[31] casts out fear; for fear has to do with punishment, and whoever fears has not reached perfection in[32] love. [19] We love,[33] because he first loved us.

31. Perhaps more idiomatic in terms of contemporary English would be 'love in its fullness', because for many people 'perfect' (*teleios*) in a moral and spiritual context can have a somewhat unreal and even undesirable (static, rigid, fragile) ring to it.
32. Or 'grown to fullness of love'.
33. Or 'so let us love'. The text reads naturally as an exhortation based on what has just been said. The presence of 'so'/'therefore' (*oun*) in some manuscripts may be a way of making more explicit such a construal of the text.

One consequence of the mutual indwelling of believer and God is that love can reach its full fruition, with the further consequence that the future and God's final reckoning can be faced with confidence – because believers replicate the qualities of Christ (i.e. supremely love) within the world. A further mark of love reaching its full fruition is that it removes inappropriate fear, fear focussed on punishment (4:17–18). These marks of mature love enable further critical discernment, though in this case less between true and false than between differing levels of growth and maturity within the true. A further incentive to grow in love is the reminder that it is a response in kind to the initiative which God has taken in the mission of Jesus (4:19); that is, 'his commandments are not burdensome' (to use the language of 5:3), for living and growing in love is the continuing and growing in that reality which has constituted believers as those who are from God in the first place.

> [20] Those who say, 'I love God', and hate their brothers or sisters, are liars; for those who do not love a brother or sister whom they have seen, cannot love God whom they have not seen. [21] The commandment we have from him is this: those who love God must love their brothers and sisters also.

John now amplifies the point expressed briefly in 4:12, the problem of testable knowledge when the reality in question, God, is invisible (and so not amenable to conventional forms of verification via the senses). John is not simply reaffirming the dominical double commandment to love God and neighbour in his own particular form, with 'brother(s and sisters), *adelphos*' instead of 'neighbour', but is rather making a point about the nature of that which is visible and accessible to test claims to the invisible and, in conventional terms, inaccessible. His point is that the visible and accessible practice of love for brother/sister (i.e. moral practice) is what enables one to rebut, or confirm, claims to knowledge and love with regard to the invisible and otherwise inaccessible (spiritual) reality of God. As in 4:3 and 4:8, the primary formulation is pointedly negative – this is how one can know whom to disregard, those false prophets against whom John warns at the outset of the chapter. Lack of love of the visible brother/sister disqualifies claims to love the invisible God. Positively, those who love God must love their brothers/sisters also – where the point is that those who love are those who know God (4:7b).

In sum, the way to know that one knows God is to display that love for one's brothers/sisters which is not only embodied by Jesus in his earthly life ('in the flesh') as the epiphany of God's love, but also mandated by Jesus as the continuing form that the knowledge of God must take; and the way to test those who would speak for God is to look for the signs of the knowledge of God.

Conclusion: patterns of discernment in Jeremiah and John

The way in which the New Testament both continues and transforms the Old Testament criteria for critical discernment of God is well illustrated by John. The continuity is clear when one compares John's mode of thinking with that of Jeremiah. For example, we can set alongside each other Jer. 23:18a, 21–2 and 1 John 4:1, 20 and see, amidst, all their differences, important commonality.

> For who has stood in YHWH's council
> so as to see and to hear his word? . . .
> I did not send the prophets,
> but they for their part went eagerly to the task;
> I did not speak to them,
> but they for their part delivered prophecies.
> But if they had stood in my council,
> then they would have proclaimed my words to my people,
> and they would have sought to turn them from their wicked way,
> and from their evil deeds.[34]

> Beloved, do not believe every spirit, but test the spirits to see whether they are from God; for many false prophets have gone out into the world . . . Those who say, 'I love God', and hate their brothers or sisters, are liars; for those who do not love a brother or sister whom they have seen, cannot love God whom they have not seen.

In each context there is a concern to clarify that the spiritual reality of a prophetic message, i.e. whether or not it is from God, is determined by its moral content and accompaniment. Claims about the invisible and spiritual realm are validated (or not) by the visible and accessible realm of character, conduct, speech, and priorities.

Moreover, there is similarity in terms of what constitutes that moral practice which exemplifies knowledge of God (and it is striking that it is the same idiom 'knowing God' that features as a key category in both

34. Both here and in the subsequent Jeremiah quotation, the translation is NRSV with my suggested emendations incorporated.

Jeremiah and John). This is perhaps clearest if one compares the critique of Jehoiakim, and praise of Josiah, in Jer. 22:16, and the conceptually related 9:5 (ET 6), with John's affirmation in 1 John 4:7–8.

> Did not your father [Josiah] practice justice and righteousness
> as naturally as eating and drinking?
> Then he was a true king.
> He judged the cause of the poor and the needy;
> then kingship was true.
> Is not this to know me? says YHWH.
>
> Oppression upon oppression, deceit upon deceit!
> They refuse to know me, says YHWH.

> Beloved, let us love one another, because love is from God; everyone who loves is born of God and knows God. Whoever does not love does not know God, for God is love.

In each context knowledge of God is given content by human behaviour, which should focus upon promoting the well-being of others. Jeremiah's shorthand summary term is 'justice' and John's is 'love'. Although the meanings of these terms are not identical, they are clearly similar in the mode of living which they envisage. When 1 John 4:8 is read in the context of what John says elsewhere about the demanding nature of love, it is apparent that what John means by 'love' is not different in kind from what Jeremiah means by 'justice and righteousness': so 3:16–18, 'We know love by this, that he laid down his life for us – and we ought to lay down our lives for one another. How does God's love abide in anyone who has the world's goods and sees a brother or sister in need and yet refuses help? Little children, let us love, not in word or speech, but in truth and action.' That particular demonstration of the knowledge of God which is appropriate for a king (or someone in a position of power) would not be available/accessible to all; but John's shorthand summary of God's action in Christ, 'love', makes clear (if understood) that the qualities of integrity and concern for others are demonstrations of God's presence and power without, in principle, restriction of person, or place, or time.

Nowhere in his exposition of critical discernment does John cite, or even allude to, Jeremiah. Yet John's understanding that (a) the moral and visible gives critical purchase on claims to the spiritual and invisible, and (b) that self-giving concern for the well-being of others is that form of moral practice which most displays the character of God is, *mutatis mutandis*, the same understanding that we see in Jeremiah. The continuity between these books of Old and New Testament is clear.

Continuity of understanding is also combined with transformation, most obviously in the strong focus upon the person of Jesus as the one who gives definitive content to the knowledge of God. John also combines the practice of love with credal affirmation in a way that is not characteristic of Jeremiah. To be sure, Jeremiah's vision of appropriate human practice is implicitly premised upon a particular vision of the nature of YHWH, and the linkage between the two becomes explicit in Jer. 9:22–3 (ET 23–4). Nonetheless, John's giving emphasis to explicit recognition of Jesus (4:2–3) as the basis upon which love is to be understood and practised introduces a distinctive note, one that would over time be strongly developed within Christian faith and contribute to its having an overall shape and logic distinct from those of Judaism.[35]

35. I had originally hoped to include a chapter on John's Gospel, where discernment of Jesus and his message is a prominent theme (e.g. 17:8, [Jesus says] 'the words that you gave to me I have given to them, and they have received them and know in truth that I came from you; and they have believed that you sent me'). However, the relationship between prophetic conceptuality and other dimensions of Johannine christology would demand a fuller discussion than was possible in the present context.

6

Paul: cruciformity and the discernment of apostolic authenticity

> The theological reasoning of our time shows very clearly that the particular form of the death of Jesus, the man and the messiah, represents a scandal which people would like to blunt, remove or domesticate in any way possible. We shall have to guarantee the truth of our theological thinking at this point. Reflection on the harsh reality of crucifixion in antiquity may help us to overcome the acute loss of reality which is to be found so often in present theology and preaching.
>
> – MARTIN HENGEL (1977:89–90)

Introduction

After some consideration of the Johannine understanding of criteria for discernment, I propose now to look at Paul's treatment of the issue. Paul, like John, both continues and transforms the characteristic Old Testament criteria, though with distinctive emphases. Paul's most extended engagement with critical discernment of claims to speak for God comes in 2 Corinthians, and so a study of 2 Corinthians will constitute the core of this chapter. Nonetheless, there is much other material in Paul which is pertinent to the issue, and so a brief consideration of three passages, from 1 Thessalonians, 1 Corinthians, and Philippians, will preface the study of 2 Corinthians.

The way in which Paul, like Jesus and John, has absorbed, and takes as established, what one finds in the Old Testament can be seen from a passage such as 1 Thessalonians 5:19–22:

> [19] Do not quench the Spirit. [20] Do not despise the words of prophets [*or* despise prophecies], [21] but test [*dokimazete*] everything; hold fast to what is good [*to kalon*]; [22] abstain from every form of evil.

Within a context of general exhortation with which Paul concludes the letter, we encounter these specific admonitions where the five successive imperatives are revealing for Paul's general pattern of thinking. First, Paul wants his readers to be open to the initiative of God (verse 19), expressed in terms of responsiveness to *pneuma* (Spirit/spirit). The metaphor of 'quench' not only resonates with a characteristic biblical association of God's presence with fire, but also recognizes the role that human responsiveness, or lack of it, plays in relation to the fruition of God's work in human lives. The spiritual gift of prophecy is a particular form of God's work in Christian believers, and its manifestations must not be treated lightly or disparagingly (verse 20). Although 'prophecy' as a spiritual gift within the New Testament is much more narrowly defined than 'prophecy' as a vocation in the Old Testament (though apparently more widely distributed), it still involves speech on God's behalf in some form or other. Why the Thessalonians might have been minded to disdain prophetic utterances[1] is unclear, but does not affect the way in which Paul sees the exercise of the gift of prophecy as a natural corollary of openness to God's initiative; when God leads, and people are responsive, speech on God's behalf is to be expected and encouraged.

This, however, leads directly to the problem of possible misuse of God's gift. Since the obedience of faith does not require the abandonment of critical faculties, and since misuse of God's gifts was clearly a common problem in the churches Paul addresses, Paul does not simply urge submission to prophecies, but rather counsels thorough testing (*dokimazō*),[2] i.e. critical discernment (verse 21a). Two final imperatives with strong moral content then follow (verses 21b, 22), and the strong likelihood is that Paul sees these as the means by which the critical sifting is to be carried out.[3] If prophecies are to be evaluated, it is through the affirmation of what is upright and praiseworthy,[4] and the eschewal of wrong in any and every form.[5]

1. The plural *prophēteias* makes clear that Paul is speaking about specific prophetic utterances, rather than the gift of prophecy as such.

2. 'Thorough testing' is my gloss on the likely sense of 'test everything'.

3. This point is regularly overlooked. Best 1972:240, for example, says of verse 21a, 'Paul lays down no criteria here on how the tests are to be made' and sees the content of verses 21b, 22 as 'the end result of testing' (similarly, to some extent, Malherbe 2000:333). But if the moral concerns of verses 21b, 22 are the means of testing, they will not thereby cease also to constitute its result. Alternatively Aune 1983:220 speaks of the testing as 'a fully rational procedure whereby prophetic utterances (among other things) are judged on the basis of their coherence with accepted customs and norms'. But Paul says nothing about 'accepted customs and norms' (or if that is Aune's gloss on the sense of verses 21b, 22 then it is misleading). It makes best sense if Paul's criteria of testing are of a piece with the outcome of the process.

4. One possible reason for Paul's choice of *to kalon*, rather than some other term of moral uprightness (e.g. *to agathon*), might be that it can combine the sense of being moral with that of being attractive to those who see it (cf. Rom. 12:17, 2 Cor. 8:21, where *kala* is combined with 'in the sight of' [*enōpion*] people and God).

5. I follow the general consensus (e.g. *BAGD*:280) that, despite the venerable precedent of the AV, *eidos* in this context most likely does not mean 'appearance' – i.e. reject everything that

Although Paul is speaking generally, it is revealing that his criterion for the critical evaluation of the 'spiritual' (Spirit, prophecies) is the 'moral' (embracing good, rejecting evil). What Paul assumes is the pattern of thinking which we have found to be characteristic of other biblical writers in both Old and New Testaments.

Spiritual discernment in 1 Corinthians 12–14

Probably the best-known material on spiritual discernment within the Pauline writings is the discussion of spiritual gifts in 1 Corinthians 12–14.[6] Since the two spiritual gifts on which Paul primarily focusses are prophecy and speaking in tongues, some attention to what he says here is clearly germane to my thesis – and, indeed, will assist with the comprehension of 2 Corinthians.[7] Rather than offer a systematic exposition of the whole, I propose to concentrate on Paul's introduction to his discussion (12:1–3); for a right understanding of this, I suggest, unlocks Paul's thesis in the whole.

> [1] Now concerning spiritual gifts,[8] brothers and sisters, I do not want you to be uninformed. [2] You know that when you were pagans,[9] you were enticed and led astray to idols that could not speak. [3] Therefore I want you to understand that no one speaking by the Spirit of God ever says 'Let Jesus be cursed!'[10] and no one can say 'Jesus is Lord' except by the Holy Spirit.

even looks wrong – for that would bespeak a moral timidity that is not Pauline, and is also likely to inhibit moral and spiritual growth; rather it means 'kind' or 'form' – i.e. reject what is wrong in whatever form it takes.

6. Concern with discerning what is genuinely spiritual in a Christian sense characterizes 1 Corinthians as a whole, and receives well-known emphasis in the early chapters, as focussed in, for example, 2:12, 3:1–3.

7. The continuity of concerns between 1 and 2 Corinthians is more or less self-evident. As, for example, Gorman 2001:59 puts it: 'Paul finds it necessary to connect cross and Spirit in his letters to the Corinthians, where he insists that the Spirit's power is bankrupt without the Spirit's cruciformity. In both 1 and 2 Corinthians, this symbiosis of power and cruciformity becomes the criterion for judging all supposed experiences of God's Spirit.'

8. Although the genitive plural (*peri de tōn pneumatikōn*, cf. 7:1, 25, 8:1) could be either neuter ('spiritual things') or masculine ('spiritual people'), I follow NRSV text in thinking that the neuter is more likely. The neuter form *ta pneumatika* in 14:1 tells strongly in its favour, since, in terms of the structuring of chs. 12–14, 'Only in chapter 14 does the "presenting problem", the role of tongues and prophecy in worship, come to the surface of the discussion. Nevertheless, the theological reflections in chapters 12 and 13 provide the essential presuppositions for the specific advice that is finally given in chapter 14' (Hays 1997:206).

9. 'Pagan' is an anachronistic term from later Christian parlance, and as a translation may be misleading in a contemporary context where the term 'pagan' is enjoying some revival. Paul's term is *ethnē*, 'Gentiles', and he is using a standard Jewish depiction of Gentile turning from idols to serve the living God, as in 1 Thess. 1:9 (cf. Hays 1997:209).

10. Most likely correct is 'Let Jesus curse' or 'May Jesus curse.' See below.

Paul starts a new section in the letter with an introductory heading, 'Concerning spiritual gifts', and what is clearly a euphemism for 'You greatly need to improve your present understanding' (verse 1).[11] He then proceeds to allude to the former state of the Corinthians (verse 2), where 'spiritual experience' was undoubtedly real but was nonetheless fundamentally misleading ('led astray').[12] Perhaps Paul mentions this former state because it may have left the Corinthians with assumptions about the nature of spiritual things that have been carried over into their Christian context in a way that is pernicious and in need of basic revaluation. Hence Paul's positive concern in verse 3 to give a criterion for assessing the authenticity of spiritual experience.

The understanding of Paul's criterion is greatly hampered by a problem of translation. That which cannot be said by the leading of the Spirit is, in Greek, just two words, *anathema Iēsous*, just as is its opposite, which requires the Spirit in order to be spoken, *kurios Iēsous*. The universal assumption of translators has been that in each phrase 'Jesus' is the subject and the other term the predicate, with an implicit verb 'to be' in either the indicative or the subjunctive (or perhaps the imperative) mood. Thus *kurios Iēsous*, by analogy with other Pauline usage (Rom. 10:9, Phil. 2:11), is an indicative affirmation, 'Jesus is Lord', while *anathema Iēsous* could be either 'Jesus is cursed' or 'Jesus be cursed.' The trouble is, it is not easy to see why anyone in a Christian context at Corinth might be envisaged as saying 'Jesus is/be cursed', and why this should be mentioned by Paul as the antithesis of 'Jesus is Lord.'[13]

The problems appear to be solved at a stroke in a recent essay by Bruce Winter (2001). Winter draws on ancient inscriptions of imprecation. Although there is no exact parallel to the Pauline wording, in terms of an inscription with the formula *anathema X*, there are equivalent formulations (sometimes, as in Paul's wording, with no verb).[14] In these, the

11. Nasrallah 2003:77 sees 12:1 as a probable 'shock' to the Corinthians on the grounds that they 'likely understood themselves to be quite well informed about spiritual gifts'.
12. Both the language and the referent of the sentence are open to more than one interpretation, but the gist of the sentence seems reasonably clear.
13. Scholars have, of course, rightly exercised their informed historical imagination to adduce possible religio-historical analogies or contexts which might provide an explanation, though none as yet has been able to command a consensus. Thiselton 2000:917–24 gives a valuable survey and exposition of twelve suggested explanations. Of these twelve, some are variants on four leading proposals, which are: (1) Renunciation of Jesus under persecution; (2) Some kind of 'ecstatic' utterance; (3) Some kind of Jewish denial of Jesus; (4) Expression of a deficient christology.
14. So, for example (2001:168,176), 'Hermes of the Underworld [grant] heavy [sc. curses]' (*Ermē chthonie ta megala*).

deity named is the active subject who is called upon to enact a curse upon someone specified by the imprecator. The point of such imprecations becomes clear from the contexts in which they were used. These are predominantly contexts of sport, love, commerce, and litigation, where the point of the curse was in some way to disable the opposition and so enable the person invoking the curse to be appropriately successful and triumphant. (I imagine that Balak, king of Moab, would have heartily endorsed the practice – unless, perhaps, he had begun to have second thoughts.)

It follows from this that, syntactically, 'Jesus' should be the subject and 'curse' the object, with an implied verb 'give/pronounce/enact'; the correct translation of *anathema Iēsous* would then be 'May Jesus curse.'[15] On the lips of a Christian it would be an attempt to invoke Jesus so as to gain some personal advantage over somebody else (Christian or otherwise), to promote oneself at the expense of someone else. In other words, a Christian attempting to use Jesus for success or gain would be understanding Jesus as just another (perhaps more fashionable?) spiritual power or deity; that is, they would be fitting Jesus into a frame of reference brought over from their previous Gentile experience.[16] But Paul is clear that to do this would be so fundamentally to deny what Jesus means that it could in no way be ascribed to the spiritual realm identified by knowledge of God through Jesus and the Spirit.[17]

15. To be sure, the lack of exact parallel to the Pauline formulation remains a difficulty for this proposed rendering. Nonetheless, I confess that, for myself, I feel about Winter's proposal somewhat as Wellhausen felt about hearing from Ritschl that Graf placed the law later than the prophets – this solved so many problems at a stroke that Wellhausen commented that 'almost without knowing his reasons for the hypothesis, I was prepared to accept it' (1973 [1878]:3).

16. When Paul himself uses *anathema* his concern is not to gain advantage over others but rather to provide definitional boundaries of what constitutes Christian faith – to go beyond which is thereby to cut oneself off from God's grace in Christ (so, in differing ways, both 1 Cor. 16:22, Gal. 1:8–9).

17. A fine intertextual commentary is provided by Luke 9:55. When Jesus' disciples wish to incinerate some unreceptive Samaritans, Jesus rebukes them. At this point some ancient manuscripts (of which D is the most significant) add the wording of Jesus' rebuke: 'You do not know of what sort of spirit (*[p]oiou pneumatos*) you are.' At this point most scholars do no more than note that, by the recognized principles of textual criticism, this reading is unlikely to be original to Luke – a judgment with which I agree – and so remove it from the text – a judgment which I am less sure about. The wording of Jesus' rebuke resonates strongly with 1 Cor. 12:3, and may well represent an early interpretative reading of the gospel text in the light of Paul, one that is surely rich and entirely well taken. If the nature of the biblical text as canonical literature gives reason for reconceiving the work of textual criticism, so that one's goal becomes the critical establishment not of the original text (itself often a problematic concept) but of the *best received text* (see Childs 1984:518–30 for the conceptual shift; also the

By contrast, authentic spiritual experience is marked by the confession 'Jesus is Lord.' Obviously Paul's words here are not to be understood in the superficial sense that the very words 'Jesus is Lord' could not be uttered except at the prompting of the Holy Spirit, for that would be patently false; or that it would not be possible to utter the words insincerely or inappropriately.[18] Their meaning will best be appreciated by considering briefly one of their other contexts of use – Paul's dense but famous quasi-poetic account of Jesus' self-emptying and exaltation in Phil. 2:5–11:

> 5 Let the same mind be in you that was [*or* that you have][19] in Christ Jesus,
> 6 who, though he was in the form of God,
> did not count equality with God
> as something to be exploited,
> 7 but emptied [*ekenōsen*] himself,
> taking the form of a slave,
> being born in human likeness.
> And being found in human form,
> 8 he humbled himself
> and became obedient to the point of death –
> even death on a cross.
> 9 Therefore God also highly exalted him
> and gave him the name
> that is above every name,
> 10 so that at the name of Jesus
> every knee should bend,
> in heaven and on earth and under the earth,
> 11 and every tongue should confess
> that Jesus Christ is Lord [*kurios Iēsous Christos*]
> to the glory of God the father.

The progress of Jesus starts with 'equality with God'. Whatever precisely this envisages, it is clearly a position of supreme value and honour. Yet

passing observation of Johnson 2002:23), then a good case can be made for retaining the longer text as authentic in relation to Luke's portrayal of Jesus, analogous to the famous 'Father, forgive them . . .' in Luke 23:34.

18. It is only if the words are taken superficially that there is an apparent conflict between 1 Cor. 12:3 and Matt. 7:21 ('Not everyone who says to me, 'Lord, Lord' will enter the kingdom of heaven . . .'), though Luz 1989:446 observes that 'the history of interpretation has again and again dealt with the relationship between Matt. 7:21 and 1 Cor. 12:3'.

19. The noting of an alternative translation is in recognition of a debate about alternative construals ('ethical' versus 'kerygmatic') of the appeal to Christ as a whole. However, Bockmuehl 1997:122–4 has shown that there is less at stake than sometimes supposed.

what motivates Jesus' progress is his construal of the significance of 'equality with God' as not being 'something to be exploited',[20] that is used to his own advantage or self-aggrandizement. Rather it involves self-emptying (where the Greek verb used has been taken up in noun form as a major term within Christian theology and spirituality, *kenōsis*) and service of others in a total and unreserved form – so much so that his construal of 'equality' as self-giving and service leads to death in a form that was uniquely cruel and shameful. Yet a death that might be expected to be the end is not. Rather God in a total and unreserved way embraces Jesus' construal of his vocation and demonstrates this through exaltation of Jesus to the highest imaginable position. The purpose of this is to give human beings an appropriate focus for their worship of God, since the confession that 'Jesus Christ is Lord' is to be the intended human response, and its ultimate focus is on God, who is now more truly understood through what has been seen in Jesus. Clearly the meaningful use of the words 'Jesus Christ is Lord' is inseparable in Paul's mind from the recognition of the self-emptying of Jesus as the only appropriate way to his present exaltation.

The implications of having 'the mind of Christ' (2:5) are spelled out not only in the immediate sequel, where appropriate Christian living in the pattern of Christ is seen as an outworking of the will and power of God (2:12–13), but more fully in the following chapter (3:2–4:1). Here, Paul offers a personal testimony, in which the priorities of his own life can be seen to embody the mind/pattern of Christ. Towards the beginning he offers a kind of functional equivalent to Jesus' 'equality with God', in terms of enumerating human privileges and moral and spiritual qualities:

> [4] If anyone else has reason to be confident in the flesh, I have more:
> [5] circumcised on the eighth day, a member of the people of Israel, of the
> tribe of Benjamin, a Hebrew born of Hebrews; as to the law, a Pharisee;
> [6] as to zeal, a persecutor of the church; as to righteousness under the
> law, blameless.

One can discern a certain sense of pride in Paul's words. These were things which he genuinely considered valuable, because of their obvious rootedness in regard for, and fidelity to, Israel's traditions. Yet just as

20. NRSV is surely correct in this construal of the much-debated *harpagmos* (Wright 1993 makes the case).

Jesus construed 'equality with God' not in terms of self-aggrandizement but in terms of self-giving, so, because of Jesus, Paul has learned to revalue that which once was precious to him:

> 7 Yet whatever gains I had, these I have come to regard as loss because of Christ. 8 More than that, I regard everything as loss because of the surpassing value of knowing Christ Jesus my Lord. For his sake I have suffered the loss of all things, and I regard them as rubbish ...

This is Paul's functional equivalent, or non-identical imitation, with regard to Jesus' *kenōsis*: the surprising relinquishing of what he might have been expected to hold on to. This is not, however, something negative (a mark of self-denigration, or something comparable), but is rather undertaken with a clear goal in mind – to know Christ now, and to grow in that knowledge[21] – a goal that can only be reached by progressing along this particular way of self-emptying:

> ... in order that I may gain Christ 9 and be found in him, not having a righteousness of my own that comes from the law, but one that comes through faith in Christ [*or* the faith of Christ], the righteousness from God based on faith. 10 I want to know Christ and[22] the power of his resurrection and the sharing of his sufferings by becoming like him in his death, 11 if somehow I may attain the resurrection from the dead.

For Jesus self-emptying has led to exaltation by God. This was through death. Paul is still part of life within this world, but that does not mean that exaltation is solely something to hope for in the future beyond the constraints of this present existence. For Jesus' death is a symbolic reality, a metaphor for that which happens already, here and now, to the Christian believer, and resurrection likewise becomes a presently operative reality.[23] Paul's goal is conformity to Christ, and that conformity must in the first place be to the self-emptying ('the sharing of his sufferings') if the exaltation, which is the fruit of that self-emptying, is also to

21. 'At the heart of Paul's "Christian" identity is a matter of knowledge, a knowledge of Christ, the value of which exceeds all else. The way the epistemological issue is worked out indicates that "knowing" Christ is not thought of in terms of acquiring information about or of developing a proper attitude toward, as if the locus of knowledge were the brain or the emotions ... Rather, knowing Christ is elaborated in terms of participation in Christ ... This engages not one particular faculty of knowing, but the whole person' (Cousar 1990:160–1).
22. Or 'that is'. The connective *kai* is most likely not a connective of two distinct objects that Paul desires to know, but rather is explanatory or epexegetic of the meaning of the single reality of knowing Christ (cf. Gorman 2001:330, n. 45).
23. Compare Gal. 2:20, 6:14–15.

be realized ('the resurrection from the dead'). Thus what one can see as a completed progress/movement in Jesus is something still incomplete and in the process of being worked out within Paul. Indeed, the incomplete nature of the process, with its corollary of the need to remain on his present course and not to waver from it, is emphasized strongly by Paul:

> [12] Not that I have already obtained this or have already reached the goal; but I press on to make it my own, because Christ Jesus has made me his own. [13] Beloved, I do not consider that I have made it my own; but this one thing I do: forgetting what lies behind and straining forward to what lies ahead, [14] I press on towards the goal for the prize of the heavenly call of God in Christ Jesus. [15] Let those of us then who are mature be of the same mind; and if you think differently about anything, this too God will reveal to you. [16] Only let us hold fast to what we have attained. [17] Brothers and sisters, join in imitating me, and observe those who live according to the example you have in us.

Paul underlines that what is at stake is the ever-fuller personal appropriation ('make it my own') of the reality of God in Christ, the one who has shown most fully the true construal of human life and has called Paul to it ('because Christ Jesus has made me his own'). Moreover, if life in Christ is like running a race ('straining forward', 'press on towards the goal for the prize'), then there can be no place for complacency or slackening in the continuing process of transformation in Christ. And although Paul has been speaking for himself of what it means to know Christ, he is clear that what he says is not just for himself alone (as though it were some kind of apostolic privilege); rather, his embrace of the pattern of Christ is to enable others too to see and understand the new kind of life to which Christ calls his followers (verses 15–17; cf. 1 Cor. 11:1). This living model is necessary not least because the way of Christ is strongly contested:

> [18] For many live as enemies of the cross of Christ; I have often told you of them, and now I tell you even with tears. [19] Their end is destruction; their god is the belly; and their glory is in their shame; their minds are set on earthly things. [20] But our citizenship is in heaven, and it is from there that we are expecting a Saviour, the Lord Jesus Christ. [21] He will transform the body of our humiliation so that it may be conformed to the body of his glory, by the power that also enables him to make all things subject to himself. [4:1] Therefore, my brothers and sisters, whom I love and long for, my joy and crown, stand firm in the Lord in this way, my beloved.

Paul uses strong language reminiscent of Jesus' warning about the easy road that leads to destruction (Matt. 7:13–14). The way of Christ involves a transforming of human priorities that is always demanding. Yet its goal, that to which it intrinsically leads – as athletic training leads to fast running or long jumping, or musical practice leads to the ability to produce beautiful music, or a well-watered plant can produce a beautiful flower – is becoming like the glorified Christ (verse 21); so it is in this way, and no other, that Paul's readers must continue resolutely (4:1).

This brief exposition of Philippians shows that the confession that 'Jesus is Lord' is for Paul a dense summary shorthand for his understanding of life in Christ. It becomes clear that to confess Jesus as Lord is to acknowledge the crucified and risen Jesus as the key to understanding both God and the deepest meaning of human glory, honour, and exaltation (those things for which people naturally long). Moreover, this confession is intrinsically self-involving, in that it can only be meaningful on the lips of those who will appropriate the way of Christ as their own, as Paul himself has done and as he models it for others. In this it is fully comparable to John's confession of 'Jesus Christ come in the flesh' (1 John 4:2–3), which again is a dense summary shorthand for the knowledge of God in Christ whose spiritual reality is displayed (or not) in the appropriation and demonstration of that quality of love which characterizes God's self-revelation in Jesus.[24]

In the light of this we can see the full force of 1 Cor. 12:3. Paul contrasts two ways. On the one hand, one might suppose that Jesus is there to enhance one's personal standing (wealth, success, reputation) at the expense of others, since helping one to compete more successfully in life is what people readily suppose their deity should do for them; this is the mindset that in some situations could seek advantage over others through saying 'Let Jesus curse.' On the other hand, there is acknowledgement of Jesus on his own terms, where a life of honour means self-emptying and the service of others; here glory is received from God only in and through such a mode of living; those who are embracing this mindset are those who appropriately say 'Jesus is Lord.' For Paul, it is the difference between these two mindsets and lifestyles that enables discernment of spiritual things. As elsewhere, it is the moral, i.e. the nature

24. Modern tendencies to polarize 'dogma' and 'experience' and to argue about their relative priority will never do justice to the way in which, for both Paul and John, knowledge ('dogma') and love ('experience') are inseparable for critical awareness of divine truth.

of human priorities and mode of living, that displays the presence, or absence, of the spiritual, i.e. the reality of God.

The logic of the remainder of 1 Corinthians 12–14 then unfolds straightforwardly. Spiritual gifts, although diverse, are complementary in the kind of way that should exclude feelings of superiority or inferiority (12:4–31). Love, that is a practical attitude emptied of self-seeking and (implicitly) modelled on Jesus, is *the* key to spirituality (13:1–13). Of the two spiritual gifts that are an issue within the church in Corinth, prophecy is more valuable than speaking in tongues for the basic reason that it 'builds up' others (*oikodomei*, 14:3, 4, 5, etc.), i.e. it is oriented towards others' benefit; and, in the case of an unbeliever entering a Christian gathering, prophecy can cut to the heart in such a way as to bring acknowledgement of God (14:24–5). By contrast, speaking in tongues is primarily of benefit to the speaker (14:2, 4a). Paul of course includes various qualifications: speaking in tongues is a gift from God and so not to be despised (14:5a, 18, 39), and it can be of benefit to others if interpreted (14:13, 27). Nonetheless, the fact that speaking in tongues is an exercise of individual, indeed private, worship (14:2, 28), and lacks intrinsic orientation towards the well-being of others, lays it peculiarly open to self-seeking misuse.

It is difficult to escape the impression that Paul is saying all he says in 1 Corinthians 12–14 because some of the Corinthians were using speaking in tongues as a kind of spiritual ego-trip through drawing attention to themselves as the exercisers of an ability whose uncommon, and intrinsically unusual, nature might seem to imply the privileged and superior character of those who could display it. Yet to use tongues thus is to display the mindset of 'Let Jesus curse', not of 'Jesus is Lord.' It is a use of religious language and a form of religious experience that displays a spurious, not a genuine (i.e. loving), spirituality.

Criteria for recognition of an apostle in 2 Corinthians

Introduction to 2 Corinthians

Paul's second letter to the Corinthians is a rich letter; but it is not always easy to understand. Primarily this is for reasons that have always been recognized. On the one hand, some of the Greek is quite simply difficult to construe. On the other hand, Paul's train of thought can be elusive. In modern scholarship, however, the latter problem has been sharpened through two further issues. First, there is a widespread consensus that

2 Corinthians is likely to be a composite of two or more Pauline compositions.[25] Secondly, many feel that an understanding of Paul's argument depends on being able to identify the stance of those against whom he argues[26] – even though there is no consensus as to this identity.[27] Nonetheless, I do not think that an understanding of Paul need wait upon being able satisfactorily to resolve these problems,[28] for what matters most is being able to trace the intrinsic logic of Paul's thought,[29] and being sensitive to his rhetorical conventions.[30] It is not inconceivable that the situation in Corinth should remain opaque to the modern interpreter even while Paul's thought can be adequately understood.[31] My focus, therefore, will be upon teasing out Paul's own logic and rhetoric in the received form of the text.

The central issue within 2 Corinthians is that Paul's apostolic ministry to the Corinthians is under fire. The situation is spelled out most explicitly towards the end of the letter:

25. This may well be so, though it is difficult to be sure. For example, the highest level of agreement relates to the original separateness of chs. 10–13. Yet although the tone of chs. 10–12 is indeed highly charged (ironic, indignant, scathing), the tone of ch. 13, which is not usually dissociated from chs. 10–12, is entirely comparable to the more measured, though still firm, tone of chs. 1–9. More generally, Young and Ford 1987:27–60, and most recently Long 2005, make a good case that the differences of tone are explicable in terms of the conventions of ancient rhetoric.

26. Almost everything that Paul affirms or denies has been read as an implicit response to things denied or affirmed by others, and full details of such proposals can be found in the major commentaries, e.g. Furnish 1984, Thrall 1994, 2000.

27. For the range of options see Georgi 1964, Gunther 1973; Sumney 1990, 1999 also reviews the options in the context of querying the methods by which conclusions in this area tend to be reached.

28. Sumney 1990:190, 1999:131 accepts that 2 Corinthians is a composite of two letters, yet finds 'the same kind of opponent in both' in a way that diminishes the heuristic significance of the problem.

29. It is likely that the issue of compositional unity is mainly significant for reconstructing the history of Paul's dealings with the Corinthian church. With the possible exception of 6:14–7:1, there is a strong consensus that all the content originates from the same author, Paul, over a short period of time. Sequential and chronological uncertainties may have limited bearing upon the nature of Paul's account of his apostleship; though of course one must always remain open to the possibility that puzzles within the text might best be ascribed to compositional complexity and/or to our relative ignorance of the originating historical context.

30. Forbes 1986 is more succinctly illuminating than most on the rhetorical conventions of Paul's world.

31. 'In order to grasp the fundamental lines of Paul's self-defence, we do not in fact need to know who his opponents were or what in fact they represented. All we need to know is what Paul thought of them . . . What the text is about is Paul, not his opponents, and its thrust is discernible without precise knowledge of the situation' (Young and Ford 1987:54). Although probably the single most influential and significant essay in modern debate, Käsemann 1941, is structured around the issue of the identity of Paul's opponents, much in the essay remains valuable even if one is not persuaded by Käsemann's historical reconstruction.

> 11:4 For if someone comes and proclaims another Jesus than the one we proclaimed, or if you receive a different spirit from the one you received, or a different gospel from the one you accepted, you submit to it readily enough. 5 I think that I am not in the least inferior to these super-apostles.

Although the form of the sentence in verse 4 is hypothetical, it clearly speaks of established fact. Someone has come to Corinth with 'another Jesus', 'a different spirit', 'a different gospel', and this someone is clearly 'another apostle' (where the singular is just a convenient personification for a number of people, verse 5). Here we have the Pauline equivalent to the situation in which Jeremiah found himself. As with prophet, so with apostle: the message spoken for God may be contested. An alternative account may be offered, one which may displace Paul's initial message; how then can truth (according to Paul) be established?

The consequent issue of discernment is succinctly formulated (albeit not with structural weight in its actual context):

> 13:3 You desire proof [*dokimē*] that Christ is speaking in me.

Here we find both the (prophetic/apostolic) claim that Paul's words are not solely his own, but rather convey the address of the risen Christ, and the desire for critical testing[32] of that claim on the part of those who, for whatever reason, have begun to doubt it. Elsewhere within the letter Paul formulates essentially the same issue from a different angle; he says what he says to the Corinthians, 'so that you may be able to answer those who boast in outward appearance and not in the heart' (5:12b). Just as words can easily sound plausible, and yet be superficial and deceptive in terms of the reality of a person's heart and mind (which is the recurrent form of the problem of authenticity in Jeremiah), so appearances may equally deceive. What looks good and attractive may not in its reality be so – otherwise the wolf in sheep's clothing would not be a problem. The problem is how an unseen reality, the state of the human heart and mind, might be made accessible, if what is already visible (outward appearance, demeanour) is not in itself a reliable guide but needs critical scrutiny – even

32. The Greek root – in nominal form *dokimē*, in verbal form *dokimazō* – is the same as in 1 Thess. 5:21, where we began this chapter. It is a root that is difficult to translate, but whose general sense is not difficult to establish: 'the issue of *dokimē*, who needs to be "proved", and the criteria by which this "proving" is to be carried out, is at the heart of the argument of this epistle. Whether the Corinthians are *dokimoi* or not depends on whether they concede *dokimē* to Paul or to his opponents. So this untranslatable word lies at the heart of Paul's apology' (Young and Ford 1987:99).

though with regard to those displacing Paul the Corinthians apparently do not seem to feel the same need to exercise critical scrutiny that they feel with Paul. Critical purchase on invisible reality is what Paul must enable the Corinthians to obtain and practise.

The trouble is, he must do it with reference to himself. In this regard it was perhaps easier for Jeremiah. Since people generally had never heeded Jeremiah or recognized his authority anyway, he could concentrate on saying why it was foolish to trust other prophets with their more acceptable message. But Paul is being displaced from a position of trusted authority over the Corinthians, and so feels the need to give grounds not only for distrusting those who are trying to displace him, but also for renewing trust in himself. He must, therefore, *commend* himself.[33] But Paul has the wisdom to know that self-commendation is worthless. Anyone can claim anything for themselves, and the problem of knowing what is genuine is especially acute in self-commendation. As a general rule, commendation comes best from others; but the problem for Paul is that it is precisely those who should be commending him (and whose very faith is in fact a living letter of commendation, 3:1–3) who have become doubtful about him and are causing the problem: 'Indeed you should have been the ones commending me' (12:11). Of course, the commendation that really matters is that from God: 'For it is not those who commend themselves that are approved [*dokimos*, i.e. shown to have withstood scrutiny and passed the test], but those whom the Lord commends' (10:18). And yet to recognize this is to pose again the basic problem – *how* is one to know those whom the Lord does, and does not, commend?

There is, therefore, an intrinsic tension running through what Paul says. On the one hand, because self-commendation is worthless, Paul will not practise it. More than once he says or implies this: 'We are not commending ourselves to you again' (5:12, cf. 3:1); Paul is not concerned with self-promotion. On the other hand, he must commend himself, because only so can he help the Corinthians learn how to practise appropriate discernment.[34] Thus twice Paul says: 'We commend ourselves' (4:2, 6:4). As will be seen, each time Paul says this he combines it with giving

33. The key Greek verbs for 'commend' are the cognate *sunistēmi*, *sunistanō*, which recur throughout the letter, and underlie every English usage of 'commend' in this exposition.
34. The kind of dilemma in which Paul finds himself is nicely encapsulated in Prov. 26:4–5: 'Do not answer fools according to their folly, or you will be a fool yourself. Answer fools according to their folly, or they will be wise in their own eyes.'

criteria whereby the Corinthians can evaluate his ministry, so that the self-commendation is always and only in terms of promoting critical discernment. The result of all this will be to put the question back to the Corinthians – and, by extension, to all who have come to accept 2 Corinthians as Holy Scripture: 'Examine yourselves to see whether you are living in the faith. Test [*dokimazō*] yourselves. Do you not realize that Jesus Christ is in you? – unless, indeed, you fail to pass the test' (13:5).

I will now offer a brief and selective exposition of three passages in which we can see how Paul develops his critical account of the discernment of apostolic authenticity.

1 2 Cor. 4:1–12

In ch. 3, after initially raising the issue of commendation, Paul begins to offer an account of his ministry via a subtle rereading, in the light of Christ, of the scriptural account of Moses' ministry at Sinai.[35] The key term, that which ministry from God should promote, is one of the prime biblical terms associated with God – glory – which is here seen in terms of human transformation into the likeness of God through appropriation of that which is from God. Although Moses in his ministry was an agent of glory, he was reserved about its display, and his veiling of his face (for which no motive is specified in Exodus) raises the possibility that he was lacking in openness (*parrēsia*, 3:12–13) through concealing the implied fading of glory between his encounters with God; and this is parabolic of the status of Torah itself, which by itself conceals its own transitoriness in relation to Christ. However, the glory is now freshly, and more fully, available to those who turn to the Spirit who mediates the life of the risen Christ – via the ministry of Paul. Against this background Paul leaves the comparison with Moses and speaks of his ministry from a different angle:

> [1] Therefore, since it is by God's mercy that we are engaged in this ministry, we do not lose heart. [2] We have renounced the shameful things that one hides; we refuse to practise cunning or to falsify God's word; but by the open statement of the truth we commend ourselves to the conscience of everyone in the sight of God.

'Losing heart' might be a natural and understandable response to the extreme affliction which Paul had recently endured, so extreme that he

35. Watson 2004:281–98 makes sense of Paul's reading of Exod. 34:29–35 in a way that has generally eluded modern interpreters.

was pushed to the very edges of life and hope (1:8–9), quite apart from the Corinthians' failure to recognize Paul's ministry as they should; but the transformative glory of the ministry that God has mercifully given to him makes Paul confident rather than despairing (4:1). The first and fundamental mark of this confidence is that it is displayed through openness and integrity. Here is one of the occurrences of Paul's saying 'we commend ourselves', because he is speaking of the moral quality of his ministry. He has renounced an existence in which there might be any disparity between what is apparent to others and what he might feel obliged to conceal in secrecy; he will neither live in an underhanded way ('practise cunning') nor speak in a such a way as to adulterate divine truth ('falsify God's word').[36] On the contrary, he speaks as one accountable to God ('in the sight of God' – for he knows that it is God's commendation which counts, 10:18) with an integrity that has a moral power to touch the heart and mind ('the conscience of everyone').[37]

In this, Paul speaks as Jeremiah or Micaiah might speak. 'Shameful things that one hides' resonates readily with the adulterous behaviour ascribed to certain prophets (Jer. 23:14), while 'to falsify God's word' is to speak *sheqer*. To speak with integrity and appeal to the conscience is exactly what Micaiah does with Ahab. So despite Paul's ambivalent-sounding evaluation of Moses, he nonetheless is still very much standing within the categories of prophetic authenticity formulated in Israel's scriptures, and is continuing them.[38]

> 3 And even if our gospel is veiled, it is veiled to those who are perishing.
> 4 In their case the god of this world has blinded the minds of the unbelievers[39] to keep them from seeing the light of the gospel of the glory of Christ, who is the image of God.

36. If 'word of God' here is not just a general reference but specifically envisages Israel's scriptures as interpreted by Paul, which could be indicated by the context of the discussion of Moses in 3:7–18 and the use of *ho logos tou theou* for Israel's scriptures in Rom. 9:6 (cf. Martin 1986:77), it is a reminder that serious Christian biblical exegesis must always be *Sachexegese* (on which see, e.g., Morgan 2003:26), in which, among other things, the faithful construal of the substantive content of the Old Testament in the light of Christ remains an enduring challenge.

37. 'Paul commends himself not by spinning a tale about his own importance but simply by telling the truth' (Barrett 1973:129).

38. 'Paul's self-understanding and his perception of what was going on in Corinth were grounded in a deep assimilation of certain parts of Scripture and certain scriptural models. Paul is illuminated by the observation that he has "lived in the Bible" to the point where the Bible has formed his whole outlook on how the world is and what his place in it might be' (Young and Ford 1987:63).

39. Although the Greek *apistoi* could refer to those without faith whom Paul evangelizes (i.e. 'unbelievers'), it may well be that in this particular context the implicit reference is to the

If Paul's ministry surpasses that of Moses in terms of its glory, why then does it appear to be 'veiled', which was precisely the problem that afflicted Moses' ministry (3:13–15)? This is certainly not because of any deliberate veiling on Paul's part (such as he ascribes to Moses, 3:12–13). Rather the veiling, which makes Christ's light and glory invisible, is ascribed to 'the god of this world'. If a typical gloss on this – 'they have been blinded by an alien power' (Barrett 1973:131) – is taken to mean some kind of extrinsic force causing people to do what they would not do otherwise, then Paul is most likely misunderstood. Rather, as Bultmann (1985:104) puts it: 'The "god of this aeon", however much Paul will have conceived it as a personal "evil", is not a causative power back of the human will [*nicht eine kausierende Macht hinter dem Willen des Menschen*], but is at work in the will's deciding for evil.' Just as the Spirit is actively present in the human doing of God's will, so is Satan actively present in the human choice of self-will and evil. The Old Testament narratives we have considered illuminate what causes blindness to God's light: Balaam is blinded to the presence of the angel by his greed; Ahab is blinded to the truth of Micaiah's words by his ambition and pride.[40] 'The god of this world' is less an 'alien power' than a different dimension of the one reality of the human embrace of self-will. The 'unbelievers/unfaithful' who 'are perishing' are blinded by 'the god of this world' because (to use a different idiom) they idolatrously focus upon the distorted priorities of this world and treat as god what is not God – if they treat this world as god (cf. Phil. 3:19, 'their god is the belly'), then the god which this world becomes blinds them. If the implicit reference is to the Corinthians themselves, then it is their misguided esteem of the 'worldly' (*kata sarka*) priorities advocated by Paul's opponents that is the problem.

> [5] For we do not proclaim ourselves; we proclaim Jesus Christ as Lord and ourselves as your slaves for Jesus' sake. [6] For it is the God who said, 'Let light shine out of darkness', who has shone in our hearts to give the light of the knowledge of the glory of God in the face of Jesus Christ.

Although Paul's ministry meets with a mixed response, and this might be attributed to his being too interested in self-promotion, he explains

Corinthians themselves, whose transfer of allegiance from Paul to his opponents is seen by Paul as a move from being 'faithful' (*pistoi*) to 'unfaithful' (*apistoi*); and so 'unfaithful' may be a preferable rendering.

40. I am not unaware of the differences between Paul's ('apocalyptic') frame of reference and that (or those) of the Old Testament writers we have looked at, but am not persuaded that in this context they make a significant difference.

things otherwise. His ministry is not about self-promotion but rather the opposite. Because his message is 'Jesus Christ is Lord', its corollary is that Paul's role entails not mastery over others, but rather service of them.[41] The sense of Paul's message has already been seen in the context of 1 Cor. 12:3 – to proclaim the lordship of Christ entails a revaluation of human priorities in the way of Christ, the renunciation of self-will and self-aggrandizement and the embrace of self-emptying and self-giving for the welfare of others. This is only possible for Paul because he has 'seen the light' – the light of God's glory revealed in the person of Jesus; it is this knowledge of God that determines Paul's priorities.

> 7 But we have this treasure in clay jars, so that it may be made clear that
> this extraordinary power belongs to God and does not come from us.
> 8 We are afflicted in every way,[42] but not crushed; perplexed, but not
> driven to despair; 9 persecuted, but not forsaken; struck down, but not
> destroyed; 10 always carrying in the body the death of Jesus, so that the
> life of Jesus may also be made visible in our bodies. 11 For while we live,
> we are always being given up to death for Jesus' sake, so that the life of
> Jesus may be made visible in our mortal flesh. 12 So death is at work in
> us, but life in you.

The apostle who speaks for God, and whose message has the power to transform human life so that it becomes 'glorious', might naturally be considered a person of 'power'. So Paul explains that, although there is indeed power, it is not the kind of power that makes a person powerful. On the contrary, the power is God's, and it is the image of clay and potter which specifies for Paul, as for Jeremiah, the respective roles of human apostle (prophet) and the divine Creator who uses what he has made. The point that divine power does not translate into human power is underlined by the characteristic pattern of Paul's ministry – afflicted, perplexed, persecuted, struck down. These are not the marks of someone who can stand above the fray or who is strong and victorious within the fray; rather they are the marks of someone who is entirely vulnerable because he does not possess unusual power. What is distinctive for Paul is not that he escapes affliction, perplexity, persecution, and striking down, but that within them there is always a resource (implicitly, divine power

41. 'Paul's opponents, of course, assert that he slyly labors only for himself, to make himself lord of the community, cf. 1:24; 10:8; 13:10' (Bultmann 1985:107).
42. NRSV has misplaced this phrase. In the Greek it stands at the outset of the sentence and almost certainly qualifies all four antitheses, and not just the first.

appropriated by faith) so that they do not have the last word, indeed that they become the means of transformation 'from one degree of glory to another' (3:18).

The key to this strange portrayal of power is then made explicit: the pattern of Jesus crucified and risen (verses 10–11). Paul's thought here is akin to what he says in Philippians 3. The death and resurrection of Jesus is not only a fact of the past but a present reality which becomes the definitive symbol by which Paul's life is to be understood.[43] Indeed, what Paul says has profound affinity with the gospel account of Jesus' call to discipleship (Matt. 16:24–6 and parallels):

> [24] Then Jesus told his disciples, 'If any want to become my followers, let them deny themselves and take up their cross and follow me. [25] For those who want to save their life will lose it, and those who lose their life for my sake will find it. [26] For what will it profit them if they gain the whole world but forfeit their life? Or what will they give in return for their life?'

Jesus here treats the way to crucifixion as a metaphor for discipleship. He extends what applies to himself (suffering, death, and resurrection, Matt. 16:21) to those who would follow him, making clear that the way of the master must be the way of the disciple also. And the discipleship is indeed stark, for the disciple is to be as one whose life is forfeit, subject to ridicule and abuse, en route to their own brutal execution; all conventional hopes and expectations with regard to this life must be abandoned. Yet precisely here lies a paradox – that attempts to resist this reckoning of one's life as forfeit will in fact lead to the loss of that life, while willingness to embrace loss of life because of following Jesus will lead to the finding of that life. Although this is formulated as a general axiom, it is clearly dependent upon the specific pattern of Jesus as messiah for its sense and truth to be grasped. Paul's language shows his own thorough appropriation of this pattern: 'the message and the messenger are drawn together into a remarkably tight relationship' (Cousar 1990:154).

Into this context of concern for the nature of Christian apostleship, however, Paul injects a distinctive note. The purpose of the faithful embrace of a pattern of dying is that 'the life of Jesus may be made visible [*phanerōthē*, verses 11, 12]' in him.[44] That is, Paul's concern is with the visibility and accessibility of what might be considered to be invisible and

43. Resurrection in its fullness is also a future hope (4:14; cf. Phil. 3:11–12).
44. Compare 4:2 'the open statement [*phanerōsis*] of the truth'. There is an implicit verbal parallel between Paul's speaking and living as alike revealing Christ.

inaccessible – the life of the crucified and risen Jesus whom Paul proclaims. Paul wants Jesus Christ to be seen and heard. So his point is that as he (non-identically) replicates Jesus' own pattern of death and resurrection, the master becomes visible, able to be discerned, in his servant. 'The proclaimer must reflect the proclaimed' (Lambrecht 1999:77); 'Paul has to assume the responsibility of *being Jesus* for his converts' (Murphy-O'Connor 1991:144).[45]

Paul then finishes with a characteristic rhetorical flourish (verse 12). Although, as he has just made clear, both death and life are at work in him, the whole purpose of his ministry is to bring the life of God in Christ to others. So he rhetorically separates death from life, reserving that which is costly and painful to himself so that its fruit of life should become real for the Corinthians – for he is there to serve them because of Jesus.

In these twelve verses Paul's understanding of how one should discern authenticity in an apostle begins to emerge. On the one hand, he stands in clear continuity with the characteristic Old Testament emphasis on searching integrity as a *sine qua non* for the one who would speak for God, with some kind of moral failure as the chief obstacle. On the other hand, he transforms this moral concern in a christocentric and cruciform way, by making Jesus' faithfulness to God in death and resurrection the key to knowledge and discernment of God. We must remember, however, that the pattern of faithfulness in suffering is already present in both Jeremiah and Micaiah (implicitly, for each, to death), so the way of Jesus intensifies what was already present. In the familiar Matthean terminology, Jesus comes 'not to abolish but to fulfil' the content of Israel's existing knowledge of God as depicted in its scriptures.[46]

2 2 Cor. 5:11–6:13

In order to keep a clear focus on our prime concern, I pass over a section of Paul's argument (4:13–5:10) and resume at 5:11.

> 11 Therefore, knowing the fear of the Lord, we try to persuade[47] others; but we ourselves are well known [*phaneroō*] to God, and I hope that

45. Cf. Käsemann 1941:53 on Paul, through his suffering, becoming 'the earthly manifestation of Christ himself'.
46. Of course, as 2 Corinthians 3 (among many other texts) shows, Paul is more dialectical about the continuing value of Moses than is Jesus in Matthew's Gospel.
47. This is a good idiomatic and contextual translation of the Greek *peithomen*, which decontextualized is just 'we persuade': cf. Barrett 1973:163, who glosses the translation 'we persuade' with 'conative, perhaps: we try to persuade' (also Furnish 1984:306, Martin 1986:117, 121). The point is significant because of the obvious similarity to the translation of

> we are also well known [*phaneroō*] to your consciences. [12] We are not commending ourselves to you again, but giving you an opportunity to boast about us, so that you may be able to answer those who boast in outward appearance and not in the heart.

It is because of a strong sense of accountability to God whose final judgment will be mediated through the person of Christ (5:10) that Paul speaks as he does so as to persuade others about the ultimacy of God's glory in Christ. In doing this Paul stands open to God, is seen for what he is by God (for, as he has said earlier in 4:2, he will have nothing to do with the shifty or secretive). As ever in this letter, however, Paul's concern is that the Corinthians should be able to see him for what he is, to discern his apostolic authenticity (verse 11b).[48] This they can do only by using their faculty of moral evaluation, their consciences, for the right seeing of Paul is intrinsically a moral seeing.[49] But in directly asking for such recognition from the Corinthians, Paul is aware that he may get a suspicious response – this is self-seeking, self-commendation. So he spells out as clearly as he can that what he is trying to do is to give them grounds for having confidence in him in the face of an alternative that is superficially more attractive but does not withstand real scrutiny, if only they know how to scrutinize; i.e. he is saying all this to enable the Corinthians to practise informed discernment (verse 12).

> [13] For if we are beside ourselves, it is for God; if we are in our right mind, it is for you. [14] For the love of Christ urges us on, because we are convinced that one has died for all; therefore all have died. [15] And he died for all, so that those who live might live no longer for themselves, but for him who died and was raised for them.

Jer. 23:22, where I have argued that 'they would have turned' should be translated and understood as 'they would have sought to turn'. Paul, like Jeremiah, was well aware that his speaking often failed to achieve its desired goal, and yet this did not affect its intrinsic nature.

48. Paul's repeated use of the verb *phaneroō*, as in 4:2, 10, 11, continues the concern with that which is able to be discerned by the onlooker.

49. It is difficult to catch the right tone for verse 11b, given the fact that it is the Corinthians' current failure rightly to understand Paul that is causing the problem. Bultmann 1985:147 thinks the text 'expresses Paul's optimism. It cannot be otherwise; the Corinthians must certainly understand him!' Yet it could equally be read as an ironic euphemism for 'I wish you would see what you seem incapable of seeing.' Perhaps the best clue is the unusual first-person singular 'I hope' (instead of 'we'), which may 'express a deeply felt concern' (Furnish 1984:307). Paul is hardly optimistic; but he does have a longing that the Corinthians' initial discernment of him, which led to their conversion, should be renewed through what he is now saying to them (the perfect infinitive form of 'be open' (*pephanerōsthai*, 5:11b) may indicate a present recognition that is rooted in the past).

Whatever the difficulties of detail (especially the logic of 'therefore all have died'), the general thrust of Paul's words is clear. He is giving the Corinthians reasons for having confidence in him (NB the repeated 'for') – with, correspondingly, grounds for practising discernment. His seemingly puzzling behaviour (verse 13) is explained by the logic of faith in Christ crucified and risen (verses 14–15). Christ's death is the great transformative reality whereby the focus of human life is shifted from self-seeking to orientation towards others – fundamentally towards God in Christ, but also correlatively towards other people, especially the Corinthians. This is the key to understanding Paul and so also, implicitly, to understanding what constitutes genuine apostolic ministry.

> 16 From now on, therefore, we regard no one from a human point of view [*kata sarka*, 'according to the flesh']; even though we once knew Christ from a human point of view, we know him no longer in that way. 17 So if anyone is in Christ, there is a new creation: everything old has passed away; see, everything has become new!

These and the following verses are not straightforward to understand, not least because of the much-quoted nature of much of their content as (very often) a free-standing summary of Pauline theology. My concern is to understand their general tenor in relation to their context, that is the challenge to Paul's apostleship and Paul's giving the Corinthians criteria for critical discernment of apostolic authenticity; though because of the difficulties my reading must needs be heuristic.[50]

Paul draws a consequence from life in Christ, a consequence that relates directly to the issue of how the way one looks at[51] another person should be transformed (verse 16a, picking up the concern in verse 12b); thus it is clear that the dynamics of discernment are at the forefront of his thought. The difference Christ makes is that Paul no longer regards anyone 'from a human point of view' – which seems a reasonable interpretative translation of the Pauline idiom, *kata sarka*, 'according to the flesh'. In this use of 'flesh' we have one of Paul's basic categories for life lived apart from God, whose implicit opposite is life and knowledge *kata pneuma*, 'according to the spirit' (and perhaps also, in this context, *kata stauron*, 'according to the

50. It will also be clear that I differ from many modern commentators who tend to read the text in rather more generalizing terms with less sense of the sharpness of the claims Paul is making about the nature of his apostolic ministry.
51. The Greek verb used, *oida*, has no special freight, and appears to be a general term for knowing or appraising, which is well captured by NRSV 'regard'.

cross'; so Martyn 1967:285). In this context to know someone *kata sarka* 'means that one's estimates are based upon purely human, and especially self-regarding, considerations. The man who knows his fellows thus will behave towards them in a corresponding way' (Barrett 1973:170). Paul has renounced such self-regarding evaluation of others (e.g. 'How will they further my desires/projects?', 'How can I be attractive and successful like them?').

Such a false, because self-seeking, mode of evaluation could be applied even to Christ, and Paul has renounced that too. The general point seems to be that 'what Paul rejects is man's habit . . . of making a Messiah in his own image' (Barrett 1973:171) – or, in the terms which we saw in 1 Cor. 12:1–3, Paul rejects the understanding that what a saviour or deity should do should be determined by general human expectations of what saviours or deities should do, since these so regularly fit the deity into human projects (individual, familial, tribal, civic, national) of self-aggrandizement. On the contrary, all this is entirely swept away and replaced for anyone who is 'in Christ'.

Although Paul has expressed this matter in a way that is (a) general, and (b) personal and confessional, it clearly should be read with an eye to the problem at hand. What this means is that what Paul says of himself he is implicitly urging upon the Corinthians.[52] They should cease regarding people in self-promoting ways because they should cease regarding Christ in a self-promoting way. And the specific point of this is that they should cease regarding Paul in a self-promoting way, as though his ministry should promote what they by conventional criteria (i.e. *kata sarka*) consider to be best for them. They should cease because otherwise they are living in fundamental contradiction of the new reality given to them in Christ.

> 18 All this is from God, who reconciled us to himself through Christ,
> and has given us the ministry of reconciliation; 19 that is, in Christ God
> was reconciling the world to himself, not counting their trespasses
> against them, and entrusting the message of reconciliation to us. 20 So
> we are ambassadors for Christ, since God is making his appeal through

52. This makes sense of the otherwise puzzling reference (why specify at all? and why here?) to not having a *kata sarka* knowledge of Christ. For this implicit mode of argument 'a precise parallel is furnished by 1 Corinthians 8:13. At the end of a discussion concerning the principles governing the legitimacy of eating meat offered to idols, he refuses to tell the Corinthians what to do. Instead he tells them what he would do in the same circumstances' (Murphy-O'Connor 1991:58–9).

> us; we entreat you on behalf of Christ, be reconciled to God. [21] For our sake he made him to be sin who knew no sin, so that in him we might become the righteousness of God.

The concern for the authenticity of Paul's ministry becomes explicit again. God's gift of reconciliation in Christ (verse 18a), which transforms one's whole way of looking at life (verses 16–17), has been entrusted to Paul in his ministry (verse 18b). This point is so crucial that Paul repeats and amplifies it for emphasis – *the wonder of God's reconciling work in Christ resides in the message which God has given to Paul.* Although the first half of verse 19 has been extensively used in Christian theology, often with minimal, or even no, reference to verse 19b, in context the emphasis lies on verse 19b: it is *here*, in what Paul says, and not elsewhere (i.e. in the message of those seeking to displace Paul), that the true message of God's reconciling work in Christ is to be encountered.

The immediate consequence of this, both existential and practical, is spelled out. On the one hand (verse 20a), Paul as the representative of Christ is speaking for God – here is a claim about the word of God in human words as frank and unambiguous as that in 1 Thess. 2:13; and in this context the claim is as freighted as it could possibly be: 'When Paul preaches, his hearers ought to hear a voice from God, a voice which speaks on behalf of the Christ in whom God was reconciling the world. Astonishingly, the voice of the suffering apostle is to be regarded as the voice of God himself' (Wright 1993:205).

On the other hand, the message of reconciliation to God on Paul's lips requires response – they, the Corinthians, are being urged to be reconciled to God.[53] The logic of this is striking, and needs comment. For Paul is writing to those who had already come to Christian faith through his ministry (cf. 3:1–3). So reconciliation in an initial way ('justification' in classic terms) is not at stake, nor would it be relevant in context. Rather the contextual issue is the Corinthians' reconciliation with Paul himself. Thus Paul's logic appears to be as follows. The Corinthians had been reconciled to God through Christ by the means of Paul's earlier ministry among them. However, their recent giving heed to accounts of the Christian faith that called in question what Paul had said to them has to some extent distanced them again from God's reconciling work in Christ. The only way for God's reconciliation to be appropriated in this

53. Commentators tend to take Paul's words here as a general statement about his ministry in a way that detaches them to a greater or lesser extent from the context of argument.

context is to trust Paul again and so act upon his words as the very words of God. Reconciliation with God and reconciliation with Paul are two sides of the same coin.[54] After something of an aside, difficult in its brevity, in which Paul appears to make the point that his ministry embodies God's righteousness (verse 21),[55] Paul reiterates and develops this challenge to be reconciled.

> [6:1] As we work together with him, we urge you also not to accept the grace of God in vain. [2] For he says,
> 'At an acceptable time I have listened to you,
> and on a day of salvation I have helped you.'
> See, now is the acceptable time; see, now is the day of salvation!

The self-promoting account of Christ, which has been displacing Paul's message, has been nullifying[56] authentic renewal among the Corinthians. There is the danger that, like the Galatians, they may lose the gift they had been given, and what had happened to them might be 'for nothing/in vain' (*eikē*, Gal. 3:4). Paul cites a passage from Isaiah (49:8, LXX) so as to sharpen the existential challenge: *now* is the moment of salvation, as Paul makes his appeal to the Corinthians. Their renewed reconciliation to God, through renewed responsiveness to Paul and his message, constitutes their possible 'day of salvation'.

> [3] We are putting no obstacle in anyone's way, so that no fault may be found with our ministry, [4] but as servants of God we have commended ourselves in every way: through great endurance, in afflictions, hardships, calamities, [5] beatings, imprisonments, riots, labours, sleepless nights, hunger; [6] by purity, knowledge, patience, kindness, holiness of spirit, genuine love, [7] truthful speech and the power of God; with the weapons of righteousness for the right hand and for the left; [8] in honour and dishonour, in ill repute and good repute. We are treated

54. Compare Gaventa 1993:195–6: 'The call for reconciliation *with Paul*, therefore, stands in parallel with the call for reconcilation *with God*. While it would be too much to say that these two forms of reconciliation are equally important, for Paul they are directly linked with one another'; or Bash 1997:106: 'Paul probably intended to communicate that to reject him was to reject God and his grace.'

55. For the likely contextual sense of 5:21 I follow Wright 1993 in general terms. The important point to recognize is that, as in verses 18, 19, 20, the contextual weight is not on the first half of the verse but on the second half, that is the significance of Paul's ministry in the present context. The point is to underline why it is appropriate for the Corinthians to trust Paul – because 'the covenant faithfulness [i.e. righteousness] of the one true God [is] now active through the paradoxical Christ-shaped ministry of Paul' (Wright 1993:206).

56. 'Nullifying' seems to me the closest English conceptuality for *eis kenon* (NRSV 'in vain').

> as impostors, and yet are true; [9] as unknown, and yet are well known; as dying, and see – we are alive; as punished,[57] and yet not killed; [10] as sorrowful, yet always rejoicing; as poor, yet making many rich; as having nothing, and yet possessing everything.

Because what is at stake is no less than life and death, since the Corinthians' reconciliation and salvation are dependent upon their recognition and discernment of the authenticity of Paul's apostolic ministry, Paul sounds the note of integrity he has sounded before (verse 3); he will not permit any 'obstacle' (*proskopē*) to dim the light of Christ in his ministry. This is not, of course, to deny the intrinsic 'obstacle' of Christ crucified (*skandalon*, 1 Cor. 1:23), but to make the point that the character of Paul's ministry is not at odds with the message in the kind of way to which people might legitimately take exception – in essence, if Paul did not live in accord with what he preached. On the contrary, he 'commends himself' in every way. As before (4:2), Paul says this in a context which makes clear that what he is doing is not seeking self-promotion but rather specifying characteristics of an authentic apostolic ministry – 'commending ourselves as servants of God'. So as soon as he mentions self-commendation he begins to list marks of a lifestyle that is conformed to the pattern of Christ – as the Lord, so his servant.

First, there is faithful endurance of hardship, hardship that (implicitly) comes upon him because of his ministry and constitutes a way of the cross (verses 4b–5). Secondly, Paul displays qualities of moral integrity (verses 6–7), qualities that replicate the qualities of his Lord. Thirdly, Paul displays a life that overcomes death in all its symbolic forms; that is, those things which usually quench and diminish life engender an opposite response in Paul (verses 8–10). Here the pattern of Jesus' death and resurrection gives the apostle's life a more paradoxical and surprising character than might be the case from qualities of moral integrity on their own. The bottom line is that Paul's apostolic lifestyle unreservedly embodies and displays, in metaphorical mode, the dying and living of Jesus.

> [11] We have spoken frankly to you Corinthians; our heart is wide open to you. [12] There is no restriction in our affections, but only in yours. [13] In return – I speak as to children – open wide your hearts also.

Paul has just depicted at some length what characterizes apostolic authenticity, so as to enable the Corinthians to practise discernment

57. Preferable is 'disciplined'. 'Punish' in NT Greek is *kolazō*, not *paideuō* as here.

and be capable of distinguishing between the superficially attractive and the genuine (cf. 5:12). He has spoken passionately, both about himself and in appealing to the Corinthians to respond. So he concludes this whole section with a simple statement and appeal. He has spoken without reserve because this corresponds to the nature of his affection for the Corinthians. If there is reserve and restraint in their relationship, then it lies within them. So all he asks for – in the mode of a parent seeking to coax a reluctant child into action – is a comparable openness and responsiveness on their part.

3 2 Cor. 11:4–7, 11:12–12:10

From the beginning of chapter 10 the tone of the letter changes. Paul indeed wrote passionately previously, but now there is a sharper polemical edge to much that he says. This corresponds to the fact that he now focusses on explicit comparison between himself and those who are undermining his position among the Corinthians, who hitherto have only been alluded to somewhat obliquely (e.g. in 5:12):

> 11:4 For if someone comes and proclaims another Jesus than the one we
> proclaimed, or if you receive a different spirit from the one you
> received, or a different gospel from the one you accepted, you submit to
> it readily enough. 5 I think that I am not in the least inferior to these
> super-apostles. 6 I may be untrained in speech, but not in knowledge;
> certainly in every way and in all things we have made this evident to
> you. 7 Did I commit a sin by humbling myself so that you might be
> exalted, because I proclaimed God's good news to you free of charge?

Paul here says nothing about the content of this alternative message, other than to depict it negatively, as other than what he had preached. But the clear presumption (from what he says elsewhere) is that it represents a less demanding, more readily palatable account of Jesus than that which Paul had proclaimed. The trouble is – and for this Paul considers the Corinthians gullible – this alternative message appears to have found a ready reception in Corinth. And it carried with it, naturally enough, an adverse revaluation of Paul, which has posed the need for his 'self-commendation' (verse 5). Clearly part of the problem is that Paul as a speaker sounded less impressive that these others (verse 6, cf. 10:10, 'his speech is contemptible'). The criticisms of Paul included also his having made no financial demands of the Corinthians as he was in the process of evangelizing them, as the following paragraph makes clear

(11:7–11) – perhaps (since the nature of the criticism is not specified) on the basis of some form or other of 'If it is worth something, it should cost something', though complex social conventions were also at stake in acceptance of financial support. Paul, however, sees his practice of making no financial charge as symbolic of the gospel message (11:7) – his self-humbling so that others might be exalted embodies the self-giving for others that is the consequence of Christ's death and resurrection (5:15), and replicates the pattern of Christ himself, who 'though he was rich, yet for your sakes became poor, so that by his poverty you might become rich' (8:9). So Paul will give no ground here:

> 12 And what I do I will also continue to do, in order to deny an
> opportunity to those who want an opportunity to be recognized as our
> equals in what they boast about. 13 For such boasters are false apostles,
> deceitful workers, disguising themselves as apostles of Christ. 14 And
> no wonder! Even Satan disguises himself as an angel of light. 15 So it is
> not strange if his ministers also disguise themselves as ministers of
> righteousness. Their end will match their deeds.

The very fact that Paul's practice of evangelizing without financial charge symbolizes the truth of the gospel means that it provides a way of distinguishing between an authentic apostle and those who would aspire to genuine apostleship without embracing its consequences (verse 12).[58] Paul now rounds on those who have been displacing him, and denounces them as 'false apostles' (*pseudapostoloi*, an exact counterpart to 'false prophets', *pseudoprophētai*, in Matt. 7:15). They are false because they are 'deceitful' (*dolioi*), displaying that failure of integrity with God's message which Paul himself has renounced (4:2);[59] and so their would-be apostolic character is merely a disguise ('appearance', not 'heart', 5:12).

The trouble is, the disguise is a plausible one, indeed as good as it could be; for 'minister of righteousness' (*dikaiosunē*) in effect represents Paul's own self-depiction (3:9, 5:21). Paul sees a basic principle here. Those who come to exploit and use others for their own purposes do not announce the fact but disguise themselves as the opposite of what they really are, because this is what the archetypal deceiver does; the one whose reality is

58. 'It must not be forgotten that Paul himself argued in 1 Cor. ix for the principle that the apostle was entitled to support. The real point is that the requirement of self-sacrifice . . . marks out the true apostle from the false' (Barrett 1973:285).

59. Paul's verbal resonance of verb *doloō* (4:2) and adjective *dolios* (11:13) is lost in NRSV with its rendering of the verb as 'falsify' and the adjective as 'deceitful'.

to bring darkness disguises himself as a dazzling figure of light. So those who deceive, these false apostles, naturally seek to appear as people of integrity, who further the cause of integrity / righteousness. In their ability to appear attractive these false apostles are no different from the false prophets of whom Jesus speaks – for the wolf who comes to the sheep looking like one of them has likewise adopted the best possible disguise.

Although Paul's immediate comment is a snort of dismissal – 'they won't get away with it' (verse 15b) – he knows full well that the real issue is how to penetrate the disguise. For if he cannot enable the Corinthians to see through to the reality, to discern the heart, of these others, then they will see no reason to treat what Paul says about them as anything more than the rhetoric of sour grapes (or mere ideological slanging, or *odium theologicum*, or whatever). So he directly moves on from his denunciation to address the heart of the matter – providing criteria for discernment.

But because Paul's preferred method is to portray and commend the true rather than to analyse and dissect the false (though of course there are elements of the latter), there is an obvious problem. He must speak about himself as the one authentic apostle whom the Corinthians know. That, however, will appear to be self-commendation, self-promotion, in the questionable sense. And if he can only overcome others by accepting their frame of reference in the first place, i.e. win by playing by the wrong rules, then he will have lost before he even begins; even if he was successful in persuading the Corinthians in the short term, he would win a battle at the cost of losing the war. So before he gets to the points of substance, Paul must say something about method. What he does is to subvert the method of self-commendation that he must adopt by calling it no longer 'self-commendation' (*sunistēmi, sunistanō*) but rather 'boasting' (*kauchaomai*) and by saying as strongly and ironically as he can that only a fool (*aphrōn*) speaks thus:

> 16 I repeat, let no one think that I am a fool; but if you do, then accept
> me as a fool, so that I too may boast a little. 17 What I am saying in
> regard to this boastful confidence, I am saying not with the Lord's
> authority, but as a fool; 18 since many boast according to human
> standards [*kata sarka*, 'according to the flesh'], I also will boast. 19 For
> you gladly put up with fools, being wise yourselves! 20 For you put up
> with it when someone makes slaves of you, or preys upon you, or takes
> advantage of you, or puts on airs, or gives you a slap in the face. 21 To my
> shame, I must say, we were too weak [*astheneō*] for that!

In terms of method and approach, this is a fool's game (verses 16–19). Paul cannot, however, resist a pointed matter of substance, mentioning to the Corinthians their preference for time-honoured patterns of what amounts to manipulation and abuse on the part of these pseudo-apostles (verse 20); preferred presumably because then 'one knows where one stands' without being unsettled by the disturbing paradoxes of Christ crucified and risen. And in saying that he was too 'weak' [*astheneō*] for conventional dominating behaviour – which might appear simply to mean that he was not up to it – Paul tacitly introduces what will become one of his key criteria of authenticity.

In any case, after this 'methodological introduction', Paul now comes to his substantive thesis:

> But whatever anyone dares to boast of – I am speaking as a fool – I also dare to boast of that. [22] Are they Hebrews? So am I. Are they Israelites? So am I. Are they descendants of Abraham? So am I. [23] Are they ministers of Christ? I am talking like a madman [*paraphrōn*] – I am a better one: with far greater labours . . .

With a reiteration that such boasting is a fool's game, Paul comes to the comparison between himself and the others. Initially he starts slowly with variations on the theme of his Jewish credentials (verse 22). That such credentials could be significant is clear in Phil. 3:4–6. Yet that context, like 2 Cor. 11:18, makes clear that for Paul these credentials are merely *kata sarka* ('according to the flesh'; NRSV 'according to human standards'), and so do not count for any kind of authentic discernment. He mentions them here as a kind of rhetorical warm-up, to get the Corinthians thinking positively about Paul's credentials, even the ones that do not count, so that they will be better able to think positively about the credentials that do count.

In verse 23 Paul comes to the real point: evaluation of the service of Christ. Whatever the others are, Paul is 'better' (or perhaps 'more'). But he knows that in the service of the one who redefined greatness in terms of humility and self-giving for others all talk of 'superiority' in any conventional sense is a category mistake.[60] So his definitive self-commendation in relation to others has two markers to minimize

60. Perhaps this is why Paul does not say that he is 'better'/'more' with a conventional comparative adjective (*beltiōn*, *kreittōn*) but uses an adverbial *huper*, which may just carry an adverbial nuance that it is how he lives, rather than who he is in himself, that is the point of comparison.

misunderstanding. First, he intensifies his claim that only fools speak thus; previously he spoke 'as a fool'/'in folly' (*aphrōn, en aphrosunē*), now he prefaces his crucial claim to be 'better' by saying that he can only speak thus 'as an utter fool/madman' (*paraphrōn*)[61] – for it is wholly outrageous to make such a claim. Secondly, as soon as he makes the claim, he moves directly into offering a warrant for it – for the only way in which such an outrageous claim can make sense is in terms of conformity to the way of Christ, the way of the cross: 'with far greater labours . . .'.[62] That which is more briefly specified as the mark of the true apostle in 2 Corinthians 4 and 6 is now spelled out with rhetorical fullness:[63]

> . . . with far greater labours, far more imprisonments, with countless
> floggings, and often near death. 24 Five times I have received from the
> Jews[64] the forty lashes minus one. 25 Three times I was beaten with
> rods. Once I received a stoning. Three times I was shipwrecked; for a
> night and a day I was adrift at sea; 26 on frequent journeys, in danger
> from rivers, danger from bandits, danger from my own people, danger
> from Gentiles, danger in the city, danger in the wilderness, danger at
> sea, danger from false brothers and sisters; 27 in toil and hardship,
> through many a sleepless night, hungry and thirsty, often without
> food, cold and naked. 28 And, besides other things, I am under daily
> pressure because of my anxiety for all the churches. 29 Who is weak, and
> I am not weak? Who is made to stumble, and I am not indignant?
>
> 30 If I must boast, I will boast of the things that show my weakness.
> 31 The God and Father of the Lord Jesus (blessed be he for ever!) knows

61. The verb *paraphroneō* is a *hapax legomenon* in the New Testament (though reasonably attested elsewhere). Contextually, the added *para* must be intensifying.

62. Although by now Paul's pattern of thought should be clear, since his move here is identical to that in 6:4 (and, in effect, 4:7–12), an understanding of Paul should never be taken for granted. It is remarkable, for example, that Lambrecht (1999:206, 191) can reach this point in his commentary and say in his general interpretation: 'He then goes on: he is a much better "servant of Christ" than the opponents (11:23a); then, quite unexpectedly [!], he provides a list of hardships (11:23b–29)' and in his detailed comment: 'By this self-assured statement Paul introduces a whole "list of circumstances", a *Peristasenkatalog*, which has to do only [!] with hardships, sufferings, and care. This catalogue of trials should provide proof of Paul's daring conviction "I am more!" but that comparison with the opponents will recede into the background [!].' It is the more remarkable since earlier (p. 114), when commenting on 2 Corinthians 6, Lambrecht rightly says: 'Paul thus sees his suffering in connection with the death of Christ. To be united with Christ means that the minister will have to suffer as Christ did. Through all his trials he really participates in the suffering of Christ.'

63. It might be worth noting that had Paul been speaking in 'conventional' (*kata sarka*) categories, he could have mentioned the numbers of converts he had made, the communities he had founded, the recognition he had (at least sometimes) received from other Christian leaders, and so on.

64. The Greek lacks the definite article, and Paul is not here generalizing about 'the Jews' in a distancing way. Correct is 'from Jews' (Watson 2004:291).

> that I do not lie. [32] In Damascus, the governor under King Aretas set a guard on the city of Damascus in order to seize me, [33] but I was let down in a basket through a window in the wall, and escaped from his hands.

Illuminating points of background detail can be found in all the commentaries: for example that beating with rods was a Roman punishment, which thus complements the Jewish floggings and underlines the ubiquity of contexts where Paul's ministry got him into trouble with established authorities; or that a single flogging/beating could suffice to cause death.[65] For present purposes it suffices to note that, in this account, whose truthfulness Paul underlines in the strongest possible terms (verse 31), his sufferings were in effect relentless; the pressures were not only bodily (verses 25–7) but also mental and spiritual (verses 28–9); and – lest one perhaps be tempted somehow to romanticize the range and scope of things that happened to Paul (though this may be more of a temptation for the modern than the ancient reader) – afflictions could, paradoxically, be merely ignominious and uncomfortable (if that is a right reading of the puzzling verses 32–3).[66] The key thought is verse 30 – if boasting is the required activity, then Paul will boast only of 'the things that show my weakness' (*astheneia*).[67] Since one only boasts of those things that show one in a good light, this is a reminder, in mid flow, of Paul's subversion of the exercise. For what shows Paul in a good light, i.e. what shows him to be an apostle, is only those things that 'according to human standards' (*kata sarka*) would appear thoroughly undesirable.

65. Also noteworthy is Glancy 2004, which has a suggestive argument for a particular first-century cultural resonance for Paul's references to what had happened to his body, on the basis of a distinction between battle scars (on one's front) and disciplinary stripes (on one's back): 'Display of war wounds was a common feature of Roman somatic rhetoric. Those habituated to a first-century corporal idiom distinguished between a breast pierced in battle and a back welted by a whip . . . Whippability was a token not of honor, excellence, or virility, but of dishonor, abasement, and servility' (p. 134).
66. Alternatively, it may well be that Paul's words in verses 32–3 are meant implicitly to overturn conventional claims to honour based upon military prowess. To be the first to climb the wall of the enemy's fortification was the occasion of special honour in the Hellenistic world (Savage 1995:63, citing Livy 28.48.5) as also in ancient Israel (so 2 Chron. 11:6, which is more explicit in this regard than 2 Sam. 5:8). It is also suggestive to read Paul's whole catalogue as a parodic counterpart to the most famous list of heroic achievements in the first-century world, the *Res Gestae Divi Augusti* (so Fridrichsen 1929). The basic point is that in most known cultures men boast of acts of strength and of conquest of others, and Paul's pattern of life in Christ stands over against, and if appropriated subverts, all such conventional patterns.
67. 'Paul's point is not that he is superior to his rivals because he has suffered more than they, but rather that being a "servant of Christ" is defined by weakness, not the qualities which they boasted about' (Pickett 1997:179).

> 12:1 It is necessary to boast; nothing is to be gained by it, but I will go on to visions and revelations of the Lord. 2 I know a person in Christ who fourteen years ago was caught up to the third heaven – whether in the body or out of the body I do not know; God knows. 3 And I know that such a person – whether in the body or out of the body I do not know; God knows – 4 was caught up into Paradise and heard things that are not to be told, that no mortal is permitted to repeat. 5 On behalf of such a one I will boast, but on my own behalf I will not boast, except of my weaknesses. 6 But if I wish to boast, I will not be a fool, for I will be speaking the truth. But I refrain from it, so that no one may think better of me than what is seen in me or heard from me, 7 even considering the exceptional character of the revelations.

It seems a reasonable inference that 'spiritual experiences', in the form of enjoying 'visions and revelations', constituted one of the issues of contention in the Corinthians' evaluation of Paul and the other would-be apostles. Presumably unusual spiritual experiences were taken as evidence of spiritual stature. Paul's opponents presumably either claimed extensive such experiences themselves or were enabling the Corinthians to have them – or both. Paul may have appeared deficient by contrast. So this is the final issue on which he sees the need to provide criteria for discernment. He makes two basic moves.

First, he says that he has indeed had unusual, even astonishing, spiritual experiences.[68] One in particular involved rapture to an exalted spiritual realm ('the third heaven', 'Paradise'),[69] a rapture so overwhelming that it was not possible to be sure what was happening ('whether in the body or out of the body, I do not know'). Yet Paul mentions this experience not so as to glory in it (though one could read verse 5 as conveying some sense of trumping his opponents on their own terms), but so as to play it down.[70] This he does for two reasons. One is that he

68. I follow the consensus that 'a man in Christ' is Paul himself. Why he should have chosen this periphrasis can, of course, be explained in more than one way; though probably its most obvious rhetorical function is to create a certain distance between Paul and the experience recounted – which would be consonant with the diminished significance he ascribes to it.
69. These categories are well attested in other ancient Jewish literature. Their precise significance in Paul's use is open to debate. The likelihood, both from the present context and from Luke 23:43, is that they depict the most exalted possible context in the presence of God.
70. Misreading of the tenor of Paul's discussion is, unfortunately, not uncommon. So, for example, Albert Schweitzer (1953 [1930]:137): 'The high importance which Paul always attached to it [sc. the "ecstatic experience" in 12:2–4] is to be judged from the fact that in his struggle to vindicate his Apostolic authority he makes references to it, holding it to be a unique distinction, from which at once must be evident his equality with other Apostles, if not indeed his superiority to them. It was to Paradise that Enoch was translated when he was

does not want evaluations of himself to be based upon unverifiable claims – they only have his word for such a rapture, and they cannot check it – for he wants them rather to be able to evaluate him on the basis of what is accessible to their eyes and ears (verse 6b). The other reason is that what he heard in his rapture cannot be spoken of. Although on one level its content is unutterable because 'no mortal is permitted to repeat it', on another level Paul could still say plenty about the total experience (as can be appreciated from comparison with other ancient accounts which expatiated on many aspects of journeys to the heavenly realms and what was encountered there).[71] But Paul uses here the logic which he applies in 1 Corinthians 14 to speaking in tongues (cf. Käsemann 1941:68); it is indeed of value to the worshipper, but it is intrinsically of no value to others (unless made accessible through interpretation). What he experienced was of value to himself, but is of no value to others. Therefore to seek to draw attention to it and lay weight upon it would be to show mistaken, and fundamentally unspiritual, priorities – for the reasons set out in 1 Corinthians 12–14.[72] Thus Paul's first move is: astonishing spiritual experiences count for little in discerning apostolic authenticity.

> Therefore, to keep me from being too elated, a thorn was given to me in the flesh, a messenger of Satan to torment me, to keep me from being too elated. [8] Three times I appealed to the Lord about this, that it would leave me, [9] but he said to me, 'My grace is sufficient for you, for power[73] is made perfect[74] in weakness.' So, I will boast all the more gladly of my weaknesses, so that the power of Christ may dwell in me.

rapt away (Enoch lx.8, lxx.3). Paul had thus had an experience comparable to that of these pious men of early times, and remained for a time in the place which he visited! Which of the original Apostles had been granted such a favour!'

71. 'I am convinced that ascent to heaven is a *characteristic* expression of Hellenistic piety' (Tabor 1986:58). Tabor (pp. 57–111) provides extensive documentation of heavenly journeys in antiquity. See also Rowland 1996 for the general Jewish and early Christian context for such 'mysticism'.

72. It is hardly accidental that the keynote of 1 Corinthians 14, 'building up' of others (*oikodomē/mein*), recurs in a summary way in 2 Cor. 12:19: 'Everything we do, beloved, is for the sake of building you up.'

73. There is a well-attested textual variant, 'my power', which is probably an early gloss to bring out the implied sense. Dawn 2001:37–41 sees 'my' as most likely a mistake which obscures an implicit 'your', i.e. a sense of power 'as Paul's rather than God's'; but that way of formulating an antithesis between Paul and God does not do justice to Paul's consistent christological patterning of his apostolic ministry. Paul only embraces weakness for himself because of the precedent of Christ in his death and resurrection.

74. The reading *teleitai*, from *teleō*, is better attested than *teleioutai*, from *teleioō*, but it is likely that there is no significant difference of meaning between the verbs, each having here the sense of 'fulfil', 'bring to completion'. Dawn 2001:37–41 accepts *teleitai*, but argues that it should have its 'usual' sense of 'finish' as distinct from 'bring to fruition', which she reserves to *teleioō*; the point being that it is only when Paul's power is brought to an end in weakness

[10] Therefore I am content with weaknesses, insults, hardships, persecutions, and calamities for the sake of Christ; for whenever I am weak, then I am strong.[75]

The danger of attributing the wrong significance to such rapture is recognized by Paul as having been a real temptation for himself. But Paul was given a divine discipline to prevent it, though the discipline was a painful one: a thorn in the flesh.

What the 'thorn in the flesh' was has been discussed at great length, and an astonishing range of possibilities has been canvassed. We will never know, because there is no unambiguous evidence. My own inclination, for what it is worth, is to follow St John Chrysostom in his *Homily XXVI* (Chrysostom 1848:293–4) and construe the thorn as the opposition faced by Paul. Contextually, opposition to Paul is the general issue, and the association of Satan with Paul's opponents is explicit in 11:13–15.[76] Moreover, where one might expect reference to Paul's acceptance of the thorn in 12:9b–10 we find reference to his acceptance of the sufferings caused by opposition to his apostolic message, in the kind of way that suggests that the latter is an equivalent of the former. Existentially, one of the hardest things for someone who has 'seen the light' (cf. 4:6) can be to be confronted by those whose own failure to see the light leads them solely to resist, rather than open themselves to, the message;[77] such resistance, if sustained, can not only lead to the kind of extensive persecution which Paul speaks of; it also leads (according to personality) to intense frustration and sometimes to self-doubt, and even, over time, may threaten to erode the significance ascribed to the light that has been seen.

(verse 9a) that Christ's power is able to tabernacle on him (verse 9b). However, although the basis of the argument is a list of all the uses of *teleō* in the New Testament, Dawn surprisingly offers no discussion of the Pauline uses in Rom. 2:27 and Gal. 5:16, whose translation she glosses with 'fulfil', and whose sense in context is clearly 'bring to fruition' rather than 'bring to an end'. Nonetheless, Dawn's wider thesis (pp. 35–49) about the significance of divine power in human weakness can stand without this wobbly bit of foundation. Compare, for example, Barclay's interpretation of the NRSV translation (Barclay 2003:1371): 'The "perfection" of Christ's power means not only its *display*, the revelation of divine power where human power is clearly missing; it means also its *actualization*, its becoming effective, in the sense that only an empty container can be filled and only a powerless human life is empty enough to receive grace.'

75. Better would be 'powerful', since the adjective here (*dunatos*) is related to the noun for 'power' (*dunamis*) in verse 9. The regular adjective for 'strong' (*ischuros*) is eschewed.

76. Chrysostom also rightly points out the significance of *sātān* in the Old Testament.

77. *Contra* Furnish 1984:549–50, who objects that 'the imagery of a *thorn in the flesh* requires us to think of some affliction more directly personal than persecution, which Paul shared with the whole church'.

What probably matters most, however, for appreciating Paul's thought is the logic of the metaphor itself. A sharp incision in the flesh hurts in an inescapable and insistent way. You cannot but be aware of it (if you do not have the benefit of an anaesthetic); whatever you may be doing or thinking, by day or by night, you know its pain. The pain only ceases when the thorn is removed; without its removal life is permanently and searingly changed, apparently for the worse. Hence Paul's repeated request to the Lord for its removal. In the explanation that the Lord (presumably, in context, the risen Christ) gives for refusing to remove it,[78] we have the climactic reason for Paul's understanding of authenticity.

The wording is pithy and epigrammatic. It encapsulates in a few words what Paul himself expounds at length. In a sense, the whole of 2 Corinthians could be read as a gloss on these words of the risen Lord. The key to understanding why 'grace' is sufficient is the explanatory 'for power is made perfect in weakness'. This is the heart of the matter, and power and weakness, rather than grace as such, is what Paul develops in his immediate comment on, and response to, the Lord's words (verses 9b–10), in which he appropriates his Lord's axiom in such a way as to formulate his own axiom, 'whenever I am weak, then I am powerful'; for weakness and power are not successive but simultaneous. As elsewhere, it is Christ crucified and risen who is the model for Paul's appropriation; 'For he [Christ] was crucified in weakness, but lives by the power of God. For we are weak in him, but in dealing with you[79] we will live with him by the power of God' (13:4). Through the cross, which is the extreme place of Christ's weakness, the power of God is realized in resurrection; if this is the definitive way of the master, so too it must be for the servant and representative. Instinctive expectations of what might naturally follow from faith in a sovereign God who has power to raise the dead need to be rethought in the light of the specific event of Jesus; and life must be refashioned accordingly.[80] Even pain as acute as that of the thorn in the

78. 'The use of the perfect tense (*eirēken*), conventional in reporting solemn (especially divine) decrees (e.g. Acts 13:34), indicates that what had been once said is understood to have lasting significance' (Furnish 1984:530).

79. This is a questionable translation of the Greek *eis humas* ('to you'), which comes at the end of the sentence and probably serves to underline Paul's reiterated point that his life in Christ is for their benefit, even though in context there is a note of warning.

80. The language of weakness and power can legitimately be construed in a variety of ways. Within Paul's own context it is likely that socio-cultural resonances are well to the fore.

flesh can become, in Christ, a channel for the power of God which brings life to others.

The context for this is still the 'visions and revelations of the Lord'. So part of the point of the divine words of verse 9a is the contrast with the 'things that are not to be told' of verse 4. Again, Paul's handling of tongues and prophecy in 1 Corinthians 14 is heuristically valuable here. One revelation is incommunicable, the other communicable. The revelation which would prima facie seem more indicative of spiritual stature is, like tongues, a genuine gift but of limited significance. The revelation which underlines and confirms Paul's weakness, and so prima facie could seem spiritually inferior, is the revelation which, like prophecy, represents a fundamental truth of God in Christ which is not only for Paul's benefit but also for the building up of others. Thus Paul's second move is: the spiritual experience that does count in discerning apostolic authenticity is solely that which enhances conformity to Christ in his death and resurrection.

Finally, something of the significance of verses 7–10 can be further appreciated if the passage is read as Paul's Gethsemane. Although the suggestion of possible links between this passage and the gospel accounts of Jesus in Gethsemane is not novel,[81] it usually represents a suggestion about Paul's possible authorial intention. On that level, however, the suggestion can only be somewhat tenuous at best and so difficult to do much with.[82] My proposal is that this should be a reading strategy, which arises out of the location of 2 Corinthians within the collection of texts that is the canon of the New Testament: does the contextual proximity of gospels and letters create resonances which are genuinely illuminating in that they enable one to penetrate more fully the subject matter of the text, even if in a way not necessarily intended by Paul (yet still congruous with his concerns)?

The most obvious resonance with Jesus in Gethsemane is the threefold request to be spared something terrible. Although Paul does not put his request in direct speech, it could easily be rendered thus: 'Lord, if it be possible, let this thorn be taken from me.' Further, although Paul does

81. 'The number three is a reminder of Jesus' temptations in the Garden of Gethsemane and the three times he petitioned the Father to remove the cup from him' (Martin 1986:417).
82. 'It is not certain whether he knew the Gethsemane tradition' (Thrall 2000:819, n. 383); 'Some commentators see in "three times" a parallel to Jesus' prayer in Gethsemane . . . But it is rather unlikely that the word *tris* is intended by Paul as an allusion to this event' (Lambrecht 1999:203).

not include in his prayer 'Yet not my will but yours be done', that is precisely the attitude which he displays in making his own an answer which was not the one he hoped for. Although no answer to Jesus' prayer is recorded, its result is Jesus' unreserved embrace of his Father's purpose that he should fulfil his vocation to bring life to others through his own suffering and death; Paul does receive an answer, whose result is similar to that in the gospel narrative – the following of a path in which the life-giving power of God will be realized only in and through the apparent helplessness of suffering the thorn in the flesh. And the thorn in the flesh, although a metaphor, nonetheless resonates with Jesus' crown of thorns (though the Greek for 'thorn' differs) and with the nails that transfixed Jesus on the cross. So just as Gethsemane represents a definitive moment in which Jesus embraces his Father's painful but life-giving will, so Paul's prayer and the answer he receives become a revelation and appropriation of the will of God in Christ that is definitive for constituting, and discerning, Christian apostolic ministry.

Conclusion

Although there is much further rich content in 2 Corinthians, the nature of Paul's criteria for critical discernment should by now be clear. It may therefore be appropriate to conclude this consideration of Paul by returning to the text from which the argument of this book set out, 1 Thess. 2:13:

> [2:13] We also constantly give thanks to God for this, that when you received the word which you heard from us, which is from God, you accepted it not as a human word but as what it really is, God's word, which is indeed at work in you believers.

Then, the context of the passage was noted only in passing; but it deserves fuller notice. This is so not least because in many recent discussions of these words the focus of interest is mainly on their being the beginning of a discrete paragraph, 2:13–16.[83] This means that the

83. Modern biblical translations consistently start a new paragraph with 2:13, a paragraph which continues to 2:16. Some scholars (esp. Pearson 1971, on whose thesis see Bockmuehl 2001) have suggested that 2:13–16 is a secondary interpolation (Pearson, like others, observes how well 2:17 follows 2:12, with no apparent thought for how well 2:13 follows 2:12). This suggestion focusses the common tendency of debate to engage at length with linguistic, historical, and ideological issues in 2:14–16; in such debate 2:13 is more or less neglected, but gets included by virtue of being in the same paragraph (Pearson says nothing about the content of verse 13 beyond a form-critical observation that it introduces a section of thanksgiving, pp. 88, 91).

divine-in-the-human issue tends to be subordinated to interest in Paul's problematic words about extensive Jewish faithlessness and transgressions in verses 14–16, and the significance afforded for an understanding of 2:13 by what precedes in 2:1–12 is diminished.

> 2:1 You yourselves know, brothers and sisters, that our coming to you
> was not in vain, 2 but though we had already suffered and been
> shamefully maltreated at Philippi, as you know, we had courage in our
> God to declare to you the gospel of God in spite of great opposition.
> 3 For our appeal does not spring from deceit or impure motives or
> trickery, 4 but just as we have been approved by God to be entrusted
> with the message of the gospel, even so we speak, not to please mortals,
> but to please God who tests our hearts. 5 As you know and as God is our
> witness, we never came with words of flattery or with a pretext for
> greed; 6 nor did we seek praise from mortals, whether from you or from
> others, 7 though we might have made demands as apostles of Christ.
> But we were gentle among you, like a nurse tenderly caring for her own
> children. 8 So deeply do we care for you that we are determined to share
> with you not only the gospel of God but also our own selves, because
> you have become very dear to us.
>
> 9 You remember our labour and toil, brothers and sisters; we worked
> night and day, so that we might not burden any of you while we
> proclaimed to you the gospel of God. 10 You are witnesses, and God also,
> how pure, upright, and blameless our conduct was towards you
> believers. 11 As you know, we dealt with each one of you like a father with
> his children, 12 urging and encouraging you and pleading that you
> should lead a life worthy of God, who calls you into his own kingdom
> and glory.

Here Paul gives a striking account of his dealings with the Thessalonians, striking not least because he regularly appeals to the Thessalonians themselves as being in a position to vouch for the truth of what he is saying (verses 1, 2, 5, 9, 10, 11), and more than once he appeals to God as witness (verses 5, 10). How did Paul conduct himself when with the Thessalonians? What he says has many and strong resonances with what we have seen in 2 Corinthians, although there is no comparable emphasis upon the paradoxes of cruciformity.[84] Paul displayed endurance in suffering (verse 2), honesty and purity of purpose in speech (verse 3), lack of concern to curry favour (verses 4a, 5a), concern rather to please a

84. However, Gorman 2001:192–5 (cf. 216–18) offers a suggestive heuristic reading of 1 Thess. 2:5–12 in parallel with Phil. 2:6–8.

God who looks beyond appearances to one's inner reality (verse 4b); he refused to exploit listeners for personal gain (verse 5b), was uninterested in human acclaim from any source (verse 6), was gentle in practical dealings (verse 7), gave of himself in love (verse 8), and worked constantly to pay his own way and so not be a burden on others in upkeep (verse 9). In all, he lived with an integrity to which both God and humans can testify (verse 10), and nurtured the Thessalonians with paternal admonition and encouragement (verses 11–12).

It is surely not accidental that it is in this specific context of self-giving integrity that Paul is able to continue with giving thanks that when the Thessalonians heard his message they heard it for what it really was, the word of God. As elsewhere, a particular kind of (moral) human reality is the necessary corollary for (spiritual) claims to speak on God's behalf to be valid.

Excursus 1: the transferability of Paul's criteria of discernment of authenticity

Paul's argument in 2 Corinthians relates to discernment of the authenticity of his own apostolic ministry. One obvious question to put to his account, especially in the present context, concerns whether what he says of himself applies to others also;[85] and, if it does so apply, whether solely to those in a Christian ministry in some ways analogous to that of Paul, or more widely.

To be sure, the fact of the preservation of 2 Corinthians within the canon of Christian Scripture reflects and generates expectations as to the enduring significance of what Paul says in contexts and for persons other than those originally envisaged. Yet already within Paul's own text there are indications about the transferability to others of what he says of himself.

In the first place, there are Paul's explicit statements in 1 Corinthians. The discussion of food sacrificed to idols (1 Cor. 8:1–11:1) engages with deeply problematic issues of 'faith and culture' in the Corinthian context, and one of the prime ways in which Paul gives guidance to the Corinthians is by appealing to the way in which he conducts his own apostolic ministry (9:1–27).[86] Paul concludes the whole discussion (11:1): 'Be imitators of me, as

85. Güttgemanns 1966:323–38, for example, so distinguishes between apostolic suffering and general Christian suffering that continuity between the two is diminished.

86. The logic of Paul's argument has often been missed, and the sequence within the text has correspondingly been thought to be rather fragmented and lacking coherence. Yet there is now a renewed recognition of the centrality of Paul's account of his ministry for his discussion of idol meat (e.g. Wright 1991b, Barton 2003:1330–6).

I am of Christ.' Paul seeks to model for the Corinthians the new life in Christ with its new priorities, so that they can see for themselves something of what is entailed in faith in Christ. The distinctive practices of Paul's apostolic ministry – especially giving up one's rights for the sake of others – can enable the Corinthians to see how they should conduct themselves in the different sphere of food and social life. Paul takes for granted that imitation is not wooden or slavish but imaginatively non-identical as the priorities of faith in Christ are worked out in the Corinthians' context.

Related to this is Paul's earlier statement (4:6): 'I have applied all this to Apollos and myself for your benefit, brothers and sisters, so that you may learn through us the meaning of the saying, "Nothing beyond what is written",[87] so that none of you will be puffed up in favour of one against another.' The rivalries and divisions to which the Corinthians were clearly prone, not least in thinking about leadership, receive a corrective from Paul and Apollos, who model for the Corinthians what a lifestyle in accordance with Scripture, as understood in the light of Christ, now means. From these explicit statements it is apparent that Paul sees his apostolic lifestyle as having authoritative implications for the Corinthians in their non-identical setting and lifestyle.

Secondly, it is hardly surprising that commentators have followed Paul's lead, where Paul is explicit, so as to infer similar implications elsewhere. Running through Bultmann's commentary on 2 Corinthians, for example (Bultmann 1985:116, 120, 129, 139, 151, 228), is a recurrent emphasis that what Paul says of himself applies to Christians generally. So, for example, in the course of discussing 4:10 Bultmann (p. 116) says:

> What Paul says here of himself as apostle is of course fundamentally true of all believers, not, say, merely of those who labor for Jesus as apostles. In Phil. 3:4–11 Paul is not speaking as an apostle, but sets himself as a type of believer in whom faith as surrender of the *pepoithenai en sarki* ['confidence in the flesh'] becomes visible.[88] In the same way, the statements in 2 Cor. 12:5–10 about God's *dunamis* in *astheneia* ['power' in 'weakness'] are on principle and not especially oriented to the apostle. In particular, the *skolops tē sarki* ['thorn in the flesh'] is clearly a bodily malady and not a consequence of Paul's apostolic activity.[89] After all (when correctly understood), human life is

87. The likely sense of this is 'Not to go beyond what is said in Scripture' (Hays 1997:68–9; with a little qualification, Thiselton 2000:351–6).
88. Compare our discussion of Philippians (above, pp. 174–8).
89. I disagree with this construal; but do not think that this affects the basic point.

> already a participation in Christ's death, for his passion begins with his incarnation.[90]
>
> The sufferings in which the *nekrōsis tou Iēsou* ['dying of Jesus'] is at work are therefore sufferings which may happen to anyone, the Christian in particular, since he must suffer precisely as Christian. The apostle, of course, must suffer all the more. These sufferings become the sufferings of Christ, the *nekrōsis tou Iēsou* by the fact that the one who suffers is in fellowship with Christ and thus can understand his sufferings as those of Christ, can appropriate them in understanding (by faith).

Various of Bultmann's particular points are open to debate. Nonetheless, his sense of how Paul's apostolic ministry is, *mutatis mutandis*, a model for all Christians is recognizably seeking to develop concerns within Paul's writings.[91]

Thirdly, it may be that 2 Corinthians contains a specific application to the Corinthians of the Pauline pattern. This can be found in what Paul says about the collection (2 Cor. 8–9), material whose presence within the letter can often seem a little puzzling: even if the collection was a live issue in Paul's ministry at Corinth, why is it in this letter at this point?[92] It has already been seen that testing (*dokimē*) of Paul is a key issue. With regard to the collection Paul says of his desire that the Corinthians participate (8:8):

> I do not say this as a command, but I am testing [*dokimazōn*] the genuineness of your love [*agapē*] against the earnestness of others.

If love (*agapē*) after the pattern of Christ is *the* key test of authentic Christian spirituality (cf. 1 Corinthians 13 in the context of 1 Corinthians 12–14), then Paul here is using the willingness of the Corinthians to show generosity of spirit to others as a test of the authenticity of their faith in a way that is directly comparable to the testing elsewhere of the authenticity of his apostolic ministry. As Paul's *agapē* is shown in his apostolic

90. A fascinating example of Bultmann the theologian contextualizing, and seeking appropriation of, all his exegetical work within a frame of reference of systematic theology.
91. So too Käsemann 1971:58: 'True apostleship may involve tasks which are different from the tasks of all other members of the church. But its absolutely decisive criterion does not divide the apostle from other Christians. It is the discipleship of the one who was crucified.' Similarly Murphy-O'Connor 1991:147: 'The most fundamental form of the apostolate is existential, which means that it is nothing but the Christian life looked at from another angle. They are two sides of the same coin. Thus, if we abstract from the authority accruing to Paul as the founder of churches, what he says of himself is true of all sincere believers.'
92. The force of this question is of course weakened if 2 Corinthians is seen as a composite collection of Pauline material.

faithfulness, so the Corinthians' *agapē* is to be shown in their joyful generosity; the same core reality will receive differing embodiments and outworkings.

Moreover, just as Paul's understanding of his ministry is at every point patterned on conformity to Christ crucified and risen, so he sees his test of the Corinthians in the same way, for he continues by giving the same christological grounding to his test of them as he employs for himself (8:9):

> For you know the generous act [*charis*][93] of our Lord Jesus Christ, that though he was rich, yet for your sakes he became poor, so that by his poverty you might become rich.

Here Jesus' self-giving is not expressed in terms of death and life, or weakness and strength, because the contextual issue of giving money makes poverty and wealth the appropriate formulation. But the point remains the same. Jesus' self-emptying for the sake of others is what Paul has held up as the rationale for, and critical test of, apostolic authenticity. Yet it is no less the rationale for, and critical test of, the authenticity of the Corinthians' faith.

Excursus 2: does Paul deconstruct his own criteria of apostolic authenticity?

Paul is a controversial figure who provokes strong reactions. Among various negative reactions in modern times, one increasingly common approach has been a suspicious reading of Paul as someone who was self-interested and power-seeking, and correspondingly manipulative and oppressive of others.

It may be appropriate to start with Nietzsche, who had an ability to articulate very forcefully what others tend to say less forcefully. For example, in the course of a slashing and suspicious account of Christianity, *The Antichrist*, which characteristically combines acuteness and obtuseness, Nietzsche says (#42; 1969 [1888]:214):[94]

> The 'good news' was followed closely by the very worst – that of Paul. The opposite type to the 'teller of good news' is embodied in Paul, the genius in hatred, in the vision of hatred, in the relentless logic of

93. *Charis* (classically translated 'grace') is used repeatedly by Paul in this section in a variety of different senses, and it is probably impossible to find a translation that keeps all the rich resonances of the term.
94. ET by Jennifer Moberly.

> hatred ... To take a Paul as being sincere ... when he cobbled together for himself from a hallucination the proof that the Saviour was still living, or even to believe his story that he had this hallucination, would be a true silliness on the part of a psychologist. Paul wanted the end, consequently he also wanted the means ... [Nietzsche's ellipsis] What he himself didn't believe, the idiots among whom he cast his teachings did believe. – His need was power; with Paul the priest wanted to regain power, – he could only use terms, doctrines and symbols, with which one can tyrannize masses and form herds.

A recent intellectual heir of Nietzsche, via the mediation of Foucault, seems to me to be Elizabeth Castelli (1991). Although her work is a study of Paul in general, with special reference to Paul's occasional appeals to his readers to imitate him (*mimēsis*), and there is no specific reference to 2 Corinthians, much of what she says has obvious applicability to an evaluation of that letter. Her basic thesis is (p. 15):

> The notion of mimesis functions in Paul's letters as a strategy of power. That is, it articulates and rationalizes as true a particular set of power relations within the social formation of early Christian communities.

The problem for Castelli is that what Paul is doing through his appeal to his readers to imitate him is to try to establish as natural, and beyond debate, a narrowing 'sameness' which obliterates 'difference', even though the promotion and celebration of 'difference' is humanly enriching – a conceptuality which Castelli has learned and appropriated from Foucault and Derrida (among others).[95] So she regards it as vital to read Paul with an 'ironic distance' (pp. 29, 32, 97) that preserves the reader from succumbing to or replicating Paul's problematic ideology. She sums up her analysis of the significance of Paul's appeals for imitation thus (pp. 103, 115):

> Sameness, unity, and harmony are to be achieved through imitation; they also circumscribe the community which is unified, in contrast to those who are different. By implication, difference is equated with

95. Compare Adele Berlin's observation (2002:188–9) about the conduct of biblical criticism and interpretation: 'We may characterize an overarching tenet of the middle of the twentieth century as the suppression of difference [in study conducted in historical-critical mode], to be compared with the tenet at the end of the twentieth century – the celebration of difference [in study conducted in postmodern mode]. In biblical studies the suppression of difference manifests itself as academic ecumenism and the celebration of difference as academic multiculturalism.'

> diffusion, disorder, and discord. So, difference is placed outside of the community, and literally has no place in the community . . . 'Become imitators of me' is a call to sameness which erases difference and, at the same time, reinforces the authoritative status of the model . . . It is the Christians' sameness that is their salvation, while it is the non-Christians' difference that is their damnation.

Although Castelli roots what she says in a study of *mimēsis* in antiquity, it is clear that she is concerned to address contemporary culture, which continues, *mutatis mutandis,* to promote a biblical/Pauline conceptuality (p. 124, cf. pp. 127, 131): 'Western culture embraces identity and sameness while it rejects difference, which is generally figured either as the failure to achieve identity or as a threatening challenge to identity.' Her ultimate goal is not simply to promote difference over sameness, for that would preserve the conceptualization that has given rise to the problem, but rather to replace thinking in terms of sameness and difference altogether (p. 134):

> Reinscribing difference – diffusing the question of identity through multiple differences – remains the next, if almost unthinkable, step in Western (Christian) culture, a culture that has reached certain limits through its continued allegiance to totalizing positions and unproblematized notions of identity.

Thus for Castelli, as for Nietzsche, one central interest in Paul (or other biblical writers/texts)[96] is the overcoming of what are perceived to be the malign effects of Christianity in some of the fundamental structuring assumptions of contemporary culture.

Suspicion of Paul, however, has been internalized in one way or another by a good number who live and write actively from within the Christian faith. One well-known work, prior to that of Castelli, is Graham Shaw 1983. Influenced in particular by Tolstoy and Dostoyevsky, Shaw utilizes a particular notion of freedom to practise a kind of extensive *Sachkritik* in New Testament interpretation,[97] in which his concern is to challenge the dishonesty and unacknowledged self-interest that characterize much Christianity and 'to write a genuinely evangelical theology,

96. This wider biblical engagement is provided by The Bible and Culture Collective 1995, where Castelli was both contributor and editor; on which see my comments in Moberly 2000:26–37.

97. 'It is only by identifying the witness in the New Testament to authentic authority which both frees and reconciles, and using that as a criterion for interpreting the New Testament as a whole, that we may hope not to repeat the old mistakes of Christian history' (p. 23).

which makes a concern for the gospel the key to the scriptures' (p. 276).[98] The problem is, he alleges, that, although there is indeed material in Paul which truly points the way to genuine freedom (pp. 182–4), most of what Paul says points in less healthy directions, which are predominantly both self-regarding and manipulative ('bullying', p. 119). Thus Shaw concludes his exposition of 2 Corinthians (p. 125):

> Paul's dilemma is that his use of authority to improve is dependent on the effectiveness of his threat to destroy. For all his talk of weakness and identification with the cross, it is by no means clear that he stands with the crucified. There is a horrid suspicion that he ultimately stands with those who were prepared to crucify in order to defend and preserve their position. In this the Christian Paul is not perhaps so different from the persecuting Saul.[99]

More locally, I would also note the work of a colleague and friend in Durham, David Brown, a systematic theologian who works substantively with Scripture, and whose recent work has been commended by James Barr (1999:603) as an 'ideal example' of the kind of work that holds promise for the future in biblical theology. In the course of a recent review of Garrett Green's *Theology, Hermeneutics, and Imagination* (2000), Brown focusses on the inadequacy (in his judgment) of Green's handling of Nietzsche's suspicious approach to the Bible and raises this objection (Brown 2001:658):

> What, for instance, of all those situations in which the Bible appears to read not as a great summons to an alternative morality but more as a rather sad attempt by the weak to manipulate situations to their own advantage? An obvious example would be the attempts of Paul to bolster his own status by undermining, either explicitly or implicitly, the authority of others.

Since there is more undermining of the authority of others in 2 Corinthians than elsewhere in the Pauline corpus, this letter seems to me a prime example of what Brown finds questionable. It is particularly

98. This 'evangelical' concern for 'the gospel' is, however, combined with an understanding that 'the only reality of God lies in the use of that word by human beings', so that the word 'God' is a verbal 'means by which we transcend the given and transform ourselves and the world' (p. 282).

99. Comparable is the way in which Stuart 1991 makes appreciative use of Shaw's work. Stuart argues the thesis that, contrary to popular supposition, the famous material about love in 1 Corinthians 13 is 'Paul at his most manipulative' and that it is her task in the article 'to expose what Paul is really up to under the mask of sublimity' (p. 265).

striking that Paul's self-interested manipulativeness is, apparently, so 'obvious' that it needs no argument; at least to some extent Nietzsche was undoubtedly right.

Is it therefore the case that Paul's account of his apostolic authority is only coherent or plausible on a superficial and blinkered reading? If one probes the rhetoric and the implied power relations within Paul's text, does a rather different account emerge in which the reality of what is going on exposes a fundamental contradiction within Paul's theology, which renders it either empty or sinister? Does Paul preach love and reconciliation, but practise egotism and manipulation? Although these issues cannot be fully dealt with here,[100] it is nonetheless important to give some indication of how best I think they should be approached.[101]

In the first place, it must be entirely acknowledged that what Paul says is open to egotistical and manipulative use, and has been so used in the history of the Church. As Albert Camus (1963:84) once nicely put the egotistical point: 'Too many people now climb on crosses merely to be seen from a greater distance, even if they have to trample somewhat on the one who has been there so long.' Indeed it is hard to see how matters could be otherwise, for the greater and more weighty the truth claim, the greater the possibilities of using it for aggrandizement of self and to deceive or impose upon others. However, the ancient axiom *abusus non tollit usum* remains a reminder that one must always seek to distinguish right and understanding use from wrong and more or less incomprehending misuse. To be sure, Castelli and Shaw in their differing ways each give the impression that Paul is so intrinsically manipulative that there is little or no right and non-manipulative use of him from which misuse could be distinguished;[102] but I cannot find that they properly argue this, rather than assume it and then exemplify their assumption.

For my second observation is that one would hardly know from any of the above that there is other than a manipulative claim to authority in what Paul says and does. That is, the very notion that Paul is at pains in 2 Corinthians to articulate criteria of critical discernment whereby

100. On Shaw and/or Castelli see further, for example, Thiselton 1995:137–44, Thrall 2000:955–60.

101. I will not engage with Nietzsche, for that would be a major discussion in itself, or with Brown; but parts of what I say with reference to Castelli and Shaw would apply equally to these others.

102. The exception is Shaw's allowance that there is at least a little material in Paul that genuinely points the way to freedom.

the Corinthians could be enabled *to discern for themselves* who does, and who does not, speak for Christ is entirely lacking in both Castelli and Shaw.[103] To be sure, Paul articulates these criteria with reference to himself as role model for the way of Christ crucified and risen. Nonetheless, the fact that he wants to enable the Corinthians to know how to discern does not suggest a desire to keep them in uncritical subjection; for once they realize that discernment is possible, and know how Paul says it should be achieved, then it could readily be used against him. For Paul himself is emphatic that it is only as he demonstrates conformity to the pattern of Christ that he is to be acknowledged as authentic; and I do not think it is mere fantasy to suppose that Paul would have acknowledged, indeed welcomed, criticism of himself by his own criteria should he at some point have faltered in living by them (cf. 1 Cor. 9:27, Gal. 1:8).[104]

Following from this, my third concern is that neither Castelli nor Shaw allows Paul's voice to be heard. Paul's concern, that familiar exploitative and competitive patterns of human life should be fundamentally reconfigured in the light of Christ so that people can be set free to become more truly that which the Creator wills for his creation, ought to be recognizable as a concern for human flourishing which, *mutatis mutandis*, Castelli and Shaw also share. Yet their readings are so unsympathetic that a time-honoured principle – that those with whom one wishes to disagree or whom one wishes to rebut should be allowed a fair hearing – is not observed. In this regard it is interesting to see how strong ideological suspicion functions so similarly to some theological dogmas; because in certain important senses one knows in advance what a reading of the text is going to come up with, it is almost impossible to get sufficiently close to the text genuinely to hear its voice and allow oneself to be open to be

103. Shaw (pp. 122–3), for example, can only see the criterion of 'power in weakness' in 2 Corinthians 12 as yet one more clever ploy: 'Since identification with the sufferings of Christ seems to have been one of the ways in which Paul established his own apostolic authenticity, it may be that his distinctive perspective of death and resurrection is itself related to his own position . . . It may be that the selection he made [sc. of references to Jesus' life] did not represent so much an early Christian consensus about what was most important in the new religion [though why should such consensus be the criterion of true insight?] as a Pauline perception of these elements in the new religion which were most compatible with his own claims and might be exploited for his own advantage.'

104. My concern is not to try to maintain that what Paul says should be construed as somehow devoid of dimensions of 'interest' or 'power', but rather that Paul's theological language genuinely and consistently 'attempts . . . [both] transparency to God's power (God's endless resource and accessibility) . . . [and] the *giving* of power to those addressed (the resource of God offered for liberation or renewal)' – if I may utilize the wording of Rowan Williams' searching essay on theological integrity (Williams 2000:8).

surprised or challenged by what one hears.[105] Some of the battles that were fought in the nineteenth century to permit the biblical text to be heard in its own right (even if such a notion may in fact be much more complex than many of its advocates realized) may need to be fought again, *mutatis mutandis*, in relation to ideological suspicion.

Fourthly, another facet of this same issue becomes apparent within Castelli in relation to her repeated rhetoric concerning 'sameness' and 'difference'. For all that she emphasizes that Paul should not be read in an abstract way but in relation to on-the-ground social processes in which people's lives can be affected by what Paul says, she never stops to ask how he might have envisaged compliance with his injunctions to imitation.[106] For example, Paul clearly does not want the Corinthians to become apostolic missionaries like himself, even though that would arguably be the most obvious, prima facie sense of his injunction. Or, in other words, the notion of non-identical imitation, which Paul clearly takes for granted, is never mentioned, still less explored, by Castelli;[107] would the expression of love in generous giving (2 Cor. 8:8–9) be recognized by her as an appropriate imitation of Paul's apostolic sufferings, and, if so, would it still qualify solely as exemplifying 'sameness'? Alternatively, one might suppose that an account which emphasizes Pauline attachment to 'sameness' and hostility to 'difference' would at least give some space to Paul's conception of diversity within the body of Christ (1 Corinthians 12). Castelli only mentions this in passing (p. 130), and then solely to make the point that 'this organic model [sc. of the body, used by Aristotle as well as by Paul] not only inscribes a naturalness within socially-constituted relations, it also implies that social order is self-evidently a unity, a closed system with no loose ends, no remainder. However, no social organization begins as a systemic or structural unity.'

105. A genuinely heuristic use of suspicion would not be open to this criticism. For the present, the point is that neither Castelli nor Shaw uses it heuristically.
106. Nor does she engage with Paul's explicit repudiation of groupings whose identity is defined in relation to himself (1 Cor. 1:11–15) – though she dismissively depicts what Paul says as a whole in 1:10–18 as a 'clever rhetorical gesture' (p. 99).
107. Compare the strikingly different reading of Paul in Gorman 2001:382–3: 'Cruciformity is both predictable and unpredictable in its comprehensiveness. It is predictable in that it always excludes certain options, such as vengeance; it is unpredictable in that it is the work of the Spirit of the living Christ, whose faithful act of self-giving on the cross can never be replicated but is always being reactualized. By its very nature – its inability to be repeated – the cross must always be new and different even as it is consistent with the unrepeatable act of the Son of God. Thus cruciformity cannot be inscribed or legislated; it cannot be codified or routinized. It can only be remembered and recited, hymned and prayed, and then lived by the power of the Spirit and the work of inspired individual and corporate imagination.'

Castelli's rhetoric of 'sameness' is not allowed to be tested by probing the possible implications of all that Paul says.[108]

Fifthly, one gets no sense in either Castelli or Shaw of how Paul might be expected to handle a conflictual situation in which life-giving truth is at stake. Because Castelli and Shaw do not accept the premise that life-giving truth is at stake in what Paul says about his witness to Christ crucified and risen, and correspondingly do not attempt imaginatively to place themselves in Paul's situation, they do not address, even hypothetically, the question of what might be necessary to maintain the kind of truth to which Paul bears witness. If (let one imagine) the Corinthians are confused as to the implications of their new faith and are inclined to import assumptions and practices from their pre-Christian lives which unwittingly undermine their new faith, then how might Paul appropriately deal with this? Among other things, if they badly need an actual example of the transformed way of life which marks faith in Christ so that they might be enabled better to realize what is involved, then should Paul's offering of himself as such an example be intrinsically incapable of a positive interpretation? Alternatively, if (let one imagine) the fundamental reconstrual of the purpose and priorities of human life that arises from faith in God through Christ is being actively attacked and undermined by those who would prefer a less demanding understanding of faith, then how is Paul to keep in place that frame of reference and those practices which would genuinely demonstrate the full scope and meaning of Christ's death and resurrection? Is there no way in which a firm exercise of authority and discipline in such a situation, alongside appropriate attempts at reasoned persuasion (together with a strong ironic recognition of the dynamics of the situation), could be understood as the least bad, or at least a not unacceptable, procedure for seeking to resolve the conflict? To entertain such possibilities is not to resolve all the problems, but it should at least make it possible for Paul's approach to be taken seriously.

For, sixthly, there are indeed difficulties for many a reader in knowing what to make of Paul's rhetoric and tone in some passages, not least 2 Corinthians 10–12. Although some of the difficulties may be caused by

108. One might also note that Castelli's analysis is entirely directed towards the 'historical' Paul and not the 'canonical' Paul; that is, she does not reflect on the possible difference made by Paul's placement within the New Testament canon where other, distinct, voices are recognized as authoritative alongside his.

a failure to catch Paul's precise meaning,[109] there remain at least two problems. On the one hand, there is the strongly polemical language, which sounds far from gracious; on the other hand, there are warnings of discipline and exclusion, which sound far from self-giving service of others; neither sounds like an embodiment of *agapē*. With regard to the former, it must be recognized that conventions for language considered appropriate to controversy vary greatly from culture to culture and from context to context. Since Luke Johnson (1989), among others, has shown that conventions throughout the Hellenistic world were 'robust' in this regard,[110] it is important not to import anachronistic standards of evaluation, however much we may not consider it appropriate to practise Paul's kind of rhetoric ourselves. With regard to the latter, there is no simple answer. It remains the case, however, that the value of discipline is usually only seen in the long term rather than the short term;[111] and so it needs to be evaluated not by how pleasant or nasty it seems at the time but whether in the long run it succeeds in moulding often-recalcitrant people into patterns of more genuine human flourishing (even if this may include a parting of the ways with those who resist those particular patterns). Or, in other terms, the display of love may be a complex matter in many situations of life (cf. the contemporary idiom of 'tough love'). I have argued, for example, that Micaiah's encounter with Ahab is a demonstration of love and compassion (both divine and human) towards Ahab, even though the dynamics of the moment make it entirely inappropriate for anything overtly 'loving' to be said. So too, it may be that Paul's disciplinary warnings express an *agapē*, which could not be expressed in more overt ways in such a conflictual context.

Finally, much comes down to the question of whom one trusts in life, and why. Castelli and Shaw do not trust Paul, and so practise a suspicious reading with 'ironic distance'. Yet it is notable that they do not practise a

109. So, for example, Paul's depiction of his opponents as, *inter alia*, 'ministers of Satan' (2 Cor. 11:15) is sometimes taken to be denying the Christian faith of such people and simply consigning them to perdition. Yet it is likely that Paul's language is more *ad hoc*, its point being that these 'false apostles', in what they are currently doing in Corinth, are furthering the purposes of deception of themselves and others and, consequently, are 'serving Satan'. To be sure, if they persist then the result will be disastrous ('their end will match their deeds'); but Paul need no more be denying the Christian profession (and hope) of these opponents than he denies it to the Corinthians themselves when he appeals for them to be reconciled to God alongside reconciliation with himself (5:18–6:3).

110. 'Readers today hear the NT's polemic as inappropriate only because the other voices are silent' (1989:441).

111. One might compare the account of paternal discipline in Heb. 12:5–11 as something only really appreciated in the long term.

suspicious reading or keep an ironic distance with regard to their preferred 'authorities' (Foucault and Derrida for Castelli, Tolstoy among others for Shaw – even though each is careful not to treat them as 'authorities' in a traditional sense). Those who are challenged for a failure to maintain 'ironic distance' (or equivalent)[112] with regard to Paul (or other biblical writers) are entitled to put a comparable challenge to their interlocutors with regard to those writers whose insights they themselves appropriate: why do they trust the insights of, e.g., Foucault and decline to read him with 'ironic distance'? Of course, all such questions of where, and why, one places trust are enormously complex; and the trust itself can be of varying degrees, with no need to be all or nothing. But one must stand somewhere: one must trust some account of what the priorities of life and thought should be. My point at present is solely that to trust Paul – which includes trusting the historic decision of the Church to include Paul's writings within Scripture as a true revelation of the mind of Christ, whether or not this was entirely appreciated by those to whom he wrote – is no more unreasonable, and need be no less discerning, than the decision to trust any other person, or community, in their vision of life. Which recipient of trust is a *better*, more deserving, recipient still of course remains an open question; but this book as a whole is an attempt to show how one might begin to offer an answer.

112. I think, for example, of the common contemporary urgings to read 'against the grain' of the biblical text.

7

Prophecy and discernment today?

> I am not by any means suggesting that the experience of God in the world is accessible for casual perusal. These matters require careful attention and delicate diagnosis. The process of discernment is risk-filled, and never self-validating. The interpretation of the present moment in terms of God's activity is perilous, prone to error and false prophecy, and at the very least requires constant renewal and revision. But such discernment, such interpretation of God's word as speaking through the fabric of human lives is the absolutely fundamental and necessary task of theology. Without it, there is no subject matter.
>
> – LUKE TIMOTHY JOHNSON (JOHNSON 1995:283; cf. JOHNSON 1996:31)

In this final chapter I will seek briefly to do five things. First, I will draw together the threads of the preceding argument. Secondly, I will argue that some common assumptions about the nature of prophecy and its evaluation are mistaken. Thirdly, I will seek to clarify the nature of the biblical criteria of discernment through consideration of possible difficulties affecting their use. Fourthly, I will present some case studies that illuminate the possible use of the criteria. Finally, I will offer some concluding reflections on what is at stake in the whole discussion.

1 The question, the approach, and the thesis: a summary

Restatement of the problem

My focal concern throughout has been prophetic authenticity and the criteria for its discernment within both Old and New Testaments. The customary approach to prophecy in modern scholarship has been to give a historical, comparative, and developmental account – unarguably an exercise with obvious strengths. In this, however, questions of authenticity (re the claim to speak for God rather than re the composition of the literature) are usually optional and marginal. Yet part of my thesis is that if prophecy is to be other than an interesting phenomenon of the past – and its continuing validity in certain forms is a premise of Christian faith (and, *mutatis mutandis*, of Judaism and Islam also) – then the question of how it might be critically tested should be seen as integral. For if there were no rational and disciplined way of discriminating between claims to speak for God, or of knowing when human speech should and should not appropriately be recognized as being in some way a word from God, the consequences would be far-reaching. It is difficult to see how religious language could avoid being an elaborate and mystifying code which, when not merely esoteric, could hardly be recognized as more than the dressing up of human values and priorities in exotic garments; and commonly the plurality of religious voices and claims would be no better than a cacophony, a troublesome and often manipulative imposition upon life. If such were indeed the case, then one could hardly deny that the characteristic modern approach would indeed be the best approach: the redescription of such voices in social-scientific categories, especially those of psychology and sociology, that bracket out God and theology, and the marginalizing of such voices so that they no longer trouble the public sphere and can be confined to what consenting adults say and do in private (or, in some cases, in the wards of psychiatric hospitals). One would then be free to concentrate upon the real issues of life, which, however hard and intractable, may at least be amenable to some genuine amelioration if one is persistent and not distracted.[1]

If the key issue is criteria for discerning the word of God in human words, then the issue revolves around knowing what to look for and how to recognize it. What should it mean in some way to hear or see the divine in the human? Does the human somehow becomes less human ('dehumanized') if it is in any way a channel for, or locus of the presence of, God?

1. I am reminded of the concerns with which Jonathan Edwards prefaced his classic account of general spiritual discernment, the *Treatise Concerning Religious Affections*, which was written when the religious revivals in eighteenth-century New England were proving problematic: ''Tis by the mixture of counterfeit religion with true, not discerned and distinguished, that the devil has had his greatest advantage against the cause and kingdom of Christ, all along, hitherto . . . And by what is seen of the terrible consequences of this counterfeit religion, when not distinguished from true religion, God's people in general have their minds unhinged and unsettled, in things of religion, and know not where to set their foot, or what to think or do; and many are brought into doubts, whether there be anything at all in religion; and heresy, and infidelity, and atheism greatly prevail' (Edwards 1959 [1746]:86, 89).

Should God be found in phenomena or experiences that appear humanly unusual, indeed humanly inexplicable (the 'god of the gaps')? As a particular form of this last question, should human speech if it is to be recognized as God's speech be characterized by unusual mental states, such as visions, trances, or locutions, which would lead to the modern supposition that one should ascribe 'religious experience' to unusual psychology and chemically or neurologically altered brain states?

All these questions are forms of one basic issue, which in convenient theological shorthand is the relationship between 'nature' (the familiar human realm) and 'grace' (the supernatural work of God). As noted at the end of Chapter 1, one way of easily skewing reflection on this issue from the outset is the legacy of early modern philosophy and science to define 'nature' in such a way as to exclude God; for 'nature' becomes not the order created and sustained by God but rather the empirically examinable world whose analysis and explanation are to be conducted by the appropriate scientific methods, in which context all reference to 'God' contributes nothing of substance. 'God' then becomes (if not merely the famous 'unnecessary hypothesis') an outsider, an intruder, somewhat on a par with ghosts or UFOs, and divine 'transcendence' is only given substance by appeals to what generally seems to be a curious kind of 'interference' with the world. By contrast I indicated at the outset that if progress is to be made with questions of prophetic discernment and authenticity, there must necessarily be a way of understanding 'nature' in which 'grace' is not, as it were, excluded. Rather than discussing this in general terms, however, the mode of argument has been to see how the biblical texts portray 'grace' in contexts where the divine engagement with prophet and apostle is contested.

Method and approach

My selection of biblical passages for discussion has been to some extent conventional, though it is also heuristic and must be justified by its fruitfulness. I have included, I think, all the best-known and most commonly referred-to biblical texts in this general area, as well as some less well-known. I have sought to do this in such a way that it becomes clear that the primary sustained biblical engagements with the issue of critical discernment of speech for God are Jeremiah in the OT and 2 Corinthians in the NT, where the construal of particular texts belongs within an understanding of the wider context of argument. Within the OT, the story of Micaiah resonates closely with the terminology and conceptuality of

Jeremiah, and so further illustrates the nature of the conceptual foundation for my thesis. The stories of Elisha and Balaam address the question of what is necessary for seeing God, in a way that is unusual in discussions of discernment of prophetic authenticity yet is important if a major dimension is not to be neglected. Within the NT, Jesus in Matt. 7:15–23 speaks substantially within the OT's frame of reference. John in his first letter offers a distinctive voice, complementary to that of Paul; like Paul he sees Jesus as the key to discernment of God, and like Paul he offers a summary confessional formula to express this (1 John 4:2–3, 1 Cor. 12:3). To be sure, he has his own way of expounding how the reality of Jesus should be displayed in those whose speech and faith are critically scrutinized – though he, like Paul, sees love as central (1 John 4:8, 16, 1 Corinthians 13).

The general approach of my argument has been to relate the specifics of a historically aware,[2] imaginatively serious, and existentially engaged close reading of the biblical text to an attempt to think synthetically and constructively in relation to the differing voices of Scripture. One of the recurrent problems of mainstream modern biblical criticism has been that concern for analytical ability to trace distinct voices and diverse traditions in relation to their originating contexts, and more recently to analyse sophisticated literary poetics or to re-engage with reception history or to offer ideological criticism of the biblical texts, has often been at the expense of interest or confidence in synthetic ability to use the voices of Scripture in constructive moral and theological thinking – not infrequently with a suspicion that the latter is likely both to be methodologically problematic and to indulge in oversimplifications whose homiletic strength is at the expense of critical weakness. I hope to have shown – though with what degree of success the reader must decide – that attentiveness to the precise contours and distinctiveness of some of the voices of the OT and the NT is enriched by comparable hermeneutical attentiveness to overarching moral, theological, and spiritual concerns.

One issue that has deliberately been left open is the relationship between the criteria for discernment of authenticity in Old and New Testaments respectively – how, for example, does one best relate Jeremiah's criteria to those of Paul? This is because Christian appropriation of the Bible as a

2. I mean 'historically aware' in the sense that I have sought to understand each text as an ancient Hebrew or Greek composition arising out of ancient contexts of thought and practice that have coloured the texts throughout. I have not sought to contribute to debate about how the texts, and the thought within them, developed in relation to each other or to their originating contexts.

whole necessarily lives with a certain openness and constructive tension. On the one hand, one seeks to hear and respect and learn from the distinctive witness of the OT on its own terms; the integrity of the OT's witness means that patterns of spiritual life and discernment which are characterized by the searching call of the one God, even if they lack recognition of Jesus Christ, can be recognized by a Christian as in principle valid. On the other hand, one appropriates that witness only in the light of Christ, which introduces a recontextualizing, and so reconceiving and reprioritizing, of the OT; Christian discernment will most affirm those patterns that are seen as intrinsically oriented towards that which is realized in the life, death, and resurrection of Jesus.

Summary of the argument

The essence of the thesis that cumulatively runs through these texts is simple. Negatively, people too often are looking for the wrong thing. Quell (1952:67), for example, says that the core problem in true and false prophecy is that it is insoluble on internal grounds (*aus der Sache unlösbar*) because subjective genuineness/sincerity (*subjektive Echtheit*) does not guarantee objective truth (*objektive Wahrheit*). Indeed, sincerity proves nothing.[3] But sincerity or strength of conviction are beside the point,[4] for the genuinely core issue, the human appropriation of the qualities of God and its right recognition, is otherwise constituted.

Positively, the argument is that the visible gives access to the invisible; the moral gives critical purchase on the spiritual. Claims to speak for God can be meaningfully tested both in terms of the moral character, disposition, and behaviour of the speaker and in terms of the moral and theological content of the message. The related corollaries and implications of such claims – having access to the mind of God via 'standing in the divine council' or 'having the mind of Christ' (or whatever image of human proximity to the will of God is used), and speaking at divine initiative through being 'sent' by God – can also be authenticated, or discredited, in exactly the same way. Jeremiah, Micaiah, John, and Paul, for all their

3. Compare Rodinson on Muhammad and Locke on enthusiasm (above, p. 24).
4. One useful rule of thumb for recognizing anachronisms is to ask how the term/concept in question might be expressed in biblical Hebrew or Greek. I can think of no ancient Hebrew or Greek term with the same resonances as the modern notion of being 'sincere' – words like Heb. *tām* (or in Qumran texts *yētser sāmūk*) or Gk *katharos, eilikrinēs, haplous* have a moral, and sometimes ritual, register that is lacking in 'sincere', and would not, I think, be used, as 'sincere' can be, in contexts where a person is considered to be misguided or mistaken. This may perhaps serve as a further indicator that sincerity is not the concern of the biblical texts.

many differences from each other, have been seen to be in fundamental continuity with each other in their understanding of how critical discernment of authenticity in relation to speech for God should be exercised. All are entirely clear that certain claims to speak for God are spurious and should not be heeded, and this clarity is rooted in their respective understandings of the nature and character of God and of God's call upon the human.

To be sure, the speech for God that is recognized as authentic is consistently that of Jeremiah, Micaiah, John, and Paul themselves, and this fact can easily excite the suspicion that the whole exercise is viciously circular in an ideological and self-serving way.[5] Nonetheless, the texts make clear that what is at stake is far more serious than mere *amour propre* or ideological self-assertion (however common these may be among some of the epigoni). Searching language about the nature of moral truth and integrity is used in all the texts we have looked at – whether it be the difficulty of true turning to God, of resisting self-serving language, of practising justice (Jeremiah), or the costly resisting of conventional priorities and of self-promotion at the expense of others, and the embrace of the cruciform pattern of power in weakness (Paul). Moreover, Jeremiah and Paul, *mutatis mutandis*, are alike at pains not to indulge in self-justification (even if at times it can appear thus to the unsympathetic reader) but rather to articulate criteria by which *anyone* claiming to speak for God could be recognized as authentic – even if there were no obvious candidates for authenticity other than themselves in their immediate contested situations.

A related issue is that Jeremiah, Micaiah, John, and Paul generally imply or articulate in one way or other – in ways analogous to what is perhaps most clearly and memorably depicted in the Elisha and Balaam stories – that the exercise of critical discernment is itself demanding of the would-be discerner in the same basic categories as apply to the speaker under scrutiny, even if to a lesser degree. The self-seeking or complacent or compromised are, to the degree that they lack appropriate openness, less well placed to discern the extent of moral integrity and spiritual reality in others. As Paul puts it, spiritual matters and persons are spiritually discerned (1 Cor. 2:11–16). Ahab appears not incapable of

5. Of course, any world view or ultimate truth claim will always be in some sense circular, for that which is ultimate must, by definition, contain its own justification; but it remains important in the course of argument not to appeal to ultimacy prematurely.

some kind of realization of Micaiah's integrity and authenticity, but he refuses to allow this to make a difference because the personal moral cost (renouncing ambition, pride, and self-will) is too great; and so the partial perception becomes no better in its effect than no perception, and serves only to underline the cowardice of the self-deceiving king. Seeing is not straightforward, for vision and character are inextricably intertwined.

2 Three common but mistaken approaches

In the light of this overall argument, we may address three particular concerns about prophecy and its possible validation, concerns which are recurrent and yet, I suggest, misdirected.

Does God dehumanize the prophets?

The anxiety that an account of divine impact upon a prophet might in some ways dehumanize the prophet, and so diminish the intrinsic worth of being human, was forcefully expressed by McKane from a perspective of Christian faith; and seemed also to be shared, *mutatis mutandis*, by Parris as an avowed atheist. So it appears to represent a characteristic contemporary concern. Yet the enduring baneful effects of some of the early modern reconceptualizations of God and humanity are hardly more evident than in the change from seeing God as the one who enables life to become what it is meant to be (as in the classic tradition)[6] to seeing God as the one who imposes, displaces, diminishes (as in the characteristic contemporary anxiety).

It should be clear by now that the biblical material under discussion gives no grounds for the anxiety. If moral integrity (in convenient shorthand) is *the* quality that must characterize a prophet's speech and life, and represents the key to discernment of that prophet's authenticity, then life is enriched, not diminished, by the prophetic vocation; and likewise an ability to see more clearly what is there (and may not be superficially evident) is an enrichment for the person who thus sees. To be sure, the enrichment is not always straightforward, for responsiveness to God can

6. A classic axiom is that 'grace perfects nature' (cf. Aquinas, *De Veritate* 27.6 ad 1; the Latin verb is *perficio*). Like all shorthand formulations it is easily misunderstood, not least if it is taken in such a way as to minimize the possible disruptive and paradoxical nature of 'perfecting', as epitomized in the mystery of Christ's death and resurrection. The point is that, as people are transformed by divine grace, they can realize the true potential of their being – what they are 'meant to be'.

often make life harder because more demanding, and can engender costly conflict with self-will and evil; and those who respond fully to God may also defy usual expectations of what enriched human life should look like (a prophet like Ezekiel or a saint such as St Francis of Assisi would not easily take a place in regular social gatherings). Nonetheless, the anxiety that belief in God may diminish humanity has no place in the Bible because the biblical writers see coming close to God as coming close to the truth of human being. The writers of OT and NT alike see the authentic prophet as authentic because that prophet embodies and displays the character and concerns of God which also instantiate what it means for humans to be made in the image of God. As Karl Rahner (1966:12) put it (with reference to understanding what is involved in orthodox christology):

> It must always be borne in mind that for a really Christian doctrine of the world to God, the autonomy of the creature does not grow in inverse but in direct proportion to the degree of the creature's dependence on, and belonging to, God.

Greater proximity to God brings more, not less, freedom and dignity. Or as Ulrich Luz recently put it, in the context of discussing Paul and mysticism not least with reference to 2 Corinthians (Luz 2004:141):

> The fact that the suffering Christ transfers and re-forms Paul's life does not extinguish his personal existence, but forms it in an extremely demanding way. It is certainly not by chance that in the whole of the early period of Christianity, and, I think, in almost the whole religious history of antiquity, there is hardly a person who comes across to us as such an unmistakable individual as this Paul, although – or rather, precisely because – he himself no longer lives, but Christ lives in him.

When we recall McKane's contention (above, p. 30) that 'the prophet absorbs the mysterious experience into his humanity, filtering it through human modes of apprehension and evaluation, and causing it to issue in a linguistic form which is human and not divine', we can see more clearly how infelicitous is that final characterization of the form of prophetic speech as 'human and not divine', and how that particular disjunction as it were epitomizes his difficulties over dehumanizing. Of course, the linguistic form is a human linguistic form, comparable to other speech forms in Israel and elsewhere. But what matters is that the prophetic speech is most truly human when it is also most responsive to God. If the point cannot be grasped that God is the enabler of, and not the threat to, human life and speech becoming most truly itself (however disorienting and disrupting the process may be), then the whole biblical conception of revelation and grace must necessarily remain more or less opaque.

Does psychology explain prophecy?

On one level our discussion has not directly addressed the issue of the psychological conceptualities utilized by Rodinson and others to 'explain' prophecy. But this is because in all the material we have surveyed there has been no interest in, or appeal to, unusual psychological states, or practices that might induce or accompany them. Within Jeremiah, we have seen that to construe the reference to 'standing in the divine council' as depicting some kind of 'ecstasy' (or whatever) is a straight misreading of the text. Micaiah indeed speaks of two visions. But these visions are not used as a ground for giving him credence, for the dynamics of the story revolve entirely around the nature of the response to the challenging content of the visions.[7] The narratives that depict Elisha and Balaam as seeing or unseeing say nothing about mental states, but are interested rather in human dispositions. John's account of love, as the practical outworking of faith in Jesus, is not even interested in the emotions, never mind the psychology, that may accompany love. Paul indeed mentions the remarkable experience of being taken up to the third heaven (2 Cor. 12:1–4), but shows no interest in speaking of it, and clearly subordinates it to the communicable revelation of grace as sufficient and of power as realized in weakness. At most this rapture functions in the same way as speaking in tongues – those spiritual experiences to which others can lay claim, Paul lays claim to as well, and yet he does so only in order to downplay their significance and to direct attention elsewhere for the truly significant marks of spiritual authenticity.

To say this is not, of course, to deny the presence in many a biblical narrative of varying kinds of 'ecstatic' practices or behaviour accompanying the delivering of prophecy; Saul, for example, behaves remarkably (so much so as to provoke a proverb) when the spirit of God comes upon him (1 Sam. 10:10–13); or Elisha requests music for the hand of YHWH to come upon him (2 Kgs. 3:15); or, in the NT, astonishing events on the day of Pentecost precede Peter's address (Acts 2). My point is the absence of

7. It is also not unlikely that Micaiah's second vision (1 Kgs. 22:19–22) is primarily an imaginative rhetorical expedient to try to penetrate Ahab's self-will and complacency.

reference to, or the downplaying of, such things in those texts we have considered which are concerned with norms and criteria of critical discernment; 'ecstatic' practices and behaviour are recognized as sometimes happening, and yet are clearly, within the wider biblical context, to be classed among the *adiaphora*.[8]

This lack of interest in unusual mental states does not, to be sure, suffice to disprove the suspicion that claims to speak for God are entirely explicable in psychological terms, for theoretically that could still be the case. However, the consistent biblical emphasis upon the moral and theological content of what the prophet or apostle says, rather than what may or may not accompany their saying it (other than their lifestyle), strongly suggests that the biblical concern for spiritual authenticity and the psychological concern for understanding mental processes are two substantially different kinds of concern; they are better seen as complementary and mutually irreducible facets of a rich and complex phenomenon rather than as in conflict. Indeed, insofar as psychologists classify mental states as beneficial or harmful, this is done substantially in terms of the accompanying disposition and behaviour, and so there is real continuity with the biblical priorities – even if this leaves open to debate the question as to how one decides what counts as desirable dispositions and behaviours. It is also to be hoped that the sustaining of an appropriately rich and complex understanding of the mind, and of the conceptual irreducibility of its moral and spiritual dimensions, might give a little pause to some of the cruder contemporary suppositions that the stimulating of particular areas of the brain might 'cause religious experience'.[9]

8. We should also remember that in the Pentecost narrative the Spirit-filled multilingual speaking of the apostles on its own at best led to astonishment and perplexity and at worst to mocking dismissal (2:12–13).

9. I think, for example, of *Horizon*'s 'God on the Brain', shown on BBC2 on 17 April 2003, which introduced the remarkable 'science' of 'neurotheology'. The unexceptionable proposition that one should be able to demonstrate links between 'religious experience' and 'brain states' (for of course any human experience will involve the brain in some way) turned into the startling thesis that the stimulation of the temporal lobes could be the cause of 'religious experience'/'the sense of God'. The dramatic climax came when Richard Dawkins was invited to put on a kind of helmet which could direct electrical emanations to, and measure brain waves in, the frontal lobes; would the famed atheist now have a religious experience? 'My leg feels twitchy' was (if I remember rightly) his sole comment. The programme displayed astonishing conceptual naivety, seemed entirely ignorant of the long, rich, and diverse history of enquiry into 'religious experience' (apart from all too limited contributions from Stephen Sykes), and although broadcast in all apparent seriousness quickly degenerated into pure farce. The programme was not a good advertisement for science, or for television as a non-trivializing medium.

Do miracles validate prophecy?

A further point of note is that in all the material we have considered there has been no appeal whatever to the 'miraculous'[10] to validate the word of a contested prophet or apostle. Paul, to be sure, does mention in 2 Corinthians, in a passage we have not yet discussed, the way in which 'signs and wonders' accompanied his ministry in Corinth (2 Cor. 12:12):

> The signs of a true[11] apostle were performed among you with utmost patience,[12] signs and wonders and mighty works.

However, this comes only *after* the extended account of criteria of authenticity which climaxes in the embrace of power in weakness. Thus it is hardly more than an afterthought, whose force seems to be along the lines of 'And by the way, you did also get from me the conventional signs of an apostle which the super-apostles performed, so you can hardly complain of being deprived.' Insofar as Paul attributes significance to these signs (of which he appropriately speaks in the passive, thus ascribing them not to his own power, but to that of God), such significance is not separable from the manner in which they were displayed, i.e. 'with utmost endurance', with the kind of apostolic qualities of which he has already spoken, 'carrying in the body the death of Jesus, so that the life of Jesus may also be made visible in our bodies' (4:7–12). But apart from this passing reference, neither Jeremiah nor Micaiah nor John nor Paul shows any interest in trying to validate contested authenticity through 'signs and wonders'. The words of Jesus on the subject (Matt. 7:21–3) explicitly pronounce 'many deeds of power' to be worthless in comparison with obedience to his Father's will,[13] and Jesus' path to Gethsemane and Golgotha enacts the same priorities.

10. I use inverted commas to indicate that 'miracle' is in some ways a problematic category, for reasons to do with the widespread modern tendency to exclude 'grace' from 'nature'. In the present context, however, I think that nothing hangs on possible difficulties of concept or definition.

11. 'True' is not in the Greek and is a dismaying interpretative addition by the translators (NRSV here perpetuates RSV), which seriously skews the real force of Paul's argument in context. 'Signs of an apostle' is most probably a conventional phrase (e.g. Käsemann 1941:61–2, Thrall 2000:837), which Paul is willing to use because 'signs and wonders' had indeed attended his founding visit to Corinth (Thrall 2000:840). But Paul's argument in context is that such signs precisely do *not* determine true apostleship when apostleship is contested.

12. Furnish 1984:553 observes that 'the noun *endurance* [*hypomonē*] involves much more than simple "patience"… it means enduring with hope in the face of afflictions'. So 'with utmost endurance' is a preferable translation.

13. In that discussion we noted also Deut. 13:2–6 (ET 1–5), which denies probative value to 'omens or portents' if they are utilized to undermine Israel's allegiance and obedience to YHWH.

This consistent emphasis poses an interesting question in relation to the not uncommon portrayal in other biblical texts of divine acts of power as indeed having – in principle, though by no means always in practice – some kind of probative significance (e.g. Exod. 4:1–9, 1 Kgs. 18:20–40, Matt. 11:20–4, John 12:37–43, Acts 14:3). Since any thorough engagement with this question would overburden the present discussion, I will simply offer one heuristic suggestion, which I hope to develop elsewhere. The portrayals of 'signs and wonders' as having some probative value are consistently in contexts of address to people who are in one way or other reluctant to be responsive or to take seriously the divine challenge/invitation that is being mediated to them; in such situations signs and wonders may attract a more responsive hearing for the speaker; they never appear in contexts where the need is to discern between rival claims to speak for the one God.[14] What may be appropriate to one situation may be inappropriate to another.

It may be that one reason neither ecstasies nor miracles are of any interest in the material we have considered is that they would be 'extrinsic' evidence rather than 'intrinsic'. They would be extrinsic in the sense that they would bear no integral or internal relation to the content of what the prophet or apostle says and does – even though they might in principle function as pointers.[15] Only if every time a prophet or apostle spoke there were both ecstasies and miracles might one possibly suppose that there were indeed some intrinsic linkage; but this is patently not the case either within the Bible or in most contexts influenced by the biblical tradition, for ecstasies and miracles have consistently been attested as occasional, not invariable, accompaniments to speech for God. Appropriate moral and theological content and practice, to do with living rightly under God, are, however, intrinsic to prophetic utterance, and so necessarily play a role in critical discernment that neither ecstasies nor miracles could play.

3 Clarifying the criteria of discernment

I have argued that for the (would-be) prophet there are two prime criteria of discernment: on the one hand, disposition, character, and lifestyle; on

14. It is true that 1 Kgs. 18 depicts a prophetic contest; yet it is not between different claims to speak for YHWH, but between the prophet of YHWH and prophets of Baal.

15. The potentially positive role of signs and wonders is importantly articulated in Acts 14:3 in terms of 'witness' to the apostolic proclamation.

the other hand, a message whose content and searching challenge reflect God's priorities and seek to engender unreserved engagement with God. I have also argued that there are comparable, even if lesser, requirements for anyone who would engage in discernment, on the grounds that sight and character are intertwined. At this point it is appropriate to offer some brief further clarification of these requirements in relation to some obvious difficulties.[16]

Are the biblical criteria too vague for realistic implementation?

One issue is how one determines the moral content which constitutes the critical norm for discernment. For, on the whole, there is a striking lack of specificity on this issue in the texts surveyed.

Jeremiah characteristically does not enumerate specific moral qualities or appeal to a moral code – the chief exception being his temple sermon (7:1–15).[17] Within the specific indictment of prophets (23:9ff.) 'adultery' and 'lies' are singled out (23:14), but the language is for the most part even more generalized: 'wickedness', 'evil', 'ungodliness'. Likewise Jeremiah says little explicitly about the moral qualities of God (9:22–3 (ET 23–4) being the chief exception). Yet at the same time there is no implication in the text that Jeremiah is morally or spiritually vacuous. So clearly far more is *presupposed* by Jeremiah than is ever given explicit articulation. Similarly, I suggested that the figure of Micaiah in his narrative should be seen to presuppose and utilize an understanding of the moral and spiritual character of God and of human life that is much more comprehensive and systematic than is directly articulated within the narrative itself.

John in his first letter is hardly more precise. His norm for critical discernment is the love of God embodied in Jesus Christ and replicated by the Spirit in believers. His apparent two tests of discernment – on the one hand, confession of Jesus Christ come in the flesh, on the other hand, self-giving love – are in reality one test, one norm, viewed from different

16. In another context it would be interesting to compare the biblical criteria with Aristotle's account of the means by which a speaker persuades others (*On Rhetoric* 1.2.1358a2–4), as a study of the ways in which the biblical writers adopt and transform the common concerns of life. Aristotle refers to the character (*ethos*) of the speaker, the nature of the argument itself (*logos*), and the disposing of the listener in particular ways (*pathos*); thus concerns about character, content, and audience are all in some way present.

17. Jer. 7:9 can reasonably be read as an appeal to the Ten Commandments, whose transgression warrants Jeremiah's indictment; though whether that is intrinsic to the originating significance of the words or is rather a reading strategy that is dependent upon working with the canonical shape of the OT is unclear and can be argued either way.

angles. Yet he uses this norm with little concern for spelling out its precise implications, though of course he does make some specifications, such as that love must entail giving both of oneself and of the necessities of life (3:14–17). Again, more appears to be presupposed than is articulated.[18] And, of course, it is regularly the case in life that when wise and mature people speak they presuppose far more than is articulated in any specific utterance.

Paul in 2 Corinthians is hardly different. When he does present lists in the context of discernment (6:4–10, 11:23–33) they are not, other than in part (6:6–7), lists of moral qualities (as in, for example, Mark 7:21–3) but rather rhetorical evocations of the sufferings appropriate to the one who would follow a crucified Lord. Paul's portrayal of faithful conformity to Christ is specific only on the fundamentals, the replication of Christ's death and resurrection through the realization and embrace of the paradox of power in weakness (12:9–10). And Paul expects others to imitate Christ in ways that are unslavish and imaginatively non-identical.[19]

Such varied and yet consistent lack of specificity may appear to be a serious weakness. For what if the question of what constitutes the appropriate and normative moral content for discernment is itself contested? Does the whole exercise of discernment then threaten to unravel and to degenerate into interminable wrangling that can be settled only by the exercise of coercive power?

Although the issues merit extensive treatment, I will for the present just make two observations. First, the apparent weakness of relative lack of specificity is surely a strength to the extent that it directs attention to a person's/prophet's fundamental motivation and stance in life: it focusses less on the detail and more on the big picture.[20] This is important primarily because of the ever-present danger of moralism (to be discussed in the next section) and the corresponding danger of self-deception in using time-honoured words and practices to conceal a fundamental

18. It is tempting to suggest that a substantial part of what is presupposed should be seen as the Gospel of John (though even here there is famously little ethical specificity). Whether or not the first letter was written in response to problems raised by the interpretation and reception of John's Gospel (a historical question which can be argued either way because of paucity of evidence), it seems a reasonable readerly strategy (analogous to that noted in the previous footnote) to read it in its canonical placement as a certain kind of commentary on John's Gospel.

19. Cf. Chapter 6, Excursus 1.

20. There are thus important resonances with virtue ethics, which shifts the ethical focus away from the morality of particular acts (though this still plays a role) to the nature of a person's character and the question of what constitutes wise and upright decision-making and living in relation to an overall vision of life.

existential lack. The reality of engagement with the living God, and its appropriate discernment, is intensely and demandingly moral and yet not reducible to moral check-lists.[21]

Secondly, we have noted that the lack of specificity seems combined with the presupposing of a larger vision of God and life than receives specific mention. What appears to be at stake is the best way to bring this total vision to bear upon the specific act of discernment. And there is no one straightforward way to do this. On the one hand, the language of 'evil' might leave one addressee wholly unmoved (e.g. 'too vague to be helpful' or 'that clearly can't mean me'), while for another it might precisely provide the category to make them re-envisage what they had been doing in a way that moves them to cease doing it. Paul's consistent emphasis on appropriating the way of the crucified and risen Lord may not have moved the Corinthians (at any rate, no record survives of their response),[22] yet it has moved many others, secondary addressees, who have encountered it as part of Scripture. On the other hand, the texts we have been considering have only been preserved as part of a larger scriptural whole (and Scripture is itself contextualized within the continuing thought and practice of the Church). This means that, however much one seeks to hear the voices of the particular texts in their own right, the Christian reader will almost always in one way or other contextualize the particular voices within other voices that affect how one hears and utilizes any specific text.[23] Like anything else these contextualizations can be handled well or badly. When handled well they offer a deeper resonance to particular voices and can prevent relative lack of specificity degenerating into emotive but contentless rhetoric.

21. Cf. Chapter 1, p. 16, n. 33, where I suggested that Münderlein's negative conclusion that 'there are no criteria for discernment of prophets' because ultimately 'the substance of prophecy, the word of Jahweh, cannot be captured in rules' might, if reconceived, not be a bad starting point for constructive discussion about the nature of valid criteria.

22. Paul's having the collection to take to Jerusalem is usually considered to imply a positive response to him on the part of at least some at Corinth.

23. For example, the resonances between Jer. 1:9 and Deut. 18:18, together with the portrayal of Moses as archetypal prophet in relation to communication of Torah (Deut. 5:22–33), should incline the reader of the canonical OT to see the requirements of Torah as giving specificity to prophetic challenges. However, when the prophets are read as interpreters of Torah their construal is by no means wooden or predictable, as YHWH's refusal to implement the law for the stubborn and rebellious son well illustrates (Deut. 21:18–21, Hos. 11:1–9). Alternatively, if one reads Paul as an interpreter of Jesus in the gospels one should not miss his often unpredictable moves, such as, say, his sitting light at Corinth to the dominical directive about the appropriate means of support for those preaching the gospel (Luke 10:7, 1 Cor. 9:14–18) because of his awareness of the potentially problematic social dynamics that financial support can create.

How can one avoid moralism?

One of the abiding difficulties in understanding and appropriating the moral emphases in the texts under consideration is a tendency to narrow and misconstrue their scope. At the outset of this book (Chapter 1, p. 9, n. 23) I put 'moral' in inverted commas (and was strongly tempted to do so in every usage throughout the book) as a way of indicating that the term is problematic and readily misleading. It is all too easy for a robust and wide-ranging understanding of what is 'moral' – which I take to be characteristic of our texts – to be reduced to a 'moralism' which operates with an unduly narrow vision of what counts as moral, and tends to display something of a check-list mentality.[24]

Although there is no simple way of preventing this, there are some prime considerations within a biblical context which should give pause to the would-be moralizer. In the first place, it is important to take biblical rhetoric seriously without handling it woodenly. For not only, as already noted, do our texts tend to lack a certain kind of specificity, but they also tend to use robust language without qualifiers. Jeremiah not infrequently speaks of 'everyone' as corrupt (e.g. Jer. 6:13–15) and refuses to recognize any validity within an otherwise moving expression of repentance (14:7–10). Comparably, Jesus speaks of the narrow way to life which few take and the broad and easy way to destruction that many take (Matt. 7:13–14). Or Paul addresses Corinthian Christians as though they were effectively unreconciled to God (2 Cor. 5:20–6:2). All this is 'strong' language, which uses direct and unqualifed categories for the sake of existential impact, to open eyes to see things which might otherwise escape them.[25] Yet in all these contexts it would be possible to enter qualifications about the many shades of grey between black and white in relation to the varying characters and conditions of different people. The challenge is to be able to take the language seriously – which for the would-be faithful interpreter includes opening oneself to its impact – while not failing to recognize that such seriousness should not preclude a more nuanced analysis (appropriate not least in many

24. Compare one of my main criticisms of Robert Carroll in the second excursus to Chapter 2 (pp. 90–5).

25. The biblical use of paired categories – righteous and wicked, wise and foolish, believing and unbelieving, those being saved and those being lost – is in significant ways analogous to the sociological use of ideal types which are meant to be used heuristically to enable a greater clarity of vision in situations which in themselves are messy and opaque. In biblical, and biblically influenced, contexts the language also prescribes movement, and can help people to move, towards the life-giving side of the polarity.

pastoral situations) which recognizes moral complexity as well as moral simplicity.

Similarly, one must always recognize that moral challenges may be facile (e.g, on the lips of certain glib proclaimers of doom), while messages of reassurance may be searching (e.g, to people who have been so scarred that daring to hope again seems beyond them). There is no language that cannot be misused, and no general principles that cannot be misunderstood. Misuse and misunderstanding become more likely the further away that either speaker or discerner (or both) are from contexts that nurture and enable well-developed moral and spiritual understanding and practice.

Perhaps the most fundamental factor for inhibiting moralism, in the wider context of Scripture, is the priority of grace; which one can formalize theologically in terms of a doctrine of 'election'. God chooses a people, and calls particular persons, irrespective of their moral quality at the time of God's initiative. Jeremiah's vocation is traced back to before his birth in terminology which Paul also appropriates for himself (Jer. 1:5, Gal. 1:15). The supreme example of this is the eponymous ancestor of God's people, Jacob/Israel, the significance of whose choice by God while still in his mother's womb (Gen. 25:23) is succinctly spelled out by Paul: 'Even before they [Rebecca's children] had been born or had done anything good or bad (so that God's purpose of election might continue, not by works but by his call) she was told, "The elder shall serve the younger" ' (Rom. 9:11–12). The fact that Jacob/Israel is a self-seeking and dishonest character only serves to sharpen the paradox of the morally unmerited call of God. In a related vein we have also noted Jeremiah's strong statement of the initiative of God in recreating an as yet unrepentant Israel (Jeremiah 31–2);[26] to which there are strong NT analogies in, for example, John's 'In this is love, not that we loved God but that he loved us and sent his Son to be the atoning sacrifice for our sins' (1 John 4:10) or Paul's 'God proves his love for us in that while we were still sinners Christ died for us' (Rom. 5:8). Although there are almost endless ramifications to understanding God's gracious initiative, not least in holding it in appropriate tension with God's moral demand, my point at present is solely that any genuine grasp of what grace entails should be a major factor in inhibiting any facile moralism; for in any authentic biblical and/or Christian theology, grace must always be fundamental.

26. Cf. Excursus 3 to Chapter 2 (pp. 98–9).

With regard to those qualities and dispositions that should enable someone to discern, there are clear biblical recognitions, especially in the gospels, of the possible dangers of a moralism that can inhibit discernment. I offer two examples. On the one hand, in the Synoptic Gospels, there is a recurrent emphasis in the teaching of Jesus that sinners may have priority in the kingdom of God (the last becoming first, while the first become last). A typical example is the words of Jesus in the context of speaking about religious authority and John the Baptist (Matt. 21:31b–32): 'Truly I tell you [sc. chief priests and elders, verse 23], the tax-collectors and the prostitutes are going into the kingdom of God ahead of you. For John came to you in the way of righteousness and you did not believe him, but the tax-collectors and the prostitutes believed him; and even after you saw it, you did not change your minds and believe him.' Jesus' point is that people who are morally compromised in familiar categories may nonetheless retain an important openness of heart and mind in parts of their character that have not been corrupted. This can enable them to recognize goodness and truth when they are before them in ways that the more morally upright may find difficult because their rectitude can induce varying kinds of complacency and narrowness of vision.

On the other hand, John's Gospel shows how Israel's tradition as a whole may be used in such a way as to obscure rather than illuminate recognition of Jesus. Characteristic is John 9, in which the passage from blindness to sight for the man born blind is paralleled by the passage from sight to blindness on the part of the religious authorities. Why? Because Jesus' act of healing on the sabbath poses genuinely difficult issues of discernment, and yet the authorities refuse properly to exercise their responsibilities to discern. After the initial scene-setting and account of the healing and its immediate aftermath (9:1–15), the problem is succinctly formulated: 'Some of the Pharisees said, "This man is not from God, for he does not observe the sabbath." But others said, "How can a man who is a sinner perform such signs?" And they were divided' (verse 16). Since Torah specifies that wonder-working need not be heeded if it is combined with faithlessness to YHWH (Deut. 13:2–6 (ET 1–5)), and since sabbath regulations could be lifted if life was under threat, yet the man's life had not been under threat, Jesus' action, although life-enhancing, poses a genuine problem.

The authorities ask both the man and his parents for their opinion (verses 17, 18–23), though since the authorities' general disposition suggests that they would hardly consider such opinions valid anyway, the questions look like (and are construed by the parents as) a quest for self-incrimination. The authorities then pronounce confidently on the very matter with which they have not yet properly engaged: 'We know that this man is a sinner' (verse 24). And when the man born blind demurs, their questions simply cover factual, not interpretative, ground that has already been covered, as the man indelicately points out (verses 25–7). This leads to an expression of the root problem: 'You are his disciple, but we are disciples of Moses. We know that God has spoken to Moses, but as for this man, we do not know where he comes from' (verses 28b–29). The authorities take refuge in the familiar and secure. Instead of using what they know from God to engage in discernment that might enlarge their understanding further (so that they might indeed come to know where Jesus is from, as the reader of the gospel already knows, e.g. 3:31–6), they use their knowledge to pre-empt and prejudge, to close down rather than open up. Unsurprisingly, at this point even the appearance of rational enquiry breaks down and is replaced by scorn from the man and abuse from the authorities (verses 30–4). When Jesus reappears and receives the allegiance of the man (verses 35–8), his final words relate to why the authorities have become culpably blind: 'If you were blind, you would not have sin. But now that you say, "We see", your sin remains' (verse 41). In terms of the story it is their very claim to see, through God's speaking to Moses, which makes culpable their failure to use that vision so as to discern who Jesus is. It is a failure akin to moralism, when that which should enable discernment is used to inhibit it – an ever-present possibility as much within Christian as within Jewish tradition.

4 Some examples of applying criteria of critical discernment

It may be helpful at this point to offer some (all too brief) case studies and contemporary issues, to give some further suggestions as to how the thesis of this study might be applied.

An adulterous prophet? The case of Martin Luther King, Jr

My first example, which displays some of the difficulties in the relationship between the moral and moralism, is one of the most widely recognized Christian 'prophetic' voices of the twentieth century, Martin Luther King, Jr.[27] King's prolonged struggle against racial injustice

27. Amidst the mass of literature, Oates 1982 is a good biography.

creatively utilized non-violent resistance, and led to important changes in federal law and in the structures and practices of American society. His struggle was always at considerable personal cost, in the face of bitter opposition and antagonisms, and culminated in his assassination at Memphis on 4 April 1968. The legacy of his speeches and action has made him a figure of iconic status in America.

One consequence, however, of King's prolonged periods away from his wife and family is that he became sexually active away from home. Hostile police and FBI surveillance bugged King's hotel rooms, and the deeply hostile J. Edgar Hoover, the then Director of the FBI, sought to use compromising tapes to attack and undermine King, whom he suspected of communist affiliations; although almost all who became aware of this material, from President Johnson down, refused to use it (Oates 1982:264–5, 314–18).

King's being sexually active in his hotel rooms means, in traditional moral and social terminology, that he committed adultery. Since adultery is something specified by Jeremiah as a mark of a prophet who is not to be heeded (Jer. 23:14, 29:21–3),[28] does it follow from this that King (an ordained Christian minister) should not be recognized as of 'prophetic' stature? Certainly J. Edgar Hoover had no doubt that this sexual activity confirmed that King was a moral degenerate who ought not to be heeded.

The question, however, illustrates well something of the complexity of moral judgment. On the one hand, one should at least note the historical irony that, if the women with whom King had intercourse were not themselves married, then his behaviour would not have counted as adulterous in the historical context of Jeremiah;[29] only if a woman already belonged to another man, through marriage or betrothal, would sexual intercourse with her count as adultery, for it would then count as misusing another's man's property, not least through creating uncertainty as to the parentage of a child.[30] The OT does not approve of a married man having intercourse with an unmarried woman, but differentiates it from adultery and sees it as much less serious. Parity of expectation and accountability for married men and women is a post-OT development.

28. See above, p. 71, n. 80.
29. For the nature and logic of adultery in ancient Israel, see, e.g., de Vaux 1961:36–7, Countryman 1989:35–9.
30. The legal principle is that a woman could violate only her own marriage, while a man could violate only the marriage of another man.

On the other hand, it does not really help to try to excuse King's behaviour in the kinds of ways that come readily to mind. For example: sexual activity beyond marriage is so common on the part of major public figures that it should be of no real interest to anyone other than the prurient. Or, it was a private failing and made no difference to King's public significance. Or (most potently), had King remained a conventional pastor in congregational ministry then temptations to sexual activity beyond marriage might well not have arisen or might have been readily resisted, and it was only because of his willingness to renounce security and comfort and expose himself to enormous hostile pressures in obedience to a demanding divine vocation[31] that the problem arose – and those who have not made comparable sacrifices are in no position to cast the first stone. Such excuses have weight. But in the present discussion, whose purpose is not to justify or condemn King but to understand how the moral criterion of prophetic authenticity might be used without moralism, such excuses offer limited help; for they all, in varying degrees, incline to downplay the moral significance of adultery.[32] Such mitigation can tend to displace rather than to embody serious moral consideration; accordingly, it can help provoke, by way of reaction, just the kind of moralism that might seize upon King's adultery and discount all else.

The point is that although this particular moral failing does not deny King's moral stature, it does to some degree *diminish* that stature, as King himself realized. At the very least, it gave his enemies a possible stick to beat him with. When in December 1964 he was en route to Norway to receive the Nobel Peace Prize, he realized that the prize made him a moral leader on the world stage. Consequently he needed to, and apparently did, renounce a practice that was morally compromising and could to some degree discredit him (Oates 1982:318). Although his renunciation was not expressed in terms of repentance, but rather in terms of a prudential recognition of the need to be more 'spartan' in accordance with his world stature, it at least restores consistency to his conduct. It should

31. For King's experience of a divine voice calling him to stand for justice and truth and promising to be with him to the end, see Oates 1982:88–9.

32. Part of the difficulty is the greatly diminished status of marriage in much contemporary Western society. The idea of the 'sanctity' of marriage, or the importance of its familial and social role, has widely become rather less meaningful than the individualistic notion of a human right to sexual intimacy and fulfilment constrained only by the requirement of mutuality.

not, I think, permit a moralizer to seize upon isolated actions in neglect of the general and predominant tenor of his words and way of life.

In short, therefore, the powerful witness to love and justice in King's sermons and speeches, and the corresponding integrity of his actions non-violently to oppose racial injustice, remains a witness to be heeded. Although his stature is to a degree diminished by his marital infidelity, the general coherence of his speech with his action, and of both with the will of God, can rightly be recognized as 'prophetic', in authentic continuity with the biblical prophets.[33]

Does Osama bin Laden speak for God?

One reader of a draft of this book tested my thesis with helpful sharpness. A second case study can usefully focus on the question that s/he put, 'Does Osama bin Laden speak for God?'[34] For a little reflection shows that a prima facie case can be made for bin Laden in terms of my thesis, a case which depends not least upon the relative lack of specificity of moral criteria. The reader continued:

> His actions are in no obvious sense self-interested. Like Paul [and, one could add, Jeremiah or Micaiah], he has made great financial and personal sacrifices for the sake of his message. His life is fully consistent with what he proclaims. In the name of God, he prophetically challenges a worldly empire (the USA) that he regards as corrupt, lustful, violent and blasphemous. Even his use of violence is consistent with the example of the prophet Elijah, who killed the false prophets of Baal [and one could note comparably the OT's approval of Phinehas' impalement of Zimri and Cozbi (Num. 25) and of Jehu's massacre of the house of Ahab and of worshippers of Baal (2 Kgs. 10:1–30)] . What are we to say about his moral character, and how it might confirm or disconfirm the truth of his message?

I have two basic responses to this. First, one can point out that even on the OT's own terms the case for bin Laden would not be entirely straightforward. For example, there are signs within the canonical formation of

33. A biblical comparison with Martin Luther King, Jr that might be worth developing would be with King David. David's offences (2 Samuel 11) were more heinous than those of King, although there is the salient difference that he repented publicly. Despite these offences, OT tradition can depict David as a model of obedience to YHWH for whose sake YHWH may be gracious (as in Ahijah's speech, 1 Kgs. 11:31–9). David's flawed character is not understood within the OT to disqualify him from authentic speaking of and for God.

34. I am grateful to the anonymous reader for Cambridge University Press for this and other responses to a draft of my thesis.

the OT that a practice such as 'holy war' (*herem*) may be retained because of a move to construe its significance in metaphorical terms which no longer envisage actual warfare.[35] It may not be accidental that those prime OT texts about discernment of authenticity that we have considered focus upon figures, Jeremiah and Micaiah, who entirely lacked military means to implement their vision – which directs one's attention to the validity of their message in and for itself as testimony to the will of God. One should not simply assimilate bin Laden's vision of God, with its warlike elements, to the OT's vision of God, with its warlike elements, as though the respective Islamic and YHWHistic contextualizations of those visions made no real difference (since, for example, the OT does not prioritize violent struggle to impose its vision and lifestyle upon others in the mode of *jihad*; Israel's struggles are for Israel itself to remain faithful to YHWH, whatever other peoples may do). And, rather basically, bin Laden's use of violence is not simply 'consistent' with that of Elijah, for there was something intrinsically *indiscriminate* in the deaths of 9/11 (and other al-Qaeda actions, and plans that have been discovered), in a way that was not the case with the prophets of Baal (or those put to death by Phinehas or Jehu).

Secondly, a crucial consideration in a case such as this must be the general theological point that for the Christian the OT does not constitute an authority except in relationship (of a dialectical and reciprocal kind) with the NT – nor do OT and NT together function authoritatively except in dialectical relationship with the life of the Church and a rule of faith. The pattern of Christ, as displayed in the gospels and expounded by Paul, which entails self-giving for others and refusal to allow true life under God to involve benefiting at the expense of others, fundamentally invalidates the programme of bin Laden, with its prioritizing of largely indiscriminate murder, as an expression of the will of God.[36] The same

35. I have made some preliminary exegetical suggestions along these lines in Moberly 1999b:133–40.

36. Of course, there is also much in the major traditions of Islam that questions the use made of Wahhabism and Salafism in contemporary Islamism and its terrorist manifestations. In recent years some Jews have wanted to construe Judaism in ways akin to bin Laden's construal of Islam; one thinks of Baruch Goldstein murdering Muslims in Hebron or Yigal Amir assassinating Yitzhak Rabin 'for the glory of God'. It is not that the Bible does not contain elements to which they can appeal in support, but rabbinic Judaism developed (in effect) a rule of faith which rules out their reading as a misreading. Christians also have behaved comparably, as in the murder of doctors who carry out abortions in the USA. One of the most worrying aspects of our contemporary context is the superficial and attenuated understanding and use of sacred text and tradition on the part of many who think that they can practise the faith without needing to appropriate a proper rule of faith.

pattern of Christ also invalidates the all-too-numerous campaigns of murder and destruction conducted under the aegis of the Church within its history, of which the medieval Crusades to the Holy Land are only the most notorious example. If the pattern of Christ is indeed the ultimate norm for discernment of speech and action on behalf of God, then congruity with Christ (rather than the presence or absence of explicit recognition of Christ) must in one way or another be that for which one looks in the exercise of discernment.[37]

How can one discern speech for God in those of other faiths and no faith?

A third question, not unrelated to the previous one, concerns how the thesis proposed could be used in relation to people of faiths not rooted in the biblical tradition and conceptuality or to people of integrity who profess no faith. Within present constraints I will briefly offer three heuristic proposals.

First, in general terms, I hope that my thesis illustrates something of the value of constructing an argument specifically within the confines of the Bible as Christianly constituted and understood, rather than via more generalized engagement with recurrent religious phenomena in multiple geographical contexts and periods of history. To use the categories of the eighteenth century, it is no longer the case that the universal should override and displace the particular, but rather that the particular can valuably illuminate the universal. Or, in contemporary categories, instead of aspiring to a view from nowhere it is better to have a view from a well-chosen somewhere. The point of focussing upon the Bible and Christian theology is not to narrow the concerns to 'churchy matters' but rather to enable a principled approach to the understanding and appraisal of human life in general, religious or otherwise. To be sure, any tradition-specific argument will remain open to being contested from other traditions and perspectives, but what matters is the intrinsic potential of the well-chosen somewhere to be fruitful in engaging with traditions and perspectives other than its own and in demonstrating resonant and illuminative power for life and thought.

37. Compare Gorringe 1990:38 (which is taken from a useful wide-ranging discussion of discernment): 'The Spirit is the Spirit of Christ, but this does not mean that to recognize God in the world is to look for those who believe in Christ, but that we look for those whose lives resemble his, and who thus show that they have the "mind of Christ".'

Sustained engagement with key aspects of the Bible, via its specific voices in both testaments, offers a distinctive account of God and human life. At heart, the nature and meaning of human life is correlative with the vision of God. To understand humanity and to know God are different facets of a single, complex reality. Within the NT and Christian faith these two facets are focussed in the particular person of Jesus Christ as the one in whom the truth of humanity and of God is embodied and displayed – a particular person who is of life-giving significance for the world generally. This significance is articulated in many ways in terms of sin and redemption, creation and eschatology, but one undergirding concern is that God's particular revelation and salvation is to enable the whole created order to realize that meaning and potential for which it exists. Rightly to understand and practise this is demanding, and often eludes Christians, yet it remains the enduring task which gives the Church its *raison d'être*.

Secondly, concern for human integrity in both theory and practice is a general human phenomenon which is in no way restricted to the Bible and the faiths rooted in it. The Bible itself regularly recognizes the integrity of those who do not belong to the chosen people;[38] so the nature upon which grace works can be not only misguided and corrupt but also capable of goodness and truth. So, to take one example, Paul's account of his integrity in 1 Thess. 2:1–12, which we noted to have strong resonances with his account of apostolic authenticity in 2 Corinthians, has many strong resonances also with emphases found among the philosophical writers of the Graeco-Roman world. For the ancient world did not have a concept of religion in the way in which the modern West tends to understand it, and the closest ancient Mediterranean conceptuality for the kind of integration of belief and practice that characterized early Christianity was 'philosophy'. Pierre Hadot, through many works which are summed up in his luminous *Philosophy as a Way of Life* (1995), has cogently argued the thesis that, 'Ancient philosophy, at least beginning from the sophists and Socrates, intended, in the first instance, to form people and to transform souls' (p. 20), and that, 'One must always approach a philosophical work of antiquity with this idea of spiritual progress in mind' (p. 64).

38. Within the OT, for example, Job receives the highest approbation (Job 1:1); and wherever his land of Uz should be imagined to be located, Uz was not Israel. Perhaps the second-highest approbation is given to Noah (Gen. 6:9), who is also not located within Israel (for his context is pre-Israel).

Consequently, 'both Judaism and Christianity sought to present themselves to the Greek world as philosophies' (p. 72).

Thus Abraham Malherbe, for example, whose recent commentary on the Thessalonian letters (Malherbe 2000, esp. 133–63) develops his substantial earlier work on the extensive parallels between the language and concerns of the philosophers and of Paul in his engagement with the Thessalonians (Malherbe 1987, 1989),[39] not infrequently cites a striking passage from Dio Chrysostom.[40] Dio, a humane Stoic-Cynic philosopher, whose dates (c. AD 40/50–c. AD 110/120) make him a younger contemporary of Paul, discusses contemporary philosophers and their defects, and sets in contrast to them a portrayal of the qualities of the ideal philosopher with which he identifies his own work as a kind of vocation (*Oration* 32:11–12):

> But to find a man who in plain terms [*katharōs*] and without guile [*adolōs*] speaks his mind with frankness [*parrēsiazomenon*], and neither for the sake of reputation [*doxēs*] nor for gain, but, out of good will and concern for his fellow-men stands ready, if need be, to submit to ridicule and to the disorder and uproar of the mob – to find such a man as that is not easy, but rather the good fortune of a very lucky city, so great is the dearth of noble, independent souls and such the abundance of toadies [*kolakōn*], mountebanks, and sophists. In my own case, for instance, I feel that I have chosen that role, not of my own volition, but by the will of some deity. For when divine providence is at work for men, the gods provide, not only good counsellors who need no urging, but also good words that are appropriate and profitable to the listener.

Apart from the general tenor being similar to Paul,[41] the Greek words in square brackets are all characteristic of Paul's writing in this area. Clearly, those serious about exploring and enabling understanding of the truths of the human condition regularly realize the implications for themselves,[42]

39. 'Paul's description of his Thessalonian ministry in 1 Thessalonians 2 is strikingly similar to the picture sketched by Dio, both in what is said and in the way in which it is formulated' (1989:47). Throughout his work Malherbe's concern is not to portray Paul simply as one variation upon a common cultural theme, but rather to point out how Paul 'adapts contemporary conventions to express his unique self-understanding to people who were familiar with these conventions' (2000:159).

40. The Dio passage, cited in 2000:154, is also cited and more fully contextualized in Malherbe 1970 (reprinted in 1989:35–48).

41. Passages throughout Dio which resonate with the NT are set out in Mussies 1972; for similarities specifically to 2 Corinthians see pp. 170–82.

42. This is not the place to engage with the substance and rhetorical strategies of Dio in their own terms. I simply note that I see no reason not to take seriously what Dio says.

even without the benefit of biblical revelation. The biblical revelation should not close the eyes of believers to the reality of integrity wherever it appears but rather should enable its clearer perception and appreciation; dogma, rightly understood and appropriated, should enable vision.[43] And even if Dio's ascription of his speech to 'the will of some deity' and 'the gods' invites a Christian redescription in terms that Dio would not himself have acknowledged, the motive for the redescription would be to clarify why Christian faith can in principle offer a qualified recognition of Dio's speaking as deriving ultimately from none other than the source from which biblical prophecy derives.[44]

Thirdly, although it would be possible to probe the theological issues in relation to Luke's portrayal of Paul at the Areopagus (Acts 17:16–34), which is a *locus classicus* in this general context, I prefer briefly to consider John 3:19–21. This passage concludes the episode of Nicodemus' encounter with Jesus, an encounter in which a central position is held by the problematics of discerning who or what is 'from God/above' and 'born of the Spirit'. John speaks of the nature of the judgment (*krisis*) which is integral to Jesus' coming to bring eternal life (3:16–18) and concludes:

> And this is the judgement, that the light has come into the world, and people loved darkness rather than light because their deeds were evil. For all who do evil hate the light and do not come to the light, so that their deeds may not be exposed. But those who do what is

43. The point is forcefully expressed by Flannery O'Connor in the context of her articulating the task of the Catholic novelist (O'Connor 1970:178): 'There is no reason why fixed dogma should fix anything that the writer sees in the world. On the contrary, dogma is an instrument for penetrating reality. Christian dogma is about the only thing left in the world that surely guards and respects mystery. The fiction writer is an observer, first, last, and always, but he cannot be an adequate observer unless he is free from uncertainty about what he sees . . . Open and free observation is founded on our ultimate faith that the universe is meaningful, as the Church teaches.'

44. The relationship of Christian faith and revelation to the best of Graeco-Roman understandings and practices was, of course, a recurrent issue in patristic thought. A basic openness to non-Christian integrity, often conceptualized in terms of the workings of the *logos*, is perhaps nicely epitomized in the appropriation of the first-century Stoic philosopher Seneca. Tertullian (*De Anima* 20) can refer to Seneca and his thought as *saepe noster* ('often one of us'), while Jerome (*Adversus Jovinianum* 1:49) drops the qualifier and depicts Seneca as straightforwardly *noster* ('our own'). It must, however, be admitted that the appropriation, especially by Jerome, was aided by a supposed exchange of letters between Paul and Seneca (see Hennecke 1965:135–41, with introduction by A. Kurfess, pp. 133–5, which leaves open a date sometime in the third or fourth century), whose imagined construal of a suitable exchange between the great men seems widely and mistakenly to have been taken as an actual correspondence – the mistake being serious because the writer's distinctly limited imagination produced a trivial content vastly inferior to anything more reliably ascribed to Paul or Seneca. Thus the intrinsic issue of understanding and evaluation of content in Seneca became increasingly hijacked by appeal to spurious 'authority'.

true come to the light, so that it may be clearly seen that their deeds have been done in God.

John reverts to the language of the prologue (1:5, 9) in order to articulate the significance of Jesus. The coming of Jesus is a definitive embodiment of the light that constantly shines into the world. The image is not, as sometimes supposed, of the light as a gift such as reason which is generally given to humanity. Rather the image is of a torch thrust into a dark place, where those who have hitherto inhabited the darkness are compelled by the light to make some response. One possible response is to shrink back from the light and seek a corner in which the former darkness may still be relatively undisturbed. John sees such a shrinking as characterizing those who 'do evil', who for reasons of lack of integrity do not wish their exposure to the light to introduce possible change and transformation. Yet the other response is so to welcome the light that one moves out of the darkness and embraces the transformation that the light brings. This John ascribes to those who 'do the truth', those whose mode of living in the world has an integrity that is accompanied by a certain kind of openness and responsiveness. Indeed, the light shows that what they had formerly done had been 'done in God', even though at the time they may not have recognized this and the redescription only becomes apparent through their response to the light which is Christ.

In general terms, and among other things, John seems to be articulating an understanding of divine grace as present even when unrecognized ('the possibility of experiencing grace and the possibility of experiencing grace *as* grace, are not the same thing').[45] In such cases, the coming of Christ will affirm those good intuitions and practices that were already in place, and show that they have an origin in God. To be sure, the shining of the light will transform the context in which future practices are undertaken, and so things should not remain as they were before; rather, the reconstitution of human self-understanding in the light of God in Christ should enable the doing of the truth to flourish more fully and explicitly than otherwise. Nonetheless, that which is reconstituted is also fundamentally affirmed.

The point for the Christian practice of discernment should be clear. Although there is always much to confront and challenge when

45. Cf. p. 36, n. 60. This seems to me a more helpful way of posing the issue within the Johannine text which is more commonly expressed in predestinarian terms (though I lack space to engage with the interpretative debates).

self-seeking in complacent or corrupt forms predominates, there can also be much to affirm. Those who speak and act in frames of reference other than the biblical can be affirmed when their speech and practice display the kinds of qualities which in the biblical context evidence the gracious initiative of God. Of course, this will often be a complex and nuanced matter in which acknowledgement, querying, and rejection may be juxtaposed in untidy and unpredictable ways. To be sure, the enabling of people to see that their best intuitions and practices are genuinely affirmed and subsumed in Christ, and not denied, is a challenge that the Church has frequently failed to meet – for many reasons, and not least that sometimes its own intuitions and practices may be rather more distant from the reality of Christ than those of people who do not acknowledge Him. Nonetheless, recognition and affirmation of speech and action that display the reality of God, even if they are understood more or less differently by those who speak and act, remain part of a mandate for Christian practices of critical discernment.

What about the churches' understanding of gays and lesbians?

Finally, in this section, there is one topic that can hardly be avoided at the present time – the attitudes of the various churches to 'homosexuality',[46] both male and female. Yet if honesty requires some mention of the question, wisdom suggests that any contribution in this context to so controverted an issue should be brief.[47] So I will just say a few things to try to set the issue in context.

First, there can be little doubt that, prima facie, the heated disagreements in the contemporary Church over appropriate expressions of sexuality in general and over gay and lesbian issues in particular may make many wonder whether the churches do have what is necessary for discernment. Nonetheless, it is important to set current controversy in a broader historical frame of reference. For controversy of one kind or another has, for better and worse, been a regular feature of the history of the Church. The christological controversies of the fourth century, or the soteriological controversies of the sixteenth century, were even more heated than the controversies of today. Moreover, it is also important not

46. I use the inverted commas because the nature of the term used to depict the phenomenon is itself part of the problem.
47. I have discussed appropriate use of Scripture in this context in Moberly 2000.

to harbour inappropriate expectations, as though the fact that God has revealed Himself should somehow mean that Christians should never face uncertainties or disagreements, as though divine revelation were some kind of blueprint for the whole of life. The Bible indeed provides revelatory understanding of God, humanity, and the world that Christians believe to be true, and its content likewise forms the people of God in searching intellectual and moral ways. But the purpose of this is not to 'solve all our problems' but rather to enable those who believe to be equipped to tackle the challenges of life in a right and fruitful way.[48] Learning, understanding, and applying God's truth in the world is a never-ending task. So the churches will always face challenges of one kind or another in their seeking to discern what constitutes faithfulness to God and biblical revelation in the varied and changing contexts of life. Prolonged controversy over homosexuality may be a sign neither of stupidity nor of faithlessness, but of attempts to be faithful in an area whose true complexity is easily underrated.[49]

Secondly, the argument of this book focusses upon discernment of purported speech on God's behalf (i.e. evaluating a person and their message), and it would not be appropriate simply to shift the argument into the related, yet distinct, area of ecclesial decision-making (i.e. deciding moral and social issues of principle).[50] To be sure, one may still expect that in some way there should be 'prophetic' input to official ecclesial discernment, not least because penetrative understanding of the true meaning and reality of what is given to the Church is by no means straightforward or to be taken for granted. As Luke Johnson (1998:38) has put it:

> The teaching office of the church requires the voice of prophecy to be alive if it is not to grow distended: through prophets the living Jesus can speak in new ways. And the preservers of tradition need also to hear the voices of theologians whose task is not so much to preserve as it is to extend the boundaries of our understanding

48. These last two sentences are a loose paraphrase of the famous statement about Scripture in 2 Tim. 3:16–17.

49. One dimension of the complexity is the 'levitical' nature of homosexuality (Davis 2003:173–7), which relates it to debates as old as both Judaism and Christianity about what constitutes appropriate holiness of living.

50. Likewise, I do not wish here to go into the question, well-known especially in the Roman Catholic Church, of the relationship between public revelation (i.e. ecclesially recognized, doctrinally normative formulations) and private revelation (i.e. utterances of a particular person, purportedly under the influence of the Spirit); on which see, e.g., Rahner 1963.

> of the mystery of Christ. The tradition is impoverished if the voice of prophecy is stilled.

Yet although one may reasonably ask who are those people within the churches whose quality of life and witness has the kind of prophetic qualities that would give them credibility in this area also, disagreements about some of the moral pronouncements of the late Pope John Paul II underline that even here there are no easy answers. The dynamics of prophetic discernment are a necessary, but not a sufficient, element in the formation of that wisdom which the churches need in their decision-making.

Thirdly, one major danger is that the controverted issue may be invested with an importance that it does not deserve, which is surely what is happening with homosexuality (though the question of how one decides what weight to give to the controversy is not least among the controverted issues). On any reckoning – since the NT makes it definitional of the significance of Christ that he displaces divisive human identities for those who believe in him so as to replace them with recognition and reconciliation (e.g. Eph. 2:11–22) – it is not the path of wisdom either for individuals or for churches to define their identity in terms of sexual orientation and practice, any more than it is on issues such as attitudes to warfare or wealth or divorce and remarriage (where Christians recognize not only that they should but that they can, generally, remain in fellowship and communion with those from whom they differ).

Fourthly, another major danger that prolonged ecclesial disagreements pose is a narrowing of focus and vision, that is a diminishing of ability to discern well, related to a diminishing of love. Attempts to discern signs of grace in other Christians, and to hear their witness, can all too easily become displaced by attempts to show that 'we are right and you/they are wrong'. Too many in different areas of the debate know that they are right, and yet display their rectitude with an attitude of heart that suggests neither grace nor compassion; thereby their discernment and demonstration of the whole counsel of God are seriously diminished.

5 Three concluding reflections

There is much that could yet be said. For example, I am aware of not interacting explicitly with the literature and practices of contemporary charismatic and Pentecostal Christianity (although I hope that much of what has been said will be seen to have clear bearing upon many of the live issues). I have not engaged with the remarkable contemporary resurgence of interest in 'spirituality', whose various forms are largely divorced from the Bible and the institutional churches, and whose moral dimensions, where present, are much more devoted to global issues of injustice and ecology than to personal moral transformation. And there are many unmentioned facets of contemporary Western intellectual and social culture that bear upon contemporary understanding and appropriation of the issues discussed here. So debate must continue.

I close with three considerations. First, I would like to say something about the assumption made throughout about the fundamental integrity of the biblical material that has been studied. For it has become fashionable in some recent scholarship to seek to retrieve voices that were excluded and suppressed by the processes of biblical canon formation, and to uphold their dignity and value in the name both of accurate historical understanding and of justice and compassion for the 'losers' in some of history's conflicts; and correspondingly to question the integrity of the biblical canon and of the voices included in it. Such criticisms, although useful for dispelling complacency, can, however, easily lose sight of at least two important factors.

On the one hand, it is striking how few of the texts we have considered portray the authentic prophet as a 'winner' in any conventional sense. Jeremiah's ministry was largely fruitless among his contemporaries and brought great anguish to himself; the tension is acute between his 'appointment over nations and kingdoms' and his personal ignominies at the hands of others. Micaiah is unheeded and is left to die in prison. Paul's account of his ministry and travels appears the very antithesis of conventional accounts of glory or 'winning'; yet he gladly undertakes it in faithfulness to a Lord whose own life and ministry were brought to an end by the brutalities of betrayal, torture, and shameful public execution. The voices in the canon are the voices of those who suffered for the truth.

On the other hand, if these voices have been preserved as authoritative for subsequent generations, their very recognition and canonical preservation imply a remarkable process of discernment on the part of Jews and Christians. For such a discernment not only saw that failure and disappointment by many conventional standards were compatible with speaking and enacting God's truth for human life. It also built into the constitution and self-definition of future communities that would acknowledge these texts as authoritative, as Scripture, a searching criterion for the recognition of the voice of the God these communities would serve – that true self-interest lies not in self-seeking but in self-giving for the welfare of others. To be sure, the history of these communities is all too often of more or less partial recognition, sometimes indeed downright denial, of that which constitutes them. Consequently, rejection of the values of these communities, and the subjecting of their claims to a hermeneutic of suspicion, is often justified. Nonetheless, the canonical texts have already authorized precisely that exposing and confronting of human self-seeking and self-deception that a hermeneutic of suspicion, at its best, also seeks. Moreover, the way in which the biblical texts relate this to the unceasing will of God to make and remake human beings into what they ought to be means that, rightly understood, these texts will always be more searching in their confrontation with human self-will than any account which is grounded in something less than the will of God for His creation.

Secondly, I would like to transpose my argument about discernment into the metaphor of a game and say that what I have been trying to do is to articulate what the rules of the game are and how it should be played – the kind of game I have in mind is one like chess or football (where skill, learning, and discipline are constitutive) rather than one like whist or bingo (where chance predominates). For the most part, the argument has been directed against those who are doubtful about such a game; those who think that there is no such game (e.g. Rodinson), or who think that the game is a different kind of exercise (ideological assertion and manipulation) in disguise (e.g. Carroll); or those Jewish and Christian scholars who believe that there is, or at least should be, a game, but who struggle to formulate playable rules (e.g. McKane). In the course of articulating my thesis, however, I have more than once encountered a different kind of response from friends and colleagues. This has taken the form of 'If discernment is viable, then what about the Church and gays, or what about the validity of the war in Iraq?' – where there has been a clear implication that I ought somehow to be able to pronounce definitively, or tell others how to pronounce definitively, upon the discernment of the rights and wrongs of these controverted issues. In terms of my metaphor, however, this seems to me to be wanting to know not just how to play the game, but how to be sure of, as it were, winning it every time.[51] Yet that is

51. In other words, the contemporary instinct – revealingly and dismayingly – is to construe any claim to real access to the Spirit in terms of individualism and illuminism, rather than in terms of the insights that may become accessible through moral, ritual, devotional, and social living and thinking within the disciplines of ecclesial faith.

surely illegitimate. One can play the game rightly and well without being sure that one will always be clearly a winner. If my argument is at all along the right lines, then intrinsically it will not be possible to acquire some (as it were, divine) perspective from which one can look down upon the human fray and pronounce upon its rights and wrongs. Rather it is only possible for those who engage in the fray, and who seek to discern responsibly within the fray, who may be able rightly to recognize those who speak and act for God. But there is no guarantee either that their discernment will be clear and whole, rather than mixed and partial, or that their discernment, even if entirely faithful, will be heeded by those who should heed (though some at least will be rescued from the ever-present and ever-predatory wolves in sheep's clothing). In other words, the struggles of life continue. The exercise of discernment offers the hope, however, that the life-transforming and wonder-bestowing reality of God may genuinely be appropriated and make the struggles supremely worth while.

Thirdly and finally, although the whole argument has been conducted with reference to claims to speak for God, in the Bible and in Christian faith that is rooted in the Bible, this does not mean that it is an argument only for the 'religiously inclined'. For the whole question of criteria for discerning prophetic authenticity is a particular intensification of questions that, whether or not one is always conscious of them, affect every living person – Whom should I trust? or How can I know who is trustworthy? These questions, in one form or other, impact upon the friends we make, the life partner we choose, the jobs we seek to do, the advertising we heed and the ways we spend our money, the priorities we set for our life, the ways we cope with disappointment and suffering, the overall view of life and the world which we hold. In all these areas, failure to attend properly to the grounds for trust can regularly lead to pain, frustration, bewilderment, and loss, indeed tragedy. In other words, an argument as to the role of human integrity, in forms congruent with the pattern of Christ, for discerning the presence and will of God, embraces and heightens an elemental human concern. For God, in biblical revelation and in the faiths rooted in it, is that reality who enables life to become what it is meant to be.

References

Abraham, William J., 2002, 'The Offense of Divine Revelation', *HTR* 95:3, pp. 251–64.

Aharoni, Y., 1978, 'Ramat Rahel', in Michael Avi-Yonah and Ephraim Stern, *Encyclopedia of Archaeological Excavations in the Holy Land*, vol. IV, Oxford, Oxford University Press, pp. 1000–9.

Alter, Robert, 1981, *The Art of Biblical Narrative*, London and Sydney, Allen & Unwin.

2004, *The Five Books of Moses: A Translation with Commentary*, New York and London, W. W. Norton & Co.

Aune, David E., 1983, *Prophecy in Early Christianity and the Ancient Mediterranean World*, Grand Rapids, Eerdmans.

Austin, J. L., 1975, *How to Do Things with Words*, 2nd edn, Oxford, Clarendon.

Ball, E., 1977, 'A Note on 1 Kings XXII.28', *JTS* 28, pp. 90–4.

Balthasar, Hans Urs von, 1991, *The Glory of the Lord: A Theological Aesthetics*, vol. VI, *Theology: The Old Covenant*, Edinburgh, T. & T. Clark (ET by Brian McNeil and Erasmo Leiva-Merikakis from German of 1967, ed. by John Riches).

Barclay, John, 2003, '2 Corinthians', in James D. G. Dunn and John W. Rogerson (eds.), *Eerdmans Commentary on the Bible*, Grand Rapids and Cambridge, UK, Eerdmans, pp. 1353–73.

Barr, James, 1999, *The Concept of Biblical Theology: An Old Testament Perspective*, London, SCM Press.

Barrett, C. K., 1973, *The Second Epistle to the Corinthians*, BNTC, London, A. & C. Black.

Barth, Karl, 1956, *Church Dogmatics* I/2, Edinburgh, T. & T. Clark (ET from German by G. T. Thompson and H. Knight).

1957, *Church Dogmatics* II/2, Edinburgh, T. & T. Clark (ET from German by G. W. Bromiley et al).

Barton, Stephen C., 2003, '1 Corinthians', in James D. G. Dunn and John W. Rogerson (eds.), *Eerdmans Commentary on the Bible*, Grand Rapids and Cambridge, UK, Eerdmans, pp. 1314–52.

Bash, Anthony, 1997, *Ambassadors for Christ: An Exploration of Ambassadorial Language in the New Testament*, WUNT, 2nd series 92, Tübingen, Mohr Siebeck.

Berlin, Adele, 2002, 'On Bible Translations and Commentaries', in Athalya Brenner and Jan Willem van Henten (eds.), *Bible Translation on the Threshold of the Twenty-First Century: Authority, Reception, Culture and Religion*, JSOTSS 353, London, Sheffield Academic Press, pp. 175–91.

Berquist, J. L., 1989, 'Prophetic Legitimation in Jeremiah', *VT* 39, pp. 129–39 (reprinted in Orton 2000, pp. 200–10).

Berrigan, Daniel, 1999, *Jeremiah: The World, the Wound of God*, Minneapolis, Fortress.

Best, Ernest, 1972, *The First and Second Epistles to the Thessalonians*, BNTC, London, A. & C. Black.

Bible and Culture Collective, 1995, *The Postmodern Bible*, New Haven, Yale University Press.

Bickerman, Elias, 1967, *Four Strange Books of the Bible*, New York, Schocken.

Blank, Sheldon H., 1955, *'Of a Truth the Lord hath Sent me': An Inquiry into the Source of the Prophet's Authority*, Cincinnati, Hebrew Union College Press.

Blenkinsopp, J., 1996, *A History of Prophecy in Israel*, 2nd edn, Louisville, Westminster/John Knox Press.

Bockmuehl, Markus, 1997, *The Epistle to the Philippians*, BNTC, London, A. & C. Black.

2001, '1 Thessalonians 2:14–16 and the Church in Jerusalem', *TynB* 52:1, pp. 1–31.

Boring, M. Eugene, 1995, 'The Gospel of Matthew', in Leander E. Keck et al. (eds.), *The New Interpreter's Bible*, vol. VIII, Nashville, Abingdon, pp. 87–505.

Bosworth, David, 2002, 'Revisiting Karl Barth's Exegesis of 1 Kings 13', *BI* 10:4, pp. 360–83.

Boyle, Nicholas, 2004, *Sacred and Secular Scriptures: A Catholic Approach to Literature*, London, DLT.

Brenneman, James E., 1997, *Canons in Conflict: Negotiating Texts in True and False Prophecy*, Oxford, Oxford University Press.

Brichto, Herbert Chanan, 1992, *Towards a Grammar of Biblical Poetics: Tales of the Prophets*, New York and Oxford, Oxford University Press.

Bright, John, 1965, *Jeremiah*, AB, Garden City, NY, Doubleday.

Brown, David, 2001, 'Review of Garrett Green, *Theology, Hermeneutics, and Imagination* (CUP: 2000)', *JR* 81:4, pp. 657–8.

Brown, Raymond E., 1982, *The Epistles of John*, AB 30, New York, Doubleday.

Brueggemann, Walter, 1988, *To Pluck up, to Tear down: A Commentary on the Book of Jeremiah 1–25*, Grand Rapids, Eerdmans/Edinburgh, Handsel Press.

1991, *To Build, to Plant: A Commentary on Jeremiah 26–52*, Grand Rapids, Eerdmans/Edinburgh, Handsel Press.

1997, *Theology of the Old Testament: Testimony, Dispute, Advocacy*, Minneapolis, Fortress.

2003, 'Four Proclamatory Confrontations in Scribal Refraction', *SJT* 56:4, pp. 404–26.

Buber, Martin, 1949, *The Prophetic Faith*, New York and Evanston, Harper & Row.

1982 [1968/1942], 'False Prophets (Jeremiah 28)', in his *On the Bible: Eighteen Studies* (ed. Nahum Glatzer), New York, Schocken, pp. 166–71 (ET by Olga Marx from Hebrew of 1942).

1997 [1948], 'The Faith of Judaism', in his *Israel and the World: Essays in a Time of Crisis*, Syracuse, NY, Syracuse University Press, pp. 13–27.

Buckley, Michael J., 1987, *At the Origins of Modern Atheism*, New Haven and London, Yale University Press.

Budd, Philip, 2003, 'Numbers', in James D. G. Dunn and John W. Rogerson (eds.), *Eerdmans Commentary on the Bible*, Grand Rapids and Cambridge, UK, Eerdmans, pp. 125–52.

Bultmann, R., 1985, *The Second Letter to the Corinthians*, Minneapolis, Augsburg (ET by Roy A. Harrisville from German of 1976).

Calvin, John, n.d. [ET from Latin of 1560s], *Calvin's Commentaries*, vol. V, Wilmington, Associated Publishers and Authors.

1882, 'Mosis Reliqui Libri Quatuor in Formam Harmoniae', in *Calvini Opera* XXV, Corpus Reformatorum LIII, Brunswick, C. Schwetschke.

Camus, Albert, 1963, *The Fall*, London, Penguin (ET by Justin O'Brien from French of 1956).

Carroll, Robert P., 1976, 'A Non-Cogent Argument in Jeremiah's Oracles against the Prophets', *Studia Theologica* 30, pp. 43–51.

1979, *When Prophecy Failed: Reactions and Responses to Failure in Old Testament Prophetic Traditions*, London, SCM.

1981, *From Chaos to Covenant: Uses of Prophecy in the Book of Jeremiah*, London, SCM.

1986, *Jeremiah*, OTL, London, SCM.

1991, *Wolf in the Sheepfold: The Bible as a Problem for Christianity*, London, SPCK.

1995, 'Synchronic Deconstructions of Jeremiah: Diachrony to the Rescue? Reflections on Some Reading Strategies for Understanding Certain Problems in the Book of Jeremiah', in Johannes C. de Moor (ed.), *Synchronic or Diachronic? A Debate on Method in Old Testament Exegesis*, Oudtestamentische Studien XXXIV, Leiden, Brill, pp. 39–51.

1999a, 'Halfway through a Dark Wood: Reflections on Jeremiah 25', in Diamond et al. 1999, pp. 73–86.

1999b, 'Something Rich and Strange: Imagining a Future for Jeremiah Studies', in Diamond et al. 1999, pp. 423–43.

Castelli, Elizabeth A., 1991, *Imitating Paul: A Discourse of Power*, Louisville, Westminster/John Knox Press.

Cavanaugh, William T., 1995, '"A Fire Strong Enough to Consume the House": The Wars of Religion and the Rise of the State', *Modern Theology* 11:4, pp. 397–420.

Childs, Brevard S., 1984, *The New Testament as Canon: An Introduction*, London, SCM.

1985, *Old Testament Theology in a Canonical Context*, London, SCM.

1992, *Biblical Theology of the Old and New Testaments*, London, SCM.

Chrysostom, J., 1848, *The Homilies of S. John Chrysostom, Archbishop of Constantinople, on the Second Epistle of St. Paul the Apostle to the Corinthians*, LF, Oxford, Parker & Rivington (ET by members of the English Church from Greek of c. AD 400).

Clements, R. E., 1988, *Jeremiah*, IBCTP, Atlanta, John Knox Press.

Countryman, L. William, 1989, *Dirt, Greed and Sex: Sexual Ethics in the New Testament and their Implications for Today*, London, SCM.

Cousar, Charles B., 1990, *A Theology of the Cross: The Death of Jesus in the Pauline Letters*, OBT, Minneapolis, Fortress Press.

Crenshaw, James L., 1971, *Prophetic Conflict: Its Effect upon Israelite Religion*, BZAW 124, Berlin and New York, de Gruyter.

Daube, David, 1973, *Ancient Hebrew Fables*, Oxford, Oxford University Press.

Davidson, Robert, 1964, 'Orthodoxy and the Prophetic Word: A Study in the Relationship between Jeremiah and Deuteronomy', *VT* 14, pp. 407–16 (reprinted in David E. Orton (ed.), *Prophecy in the Hebrew Bible: Selected Studies from* Vetus Testamentum, Leiden, Boston, MA, and Cologne: Brill, 2000).

Davies, W. D. and Allison, Dale C., 1988, *The Gospel According to Saint Matthew*, vol. I, Edinburgh, T. & T. Clark.

Davis, Ellen, 2003, 'Critical Traditioning: Seeking an Inner-Biblical Hermeneutic', in Ellen F. Davis and Richard B. Hays (eds.), *The Art of Reading Scripture*, Grand Rapids, Eerdmans, pp. 163–80.

Dawkins, Richard, 2003, *A Devil's Chaplain: Selected Essays by Richard Dawkins*, ed. Latha Menon, London, Weidenfeld & Nicolson.

Dawn, Marva J., 2001, *Powers, Weakness, and the Tabernacling of God*, Grand Rapids, Eerdmans.

Diamond, A. R. Pete, O'Connor, Kathleen M., and Stulman, Louis (eds.), 1999, *Troubling Jeremiah*, JSOTSS 260, Sheffield Academic Press.

Dodd, C. H., 1946, *The Johannine Epistles*, London, Hodder & Stoughton.

Dodds, E. R., 1951, *The Greeks and the Irrational*, Berkeley and Los Angeles, California University Press.

Douglas, Mary, 2001, *In the Wilderness: The Doctrine of Defilement in the Book of Numbers*, Oxford, Oxford University Press (new edn of 1993 hardback pub. by Sheffield Academic Press).

Dozeman, Thomas B., 1998, 'The Book of Numbers', in Leander E. Keck et al. (eds.), *The New Interpreter's Bible*, vol. II, Nashville, Abingdon, pp. 1–268.

Dubay, Thomas, 1977, *Authenticity: A Biblical Theology of Discernment*, Denville, NJ, Dimension Books.

Duhm, Bernhard, 1901, *Das Buch Jeremia*, KHAT XI, Tübingen and Leipzig, Mohr Siebeck.

Dunn, J. D. G., 1980, *Christology in the Making*, London, SCM Press.

Edwards, Jonathan, 1959 [1746], *The Works of Jonathan Edwards*, vol. II, *Religious Affections*, ed. John E. Smith, New Haven, Yale University Press; edition of original of 1746.

Edwards, Ruth B., 1996, *The Johannine Epistles*, NT Guides, Sheffield, Sheffield Academic Press.

Ehrlich, Arnold B., 1968 [1912], *Randglossen zur Hebräischen Bibel*, vol. IV, Hildesheim, Georg Olms.

Fabry, H.-J., 1999, '*sôd*', in *TDOT*, vol. X, pp. 171–8.

Farrer, A. M., 1948, *The Glass of Vision*, London, Dacre Press.

Forbes, Christopher, 1986, 'Comparison, Self-Praise and Irony: Paul's Boasting and the Conventions of Hellenistic Rhetoric', *NTS* 32, pp. 1–30.

Forest, Jim, 1999, *The Ladder of the Beatitudes*, Maryknoll, Orbis.

Fowl, Stephen E. and Jones, L. Gregory, 1991, *Reading in Communion: Scripture and Ethics in Christian Life*, London, SPCK.

France, R. T., 1985, *Matthew*, TNTC, Leicester, IVP/Grand Rapids, Eerdmans.

Fretheim, Terence E., 1999, *First and Second Kings*, Westminster Bible Companion, Louisville, Westminster John Knox Press.

2002, *Jeremiah*, Smyth & Helwys Bible Commentary, Macon, GA, Smyth & Helwys.

Fridrichsen, A., 1929, 'Peristasenkatalog und *res gestae*. Nachtrag zu 2 Cor. 11:23ff', *SO* 8, pp. 78–82.

Funk, Robert W., 1996, *Honest to Jesus: Jesus for a New Millennium*, San Francisco, HarperSanFrancisco/Polebridge Press.

Funkenstein, Amos, 1986, *Theology and the Scientific Imagination from the Middle Ages to the Seventeenth Century*, Princeton, Princeton University Press.

Furnish, Victor Paul, 1984, *II Corinthians*, AB32A, New York and London, Doubleday.

Gaventa, Beverly, 1993, 'Apostle and Church in 2 Corinthians: A Response to David M. Hay and Steven J. Kraftchick', in David M. Hay (ed.), *Pauline Theology*, vol. II, *1 & 2 Corinthians*, Minneapolis, Fortress, pp. 182–99.

Georgi, D., 1964, *Die Gegner des Paulus im 2 Korintherbrief. Studien zur religiösen Propaganda in der Spätantike*, Neukirchen, Neukirchener Verlag.

Gibson, J. C. L., 1994, *Davidson's Introductory Hebrew Grammar – Syntax*, Edinburgh, T. & T. Clark.

Glancy, Jennifer A., 2004, 'Boasting of Beatings (2 Corinthians 11:23–25)', *JBL* 123:1, pp. 99–135.

Goldingay, John, 2001, 'What Are the Characteristics of Evangelical Study of the Old Testament?', *EQ* 73:2, pp. 99–117.

Gorman, Michael J., 2001, *Cruciformity: Paul's Narrative Spirituality of the Cross*, Grand Rapids, Eerdmans.

Gorringe, T. J., 1990, *Discerning Spirit: A Theology of Revelation*, London, SCM Press/ Philadelphia, TPI.

Grabbe, Lester L., 1995, *Priests, Prophets, Diviners, Sages: A Socio-Historical Study of Religious Specialists in Ancient Israel*, Valley Forge, PA, TPI.

Gray, G. B., 1903, *Numbers*, ICC, Edinburgh, T. & T. Clark.

Gray, John, 1977, *I & II Kings*, 3rd edn, London, SCM Press.

Green, Garrett, 2000, *Theology, Hermeneutics, and Imagination: The Crisis of Interpretation at the End of Modernity*, Cambridge, Cambridge University Press.

Gunkel, Hermann, 1917, *Die Propheten*, Göttingen, Vandenhoeck & Ruprecht.

Gunther, John J., 1973, *St Paul's Opponents and their Background: A Study of Apocalyptic and Jewish Sectarian Teachings*, SNT 35, Leiden, Brill.

Güttgemanns, E., 1966, *Der leidende Apostel und sein Herr: Studien zur paulinischen Christologie*, FRLANT 90, Göttingen, Vandenhoeck & Ruprecht.

Hadot, Pierre, 1995, *Philosophy as a Way of Life*, ed. with introduction by Arnold I. Davidson, Oxford, Blackwell (ET by Michael Chase from French of 1987).

Harrison, Peter, *'Religion' and the Religions in the English Enlightenment*, Cambridge, Cambridge University Press.

Hasel, Gerhard, 1991 [1972], *Old Testament Theology: Basic Issues in the Current Debate*, 4th edn, Grand Rapids, Eerdmans.

Hayes, John H. and Prussner, Frederick C., 1985, *Old Testament Theology: Its History and Development*, London, SCM.

Hays, Richard B., 1997, *First Corinthians*, IBCTP, Louisville, John Knox Press.

Heaton, E. W., 1958, *The Old Testament Prophets*, Harmondsworth, Penguin.

Hengel, Martin, 1977, *Crucifixion*, London, SCM (ET by John Bowden from German of 1976).

Henneke, E. and Schneemelcher, W., 1965, *New Testament Apocrypha*, vol. II, ed. R. McL. Wilson, London, Lutterworth Press (ET by Ernest Best et al. from German of 1964).

Henry, Matthew, 1960, *Matthew Henry's Commentary on the Whole Bible*, London, Marshall, Morgan & Scott (ed. by L. F. Church from early eighteenth-century text).

Heschel, Abraham J., 1962, *The Prophets*, New York, Harper & Row.

Hobbes, Thomas 1996 [1651], *Leviathan*, ed. R. Tuck, Cambridge, Cambridge University Press.

Hobbs, T. R., 1985, *2 Kings*, WBC 13, Waco, Word.

Hoffman, Yair, 1997, 'Prophecy and Soothsaying', in *Tehillah le-Moshe: Biblical and Judaic Studies in Honor of Moshe Greenberg*, Winona Lake, Eisenbrauns, pp. 221–43.

Hogenhaven, Jesper, 1987, *Problems and Prospects of Old Testament Theology*, Sheffield, JSOT Press.

Holladay, William L., 1986, *Jeremiah 1*, Hermeneia, Philadelphia, Fortress.

Hossfeld, Frank Lother and Meyer, Ivo, 1973, *Prophet gegen Prophet: Eine Analyse der alttestamentlichen Texte zum Thema: Wahre und falsche Propheten*, BB 9, Fribourg, Verlag Schweizerisches Katholisches Bibelwerk.

Houston, Walter, 1993, 'What did the Prophets Think they were Doing? Speech Acts and Prophetic Discourse in the Old Testament', *BI* 1:2, pp. 167–88.

Huffmon, H. B., Schmitt, John J., Barton, John, and Boring, M. Eugene, 1992, 'Prophecy', in David Noel Freedman et al. (eds.), *The Anchor Bible Dictionary*, vol. v, New York, Doubleday, pp. 477–502.

Jacobs, Alan, 2001, *A Theology of Reading: The Hermeneutics of Love*, Boulder, CO, Westview Press.

James, William, 1960 [1902], *The Varieties of Religious Experience*, Glasgow, Collins.

Johnson, Luke T., 1989, 'The New Testament's Anti-Jewish Slander and the Conventions of Ancient Polemic', *JBL* 108, pp. 419–41.

1995, 'Fragments of an Untidy Conversation: Theology and the Literary Diversity of the New Testament', in Steven J. Kraftchick, Charles D. Myers, Jr, and Ben C. Ollenburger (eds.), *Biblical Theology: Problems and Perspectives: In Honor of J. Christiaan Beker*, Nashville, Abingdon Press, pp. 276–89.

1996, *Scripture and Discernment: Decision Making in the Church*, Nashville, Abingdon Press.

1998, *Living Jesus: Learning the Heart of the Gospel*, San Francisco, HarperSanFrancisco.

2002, 'What's Catholic about Catholic Biblical Scholarhip? An Opening Statement', in Luke Timothy Johnson and William S. Kurz, *The Future of Catholic Biblical Scholarship: A Constructive Conversation*, Grand Rapids, Eerdmans, pp. 3–34.

Johnston, Philip S., 2002, *Shades of Sheol: Death and Afterlife in the Old Testament*, Leicester, Apollos/Downers Grove, IVP.

Jones, Douglas Rawlinson, 1992, *Jeremiah*, NCB, London, Marshall Pickering/Grand Rapids, Eerdmans.

Jones, G. H., 1984, *1 and 2 Kings*, 2 vols., NCB, London, Marshall, Morgan & Scott.

Käsemann, E., 1941, 'Die Legitimität des Apostels: Eine Untersuchung zu II Korinther 10–13', *ZNW* 41, pp. 33–71.

1971, 'The Saving Significance of the Death of Jesus in Paul', in his *Perspectives on Paul*, Philadelphia, Fortress Press (ET from German by Margaret Kohl), pp. 32–59.

Keck, Leander E. et al. (eds.), 2001, *The New Interpreter's Bible*, vol. vi, Nashville, Abingdon.

Knierim, Rolf P. and Coats, George W., 2005, *Numbers*, FOTL iv, Grand Rapids, Eerdmans.

Koch, K., 1983, *The Prophets*, 2 vols., London, SCM Press (ET by Margaret Kohl from German of 1980).

Kuenen, A., 1877, *The Prophets and Prophecy in Israel: An Historical and Critical Enquiry*, London (ET by A. Milroy from Dutch of 1875).

Lambrecht, Jan, 1999, *Second Corinthians*, Sacra Pagina 8, Collegeville, Liturgical Press.

Lange, Armin, 2002, *Vom prophetischen Wort zur prophetischen Tradition: Studien zur Traditions- und Redaktionsgeschichte innerprophetischer Konflikte in der Hebräischen Bibel*, FAT 34, Tübingen, Mohr Siebeck.

Lash, Nicholas, 1988, *Easter in Ordinary: Reflections on Human Experience and the Knowledge of God*, London, SCM.

1996, *The Beginning and the End of 'Religion'*, Cambridge, Cambridge University Press.

1997, 'The Church in the State We're In', in L. Gregory Jones and James J. Buckley (eds.), *Spirituality and Social Embodiment*, Oxford, Blackwell, pp. 121–37.

2004, *Holiness, Speech and Silence: Reflections on the Question of God*, Aldershot, Ashgate.

Levenson, Jon D., 1993, 'Historical Criticism and the Fate of the Enlightenment Project', in his *The Hebrew Bible, the Old Testament, and Historical Criticism*, Louisville, Westminster/John Knox Press, pp. 106–26.

Levine, Baruch A., 2000, *Numbes 21–36*, AB 4A, New York, Doubleday.

Levinson, Bernard, 1997, *Deuteronomy and the Hermeneutics of Legal Innovation*, New York and Oxford, Oxford University Press.

Lewis, C. S., 1963, *The Magician's Nephew*, Harmondsworth, Penguin.

Lieu, Judith, 1991, *The Theology of the Johannine Epistles*, Cambridge, Cambridge University Press.

Lightfoot, J. B., 1895, *Notes on Epistles of St Paul*, London and New York, Macmillan.

Lindblom, J., 1962, *Prophecy in Ancient Israel*, Oxford, Blackwell.

Locke, John, 1894 [1690], *An Essay Concerning Human Understanding*, ed. Alexander Campbell Fraser, vol. II, Oxford, Clarendon Press.

Long, Fredrick J., 2005, *Ancient Rhetoric and Paul's Apology: The Compositional Unity of 2 Corinthians*, SNTSMS, Cambridge, Cambridge University Press.

Lonsdale, David, 1992, *Dance to the Music of the Spirit: The Art of Discernment*, London, DLT.

Lundbom, Jack R., 1999, *Jeremiah 1–20*, AB 21A, New York, Doubleday.

2004, *Jeremiah 21–36*, AB 21B, New York, Doubleday.

Luz, Ulrich, 1989, *Matthew 1–7: A Continental Commentary*, Minneapolis, Fortress Press (ET by Wilhelm C. Linss from German of 1985).

2004, 'Paul as Mystic', in Graham N. Stanton, Bruce W. Longenecker, and Stephen C. Barton (eds.), *The Holy Spirit and Christian Origins: Essays in Honor of James D. G. Dunn*, Grand Rapids, Eerdmans, pp. 131–43.

MacDonald, Nathan, 2003, *Deuteronomy and the Meaning of 'Monotheism'*, FAT, 2nd series 1, Tübingen, Mohr Siebeck.

McKane, William, 1979, 'Prophecy and the Prophetic Literature', in G. W. Anderson (ed.), *Tradition and Interpretation*, Oxford, Clarendon, pp. 163–88.

1985, 'Is there a Place for Theology in the Exegesis of the Hebrew Bible?', *Svensk Exegetisk Arsbok* 50, pp. 7–20.

1986, *Jeremiah*, vol. I, ICC, Edinburgh, T. & T. Clark.

1995, *A Late Harvest: Reflections on the Old Testament*, Edinburgh, T. & T. Clark.

1996, *Jeremiah*, vol. II, ICC, Edinburgh, T. & T. Clark.

1998, *The Book of Micah: Introduction and Commentary*, Edinburgh, T. & T. Clark.

Malherbe, Abraham J., 1970, '"Gentle as a Nurse": The Cynic Background to 1 Thessalonians 2', *NovT* 12, pp. 203–17.

1987, *Paul and the Thessalonians: The Philosophic Tradition of Pastoral Care*, Philadelphia, Fortress Press.

1989, *Paul and the Popular Philosophers*, Minneapolis, Fortress Press.

2000, *The Letters to the Thessalonians*, AB 32B, New York, Doubleday.

Marguerat, D., 1981, *Le Jugement dans l' Evangile de Matthieu*, Geneva, Editions Labor et Fides.

Marshall, I. Howard, 1978, *The Epistles of John*, NICNT, Grand Rapids, Eerdmans.

Martin, Ralph P., 1986, *2 Corinthians*, WBC 40, Waco, Word Books.

Martyn, J. L., 1967, 'Epistemology at the Turn of the Ages: 2 Corinthians 5:16', in W. R. Farmer, C. F. D. Moule, and R. R. Niebuhr (eds.), *Christian History and Interpretation: Studies Presented to John Knox*, Cambridge, Cambridge University Press, pp. 269–87.

Matthes, J. C., 1859, *Dissertatio Historico-Critica De Pseudoprophetismo Hebraeorum*, Leiden, dissertation.

Metzger, Bruce M., 1971, *A Textual Commentary on the Greek New Testament*, n.p., United Bible Societies.

Meyer, Ivo, 1977, *Jeremia und die falschen Propheten*, OBO 13, Freiburg, Universitätsverlag/ Göttingen, Vandenhoeck & Ruprecht.

Milgrom, Jacob, 1990, *The JPS Torah Commentary: Numbers*, Philadelphia and New York, Jewish Publication Society.

Miller, Patrick D., 2001, 'The Book of Jeremiah', in Keck 2001, pp. 553–926.

Minear, Paul S., 2002, 'The Musician Versus the Grammarian: An Early Storm Warning', in his *The Bible and the Historian: Breaking the Silence about God in Biblical Studies*, Nashville, Abingdon Press, pp. 25–36.

Miranda, J., 1977, *Marx and the Bible*, London, SCM Press.

Moberly, R. W. L., 1983, *At the Mountain of God: Story and Theology in Exodus 32–34*, JSOTSS 22, Sheffield, JSOT Press.

1997, '*qyn*/Lament', in Willem VanGemeren (ed.), *New International Dictionary of Old Testament Theology and Exegesis*, vol. IV, Carlisle, Paternoster, pp. 866–84.

1998, '"God Is Not a Human that He Should Repent" (Numbers 23:19 and 1 Samuel 15:29)', in Tod Linafelt and Timothy Beal (eds.), *God in the Fray: A Tribute to Walter Brueggemann*, Minneapolis, Fortress, pp. 112–23.

1999a, 'On Learning to be a True Prophet: The Story of Balaam and his Ass', in P. J. Harland and C. T. R. Hayward (eds.), *New Heaven and New Earth: Prophecy and the Millennium: Essays in Honour of Anthony Gelston*, SVT LXXVII, Leiden and Boston, Brill, pp. 1–17.

1999b, 'Toward an Interpretation of the Shema', in Christopher Seitz and Kathryn Greene-McCreight (eds.), *Theological Exegesis: Essays in Honor of Brevard S. Childs*, Grand Rapids, Eerdmans, pp. 124–44.

2000, 'The Use of Scripture in Contemporary Debate about Homosexuality', *Theology* 103, pp. 251–8.

2003a, 'Jonah, God's Objectionable Mercy, and the Way of Wisdom', in David F. Ford and Graham Stanton (eds.), *Reading Texts, Seeking Wisdom*, London, SCM, pp. 154–68.

2003b, 'Does God Lie to His Prophets? The Story of Micaiah ben Imlah as a Test Case', *HTR* 96:1, pp. 1–23.

2004a, '"Test the Spirits": God, Love, and Critical Discernment in 1 John 4', in Graham N. Stanton, Bruce W. Longenecker, and Stephen C. Barton (eds.), *The Holy Spirit and Christian Origins: Essays in Honor of James D. G. Dunn*, Grand Rapids, Eerdmans, pp. 296–307.

2004b, 'The Canon of the Old Testament: Some Historical and Hermeneutical Reflections from a Western Perspective', in Ivan Z. Dimitrov, James D. G. Dunn, Ulrich Luz, and Karl-Wilhelm Niebuhr (eds.), *Das Alte Testament als christliche Bibel in orthodoxer und westlicher Sicht*, WUNT 174, Tübingen, Mohr Siebeck, pp. 239–57.

Montgomery, James A. and Gehman, Henry Snyder, 1951, *The Book of Kings*, ICC, Edinburgh, T. & T. Clark.

Morgan, Robert, 2003, 'Jesus Christ, the Wisdom of God (2)' in David F. Ford and Graham Stanton (eds.), *Reading Texts, Seeking Wisdom*, London, SCM, pp. 22–37.

Morrison, R., 2004, 'Cover Story: "There is no God, no Afterlife, no Paradise"', *The Times*, 11 October, T2, pp. 4–5.

Mosis, R., 2003, '*pth*', in *TDOT* XII, pp. 162–72.

Münderlein, Gerhard, 1979, *Kriterien wahrer und falscher Prophetie: Entstehung und Bedeutung im Alten Testament*, Europäische Hochschulschriften: Theologie Bd 33, 2nd edn, Bern, Frankfurt-on-Main/Las Vegas, Peter Lang.

Murphy-O'Connor, Jerome, 1991, *The Theology of the Second Letter to the Corinthians*, NTT, Cambridge, Cambridge University Press.
Mussies, G., 1972, *Dio Chrysostom and the New Testament*, SCHNT 2, Leiden, Brill.
Nasrallah, Laura S., 2003, *'An Ecstasy of Folly': Prophecy and Authority in Early Christianity*, HTS, Cambridge, MA, Harvard University Press.
Nelson, Richard D., 1987, *First and Second Kings*, IBCTP, Atlanta, John Knox Press.
Neumann, Peter H. A., 1979, *Das Prophetenverständnis in der deutschsprachigen Forschung seit Heinrich Ewald*, Wege der Forschung CCCVII, Darmstadt, Wissenschaftliche Buchgesellschaft.
Nicholson, Ernest, 1973, *The Book of the Prophet Jeremiah 1–25*, Cambridge, Cambridge University Press.
Niebuhr, Reinhold, 1938, 'The Test of True Prophecy', in his *Beyond Tragedy: Essays on the Christian Interpretation of History*, London, Nisbet, pp. 89–110.
Nietzsche, F., 1969 [1888], *Der Antichrist*, in Giorgio Colli and Mazzino Montarini (eds.), *Nietzsche Werke* VI/3, Berlin, de Gruyter, pp. 163–251.
Noth, Martin, 1968, *Numbers*, OTL, London, SCM (ET by James D. Martin from German of 1966).
Oates, Stephen B., 1982, *Let the Trumpet Sound: The Life of Martin Luther King, Jr*, London and Tunbridge Wells, Search Press.
O'Connor, Flannery, 1970, 'Catholic Novelists and their Readers', in her *Mystery and Manners: Occasional Prose*, ed. Sally and Robert Fitzgerald, New York, Farrar, Straus & Giroux, pp. 169–90.
Ollenburger, Ben C. (ed.), 2004, *Old Testament Theology: Flowering and Future*, Winona Lake, Eisenbrauns.
Osswald, Eva, 1962, *Falsche Prophetie im Alten Testament*, Tübingen, Mohr Siebeck.
Otto, R., 1924, *The Idea of the Holy*, Oxford, Oxford University Press (ET from 9th German edn of 1923).
Overholt, Thomas W., 1970, *The Threat of Falsehood: A Study in the Theology of the Book of Jeremiah*, SBT, 2nd series 16, London, SCM.
Parris, Matthew, 2003, 'Brother Charles, the Story of a Good Man out of Africa', *The Times*, 15 March.
Pearson, B. A., 1971, '1 Thessalonians 2:13–16: A Deutero-Pauline Interpolation', *HTR* 64, pp. 79–94.
Perdue, Leo G., 1994, *The Collapse of History: Reconstructing Old Testament Theology*, Minneapolis, Fortress Press.
Petersen, David L., 2001, 'Introduction to Prophetic Literature', in Keck 2001, pp. 1–23.
2002, *The Prophetic Literature: An Introduction*, Louisville, Westminster/John Knox Press.
Pickett, Raymond, 1997, *The Cross in Corinth: The Social Significance of the Death of Jesus*, JSNTSS 143, Sheffield Academic Press.
Preuss, Horst Dietrich, 1996, *Old Testament Theology*, vol. II, Edinburgh, T. & T. Clark (ET by Leo G. Perdue from German of 1992).
Provan, Iain W., 1995, *1 and 2 Kings*, NIBC 7, Peabody, Hendrickson.
Quell, Gottfried, 1952, *Wahre und falsche Propheten: Versuch einer Interpretation*, BFCT 46, Gütersloh, Bertelsmann.
Rad, Gerhard von, 1933, 'Die falschen Propheten', *ZAW* 51, pp. 109–20.
1966, *Deuteronomy*, London, SCM (ET by Dorothea Barton from German of 1964).
1975, *Old Testament Theology*, vol. II, London, SCM Press (ET from German of 1960).

Rahner, Karl, 1963, *Visions and Prophecies*, London, Nelson (ET from German by C.H. Henkey and R. Strachan); reissued in his *Studies in Modern Theology*, London, Burns & Oates, 1965, pp. 87–188.

1966, 'Thoughts on the Possibility of Belief Today', in his *Theological Investigations*, vol. v, Baltimore, Helicon Press/London, DLT (ET from German by Karl-H. Kruger), pp. 3–22.

1991, 'Book of God – Book of Human Beings', in his *Theological Investigations*, vol. xxii, London, DLT (ET by Joseph Donceel, SJ from German of 1984), pp. 214–24.

Rendtorff, Rolf, 2005, *The Canonical Hebrew Bible: A Theology of the Old Testament*, TBS 7, Leiden, Deo Publishing (ET by David E. Orton from German of 2001).

Reventlow, Henning Graf, 1985, *Problems of Old Testament Theology in the Twentieth Century*, London, SCM (ET by John Bowden from German of 1982).

Richard, E.J., 1995, *First and Second Thessalonians*, Sacra Pagina 11, Collegeville, MN, Liturgical Press.

Ricoeur, Paul, 1981, 'Toward a Hermeneutic of the Idea of Revelation', in his *Essays on Biblical Interpretation*, ed. Lewis S. Mudge, London, SPCK, pp. 73–118 (reprinted from *HTR* 70: 1–2 (1977)).

Rodinson, Maxime, 1971 [2002], *Mohammed*, London, Penguin (ET by Anne Carter from 2nd French edn of 1968; reprinted 2002).

Rowland, Christopher, 1996, 'Apocalyptic, Mysticism, and the New Testament', in Peter Schäfer (ed.), *Geschichte–Tradition–Reflexion: Festschrift für Martin Hengel zum 70. Geburtstag. Bd. 1. Judentum*, Tübingen, Mohr Siebeck, pp. 405–30.

Rudolph, Wilhelm, 1968, *Jeremia*, 3rd edn, HAT, Tübingen, Mohr Siebeck.

Sanders, James A., 1977, 'Hermeneutics in True and False Prophecy', in George W. Coats and Burke O. Long (eds.), *Canon and Authority: Essays in Old Testament Religion and Theology*, Philadelphia, Fortress, pp. 21–41.

Savage, T.B., 1995, *Power through Weakness*, SNTSMS 86, Cambridge, Cambridge University Press.

Schmid, Hansjörg, 2002, *Gegner im 1. Johannesbrief? Zu Konstruktion und Selbstreferenz im johanneischen Sinnsystem*, BWANT 159, Stuttgart, Kohlhammer.

Schneiders, Sandra M., 1999, *The Revelatory Text: Interpreting the New Testament as Sacred Scripture*, 2nd edn, Collegeville, Liturgical Press.

Schweitzer, Albert, 1953 [1930], *The Mysticism of Paul the Apostle*, 2nd edn, London, A. & C. Black (ET by William Montgomery from German of 1930).

Scobie, Charles H.H., 2003, *The Ways of our God: An Approach to Biblical Theology*, Grand Rapids and Cambridge UK, Eerdmans.

Sharp, Carolyn J., 2003, *Prophecy and Ideology in Jeremiah: Struggles for Authority in the Deutero-Jeremianic Prose*, London and New York, T. & T. Clark.

Shaw, Graham, 1983, *The Cost of Authority: Manipulation and Freedom in the New Testament*, London, SCM.

Sheppard, Gerald T., 1988, 'True and False Prophecy within Scripture', in Gene M. Tucker, David L. Petersen, and Robert R. Wilson (eds.), *Canon, Theology, and Old Testament Interpretation: Essays in Honor of Brevard S. Childs*, Philadelphia, Fortress, pp. 262–82.

Skinner, John, 1930, *Prophecy and Religion*, Cambridge, Cambridge University Press.

Smalley, Stephen S., 1984, *1, 2, 3 John*, WBC 51, Waco, Word Books.

Spinoza, Benedict de, 1951 [1670], *A Theologico-Political Treatise*, New York, Dover (ET from Latin by R.H.M. Elwes).

Stade, B., 1881, 'Deuterosacharja. Eine kritische Studie. 1 Theil', *ZAW* 1, pp. 1–96.

Strecker, Georg, 1996, *The Johannine Letters*, Hermeneia, Minneapolis, Fortress Press (ET by Linda M. Maloney from German of 1989).

Stuart, Elizabeth, 1991, 'Love is ... Paul', *ExpT* 102:9, pp. 264–6.

Stulman, Louis, 1999, 'The Prose Sermons as Hermeneutical Guide to Jeremiah 1–25: The Deconstruction of Judah's Symbolic World', in Diamond et al. 1999, pp. 34–63.

Sumney, J. L., 1990, *Identifying Paul's Opponents: The Question of Method in 2 Corinthians*, JSNTSS 40, Sheffield, JSOT Press.

1999, *'Servants of Satan', 'False Brothers', and Other Opponents of Paul*, JSNTSS 188, Sheffield, Sheffield Acacemic Press.

Sweeney, Marvin A., 2003, 'The Truth in True and False Prophecy', in Christine Helmer and Kristin De Troyer, with Katie Goetz (eds.), *Truth: Interdisciplinary Dialogues in a Pluralist Age*, Studies in Philosophical Theology 22, Leuven, Peeters, pp. 9–26.

Tabor, J., 1986, *Things Unutterable: Paul's Ascent to Paradise in its Greco-Roman, Judaic, and Early Christian Contexts*, Lanham, MD, University Press of America.

Thiselton, A. C., 1974, 'The Supposed Power of Words in the Biblical Writings', *JTS* 25, pp. 283–99.

1995, *Interpreting God and the Postmodern Self: On Meaning, Manipulation and Promise*, SJT Current Issues in Theology, Edinburgh, T. & T. Clark.

2000, *The First Epistle to the Corinthians*, NIGTC, Grand Rapids, Eerdmans/Carlisle, Paternoster.

Thomas, John Christopher, 2004, *The Pentecostal Commentary on 1 John, 2 John, 3 John*, London and New York, T. & T. Clark International.

Thompson, J. A., 1980, *The Book of Jeremiah*, NICOT, Grand Rapids, Eerdmans.

Thrall, Margaret E., 1994, *The Second Epistle to the Corinthians*, vol. I, ICC, Edinburgh, T. & T. Clark.

2000, *The Second Epistle to the Corinthians*, vol. II, ICC, Edinburgh, T. & T. Clark.

Tigay, Jeffrey H., 1996, *The JPS Torah Commentary: Deuteronomy*, Philadelphia and Jerusalem, Jewish Publication Society.

Van Seters, John, 1997, 'From Faithful Prophet to Villain: Observations on the Tradition History of the Balaam Story', in E. E. Carpenter (ed.), *A Biblical Itinerary: In Search of Method, Form and Content: Essays in Honor of George W. Coats*, JSOTSS 240, Sheffield, Sheffield Academic Press, pp. 126–32.

Vaux, Roland de, 1961, *Ancient Israel: Its Life and Institutions*, London, DLT (ET from French by John McHugh).

Vickers, Salley, 2000, *Miss Garnet's Angel*, London and New York, HarperCollins.

Volz, P., 1928, *Der Prophet Jeremia*, KAT vol. X, 2nd edn, Leipzig, Deichertsche.

Walsh, Jerome T., 1996, *1 Kings*, Berit Olam, Collegeville, Liturgical Press.

Watson, Francis, 2004, *Paul and the Hermeneutics of Faith*, London and New York, T. & T. Clark International.

Webster, John, 2003, 'Reading Scripture Eschatologically (I)', in David F. Ford and Graham Stanton (eds.), *Reading Texts, Seeking Wisdom*, London, SCM, pp. 245–56.

Wellhausen, Julius 1973 [1878], *Prolegomena to the History of Ancient Israel*, Gloucester, MA, Peter Smith (ET by Mr Black and Mr Menzies from German of 1878).

Williams, Rowan, 1979, *The Wound of Knowledge: Christian Spirituality from the New Testament to St John of the Cross*, London, DLT.

2000, 'Theological Integrity', in his *On Christian Theology*, CCT, Oxford, Blackwell, pp. 3–15.

Winter, Bruce, 2001, 'Religious Curses and Christian Vindictiveness', in his *After Paul Left Corinth*, Grand Rapids, Eerdmans, pp. 164–83.

Wright, N.T., 1991a, 'Jesus Christ is Lord: Philippians 2.5–11', in N.T. Wright, *The Climax of the Covenant: Christ and the Law in Pauline Theology*, Edinburgh, T. & T. Clark, pp. 56–98.

1991b, 'Monotheism, Christology and Ethics: 1 Corinthians 8', in N.T. Wright, *The Climax of the Covenant: Christ and the Law in Pauline Theology*, Edinburgh, T. & T. Clark, pp. 120–36.

1993, 'On Becoming the Righteousness of God: 2 Corinthians 5:21', in David M. Hay (ed.), *Pauline Theology*, vol. II, *1 & 2 Corinthians*, Minneapolis, Fortress, pp. 200–8.

Young, Frances and Ford, David, 1987, *Meaning and Truth in 2 Corinthians*, Grand Rapids, Eerdmans.

Index of authors cited

Index of scriptural references

Rabbinic texts

Index of subjects

Printed in the United States
104597LV00005B/76-87/A

9 780521 051040